LINUX

Linux File Systems

ABOUT THE AUTHOR

Moshe Bar is the author of *Linux Internals* and Linux senior editor at *Byte.com* and *Dr. Dobbs*. He is a contributor to the JFS file system project for Linux and a main contributor to the Mosix project for Linux clustering. Moshe Bar holds a Ph.D. in computer science.

LINUX

Linux File Systems

MOSHE **BAR**

Osborne/**McGraw-Hill**

New York   Chicago   San Francisco
Lisbon   London   Madrid   Mexico City   Milan
New Delhi   San Juan   Seoul   Singapore   Sydney   Toronto

Osborne/**McGraw-Hill**
2600 Tenth Street
Berkeley, California 94710
U.S.A.

To arrange bulk purchase discounts for sales promotions, premiums, or fund-raisers, please contact Osborne/**McGraw-Hill** at the above address. For information on translations or book distributors outside the U.S.A., please see the International Contact Information page immediately following the index of this book.

Linux File Systems

1234567890 DOC DOC 01987654321

Book p/n 0-07-212954-9 and CD p/n 0-07-212953-0
parts of
ISBN 0-07-212955-7

Publisher
  Brandon A. Nordin
Vice President and Associate Publisher
  Scott Rogers
Acquisitions Editor
  Michael Sprague
Project Manager
  Mark Karmendy
  David Nash

Composition and Indexing
  Apollo Printing and Typesetting
Series Design
  Peter F. Hancik
Cover Design
  Amparo Del Rio

This book was composed with Corel VENTURA™ Publisher.

To my mother for having endured hardship to raise me.
To my father for having taught me to believe in the value of principles.
To my teachers for having imbued in me a thirst for knowledge.
To my friends who have brought new colors, sounds and smells to my life.

CONTENTS

Acknowledgments xiii

▼ 1 Introduction 1

Gnu/Linux and File Systems 2
Purpose of this Book 3
   Who Should Read this Book 4
   What You Should Know Before Reading this Book 4
   What this Book Contains 4
   How to Use this Book 4
Where to Find More Information 5
   Suggestions, Comments 5
   Open Source—Implications For a Modern Operating
     System 5
History of Linux 6
   Functionality Provided by Linux Today 7
   Novelties in the 2.4 Kernel 8

▼ 2 Compiling a Kernel 11

Source Code Tree Structure 12
   The arch/ Directory 17
   The drivers/ Directory 17
   The fs/ Directory 17

The include/ Directory   17
The ipc/ Directory   17
The init/ Directory   17
The lib/ Directory   18
The kernel/ Directory   18
The mm/ Directory   18
The net/ Directory   19
Compiling It   19
The GNU gcc Compiler   20
Coding Conventions   20
Architecture Dependencies   21

▼ 3   What's a File System?   23
General Aspects of a File System   24
The Hierarchy of the File Structure   25
Objects in a File System   28
Buffers, Caches, and Memory Garbage Collection   29
The Buffer Cache   29
The bdflush Kernel Daemon   32
Kswapd   33
File System Objects   33
Files   35
File Functions   37
Inodes   40
Functions on Inodes   45
File Systems   49
Names or dentrys   52
Dentry Structure   52
Dentry Functions   55
The Linux Super-Block   57
The Super-Block Structure   57
Super-Block Functions   60
Performance Issues and Optimization Strategies   63
Raw I/O   64
Process Resource Limits   65
Extent-Based Allocation (General)   66
Block-Based Allocation (General)   67
The Transaction-Processing or Database Issue of Safety . . .   68
Advantages of Journaling over Non-Journaling   69

▼ 4   The Linux VFS   75
General Concepts   76
The VFS Source Code   76

How VFS Works 78
Source Files include/linux/fs.h (2.4.3) 86
Source file fs/ext2/super.c (2.4.3) 113
Source file fs/ext2/file.c (2.4.3) 130
Source Code open_namei() function from fs/namei.c 132

▼ 5   LVM (Logical Volume Manager) 137
Linux LVM Introduction 138
LVM Benefits 141
How does LVM work? 141
LVM Internals 142
Source Code include/linux/lvm.h 146

▼ 6   RAID with Linux 163
PCI Controllers 164
SCSI-to-SCSI Controllers 165
Software RAID 166
Striping 168
RAID 0 Configuration 168
RAID 1 Configuration 169
Limits Of RAID 170
Recovering from RAID Device Failure 171
Case A 172
Case B 173

▼ 7   The Second Extended File System (ext2) 181
New Features 182
Standard ext2fs Features 182
Advanced ext2fs Features 182
Directories 183
Blocks 184
The Super-Block 186
The Ext2fs Library 188
The Ext2fs Tools 189
The Inode in ext2fs 192
The ext2fs Super-block 192
The ext2 Group Descriptor 193
Free Blocks Count, Free Inodes Count, Used Directory
    Count 194
Changing the Size of a File in an ext2 File System 194
Group Descriptors 199
Bitmaps 200
Inodes 200

Directories 202
Allocation algorithms 203
Error Handling 204
Source Code include/linux/ext2_fs.h 205

▼ 8   IBM's JFS Journaling File System for Linux 219
The Main JFS Data Structures and Algorithms 220
    Super-blocks: Primary Aggregate Super-block and
      Secondary Aggregate Super-block 220
    Inodes 220
    Standard Administrative Utilities 221
    How JFS Is Set up at Boot Time 222
    Block Allocation Map 222
    Inode Allocation Map 223
    AG Free Inode List 224
    IAG Free List 224
    Fileset Allocation Map Inodes 224
    Design Features that Distinguish JFS from Other File
      Systems 225
    JFS's Further Extensive Use of B+-Trees 226
    Leaf Nodes 227
    Internal Nodes 227
    Variable Block Size 228
    Directory Organization 228
    JFS's Support for both Sparse and Dense Files 228
Aggregates and Filesets 229
    Files 229
    Directory 229
    Logs 230
    The File Structure and Access Control 230

▼ 9   ReiserFS for Linux 233
The File System Name Space 234
Block Alignments of File Boundaries 235
Balanced Trees and Large File I/O 236
    Serialization and Consistency 237
    Tree Definitions 238
Buffering and the Preserve List 241
    ReiserFS Structures 241
Using the Tree to Optimize Layout of Files 245
    Physical Layout 245
    Node Layout 245

Installing and Configuring ReiserFS on a Linux Kernel 251
    Linux-2.2.X Kernels 251
    Linux-2.4.0 to 2.4.2 253

▼ 10 XFS 255
The XFS Implementation 257
    Log Manager 258
    Buffer Cache Manager 259
    Lock Manager 259
    Space Manager 259
    Attribute Manager 260
    Name Space Manager 261
    Administration of XFS File Systems 262
XFS Structures and Methods 262
    Inode Data Structure 262
    Inode Life Cycle 263
    Inode Allocation 264
    Inode In-line Data/Extents/B-tree Root 265
    Inode locking 267
    Inode Transactions and Logging 267
    Inode Flushing 268
    Inode Recycling 269
The XFS Super-block Structures and Methods 269
    The Super-block Buffer 270
    Super-block Management Interfaces 271
    Structures on Disk 272
    Allocation Group Header 274
    Data Block Freelist 275
    Inode Table 275
    Data and Attribute Block Representation 277
    File System Structure 278
    Buffering vs. Allocation 278
    XFS Availability and Release Caveats 279
Working with XFS 279
    Partitioning 279

▼ A The Software-RAID HOWTO 281
Table of Contents 282
    1. Introduction 283
    2. Why RAID? 285
    3. Hardware issues 288
    4. RAID setup 290

5. Testing 302
6. Reconstruction 303
7. Performance 304
8. Credits 306

▼ **B**   References 307

▼ **C**   The Loopback Root Filesystem HOWTO 313

Table of Contents 314
1. Introduction 315
2. Principles of Loopback Devices and Ramdisks 315
3. How To Create a Loopback Root Device 317
4. Booting the System 324
5. Other Loopback Root Device Possibilities 325

▼ **D**   Linux Partition HOWTO 327

Table of Contents 328
1. Introduction 328
2. What is a partition anyway? 329
3. What Partitions do I need? 332
4. An example 336
5. How I did it on my machine 337

▼   Index 339

ACKNOWLEDGMENTS

The writing of this book required great efforts not only from me, but also from my better half. She was patient in hundreds of occasions when this book took precedence to us being together. Many thanks to her for standing by me.

Special thanks to the contributors of the OpenSource project XFS, JFS, and ReiserFS. They are too many to mention here, but they certainly include Stephen Lord and Jim Mostek who agreed to provide me with documentation about XFS. Steve Best at IBM helped me by patiently answering my many questions about JFS. Hans Reiser provided basic documentation for this project under the condition that I return the edited ReiserFS chapter of this book to him as documentation for the ReiserFS website.

Many thanks also to my friends, Roberto, Tom, and Prof. Barak for supporting me with insights, advice and good humor.

The content of this book relies heavily on the help of some of the gurus behind Linux and its file systems. People like Wietse Venema, Stepehn Tweedie, Andrea Arcangeli, Ingo Molnar, Remy Card, and others have greatly contributed through their own work and through their untiring willingness to explain things.

Other outstanding OpenSource community members like Neil Brown, Alessandro Rubini, Doug Gilbert, Louis-Dominique Dubeau, and others greatly contributed to this book with their research and documentation of some of the subsystems discussed in this book.

Most of all, it is my duty to thank God for giving me all I needed to write this book.

CHAPTER 1

Introduction

Having worked with Unix for almost 20 years, and being a Linux user for eight years, I thought I knew all about how Linux stores and retrieves data. Even so, I couldn't believe what I was hearing at a Unix conference in the Netherlands in the autumn of year 2000. Wietse Venema (the author of *TCPWrappers* and the mastermind behind the postfix MTA[1]) was the opening speaker, and stunned the audience by announcing that he had been recovering files once thought to be lost from regular Linux file systems.[2]

I grew up (not in a literal way, of course) thinking that once a file was deleted, it was gone forever—not to be un-deleted again. Wietse Venema was saying that, as a matter of fact, files can be recovered quite easily and this alone constitutes a serious security issue. Hundreds of listeners realized along with me just how little we really knew about the file systems we trust our precious data to.

GNU/LINUX AND FILE SYSTEMS

In its very early days, Linux was cross-developed under the Minix[3] operating system. Linus Torvalds chose this strategy because it allowed him to share disks between the two systems rather than to design a new file system from scratch. The Minix file system was an efficient and relatively bug-free piece of software. However, the restrictions in the design of the Minix file system were too limiting, so people started thinking and working on the implementation of new file systems in Linux.

In order to ease the addition of new file systems into the Linux kernel, a Virtual File System (VFS) layer was developed. The VFS layer was initially written by Chris Provenzano, and later rewritten by Linus Torvalds before it was integrated into the Linux kernel. It is described in the Virtual File System chapter of this book.

After the integration of the VFS into the kernel, a new file system, called the Extended File System (ext) was implemented in April 1992 and added to Linux version 0.96. This new file system removed the two big Minix limitations: its maximum size was 2GB and the maximum filename size was 255 characters. The ext file system was already quite an improvement over the Minix file system but it still had some inherent shortcomings. There was no support for separate access, inode modification, and data modification timestamps.[4] The file system used linked lists in the kernel to keep track of free blocks and inodes in the file system(s), but also introduced new inefficiencies: as the file system

---

1 An MTA is a Mail Transportation Agent and is needed to send and receive e-mails.
2 When deleting a file, the Linux ext2 file system does not wipe the directory entry. As a result, the name-to-inode mapping is preserved, at least until the directory entry is overwritten. So, if you have access to the raw directory blocks you can find the names of deleted files and their inode numbers; from there you can access the first dozen or so direct blocks.
3 Minix and its file system were developed by Prof. Andrew Tanenbaum for pedagogic purposes.
4 These features are explored in later chapters.

usage advanced, those lists became unsorted and the file system became fragmented, which resulted in impaired overall file system performance.

As a response to these issues, two new file systems were released in early 1993: the Xia file system (Xiafs) and the Second Extended File System, or ext2fs. The Xia file system was based mostly on the Minix file system code and only added a few basic improvements. It provided long filenames, support for bigger partitions, and support for the three timestamps: creation time, modification time, and access time. On the other hand, ext2fs was based on the ext file system code and had many improvements. It had been designed from the beginning to allow for future improvements.

When the two new file systems were first released, they provided essentially the same features set, although with different implementation and source code. Due to its minimal design, Xiafs was actually more stable than ext2fs. Eventually, the bugs were fixed in ext2fs and lots of improvements and new features were integrated. Today, ext2fs is very stable and has become the de facto standard Linux file system.

In addition to in-depth coverage of ext2fs, this book looks into all the important file systems now available for Linux, examines their strengths and weaknesses, and shows how to use them effectively.

PURPOSE OF THIS BOOK

This book is written to enhance the general understanding of the most important file systems available today for Linux. Sometimes, to be able to understand file systems thoroughly, we have to look at how they are written. This book is not, however, a source code commentary of these file systems. Rather, it is a book that shows when to use which file systems effectively.

The following is a review of a few broad terms:

▼ A *kernel* is the operating system software running in protected mode and having access to the hardware's privileged registers.

■ A *file system* is a logical collection of control blocks representing independent containers of user or system data. There is a possible ambiguity when referring to the term "file system." One way of using the term is when referring to a particular kind of file system, such as ext2fs or NFS. Alternatively, it can be used to refer to a particular instance of a file system, such as /usr or /boot.

■ A *name space* is a collection of uniquely assigned identifiers, such as filenames. Within a name space, there can only be one instance of a filename. Usually a name space is contained within the scope of a directory.

▲ A *directory* is a special file which is maintained by the file system, and which contains a list of entries. To a user, an entry appears to be a file and is accessed in terms of its symbolic entry name, which is the user's filename.

Who Should Read this Book

This book is targeted at system and network administrators, developers, and capacity planning managers. It will also appeal to Linux enthusiasts who have a good general understanding of hardware and software.

In the chapters that follow, system administrators learn how to prepare their kernel to be used with a particular file system, which file systems are available, and how to use them correctly. Also, they will be able to increase system throughput considerably by tuning the file system at the proper places.

Developers learn how file systems impact their applications. Although many might argue that file systems are really transparent to the developer, this is not true. For example, knowing that a lock mechanism is effectively implemented by a file system frees the programmer or developer from having to code this functionality into the application.

What You Should Know Before Reading this Book

It helps to have a good understanding of the general concepts of computer science theory, especially in the area of name space and I/O. In addition, it helps if the reader has a working knowledge of the Linux interface and a rudimentary understanding of what's involved in basic system administration. No previous knowledge about file systems is necessary.

It helps to be able to read C programs, although most of the code provided is explained. For a good introduction to C, the author of this book always strongly recommends *The C Programming Language* by Kernighan/Ritchie, the designers of C.

What this Book Contains

This book contains a short introduction to the Linux OS, and how it is organized. It also explains how to recompile a Linux kernel, which is important knowledge for using file systems not pre-compiled into a standard Linux distribution kernel.

Once the general Unix approach to file systems has been reviewed, we study the Linux abstraction of file systems through the *Virtual File System* or *VFS*. Then all the important file systems are reviewed and explained.

This book does not attempt to present an exhaustive commentary of all available Linux file systems. Rather, it focuses on the most important ones and on how to use them effectively.

Appendices are included at the end of the book for system calls, the GPL license, and other useful information.

How to Use this Book

It is best to read through this book in a linear fashion from the beginning to the end. After the first pass, readers might want to use this book as a quick reference in their day-to-day use of file systems.

WHERE TO FIND MORE INFORMATION

The most up-to-date information on Linux file systems can be found on the Internet. It is, however, essentially raw data. Gathering this information, assembling it, and putting it into a coherent format is not a trivial task. This is the biggest value of *Linux File Systems*—to provide a coherent, researched, and formatted source of information that is otherwise only available to the public through Web sites, source code, and articles.

One good source of information on the kernel is, of course, the kernel source code implementing the file systems. Subscribing to the developers' mailing lists for all the file systems mentioned in this book is a very good way to get to know all related aspects of file systems.

Suggestions, Comments

Any suggestions or comments are very welcome and can be addressed either to moshe_bar@hotmail.com or to Moshe Bar c/o McGraw-Hill, Professional Book Group, Two Penn Plaza, New York, NY 10121.

Open Source—Implications For a Modern Operating System

Without doubt, the main reason for the unusual success of Linux is the General Public License (GPL). However, the concept of Open Source, or of free software as it is sometimes called, is actually quite old. The first proponent of free software was Richard Stallman, of the Free Software Foundation (FSF). He designed the GPL license for some excellent and now widespread software that he wrote, most prominently perhaps the Emacs editing environment and the GCC compiler for C and C++. For a full list of GNU tools, visit www.gnu.org.

Richard Stallman has also been working for a long while now on a full GNU operating system, a project called GNU Hurd. Under development for nearly a decade, this OS is still not a reality, but many powerful technologies have emerged from this project which have found their way to other operating systems, such as Linux, BSD, and others.

Operating systems benefit from having an Open Source approach to development in two ways: reliability and performance. The reliability of Linux stems, in large part, from the scrutiny of hundreds (or thousands) of developers auditing the code, improving it, changing it, and trying it out. As Eric Raymond stated in his famous paper "The Cathedral and the Bazaar": *Given a large enough beta-tester and co-developer base, almost every problem will be characterized quickly and the fix obvious to someone.*

Thus, having so many eyes scrutinizing the Linux code base makes for a better QA (Quality Assurance) department than any closed model software development organization could ever afford. This, in turn, makes for better quality software.

A mere development model such as Open Source cannot, by itself, replace proper design and coding methods. But the Open Source model exceeds the proprietary one by great lengths. Consider the example of a kernel improvement in Linux.

HISTORY OF LINUX

Like many success stories, Linux began as a project sprung from necessity. In 1991, Linus B. Torvalds, then a student at the University of Helsinki in Finland, bought himself a PC based on the i386, the first Intel CPU to have on-chip support for virtual memory management. Not entirely satisfied with the MS/DOS operating system, Linus instead decided to implement the Minix OS on his PC.

Soon he was enhancing Minix to provide functions and features that he needed for his studies. Then, he decided that Minix was too much of an academic OS, and that he should create an operating system from scratch. Torvalds also decided, most importantly, to make his new OS's source code freely available over the Internet, that is, as Open Source, under the name of Linux, a contraction of Linus and Unix.

The first version 0.01 was made available for download on the Internet in August 1991. In October of the same year, Linus officially announced the availability of version 0.02. This version already could execute such Unix-user-land programs as the bash shell, the GNU gcc compiler, and other basic utilities, but not much more.

Soon, because of the Open Source nature of the project, with the source code being immediately available all over the globe, many hackers, computer freaks, and PC enthusiasts began looking at the code and enhancing it. Many began to send their suggestions to Linus, who inaugurated the "official" reference Linux source code development tree. Looking through their code suggestions, he rejected most, but some he incorporated. Development continued this way for three more years before a first production version was announced.

In March 1994, version 1.0 was made available. It still showed the occasional erratic behavioral quirk, as this author fondly remembers, but was quite usable. Linux 1.0 featured TCP/IP, SLIP, and printer support, and had enough drivers to support a wide range of the PC equipment then available.

After that, the Linux boom really began, and millions of enthusiasts in all corners of the world started using the system. A little earlier, around 1992–93, the first Linux "distributions" appeared. Distributions, the primary way to obtain a fully functional OS, include the Linux kernel, the X windowing system, and a comprehensive package of application programs and utilities, which can number in the hundreds. Distributions also include an "installer," which prepares the binary image of the OS and the boot/shutdown scripts, and makes sure that all components are compatible with and tuned for each other. Last, but not least, distributions also provide documentation. Today many distributions exist, the most successful on the market being RedHat, SuSE, and Caldera.

The highlights of the steady ascent of Linux to its status as a major power in the IT market today are listed here:

August 1991   Version 0.01

October 1991   Official announcement 0.02

November 1993   First Slackware Distribution with kernel 0.99

March 1994   Version 1.0

June 1995   First port to the Alpha architecture

October 1996   Debian Linux is used on the space shuttle in orbit (on an
                        IBM laptop)

January 1999   Version 2.2.0

January 2001   Linux 2.4.0 released

July 2001   Linux 2.4.6 released

Functionality Provided by Linux Today

Linux has come a long way from its humble beginning in 1991. As the phenomenon of Open Source has spread further and wider, more and more people have contributed to the Linux kernel and to its subsystems. At the same time, thousands upon thousands of user-space packages were added at ever-increasing frequency. With the concurrent rise of the World Wide Web, some Web sites were devoted solely to the purpose of daily announcements about new software versions available for Linux.

Today Linux is available on many platforms, including Intel, Sparc, Alpha, MIPS, the Motorola 68000 family, and PowerPC.

Early on, Linux was brought into conformance with the POSIX (Portable Operating System Interface) standard. Its POSIX-compliance allows applications developed under Linux to be very easily ported to other POSIX-compliant operating systems. On Intel CPU-based systems, the Linux binaries conform to iBSCS standards. This allows, for example, a statically linked program to run under FreeBSD or Solaris without recompilation.

Technically, Linux provides the following functions:

▼   Multi-user

■   Multi-process, multi-processor (SMP)

■   Inter-Process communication (IPC, pipes, sockets)

■   Process control

■   POSIX-style terminal management

■   TCP/IP, Ipv4, Ipv6

■   Support for a wide variety of hardware

■   Demand paging with optional LRU (Least Recently Used) algorithms and page coloring

■   Swapping

■   Buffer cache

- Dynamic and shared libraries
▲ Support for many file systems (ext2fs, UFS, NTFS, HPFS, MS/DOS, ISO9660, coda, and many more)

Novelties in the 2.4 Kernel

Linux 2.2 was a major improvement over Linux 2.0 and the Linux 1.x series. It supported many new file systems, had a new system of file caching, and it was much more scalable. Linux 2.4 builds on these improvements and more, to be the best Linux kernel yet in a wide variety of situations.

The Virtual File System (VFS) layer has also been heavily modified from earlier Linux versions. Linux 2.2 featured a number of wonderful changes to this layer that allowed for better caching and a much more efficient system overall. However, the system in Linux 2.2 still had a number of important limitations which were resolved in time for Linux 2.4. One major limitation to the way Linux 2.2 handled things was its use of two buffers for caching: one for reading and one for output. As you can imagine, this made things very complicated as the kernel developers had to code with kid gloves to always ensure that these caches were in sync when they had to be. Linux 2.4 brings this wall down completely by removing the multiple cache system and putting all the work into a single page caching layer. This change makes Linux 2.4 more efficient, the code is easier to understand for developers, and the amount of memory needed for the caches has been split roughly in two. During the course of this rewrite, many race conditions (errors caused when multiple processes "race" for access to unprotected variables) were removed and the code streamlined to allow significantly better scaling to higher-end systems and disk writes to happen faster when multiple volumes are involved.

The Linux kernel is a collection of modular components and subsystems, including device drivers, protocols, and other types of components. These are glued to the core of the Linux kernel by APIs, Application Programming Interfaces, that provide a standard method by which the Linux kernel can be expanded. Most of this book focuses on these Linux OS components that do the most work.

In the 2.4 kernel series, Linux has vastly improved its ability to handle large numbers of processes and tasks. The task limit can now grow to number beyond 4090. Additionally, the scheduler's efficiency has been improved somewhat, and Linux 2.4 can better handle systems with a large number of concurrent processes than earlier versions.

Linux 2.4 can also handle much larger "enterprise-class" hardware than could previous Linux kernel revisions. For example, Linux 2.4, with appropriate patches, can address beyond 4GB of RAM. One machine I have seen is configured with 12GB of RAM and has one address space of 8.3GB resident size.

Scalability on SMP systems has become now comparable to proprietary operating systems and, in some instances, is even better.

Support for other processor platforms has been increased too. Next to the traditional architectures, Linux 2.4 now supports the new Transmeta Crusoe processor directly. The 3Com Palm Pilot as well as Psion5, all run Linux in native mode. The new Intel IA64 (the next generation 64-bit successor to the venerable Intel x86 architecture) is not yet directly included with the kernel.

New file system support has been added (the Irix efs file system, and the UDF standard used on DVD disks), while others have been made obsolete (QNX and ext1).

The introduction of *tasklets*, a new revolutionary way of handling low-level interrupts, makes the TCP/IP stack (along with other subsystems and user programs) much more efficient. New networking protocol software has been added that is capable of handling the DECNet standard.

Linux 2.2 and Linux 2.0 included built-in support for starting a Java interpreter (if present) whenever a Java application was executed. (Linux was one of the first operating systems to do this at the kernel level.) Linux 2.4 still includes support for loading Java interpreters as necessary, but the specific Java driver has been removed and users will need to upgrade their configurations to use the "Misc." driver.

The first OS to so, the Linux 2.4 kernel includes a kernel web daemon, or kHTTPd. This facility allows the handling of more efficient static web pages.

In the chapters ahead, we shall look at all these enhancements and many more from a detailed perspective and understand the kernel dynamics involved with them.

CHAPTER 2

Compiling a Kernel

Many of the file systems discussed in this book need to have the kernel recompiled. In some cases, the kernel first needs to be patched with the new file system software (such as with JFS, ReiserFS, and XFS). It is therefore important to thoroughly understand how to create a new kernel with the desired functionality.

The prospect of having to compile and install a new kernel seems a dangerous and daunting task to many who might be afraid of doing something wrong and making it impossible to boot the machine. As with all system administrator tasks, it is true that there is a certain risk of doing things the wrong way. This is why it is best to compile the new kernel immediately after installation. If something goes wrong, the system can be reinstalled from scratch, without wasting too much of your time. Making such a mistake later on, after you have installed additional software (such as a database manager), would prove much more painful.

There is no need to be worried, however. Compiling a kernel and installing it is simpler than you might think. Follow these steps to compile a sample kernel.

CAUTION: Apply all of the necessary kernel source patches before compiling the kernel. At www.linuxhq.com, you will find links to obtain the generic kernel patches.

SOURCE CODE TREE STRUCTURE

To be able to patch a kernel and compile it, as well as to further understand this book, it is helpful to have a good overview of the source code tree structure.

```
|-- Documentation
|   |-- arm
|   |   `-- nwfpe
|   |-- cdrom
|   |-- fb
|   |-- filesystems
|   |-- i386
|   |-- isdn
|   |-- kbuild
|   |-- m68k
|   |-- networking
|   |   `-- ip_masq
|   |-- powerpc
|   |-- sound
|   |-- sysctl
|   `-- video4linux
|       `-- bttv
|-- arch
|   `-- i386
```

```
|          |-- boot
|          |   |-- compressed
|          |   `-- tools
|          |-- kernel
|          |-- lib
|          |-- math-emu
|          `-- mm
|-- configs
|-- drivers
|   |-- acorn
|   |   |-- block
|   |   |-- char
|   |   |-- net
|   |   `-- scsi
|   |-- ap1000
|   |-- block
|   |   `-- paride
|   |-- cdrom
|   |-- char
|   |   |-- ftape
|   |   |   |-- compressor
|   |   |   |-- lowlevel
|   |   |   `-- zftape
|   |   |-- hfmodem
|   |   |-- ip2
|   |   `-- joystick
|   |-- dio
|   |-- fc4
|   |-- isdn
|   |   |-- act2000
|   |   |-- avmb1
|   |   |-- divert
|   |   |-- eicon
|   |   |-- hisax
|   |   |-- icn
|   |   |-- isdnloop
|   |   |-- pcbit
|   |   `-- sc
|   |-- macintosh
|   |-- misc
|   |-- net
|   |   |-- fc
|   |   |-- hamradio
|   |   |   `-- soundmodem
```

```
|   |     `-- irda
|   |-- nubus
|   |-- pci
|   |-- pnp
|   |-- sbus
|   |   |-- audio
|   |   `-- char
|   |-- scsi
|   |   `-- aic7xxx
|   |-- sgi
|   |   `-- char
|   |-- sound
|   |   `-- lowlevel
|   |-- tc
|   |-- usb
|   |   `-- maps
|   |-- video
|   `-- zorro
|-- fs
|   |-- adfs
|   |-- affs
|   |-- autofs
|   |-- coda
|   |-- devpts
|   |-- efs
|   |-- ext2
|   |-- fat
|   |-- hfs
|   |-- hpfs
|   |-- isofs
|   |-- lockd
|   |-- minix
|   |-- msdos
|   |-- ncpfs
|   |-- nfs
|   |-- nfsd
|`  |-- nls
|   |-- ntfs
|   |-- proc
|   |-- qnx4
|   |-- romfs
|   |-- smbfs
|   |-- sysv
|   |-- ufs
```

```
|    |-- umsdos
|    `-- vfat
|-- ibcs
|    |-- Doc
|    |-- PROD.Patches
|    |-- Patches
|    |-- Tools
|    |-- VSYS
|    |-- devtrace
|    |-- iBCSemul
|    |    `-- maps
|    |-- include
|    |    `-- ibcs
|    `-- x286emul
|-- include
|    |-- asm -> asm-i386
|    |-- asm-generic
|    |-- asm-i386
|    |-- linux
|    |    |-- byteorder
|    |    |-- lockd
|    |    |-- modules
|    |    |-- modules-BOOT
|    |    |-- modules-smp
|    |    |-- modules-up
|    |    |-- nfsd
|    |    |-- raid
|    |    `-- sunrpc
|    |-- net
|    |    `-- irda
|    |-- scsi
|    `-- video
|-- init
|-- ipc
|-- kernel
|-- lib
|-- mm
|-- modules
|-- net
|    |-- 802
|    |    |-- pseudo
|    |    `-- transit
|    |-- appletalk
|    |-- ax25
```

```
|      |-- bridge
|      |-- core
|      |-- decnet
|      |-- econet
|      |-- ethernet
|      |-- ipv4
|      |-- ipv6
|      |-- ipx
|      |-- irda
|      |      |-- compressors
|      |      |-- ircomm
|      |      |-- irlan
|      |      `-- irlpt
|      |-- lapb
|      |-- netlink
|      |-- netrom
|      |-- packet
|      |-- rose
|      |-- sched
|      |-- sunrpc
|      |-- unix
|      |-- wanrouter
|      `-- x25
|-- pcmcia-cs-3.0.14
|      |-- cardmgr
|      |-- clients
|      |      `-- patches
|      |-- debug-tools
|      |-- doc
|      |-- etc
|      |      `-- cis
|      |-- flash
|      |-- include
|      |      |-- linux
|      |      `-- pcmcia
|      |-- man
|      `-- modules
`-- scripts
       |-- ksymoops
       `-- lxdialog
```

Notice how nicely Linux organizes the source code into architecture-dependent and independent code. About 95 percent of the kernel source is independent code, and thus will be exactly the same on all porting sets of Linux. The remaining 5 percent is usually assembler code or minor details, such as clock timer frequency.

The arch/ Directory

This is where the architecture-dependent code resides. Under this directory, for each existing porting set of Linux, there are three more subdirectories: kernel/, lib/, and mm/.

The kernel/ subdirectory contains architecture-dependent implementations of general kernel features, such as signals handling, clock handling, and so forth. The lib/ subdirectory in turn contains local implementations of library functions that run faster if compiled from architecture-dependent source code. Finally, mm/ contains local memory handling implementations.

The drivers/ Directory

Perhaps unsurprisingly, all the drivers' source code resides here. Due to the great variety of devices supported by Linux 2.4, this directory contains a lot of source code; actually, more than 50 percent of all the kernel source.

The fs/ Directory

fs/ is where the code for all supported file systems is included. People experimenting with new file systems, such as IBM's JFS or Hans Reiser's reiserfs, will have to patch this directory to contain the source code for those file systems.

The include/ Directory

Before a new kernel is actually compiled, it must be configured. Configuring in this context means telling the make utility which drivers, features, and modules to compile into the kernel. By default, most standard distributions come with a uniprocessor kernel. To implement the standard SMP features of the kernel, configuring with SMP is required.

The ipc/ Directory

All the code necessary for handling inter-process communication is here. The all-important semaphores-handling C code is here (sem.c). Nevertheless, this directory contains only 3751 lines of code.

The init/ Directory

Main.c, which contains a lot of very important code, such as code to implement fork() and the one piece of code most often executed, the cpu_idle() loop, resides in the init/ directory.

The code that produces the bogomips reading at boot is here for those who are still looking at it for an indication of speed. You will find that it does not actually measure processor speed:

```
void __init calibrate_delay(void)
{
        unsigned long ticks, loopbit;
        int lps_precision = LPS_PREC;

        loops_per_sec = (1<<12);

        printk("Calibrating delay loop... ");
        while (loops_per_sec <<= 1) {
                /* wait for "start of" clock tick */
                ticks = jiffies;
                while (ticks == jiffies)
                        /* nothing */;
                /* Go .. */
                ticks = jiffies;
                __delay(loops_per_sec);
                ticks = jiffies - ticks;
                if (ticks)
                        break;
        }
}
```

The lib/ Directory

In this directory is the code that is often needed by other parts of the kernel. For instance, inflate.c can be found here. This code can decompress a kernel at boot and load it into memory. It knows how to decompress standard PKZIP 8bt compression algorithms.

The kernel/ Directory

This directory is where some of the most frequently called kernel functions reside. In addition to the scheduler, fork() and timer.c can be found here. You will also find printk.c in this directory. Throughout the kernel source code, printk() is used instead of printf() because the printf() function is not SMP-capable when called from within the kernel. Therefore, various tasks running on different CPUs might write to the console or to the syslog at the same time, garbling the output.

The mm/ Directory

mm stands for memory manager. This directory contains the source code to implement the virtual memory manager in the Linux kernel.

The net/ Directory

All the code for networking support, such as TCP/IP, Netware, and Appletalk, is here.

COMPILING IT

Before you can actually compile the kernel, you must tell the compilation utilities which functionalities you want, and whether to include those functionalities built into the kernel or to configure them as dynamically loadable modules (we will see later how the kernel handles loadable modules).

The following table shows which commands need to be used to configure the kernel:

Type	Command (as root)
Text prompt	make config
Text menus (ncurses style)	make menuconfig
GUI (requires X to run)	make xconfig

Notice that make config stores your previous choices, so you can always start it again and just change what you need.

Once you have configured the kernel to your satisfaction, you can proceed with the compilation.

root@ maguro /usr/src # make dep; make clean; make bzImage; make modules-install

The directive "make bzImage" will compile the kernel, and leave a file called bzImage in arch/i386/boot'. The above steps might take some time. On a dual PIII 700 MHz with 512MB RAM, this takes about four minutes; on a slower computer, compile time will be longer.

Now it's time to install the new kernel. Most people use LILO (Linux Loader) for this. The directive make bzlilo' will install the kernel, run LILO on it, and get you all ready to boot, but only if LILO is configured in the following way on your system: kernel is /vmlinuz ' is in /sbin, and your lilo config (/etc/lilo.conf) agrees with this.

Otherwise, you need to use LILO directly. It's a fairly easy package to install and work with, but it has a tendency to confuse people with its configuration file. Look at the config file (either /etc/lilo/config for older versions or /etc/lilo.conf for new versions), and see what the current setup is. The config file looks like this:

```
image = /vmlinuz
    label = Linux
    root = /dev/hda1
    . . .
```

The "image ="' is set to the currently installed kernel. Most people use /vmlinuz. "'label" is used by LILO to determine which kernel or operating system to boot, and "root"' is the / of that particular operating system.

Make a backup copy of your old kernel and copy the bzImage which you just made into place (you would say cp bzImage /vmlinuz' if you use /vmlinuz').

Rerun LILO and you have now added the kernel to your boot manager. Alternatively, if you wanted to make a boot disk to check things out before you actually commit your new kernel to the LILO configuration, you could use the mkbootdisk utility shipped with most distributions.

The GNU gcc Compiler

The Linux kernel is written for the GNU gcc compiler. Trying to compile it with any other C compiler will result in complete failure. The source code is full of gcc-specific directives that will prevent using anything but the gcc compiler.

Because of this gcc affinity, the kernel source code might look strange to people who are used to developing for other C compilers. One such common idiosyncrasy is the use of "inline functions." An inline function is a directive to the gcc compiler to fully expand the called function in each recurrence, instead of executing a function call each time to a single, reference instance of the called function (which requires expensive stack operations).

Some might object that this will preclude achieving truly portable code. This is, however, really not the case. Since the gcc compiler exists on all platforms (inherently so) to which Linux has been ported, the code is portable across those architectures. It is, of course, not portable in the sense of being able to compile correctly under other C compilers.

On the other hand, a kernel is not something that requires portability across architectures and compilers. The Linux kernel is optimized for reliability and efficiency, and these two goals are certainly much more important.

Coding Conventions

After reading this book, you will perhaps feel ready to contribute to the Linux kernel. You are obviously welcome to do so, as long as you respect certain conventions.

Commentaries are always in /* */ style, even for one-line comments. The // comment is not acceptable.

Most often, function-opening brackets ("{") are on a separate line. Statements are coded this way:

```
if (str[0] >= '0' && str[0] <= '9') {
        strcpy(name, "ttyS");
        strncpy(name + 4, str, sizeof(name) - 5);
    } else
        strncpy(name, str, sizeof(name) - 1);
    name[sizeof(name) - 1] = 0;
```

Single-line if statements are acceptable:

```
if (!strcmp(str, "ttya")) strcpy(name, "ttyS0");ne ifs are quite OK:
```

Kernel source, since the earliest times, has always contained a lot of gotos. Linux is no exception. It contains a goto for about every 80 lines of code. This is not because of a sloppy style of programming, but rather a requirement dictated by the craving for speedy code. In a nexted while statement, it is just much easier to use goto to get out of the code rather than break.

Architecture Dependencies

Linux runs on a wide variety of processor platforms. Almost every month, you can read about a new successful porting to another architecture. Just remember that Linux originated on the i386 processor. This is clearly visible everywhere in the kernel code.

The following table illustrates the ports achieved so far:

Processor Type	Bitsize	Maintainer
Intelx86	32	Linus Torvalds
Crusoe	32	Linus Torvalds
MIPS	32/64	Alan Cox
IA64	64	The Trillian Project
PA-RISC	64	The Puffin Group
Alpha	64	Richard Henderson
ARM	32	Russell King
Sparc	32/64	David S. Miller
PPc	32	Cort Dougan
M68000	32	Jes Sorensen

CHAPTER 3

What's a File System?

In this chapter we look into what are the constituent parts of a file system and how they are implemented in Linux 2.4. Most of what is valid for other Unix file systems is valid for Linux too. However, in some cases Linux goes the extra mile to facilitate architecture independence, speed, efficiency, security, or elegance of implementation.

GENERAL ASPECTS OF A FILE SYSTEM

The structure of this chapter was inspired by Neil Brown's important document on the Linux Virtual File System at the University of New South Wales in Australia, ww.cse.unsw.edu.au. Many thanks go to Neil Brown for his important contribution to the Linux community.

A file system is the logical means for an operating system to store and retrieve data on the computer's hard disks, be they local drives, network-available volumes, or exported shares in a storage area network (SAN). In particular, a file system implements the basic operations needed for a Unix-style OS:

▼ Create and delete files (i.e., allocate and de-allocate space on the storage medium).

■ Open files for reading and writing.

■ Seek within a file (note: Linux does not provide kernel-level support for the notion of file records).

■ Close files.

■ Create directories to hold groups of files.

■ List the contents of a directory.

▲ Remove files from a directory.

These functions have evolved over the years to become what we now commonly know as the modern Unix environment, which offers complex file manipulation capabilities and provides an extensive set of data management interfaces.

Linux has, from the very beginning, sought to make accommodatations for more than one file system to be available to users. It is not uncommon, in fact, for users to have one or more non-Linux partitions, such as DOS or FAT32, on their hard disks. Should they wish to mount these volumes under Linux, they have to have the DOS or FAT32 file system loaded into their kernel.

It is only logical that Linux developers sought to simplify the interaction between the kernel and the potentially many file system implementations. Therefore, they created the Linux Virtual File System or VFS. The Linux VFS is an abstraction layer above actual file system implementations such as ext2, DOS, FAT32, OS/2 HPFS, and others. Because of the Linux VFS, the user programs do not have to know any particulars of the file system they are using on a partition; the primitives are always the same (delete, copy, create files), since the system calls are always the same. It is then the task of the file system implementations to accept the VFS primitives and carry them out according to the file system's protocol and specifications.

Therefore, the Linux VFS makes it possible to just issue a standard "vi myfile.foo" command to edit a file, be it on a DOS, OS/2 HPFS or JFS[1] partition.

Let's start by reviewing the broad concepts of a file system.

A *file* is simply an ordered sequence of elements, where an element could be a machine word, a character, or a bit, depending upon the implementation. A program or a user may create, modify, or delete files only through the use of the file system. Generally for Unixes, at the level of the file system, a file is formatless.[2] All formatting is done by higher-level modules or by user-supplied programs, if desired. As far as a particular user is concerned, a file has one name, and that name is symbolic. (Symbolic names may be arbitrarily long, up to certain limitations, and may have syntax of their own.) The user may reference an element in the file by specifying the symbolic filename and the linear index of the element within the file. By using higher-level modules, a user may also be able to reference suitably defined sequences of elements directly by context.

A *directory* is a special file which is maintained by the file system, and which contains a list of *entries*. To a user, an entry appears to be a file and is accessed in terms of its symbolic entry name, which is the user's filename. An *entry name* need be unique only within the directory in which it occurs. Therefore, in Unix and in Linux the scope of the filename space refers to a directory only. In reality, each entry is a pointer of one of two kinds. The entry may point directly to a file (which may itself be a directory), or else it may point to another entry in the same or another directory. An entry which points to another directory entry is called a *link*.

The only information associated with a link is the pointer to the entry to which it links. This pointer is specified in terms of a symbolic name which uniquely identifies the linked entry within the hierarchy. A link derives its access control information from the branch to which it effectively points.

The Hierarchy of the File Structure

A file directly pointed to in a directory is *immediately inferior* to that directory (and the directory is *immediately superior* to the file). A file which is immediately inferior to a directory which is itself immediately inferior to a second directory is *inferior* to the second directory (and similarly the second directory is *superior* to the file). The root has level zero, and files immediately inferior to it have level one. By extension, inferiority (or superiority) is defined for any number of levels of separation via a chain of immediately inferior (superior) files. (The reader who is disturbed by the level numbers increasing with inferiority may pretend that level numbers have negative signs.) Links are then considered to be superimposed upon, but independent of, the tree structure. Note that the notions of inferiority and superiority are not concerned with links, but only with branches.

---

1   JFS is the IBM Journaling File System for Linux. (The author of this book is one of the project's contributors.)
2   Many other operating systems have a notion of the format of the file's contents. For example, IBM OS/390 knows different formats for records, fixed and variable. Unix has always chosen not to let the file system know the format of the file's contents for the sake of simplicity.

In a tree hierarchy of this kind, it seems desirable that a user be able to work in one or a few directories, rather than having to move about continually. It is thus natural for the hierarchy to be so arranged that users with similar interests can share common files and yet have private files when desired. At any one time, a user is considered to be operating in one directory, called the *working directory*. He may access a file effectively pointed to by an entry in his working directory simply by specifying the entry name. More than one user may have the same working directory at one time.

An example of a simple tree hierarchy without links is shown in Figure 3-1. Non-terminal nodes, which are shown as circles, indicate files that are directories, while the lines downward from each such node indicate the entries (i.e., branches) in the directory corresponding to that node. The terminal nodes, which are shown as squares, indicate files other than directories. Letters indicate entry names, while numbers are used for descriptive purposes only to identify directories in the figure. For example, the letter "J" is the entry name of various entries in different directories in the figure, while the number "0" refers to the root.

An entry name is meaningful only with respect to the directory in which it occurs, and may or may not be unique outside of that directory. For various reasons, it is desirable to have a symbolic name which uniquely defines an entry in the hierarchy as a whole. Such a name is obtained relative to the root, and is called the *tree name*. It consists of the chain of entry names required to reach the entry via a chain of branches from the root.

However, in most cases, the user will not need to know the tree name of an entry.

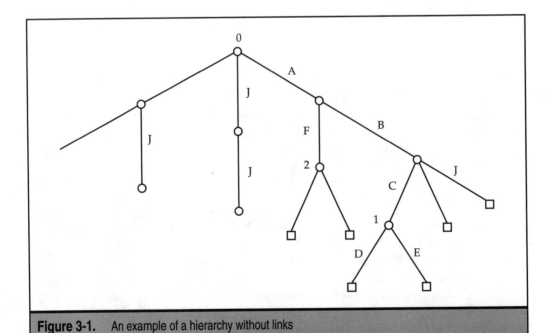

Figure 3-1.   An example of a hierarchy without links

Unless specifically stated otherwise, the tree name of a file is defined relative to the root. A file may also be named uniquely relative to an arbitrary directory, as follows.

A link with an arbitrary name (LINKNAME) may be established to an entry in another directory by means of a command:

ln -s LINKNAME, PATHNAME

The name of the entry to be linked to (PATHNAME) may be specified as a tree name relative to the working directory or to the root, or more generally as a pathname (defined below). Note that a file may thus have different names to different users, depending on how it is accessed. A link serves as a shortcut to a branch somewhere else in the hierarchy, and gives the user the illusion that the link is actually a branch pointing directly to the desired file. Although the links add no basic capabilities to those already present within the tree structure of branches, they greatly facilitate the ease with which the file system may be used. Links also help to eliminate the need for duplicate copies of sharable files. The superimposing of links upon the tree structure in Figure 3- 1 is illustrated in Figure 3-2. The dashed lines downward from a node show entries which are links to other entries. When the links are added to the tree structure, the result is a directed graph. (The direction is, of course, downward from each node.)

In the example of Figure 3-2, the entry named G in directory 2 is a link to the branch named C in directory 3. The entry named C in directory 4 (recall that entry names need

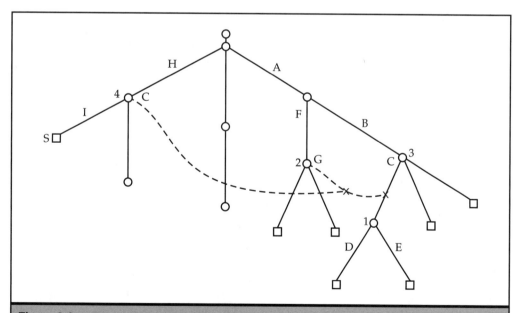

Figure 3-2.   The example of Figure 3-1 with links added

not be unique except within a directory) is a link to the entry G in directory 2, and thus acts as a link to C in directory 3. Both of these links effectively point to the directory 1.

It is desirable to have a name analogous to the tree name which includes links. Such a name is the *pathname*, and is assumed to be relative to the root unless specifically stated otherwise.

The pathname of a file (relative to the root) is the chain of entry names used to name the file, relative to the root. The working directory is always established in terms of a pathname. A user may change his working directory by means of a command such as

    cd PATHNAME

where the pathname may be relative to the (old) working directory or to the root. The definition of a pathname relative to a directory other than the root is similar to the definition of a tree name, with the following exceptions: the concept of a file immediately inferior to a directory is replaced by the concept of a file effectively pointed to by the entry. The concept of a directory immediately superior to a file is replaced by a concept, which is well-defined only as the inverse of the above effective pointer, that is, dependent on what entry in which directory was previously used to reach the file.

In general, any file may be specified by a pathname (which may in fact be a tree name or an entry name) relative to the current working directory. A file may also be specified by a pathname relative to the root. In the former case, the pathname begins with a colon, in the latter case it does not.

Objects in a File System

One can look at a file system as a container of objects. These objects are all the logical entities that such a file system abstracts to the user. One evident example of an object in a file system is the file, another is the object. Yet another is, for instance, the symbolic link. Then you have also objects not directly visible to the end-user, such as the superblock, the inode, etc.

The Linux Kernel's Relation to the File System—The Virtual File System

Since the number of files on a Unix system may easily range into the hundreds of thousands or more, the task of organizing the file system control structures is insulated from applications and yet is, strictly speaking, not a kernel thing either. The Linux kernel's file subsystem has an unusually abstract view of what a file system is. There is no knowledge whatsoever in the Linux kernel of Linux's own native ext2, or procfs, reiserfs, or any other file system; all file systems are treated equally.

The kernel provides only very basic hooks (the above-mentioned VFS) into which each file can attach itself, and provides (to both the kernel and to applications) the actual functionality via the creation and management of intermediate control structures. This level of abstraction is the key to allowing all file handling to be implemented as kernel system calls acting on instantiated control structure objects, rather than as user-space file system handling code, which in turn allows control structures for open files to be allocated and de-allocated dynamically both systemwide and per process.

An application uses the file as an abstraction to address a linear range of bytes stored on some form of I/O medium, typically a storage device such as an SCSI disk. To access a file, the OS provides file manipulation interfaces to open, close, read, and write the data within each file.

Buffers, Caches, and Memory Garbage Collection

Buffers represent not the cached contents of files, but rather cached contents of a physical disk. In contrast, caches actually cache file contents. Linux's exploitation of buffers and caches is heavily dependent on the virtual memory (VM) functionality and performance. The virtual memory is one of the most complex components of any operating system and cannot be discussed in detail here. For an in-depth treatment of the VM of Linux 2.4, refer to my book *Linux Internals*, published in July 2000 with McGraw-Hill, New York.

Figure 3-3 shows the basic organization of the VFS.

How does the kernel allocate buffers from the main memory, and how does it manage caches?

THE BUFFER CACHE

As the file systems are mounted by the user programs they generate a lot of requests to the block devices to read and write data blocks. All block data read and write requests are given to the device drivers in the form of `buffer_head` data structures via standard kernel routine calls. These give all of the information that the block device drivers need; the device identifier uniquely identifies the device and the block number tells the driver which block to read.

All block devices are viewed as linear collections of blocks of the same size. To speed up access to the physical block devices, Linux maintains a cache of block buffers. All of the block buffers in the system are kept somewhere in this buffer cache, even the new, unused buffers. This cache is shared among all of the physical block devices; at any one time there are many block buffers in the cache, belonging to any one of the system's block devices and often in many different states. If valid data is available from the buffer cache, this saves the system an access to a physical device. Any block buffer that has been used to read data from a block device or to write data to it goes into the buffer cache. Over time it may be removed from the cache to make way for a more deserving buffer or it may remain in the cache if it is frequently accessed.

Block buffers within the cache are uniquely identified by the owning device identifier and the block number of the buffer. The buffer cache is composed of two functional parts. The first is the lists of free block buffers. There is one list per supported buffer size and the system's free block buffers are queued on to these lists when they are first created or when they have been discarded. The currently supported buffer sizes are 512, 1024, 2048, 4096, and 8192 bytes. The second functional part is the cache

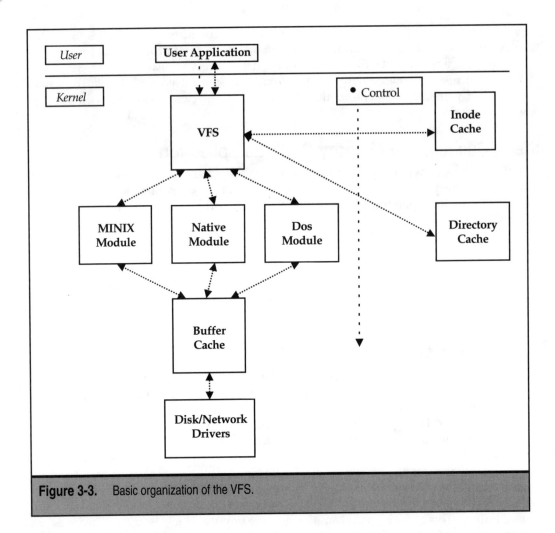

Figure 3-3.   Basic organization of the VFS.

itself. This is a hash table which is a vector of pointers to chains of buffers that have the same hash index. The hash index is generated from the owning device identifier and the block number of the data block.

Figure 3-4 shows the hash table together with a few entries. Block buffers are either in one of the free lists or they are in the buffer cache. When they are in the buffer cache they are also queued on to Least Recently Used (LRU) lists. There is an LRU list for each buffer type and these are used by the system to perform work on buffers of a type, for example, writing buffers with new data in them out to disk.

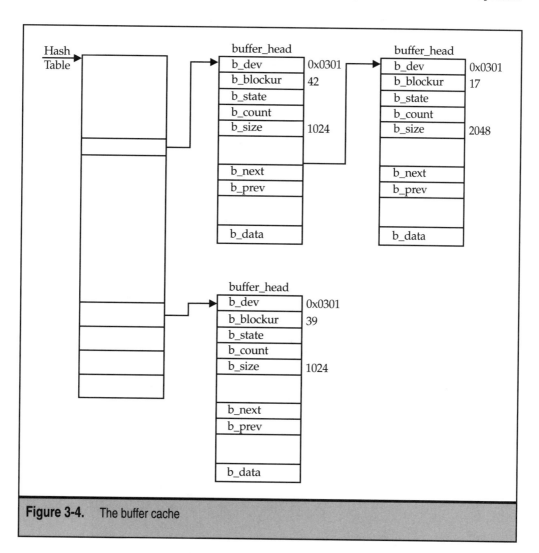

Figure 3-4. The buffer cache

The buffer's type reflects its state and Linux currently supports the following types:

clean   Unused, new buffers.

locked   Buffers which are locked, waiting to be written.

dirty   These contain new, valid data, and will be written but so far have not been scheduled to write.

shared   Shared buffers.

unshared   Buffers that were once shared but which are not now.

Whenever a file system needs to read a buffer its underlying physical device tries to get a block from the buffer cache. If it cannot get a buffer from the buffer cache then it will get a clean one from the appropriately sized free list and this new buffer will go into the buffer cache. If the buffer that it needed is in the buffer cache then it may or may not be up-to-date. If it is not up-to-date or if it is a new block buffer, the file system must request that the device driver read the appropriate block of data from the disk.

Like all caches, the buffer cache must be maintained so that it runs efficiently and fairly allocates cache entries between the block devices using the buffer cache. Linux uses the bdflush kernel daemon to perform a lot of housekeeping duties on the cache but some happen automatically as a result of the cache being used.

THE BDFLUSH KERNEL DAEMON

The bdflush kernel daemon is a simple kernel daemon that provides a dynamic response to the system having too many dirty buffers, i.e., buffers that contain data, which must be written out to disk at some time. It is started as a kernel thread at system startup time and, rather confusingly, it calls itself "kflushd" and that is the name that you will see if you use the *ps* command to show the processes in the system. Mostly this daemon sleeps, waiting for the number of dirty buffers in the system to grow too large. As buffers are allocated and discarded, the number of dirty buffers in the system is checked. If there are too many as a percentage of the total number of buffers in the system then bdflush is woken up. The default threshold is 60% but, if the system is desperate for buffers, bdflush will be woken up anyway. This value can be seen and changed using the *update* command:

```
# update -d
bdflush version 1.4
0:      60 Max fraction of LRU list to examine for dirty blocks
1:     500 Max number of dirty blocks to write each time bdflush activated
2:      64 Num of clean buffers to be loaded onto free list by refill_freelist
3:     256 Dirty block threshold for activating bdflush in refill_freelist
4:      15 Percentage of cache to scan for free clusters
5:    3000 Time for data buffers to age before flushing
6:     500 Time for non-data (dir, bitmap, etc) buffers to age before flushing
7:    1884 Time buffer cache load average constant
8:       2 LAV ratio (used to determine threshold for buffer fratricide).
```

All of the dirty buffers are linked into the BUF_DIRTY LRU list whenever they are made dirty by having data written to them and bdflush tries to write a reasonable number of them out to their owning disks. Again, this number can be seen and controlled by the *update* command and the default is 500 (see above).

As far as each file system is concerned, caching and buffer allocation are both very simple. The file system asks for a new page for the page cache or a new buffer from the buffer cache, and the cache just takes a page off the kernel's free page list to satisfy that request.

Going on like this will eventually result in all the memory being used. To avoid that, the designers of Linux provided a separate mechanism, which comprises a twofold reclamation strategy:

First: if a kernel process requests a free page and the request isn't urgent (i.e., there are no pending interrupts to handle), then the call to the memory allocator will in turn call the memory-reclaim functions to find something to evict from memory.

Second: even if there are no memory allocation calls happening, a background daemon—kswapd—regularly checks the free memory situation and starts reclaiming memory if it gets too low.

In either case, the reclamation process is the same. The kernel cycles through various data structures, including the page tables which process use to map files into virtual memory, and the page and buffer caches. It looks for pages which have not been accessed since the last time we passed over that page, and when it finds them, it removes those pages from use and returns them to the free list.

Kswapd

Kswapd cyclically goes through the pages and tries to free enough of them to ensure a smooth operation. In /proc/sys/vm/kswapd there are three parameters:

```
/proc/sys/vm/  $ cat kswapd
512  32  32
```

The first parameter is tries_base. It represents the number of pages divided by four or eight that kswapd tries to free up on each pass. A higher parameter here causes swap space to be released faster, increasing overall swap throughput.

The second parameter is tries_min and represents the minimum number of pages that kswapd should try to free up on each pass.

The third parameter is the number of pages that kswapd writes on each pass. A higher value will cause kswapd to have more pages in one I/O, increasing performance. Too high a value, however, will result in a very large I/O operation blocking everything else.

File System Objects

The Linux VFS interacts with a set of objects to store, access, and manage data on block devices. These objects are:

▼   **Files**   Files are things that can be read from or written to. They can also be mapped into memory and sometimes a list of filenames can be read from them. They map very closely to the `file descriptor` concept that Unix has. Files are represented within Linux by a `struct file` which has a number of methods stored in a `struct file_operations`.

■ **Inodes** An inode represents a basic object within a file system. It can be a regular file, a directory, a symbolic link, or a few other objects. The VFS does not make a strong distinction between different sorts of objects, but leaves it to the actual file system implementation to provide appropriate behaviors, and to the higher levels of the kernel to treat different objects differently. Each inode is represented by a `struct inode` which has a number of methods stored in a `struct inode_operations`. It may seem that files and inodes are very similar, which in fact they are, but there are some important differences. First, note that there are some things that have inodes but never have files. A good example of this is a symbolic link. Conversely, there are files which do not have inodes, particularly pipes (though not named pipes) and sockets (though not UNIX domain sockets). Also, a file has state information that an inode does not have, particularly a `position`, which indicates where in the file the next read or write will be performed.

■ **File Systems** A file system is a collection of `inodes` with one distinguished inode known as the `root`. Other inodes are accessed by starting at the root and looking up a filename to get to another inode. A file system has a number of characteristics which apply uniformly to all inodes within it. Some of these characteristics are flags such as the `READ-ONLY` flag. Another important one is the `blocksize`. I'm not entirely sure why this is needed globally. Each file system is represented by a `struct super_block`, and has a number of methods stored in a `struct super_operations`. There is a strong correlation within Linux between super-blocks (and hence file systems) and device numbers. Each file system must (appear to) have a unique device on which the file system resides. Some file systems (such as `nfs` and `proc`) are marked as not needing a real device. For these, an anonymous device, with a `major` number of 0, is automatically assigned. As well as knowing about file systems, Linux VFS knows about different file system types. Each type of file system is represented in Linux by a `struct file_system_type`. This contains just one method, `read_super`, which instantiates a `super_block` to represent a given file system.

▲ **Names** All inodes within a file-system are accessed by name. As the name-to-inode lookup process may be expensive for some file-systems, Linux's VFS layer maintains a cache of currently active and recently used names. This cache is referred to as the `dcache`. The dcache is structured in memory as a tree. Each node in the tree corresponds to an inode in a given directory with a given name. An inode can be associated with more than one node in the tree. While the dcache is not a complete copy of the file tree, it is a proper prefix of that tree (if that is a correct usage of the term). This means that if any node of the file tree is in the cache, then every ancestor of that node is also in the cache. Each node in the tree is represented by a `struct dentry` which has a number of methods stored in a `struct dentry_operations`. The dentries act as an intermediary between files and inodes. Each file points to the dentry that it has open.

Each dentry points to the inode that it references. This implies that for every open file, the dentry of that file, and of all the parents of that file are cached in memory.

In the next section we will see what these objects are in detail and how the Linux VFS interacts with these objects.

Files

The `file` structure is defined in `linux/fs.h` to be:

```
struct fown_struct {
        int pid;                    /* pid or -pgrp where SIGIO should be sent */
        uid_t uid, euid;            /* uid/euid of process setting the owner */
        int signum;                 /* posix.1b rt signal to be delivered on IO */
};

struct file {
        struct list_head        f_list;
        struct dentry           *f_dentry;
        struct file_operations  *f_op;
        atomic_t                f_count;
        unsigned int            f_flags;
        mode_t                  f_mode;
        loff_t                  f_pos;
        unsigned long           f_reada, f_ramax, f_raend, f_ralen, f_rawin;
        struct fown_struct      f_owner;
        unsigned int            f_uid, f_gid;
        int                     f_error;

        unsigned long           f_version;

        /* needed for tty driver, and maybe others */
        void                    *private_data;
};
```

The fields have the meanings explained in the following section.

f_list

This field links files together into one of a number of lists. There is one list for each active file-system, starting at the `s_files` pointer in the super-block. There is one for free file structures (`free_list` in `fs/file_table.c`). And there is one for anonymous files (`anon_list` in `fs/file_table.c`) such as pipes.

f_dentry

This field records the dcache entry that points to the inode for this file. If the inode refers to an object, such as a pipe, which isn't in a regular file system, the dentry is a root dentry created with `d_alloc_root`.

f_op

This field points to the methods to use on this file.

f_count

The number of references to this file. There is one for each different user-process file descriptor, plus one for each internal usage.

f_flags

This field stores the flags for this file such as access type (read/write), nonblocking, appendonly, etc. These are defined in the per-architecture include file `asm/fcntl.h`. Some of these flags are only relevant at the time of opening and are not stored in `f_flags`. These excluded flags are O_CREAT, O_EXCL, O_NOCTTY, O_TRUNC. This list is from `filp_open` in `fs/open.c`.

f_mode

The bottom two bits of `f_flags` encode read and write access in a way that it is not easy to extract the individual read and write access information. `f_mode` stores the read and write access as two separate bits.

f_pos

This records the current file position which will be the address used for the next `read` request, and for the next `write` request if the file does NOT have the O_APPEND flag.

f_reada, f_remax, f_raend, f_ralen, f_rawin

These five fields are used to keep track of sequential access patterns on the file, and determine how much read-ahead to do. There may be a separate section on read-ahead.

f_owner

This structure stores a process id and a signal to send to the process when certain events happen with the file, such as new data being available. Currently, keyboards, mice, serial ports, and network sockets seem to be the only files which use this feature (via `kill_fasync`).

f_uid, f_gid

These fields get set to the owner and group of the process which opened the file. They don't seem to be used at all.

f_error

This is used by the NFS client file system code to return write errors. It is set in `fs/nfs/write.c` and checked in `fs/nfs/file.c`, and used in `mm/filemap.c:generic_file_write`.

f_version

This field is available to be used by the underlying file system to help cache state, and to check for the cache being invalid. It is changed whenever the file has its `f_pos` value changed.

For example, the `ext2` file system uses it in conjunction with the `i_version` field in the inode to detect when a directory may have changed. If neither the directory nor the file position has changed, then `ext2` can be sure that the current file position is the start of a valid directory entry; otherwise it must recheck from the start of the block.

private_data

This is used by many device drivers, and even a few file systems, to store extra per-open-file information (such as credentials in `coda`).

File Functions

The list of file functions are defined in `linux/fs.h` to be:

```
typedef int (*filldir_t)(void *, const char *, int, off_t, ino_t);

struct file_operations {
        loff_t (*llseek) (struct file *, loff_t, int);
        ssize_t (*read) (struct file *, char *, size_t, loff_t *);
        ssize_t (*write) (struct file *, const char *, size_t, loff_t *);
        int (*readdir) (struct file *, void *, filldir_t);
        unsigned int (*poll) (struct file *, struct poll_table_struct *);
        int (*ioctl) (struct inode *, struct file *, unsigned int, unsigned long);
        int (*mmap) (struct file *, struct vm_area_struct *);
        int (*open) (struct inode *, struct file *);
        int (*flush) (struct file *);
        int (*release) (struct inode *, struct file *);
        int (*fsync) (struct file *, struct dentry *);
        int (*fasync) (int, struct file *, int);
        int (*check_media_change) (kdev_t dev);
        int (*revalidate) (kdev_t dev);
        int (*lock) (struct file *, int, struct file_lock *);
};
```

llseek

This implements the `lseek` system call. If it is left undefined, then `default_llseek` from `fs/read_write.c` is used instead. This updates the `f_pos` field as expected, and also may change the `f_reada` field and `f_version` field.

read

This is used to implement the `read` system call and to support other occasions for reading files, such as loading executables and reading the quotas file. It is expected to update the offset value (last argument), which is usually a pointer to the `f_pos` field in the `file` structure, except for the `pread` and `pwrite` system calls.

For file systems on block devices, there is a routine `generic_file_read` in `mm/filemap.c` which can be used for this method, providing that the inode has a `readpage` method defined.

write

This method allows writing to a file, such as when using the `write` system call. This method does not necessarily make sure that the data has reached the device, but may only queue it ready for writing when convenient, depending on the semantics of the file type.

For file systems on block devices, `generic_file_write` may be used in conjunction with `block_write_partial_page` from `fs/buffer.c` to implement this method.

readdir

`readdir` should read directory entries from the file, which would presumably be a directory, and return them using the `filldir_t` callback function. This function takes the `void *` handle that was passed along with a pointer to a name, the length of the name, the position in the file where this name was found, and the inode number associated with the name.

If the `filldir` call-back returns non-zero, then `readdir` should assume that it has had enough, and should return as well.

When `readdir` reaches the end of the directory, it should return with the value 0. Otherwise it may return after just some of the entres have been given to `filldir`. In this case it should return a non-zero value. It should return a negative number on error.

poll

`poll` is use to implement the `select` and `poll` system calls. It should add a `poll_table_entry` to the `poll_table_struct` that it is passed.

ioctl

This implements *ad hoc* ioctl functionality. If an ioctl request is not one of a set of known requests (FIBMAP, FIGETBSZ, FIONREAD), then the request is passed on the underlying file implementation.

mmap

This routine implements memory mapping of files. It can often be implemented using generic_file_mmap. Its task seems to be to validate that the mapping is allowed, and to set up the vm_ops field of the vm_area_struct to point to something appropriate.

open

This method, if defined, is called when a new file has been opened in an inode. It can do any setup that may be needed on open. This is not used with many file systems. One exception is coda which tries to get the file cached locally at open.

flush

flush is called when a file descriptor is closed. There may be other file descriptors open on this file, so it isn't necessarily a final close of the file, just an interim one. The only file-system that currently defines this method is the NFS client, which flushes out any write-behind requests that are pending.

Flush can return an error status back through the close system call, and so needs to be used if there are errors to be checked for. Unfortunately, there is no way that flush can reliably determine if it is the last call to flush.

release

release is called when the last handle on a file is closed. It should do any special clean up that is needed.

release cannot return any error status to anyone, and so should really be of type void rather than int.

fsync

This method implements the fsync and fdatasync system calls (they are currently identical). It should not return until all pending writes for the file have successfully reached the device.

fsync may be partially implemented using generic_buffer_fdatasync which will write out all dirty buffers on all mapped pages of the inode.

fasync

This method is called when the FIOASYNC flag of the file changes. The int parameter contains the new value of this flag. No file systems currently use this method.

check_media_change

This method should check if the underlying media has changed, and should return true if it has. The only place outside of disk drivers where it is called is in `read_super` when a file system is about to be mounted. If it returns true at this point, all buffers associated with the device are invalidated.

revalidate

`revalidate` is called after buffers have been invalidated after a media change, as reported by `check_media_change`. So it is only meaningful if `check_media_change` is defined. This shouldn't be confused with the `inode:revalidate` method which is quite different.

lock

This method allows a file service to provide extra handling of POSIX locks. It is not used for FLOCK style locks. This is useful particularly for network file systems where other locks might be held in ways only noticeable by the file system.

When locks are being set or removed, a lock is first obtained with this method, and then also with the standard POSIX lock code. If this method succeeds in getting a lock, but the local code fails, then the lock will never be released.

When a process is trying to find what locks are present, information returned by this method is used; the local locks are not checked.

INODES

The inode is the basic building block of any file system in Unix. It is, therefore, worthwhile to take a closer look at this important structure.

An inode can itself represent another object, e.g., a file or a directory. There is an inode for each file; a file is uniquely identified by the file system on which it resides and by its inode number on the file system.

Every inode contains pointers to various methods—or functions, if you prefer—which can operate on itself or on the object it represents. These methods can read or write data, seek to a specific offset in the file, do directory operations such as creating new files or renaming existing ones, and so on. Not all operations or methods will be valid on all inodes. For example, you can't rename on a regular file, because in Unix a rename is an operation on the parent directory, not on the file itself; and you can't seek on a pipe.

Each inode contains a count of the number of data blocks that it contains. The number of actual data blocks is the sum of the allocated data blocks and the indirect blocks. The directive fsck computes the actual number of data blocks and compares that block count against the actual number of blocks the inode claims. If an inode contains an incorrect count, fsck prompts the operator to fix it.

Each inode contains a 64-bit size field. The size is the number of data bytes in the file associated with the inode. The accuracy of the size field is roughly checked by computing from the size field the maximum number of blocks that should be associated with the inode, and comparing that expected block count against the actual number of blocks the inode claims.

Each inode contains the following information:

▼ The device where the node resides.

■ Mode of file.

■ Type of file.

■ Locking information.

■ File length (the number of bytes in the file).

■ Link count (the number of links to the file).

■ The owner's user and group IDs.

■ Access privileges.

■ Time of last access to the file.

■ The time the inode itself was last modified.

■ Time of last modification of the file.

▲ The addresses of the file's blocks on the disk (pointers to the extents that contain the file's data).

Linux keeps a cache of active and recently used inodes. There are two paths by which these inodes can be accessed. The first is through the dcache. Each dentry in the dcache refers to an inode, and thereby keeps that inode in the cache. The second path is through the inode hash table. Each inode is hashed to an 8-bit number based on the address of the file system's super-block and the inode number. Inodes with the same hash value are then chained together in a doubly linked list.

Access though the hash table is achieved using the iget function, which is only called by a file system when looking up an inode which wasn't found in the dcache, and by nfsd. Basing the hash on the inode number is a bit restrictive as it assumes that every file system can uniquely identify a file in 32 bits. This is a problem, at least of the NFS file system, which would prefer to use the 256-bit file handle as the unique identifier in the hash. The nfsd usage might be better served by having the file system provide a file handle-to-inode mapping function, which has to interpret the file handle in the most appropriate way.

During startup, the kernel initializes the table, which holds general information about the accessibility of files, by calling a routine (in the kernel's memory allocator code) that creates a cache for kernel objects. The kernel does not actually create the first object, which is a file control structure, until a file is opened.

The distinct kernel objects which are stored in said cache are called inodes. An inode is a distinct object, within the kernel, which is managed by a file system, a network redirector, or some other storage management system. Linux implements inodes in plain

C, but the design is very abstract and very object-oriented. See the code below describing the inode kernel structure.

```
struct inode {
        struct list_head        i_hash;
        struct list_head        i_list;
        struct list_head        i_dentry;

        unsigned long           i_ino;
        unsigned int            i_count;
        kdev_t                  i_dev;
        umode_t                 i_mode;
        nlink_t                 i_nlink;
        uid_t                   i_uid;
        gid_t                   i_gid;
        kdev_t                  i_rdev;
        off_t                   i_size;
        time_t                  i_atime;
        time_t                  i_mtime;
        time_t                  i_ctime;
        unsigned long           i_blksize;
        unsigned long           i_blocks;
        unsigned long           i_version;
        unsigned long           i_nrpages;
        struct semaphore        i_sem;
        struct inode_operations *i_op;
        struct super_block      *i_sb;
        wait_queue_head_t       i_wait;
        struct file_lock        *i_flock;
        struct vm_area_struct   *i_mmap;
        struct page             *i_pages;
        spinlock_t              i_shared_lock;
        struct dquot            *i_dquot[MAXQUOTAS];
        struct pipe_inode_info  *i_pipe;


        unsigned long           i_state;

        unsigned int            i_flags;
        unsigned char           i_sock;

        atomic_t                i_writecount;
        unsigned int            i_attr_flags;
        __u32                   i_generation;
```

```
        union {
                ....
                struct ext2_inode_info          ext2_i;
                ....
                struct socket                   socket_i;
                void                            *generic_ip;
        } u;
};
```

Let's look at the most important fields in that structure.

i_hash

The i_hash linked list links together all inodes which hash to the same hash bucket. Hash values are based on the address of the super-block structure, and the inode number of the inode. This hash tremendously speeds up looking for a particular node.

i_list

The i_list linked list links inodes in various states. There is the inode_in_use list which lists unchanged inodes that are in active use, inode_unused which lists unused inodes, and superblock->s_dirty which holds all the dirty inodes on the given file system.

i_dentry

The i_dentry list is a list of all struct dentrys that refer to this inode. They are linked together with the d_alias field of the dentry.

i_version

The i_version field is available for file systems to use to record that a change has been made. Typically, the i_version is set to the current value of the event global variable which is then incremented. The file system code will sometimes assign the current value of i_version to the f_version field of an associated file structure. On a subsequent use of the file structure, it is then possible to tell if the inode has been changed, and if necessary, data cached in the file structure can be refreshed.

i_nrpages

This field records the number of pages, linked at i_pages, which are currently cached for this inode. It is incremented by add_page_to_inode_queue and decremented by remove_page_from_inode_queue.

i_sem

This semaphore guards changes to the inode. Any code that wants to make non-atomic access to the inode (i.e., two related accesses with the possibility of sleeping in between) must first claim this semaphore. This includes such things as allocating and deallocating blocks and searching through directories.

It appears that it is not possible to claim a shared lock for read-only operations.

i_flock

This points to the list of `struct file_lock` structures that impose locks in this inode.

i_mmap

All of the `vm_area_struct` structures that describe mapping of an inode are linked together with the `vm_next_share` and `vm_pprev_share` pointers. This `i_mmap` pointer points into that list.

i_pages

This is the list of all pages in the page cache that refer to this inode. They are linked together on the `next` and `prev` links in the `page` structure.

i_shared_lock

This spin lock guards the `vm_next_share` and `vm_prev_share` pointers in the `i_mmap` list.

i_state

There are three possible inode state bits: I_DIRTY, I_LOCK, I_FREEING.

I_DIRTY	Dirty inodes are on the per-super-block `s_dirty` list, and will be written next time a sync is requested.
I_LOCK	Inodes are locked while they are being created, read or written.
I_FREEING	An inode has this state when the reference count and link count have both reached zero. This seems to be only used by `igrab` called from the `fat` file-system. `fat` does funny things with inodes.

i_flags

The `i_flags` field corresponds to the `s_flags` field in the super-block. Many of the flags can be set systemwide or per inode. The per-inode flags are:

MS_NOSUID	Setuid/setgid is not permitted in this file.
MS_NODEV	If this inode is a device special file, it cannot be opened.

MS_NOEXEC	This file cannot be executed.
MS_SYNCHRONOUS	All write should be synchronous.
MS_MANDLOCK	Mandatory locking is honored.
S_QUOTA	Quotas have been initialized.
S_APPEND	The file can only be appended to.
S_IMMUTABLE	The file may not be changed, even by root.
MS_NOATIME	Do not update access time on the inode when the file is accessed.
MS_NODIRATIME	Do not update access time on directories (but still do so on files unless MS_NOATIME).
MS_ODD_RENAME	Relates to NFS.

i_writecount

If this is positive, it counts the number of clients (files or memory maps) which have write access. If it is negative, then the absolute value of this number counts the number of VM_DENYWRITE mappings that are current. Otherwise it is 0, and nobody is trying to write or trying to stop others from writing.

i_attr_flags

This is never used, and is only set by ext2_read_inode to be some combination of ATTR_FLAG_SYNCRONOUS, ATTR_FLAG_APPEND, ATTR_FLAG_IMMUTABLE, and ATTR_FLAG_NOATIME.

i_generation

The intent of i_generation is to be able to distinguish between an inode before and after a delete/reuse cycle. This is important for NFS. Currently, only ext2 and nfsd maintain this field.

It is not clear that this could be exported to the VFS layer at all as it's use is so specific. Rather, each file system should have the opportunity to provide a unique file handle for a given inode, and each can then do whatever seems best to guarantee uniqueness.

Functions on Inodes

As with other objects, inodes are handled with a standard set of functions (also called methods) on them. The structure of inode operations is the following:

```
struct inode_operations {
        struct file_operations * default_file_ops;
        int (*create) (struct inode *,struct dentry *,int);
        struct dentry * (*lookup) (struct inode *,struct dentry *);
        int (*link) (struct dentry *,struct inode *,struct dentry *);
        int (*unlink) (struct inode *,struct dentry *);
```

```
    int (*symlink) (struct inode *,struct dentry *,const char *);
    int (*mkdir) (struct inode *,struct dentry *,int);
    int (*rmdir) (struct inode *,struct dentry *);
    int (*mknod) (struct inode *,struct dentry *,int,int);
    int (*rename) (struct inode *, struct dentry *,
                      struct inode *, struct dentry *);
    int (*readlink) (struct dentry *, char *,int);
    struct dentry * (*follow_link) (struct dentry *, struct dentry *,unsigned int);

    int (*get_block) (struct inode *, long, struct buffer_head *, int);

    int (*readpage) (struct file *, struct page *);
    int (*writepage) (struct file *, struct page *);
    int (*flushpage) (struct inode *, struct page *, unsigned long);

    void (*truncate) (struct inode *);
    int (*permission) (struct inode *, int);
    int (*smap) (struct inode *,int);
    int (*revalidate) (struct dentry *);
};
```

default_file_ops

This points to the default table of file operations for files opened on this inode. When a file is opened, the `f_op` field in the file structure is initialized from this, and then the `open` method in the `file_operations` table is called. That method may choose to change the `f_op` to a different (non-default) method table. This is done, for example, when a device special file is opened.

create

This, and the next eight methods are only meaningful on directory inodes.

`create` is called when the VFS wants to create a file with the given name (in the `dentry`) in the given directory. The VFS will have already checked that the name doesn't exist, and the `dentry` passed will be a negative `dentry` meaning that the inode pointer will be NULL.

`create` should, if successful, get a new empty inode from the cache with `get_empty_inode`, fill in the fields, and insert it into the hash table with `insert_inode_hash`, mark it dirty with `mark_inode_dirty`, and instantiate it into the dcache with `d_instantiate`.

The `int` argument contains the `mode` of the file, which should indicate that it is `S_IFREG` and specify the required permission bits.

lookup

lookup should check if that name (given by the dentry) exists in the directory (given by the inode) and should update the dentry using d_add if it does. This involves finding and loading the inode.

If the lookup failed to find anything, this is indicated by returning a negative dentry, with an inode pointer of NULL.

As well as returning an error or NULL, indicating that the dentry was correctly updated, lookup can return an alternate dentry, in which case the passed dentry will be released. It is unclear whether this possibility is actually used.

link

The link method should make a **hard** link from the name refered to by the first dentry to the name referred to by the second dentry, which is in the directory referred to by the inode.

If successful, it should call d_instantiate to link the inode of the linked file to the new dentry (which was a negative dentry).

unlink

This should remove the name referred to by the dentry from the directory referred to by the inode. It should d_delete the dentry on success.

symlink

This should create a symbolic link in the given directory with the given name having the given value. It should d_instantiate the new inode into the dentry on success.

mkdir

Create a directory with the given parent, name, and mode.

rmdir

Remove the named directory (if empty) and d_delete the dentry.

mknod

Create a device special file with the given parent, name, mode, and device number, and then d_instantiate the new inode into the dentry.

rename

The first inode and entry refer to a directory and name that exist. rename should rename the object to have the parent and name given by the second inode and dentry. All generic checks, including that the new parent isn't a child of the old name, have already been done.

readlink

The symbolic link referred to by the dentry is read and the value is copied into the user buffer (with `copy_to_user`) with a maximum length given by the `int`.

follow_link

If we have a directory (the first dentry) and a name within that directory (the second dentry), then the *obvious* result of following the name from the directory would be to arrive at the second dentry. If an inode requires some other non-obvious, result—as do symbolic links—the inode should provide a `follow_link` method to return the appropriate new `dentry`. The `int` argument contains a number of `LOOKUP` flags which are described in the section on `namei` lookups.

get_block

This method is used to find the device block that holds a given block of a file. The `inode` and `long` indicate the file and block number being sought (the block number is the file offset divided by the file system block size). `get_block` should initialize the `b_dev` and `b_blocknr` fields of the `buffer_head`, and should possibly modify the `b_state` flags.

If the `int` argument is non-zero then a new block should be allocated if one does not already exist.

readpage

`readpage` is only called by `mm/filemap.c` It is called by:

- ▼ `try_to_read_ahead` from `generic_file_readahead` and `filemap_nopage`
- ■ `do_generic_file_read`
- ■ `sys_sendfile`
- ■ `filemap_nopage`
- ▲ `generic_file_mmap` requires it to be non-null.

Thus it is needed for memory mapping of files (as you would expect), for using the `sendfile` system call, or if the `generic_read_file` is to be used for the `file:read` method.

`readpage` is not expected to actually read in the page. It must arrange for the read to happen. Clients wait for the page to be unlocked before using the data.

`readpage` can be implemented using `block_read_full_page` which is defined in `fs/buffer.c`. This routine assumes that `inode:get_block` has been defined and sets up buffer_heads to access the block in question. These buffer_heads will be set to call "end_buffer_io_async" on completion, which will unlock the page when all buffers on the page complete.

writepage

Writepage is called from `linux/mm/filemap.c`. It is called by `do_write_page` from `filemap_write_page`, from `filemap_swapout`, `filemap_sync_pte`, and from `generic_file_mmap`. Writepage can be implemented using `block_write_full_page` from `fs/buffer.c`. It is a close twin of `block_read_fullpage`. The important differences being:

▼ `block_read_fullpage` initiates a read with `ll_rw_block`, while `block_write_fullpage` only sets up the buffers, but doesn't initiate the write.

■ `block_read_fullpage` calls `inode:get_block` with the create flags set to zero, while `block_write_fullpage` sets it to one, and

▲ `block_read_fullpage` calls `init_buffer` to get `end_buffer_io_async` called on completion.

These two routines could be cleaned up a bit so that the similarities and differences are better defined.

flushpage

`flushpage` is called from `mm/filemap.c` and `mm/swap_state.c`.

`mm/filemap.c` is called by `truncate_inode_pages` to make sure no I/O is pending on a page before the page is released. `mm/swap_state.c` similarly calls it when a page is being removed from the swap cache—all I/O must be finished.

FILE SYSTEMS

It is probably worth starting this section on file systems by observing that there is possible ambiguity in our use of the word file system. It can be used to mean a particular type, or class, of file system, such as `ext2`, `nfs`, or `coda`, or it can be used to mean a particular instance of a file system, such as `/usr` or `/home` or *The file system on /dev/hda4*.

The first usage is implied when registering a file system, the second is implied while mounting a file system. I will continue to use this ambiguous language as most people are familiar with it and nothing better is obvious.

Linux finds out about new file system types by calls to `register_filesystem` (and forgets about them by the calls to its counterpart `unregister_filesystem`). The formal declarations are:

```
#include <linux/fs.h>

int register_filesystem(struct file_system_type * fs);
int unregister_filesystem(struct file_system_type * fs);
```

The function `register_filesystem` returns `0` on success and `-EINVAL` if `fs==NULL`. It returns `-EBUSY` if either `fs->next != NULL` or there is already a file system registered under the same name. It should be called (directly or indirectly) from `init_module` for file systems which are being loaded as modules, or from `filesystem_setup` in `fs/filesystems.c`. The function `unregister_filesystem` should only be called from the `cleanup_module` routine of a module. It returns `0` on success and `-EINVAL` if the argument is not a pointer to a registered file system. (In particular, `unregister_filesystem(NULL)` may Oops).

An example of file system registration and unregistration can be seen in `fs/ext2/super.c`:

```
static struct file_system_type ext2_fs_type = {
        "ext2",
        FS_REQUIRES_DEV /* | FS_IBASKET */,      /* ibaskets have unresolved bugs */
        ext2_read_super,
        NULL
};

int __init init_ext2_fs(void)
{
        return register_filesystem(&ext2_fs_type);
}

#ifdef MODULE
EXPORT_NO_SYMBOLS;

int init_module(void)
{
        return init_ext2_fs();
}

void cleanup_module(void)
{
        unregister_filesystem(&ext2_fs_type);
}

#endif
```

A `struct file_system_type` is defined in `linux/fs.h` and has the following format:

```
struct file_system_type {
        const char *name;
        int fs_flags;
        struct super_block *(*read_super) (struct super_block *, void *, int);
        struct file_system_type * next;
};
```

name

The name field simply gives the name of the file system type, such as `ext2` or `iso9660` or `msdos`. This field is used as a key, and it is not possible to register a file system with a name that is already in use. It is also used for the `/proc/filesystems` file which lists all file system types currently registered with the kernel. When a file system is implemented as a module, the name points to the module's address space (mapped to a `vmalloc`'d area) which means that if you forget to `unregister_filesystem` in `cleanup_module`, and try to `cat /proc/filesystems/` you will get an Oops trying to dereference name, a common mistake made by file system writers at the first stages of development.

fs_flags

A number of ad hoc flags which record features of the file system.

The file system flags, fs_flags needs some explanation. Look the table below to see the complete description of all possible flags:

FS_REQUIRES_DEV	As mentioned above, every mounted file system is connected to some device, or at least some device number. If a file system type has `FS_REQUIRES_DEV`, then a real device must be given when mounting the file system, otherwise an anonymous device is allocated. `nfs` and `procfs` are examples of file systems that don't require a device; `ext2` and `msdos` do.
FS_NO_DCACHE	This flag is declared but not used at all. From the comment in `fs.h` the intent is that for file systems marked this way, the dcache only keeps entries for files that are actually in use.
FS_NO_PRELIM	Like `FS_NO_DCACHE`, this flag is never used. The intent appears to be that the dcache will have entries that are in use or have been used, but will not speculatively cache anything else.
FS_IBASKET	Another vapor-flag. See section on `ibasket`s below, which may be a vapor-section.

next

`next` is simply a pointer for chaining all `file_system_types` together. It should be initialized to `NULL` (`register_filesystem` does not set it for you and will return `-EBUSY` if you don't set `next` to `NULL`).

read_super

The `read_super` method is called when a file system (instance) is being mounted.

The `struct super_block` is clean (all fields zero) except for the `s_dev` and `s_flags` fields. The `void *` pointer points to the data what has been passed down from the `mount` system call. The trailing `int` field tells whether `read_super` should be silent about errors. It is set only when mounting the root file system. When mounting root, every possible file system is tried in turn until one succeeds. Printing errors in this case would be untidy.

`read_super` must determine whether the device given in `s_dev`, together with the `data` from `mount`, define a valid file system of this type. If they do, then it should fill out the rest of the `struct super_block` and return the pointer. If not, it should return NULL.

NAMES OR DENTRYS

The VFS layer does all management of the pathnames of files, and converts them into entries in the `dcache` before allowing the underlying file system to see them. The one exception to this is the target of a symbolic link, which is passed untouched to the underlying file system. The underlying file system is then expected to interpret it. This seems like a slightly blurred module boundary.

The `dcache` is made up of lots of `struct dentry`s. Each `dentry` corresponds to one filename component in the file-system and the object associated with that name (if there is one). Each `dentry` references its parent which must exist in the `dcache`. `dentry`s and also record file system mounting relationships.

The `dcache` is a master of the inode cache. Whenever a `dcache` entry exists, the inode will also exist in the inode cache. Conversely whenever there is an inode in the inode cache, it will reference a dentry in the dcache.

Dentry Structure

The `dentry` structure is defined in `linux/dcache.h`.

```
struct qstr {
        const unsigned char * name;
        unsigned int len;
        unsigned int hash;
};

#define DNAME_INLINE_LEN 16

struct dentry {
        int d_count;
        unsigned int d_flags;
        struct inode  * d_inode;        /* Where the name belongs to - NULL s negative */
```

```
struct dentry * d_parent;        /* parent directory */
struct dentry * d_mounts;        /* mount information */
struct dentry * d_covers;
struct list_head d_hash;         /* lookup hash list */
struct list_head d_lru;          /* d_count = 0 LRU list */
struct list_head d_child;        /* child of parent list */
struct list_head d_subdirs;      /* our children */
struct list_head d_alias;        /* inode alias list */
struct qstr d_name;
unsigned long d_time;            /* used by d_revalidate */
struct dentry_operations  *d_op;
struct super_block * d_sb;        /* The root of the dentry tree */
unsigned long d_reftime;         /* last time referenced */
void * d_fsdata;                 /* fs-specific data */
unsigned char d_iname[DNAME_INLINE_LEN]; /* small names */
};
```

d_count

This is a simple reference count.

The count does NOT include the reference from the parent through the d_subdirs list, but does include the d_parent references from children. This implies that only leaf nodes in the cache may have a d_count of 0. These entries are linked together by the d_lru list as will be seen.

d_flags

There are currently two possible flags, both for use by specific file system implementations, and so will not be documented here. They are DCACHE_AUTOFS_PENDING and DCACHE_NFSFS_RENAMED.

d_inode

Simply a pointer to the inode related to this name. This field may be NULL, which indicates a negative entry, implying that the name is known not to exist.

d_parent

This will point to the parent dentry. For the root of a file system, or for an anonymous entry like that for a file, this points back to the containing dentry itself.

d_mounts

For a directory that has had a file system mounted on it, this points to the root dentry of that file system. For other dentries, this points back to the dentry itself.

It is not possible to mount a file system on a mountpoint, so there will never be a chain of d_mount entries longer than one.

d_covers

This is the inverse of d_mounts. For the root of a mounted file system, this points to the dentry of the directory that it is mounted on. For other dentrys, this points to the dentry itself.

d_hash

This doubly linked list chains together the entries in one hash bucket.

d_lru

This provides a doubly linked list of unreferenced leaf nodes in the cache. The head of the list is the dentry_unused global variable. It is stored in Least Recently Used order.

When other parts of the kernel need to reclaim memory or inodes, which may be locked up in unused entries in the dcache, they can call select_dcache which finds removable entries in the d_lru and prepares them to be removed by prune_dcache.

d_child

This list_head is used to link together all the children of the d_parent of this dentry. One might think that d_sibling might be a better name.

d_subdirs

This is the head of the d_child list that links all the children of this dentry. Of course, elements may refer to files and not just sub-directories, so d_child may be a better name, but that is already in use.

d_alias

As files (and some other file system objects) may have multiple names in the file system through multiple hard links, it is possible that multiple dentrys refer to the same inode. When this happens, the dentrys are linked on the d_alias field. The inode's i_dentry field is the head of this list.

d_name

The d_name field contains the name of this entry, together with its hash value. The name subfield may point to the d_iname field of the dentry or, if that isn't long enough, it will point to a separately allocated string.

d_time

This field is only used by underlying file systems, which can presumably do whatever they want. The intention is to use it to record something about when this entry was last known to be valid to get some idea about when its validity might need to be checked again.

d_op

This points to the `struct dentry_operations` with specifics for how to handle this `dentry`.

d_sb

This points to the super-block of the file system on which the object referred to by the `dentry` resides. It is not clear why this is needed rather than using `d_inode->i_sb`.

d_reftime

This is set to the current time in `jiffies` whenever the `d_count` reaches zero, but it is never used.

d_fsdata

This is available for specific file systems to use as they wish. This is currently only used by `nfs` to store a file handle. (I would have thought that the file handle is per-inode, not per-name, but I gather some nfs servers don't agree.)

d_iname

This stores the first 16 characters of the name of the file for easy reference. If the name fits completely, then `d_name.name` points here, otherwise it points to separately allocated memory.

Dentry Functions

Most handling of dentries is common across all file systems, so most operations that you would expect to do on dentries do not have methods in the `dentry_operations` list. Rather, it provides for a few operations which may be handled in a non-obvious way by some file system implementations. A file system can choose to leave all of the methods as NULL, in which case the default operation will apply.

The structure definition from `linclude/linux/dcache.h` is:

```
struct dentry_operations {
        int (*d_revalidate)(struct dentry *, int);
        int (*d_hash) (struct dentry *, struct qstr *);
        int (*d_compare) (struct dentry *, struct qstr *, struct qstr *);
        void (*d_delete)(struct dentry *);
        void (*d_release)(struct dentry *);
        void (*d_iput)(struct dentry *, struct inode *);
};
```

d_revalidate

This method is called whenever a path lookup uses an entry in the dcache in order to see if the entry is still valid. It should return 1 if it can still be trusted, otherwise it will return 0. The default is to assume a return value of 1.

The int argument gives the flags relevant to this lookup, and can include any of LOOKUP_FOLLOW, LOOKUP_DIRECTORY, LOOKUP_SLASHOK, LOOKUP_CONTINUE. These will be described (if at all) under the section on namei.

This method is only needed if the file system is likely to change without the VFS layer doing anything, as may happen with shared file systems.

If d_revalidate returns 0, the VFS layer will attempt to prune the dentry from the dcache. This is done by d_invalidate which removes any children which are not in active use and, if that was successful, unhashes the dentry.

d_hash

If the file system has non-standard rules about valid names or name equivalence, then this routine should be provided to check for validity and return a canonical hash.

If the name is valid, a hash should be calculated (which should be the same for all equivalent names) and stored in the qstr argument. If the name is not valid, an appropriate (negative) error code should be returned.

The dentry argument is the dentry of the **parent** of the name in question (which is found in the qstr), as the dentry of the name will not be complete yet.

d_compare

This should compare the two qstrs (again in the context of the dentry being their parent) to see if they are equivalent. It should return 0 only if they are the same. Ordering is not important.

d_delete

This is called when the reference count reaches zero, **before** the dentry is placed on the dentry_unused list.

d_release

This is called just before a dentry is finally freed up. It can be used to release the d_fsdata if any.

d_iput

If defined, this is called instead of iput to release the inode when the dentry is being discarded. It should do the equivalent of iput plus anything else that it wants.

THE LINUX SUPER-BLOCK

Each mounted file system is represented by the `super_block` structure. The fact that it is mounted is stored in a `struct vfsmount,` the declaration of which can be found in `linux/mount.h`:

```
struct vfsmount
{
  kdev_t mnt_dev;                    /* Device this applies to */
  char *mnt_devname;                 /* Name of device e.g. /dev/dsk/hda1
/
  char *mnt_dirname;                 /* Name of directory mounted on */
  unsigned int mnt_flags;            /* Flags of this device */
  struct super_block *mnt_sb;        /* pointer to superblock */
  struct quota_mount_options mnt_dquot; /* Diskquota specific mount options
/
  struct vfsmount *mnt_next;         /* pointer to next in linkedlist */
};
```

These `vfsmount` structures are linked together in a simple linked list starting from `vfsmntlist` in `fs/super.c`. This list is mainly used for finding mounted file system information given to a device, particularly the disk quota code.

The reason why `vfsmount` is kept separate from the list of super-blocks is because if the super-block already exists then `fs/super.c:read_super()` is satisfied by `fs/super.c:get_super()` instead of going through the `read_super` file system-specific method. But the entry in `vfsmntlist` is unlinked as soon as the file system is unmounted.

Each mount is also recorded in the `dcache` which will be described later, and this is the source of mount information used when traversing pathnames.

The Super-Block Structure

A somewhat reduced description of the super-block structure is:

```
struct super_block {
        struct list_head        s_list;         /* Keep this first */
        kdev_t                  s_dev;
        unsigned long           s_blocksize;
        unsigned char           s_blocksize_bits;
        unsigned char           s_lock;
        unsigned char           s_dirt;
        struct file_system_type *s_type;
        struct super_operations *s_op;
        struct dquot_operations *dq_op;
        unsigned long           s_flags;
        unsigned long           s_magic;
        struct dentry           *s_root;
```

```
                wait_queue_head_t          s_wait;

                struct inode               *s_ibasket;
                short int                  s_ibasket_count;
                short int                  s_ibasket_max;
                struct list_head           s_dirty;          /* dirty inodes */
                struct list_head           s_files;

                union {
                        /* Configured-in filesystems get entries here */
                        void                    *generic_sbp;
                } u;
                /*
                 * The next field is for VFS *only*. No filesystems have any business
                 * even looking at it. You had been warned.
                 */
                struct semaphore s_vfs_rename_sem;          /* Kludge */
        };
```

See `linux/fs.h` for a complete declaration which includes all file system-specific components of the `union u` which were suppressed above. The various fields in the super-block are:

s_list
A doubly linked list of all mounted file-systems (see `linux/list.h`).

s_dev
The device (possibly anonymous) that this file system is mounted on.

s_blocksize
The basic block size of the file system. I'm not sure exactly how this is used yet. It must be a power of 2.

s_blocksize_bits
The power of 2 that `s_blocksize` is (i.e. `log2(s_blocksize)`).

s_lock
This indicates whether the super-block is currently locked. It is managed by `lock_super` and `unlock_super`.
  `lock_kernel`.

s_wait
This is a queue of processes that are waiting for the `s_lock` lock on the super-block.

s_dirt

This is a flag which gets set when a super-block is changed, and is cleared whenever the super-block is written to the device. This happens when a file system is unmounted, or in response to a `sync` system call.

s_type

This is simply a pointer to the `struct file_system_type` structure discussed above.

s_op

This is a pointer to the `struct super_operations` which will be described next.

dq_op

This is a pointer to disk quota operations which will be described later.

s_flags

This is a list of flags which are logically `or`ed with the flags in each inode to determine certain behaviors. There is one flag which applies only to the whole file system, and so will be described here. The others are described under the discussion on inodes.

MS_RDONLY	A file system with the flag set has been mounted read-only. No writing will be permitted, and no indirect modification, such as mount times in the super-block or access times on files, will be made.

s_magic

This records an identification number that has been read from the device to confirm that the data on the device corresponds to the file system in question. It seems to be used by the Minix file system to distinguish between various flavors of that file system. It is not clear why this is in the generic part of the structure, and not confined to the file system-specific part for those file systems which need it. Maybe this is historical.

The one *interesting* usage of the field is in `fs/nfsd/vfs.c:nfsd_lookup()` where it is used to make sure that a `proc` or `nfs` type file system is never accessed via NFS.

s_root

This is a `struct dentry` which refers to the root of the file system. It is normally created by loading the root inode from the file system, and passing it to `d_alloc_root`. This dentry will get spliced into the dcache by the mount command (`do_mount` calls `d_mount`).

s_ibasket, s_ibasket_count, s_ibasket_max

These three refer to a basket of inodes, but there is no such thing in current versions.

s_dirty

A list of dirty inodes linked on the `i_list` field.

When an inode is marked as dirty with `mark_inode_dirty` it gets put on this list. When `sync_inodes` is called, any inode in this list gets passed to the file system's `write_inode` method.

s_files

This is a list (linked on `f_list`) of open files on this file system. It is used, for example, to check if there are any files open for write before remounting the file system as read-only.

u.generic_sbp

The `u` union contains one file system-specific super-block information structure for each file system known about at compile time. Any file system loaded as a module must allocate a separate structure and place a pointer in `u.generic_sbp`.

s_vfs_rename_sem

This semaphore is used as a file system-wide lock while renaming a directory. This appears to be to guard against possible races which may end up renaming a directory to be a child of itself. This semaphore is not needed or used when renaming things that are not directories.

Super-Block Functions

The methods defined in the `struct super_operations` are:

```
struct super_operations {
        void (*read_inode) (struct inode *);
        void (*write_inode) (struct inode *);
        void (*put_inode) (struct inode *);
        void (*delete_inode) (struct inode *);
        int (*notify_change) (struct dentry *, struct iattr *);
        void (*put_super) (struct super_block *);
        void (*write_super) (struct super_block *);
        int (*statfs) (struct super_block *, struct statfs *, int);
        int (*remount_fs) (struct super_block *, int *, char *);
        void (*clear_inode) (struct inode *);
        void (*umount_begin) (struct super_block *);
};
```

All of these methods get called with only the kernel lock held. This means that they can safely block, but are responsible from guarding against concurrent access themselves. All are called from a process context, not from interrupt handlers or the *bottom half*.

read_inode

This method is called to read a specific inode from a mounted file system. It is only called from `get_new_inode` out of `iget` in `fs/inode.c`.

In the `struct inode *` argument passed to this method the fields `i_sb`, `i_dev`, and particularly `i_ino` will be initialized to indicate which inode should be read from which file system. It must set (among other things) the `i_op` field of `struct inode` to point to the relevant `struct inode_operations` so that VFS can call the methods on this inode as needed.

`iget` is mostly called from within particular file systems to read inodes for that file system. One notable exception is in `fs/nfsd/nfsfh.h` where it is used to get an inode based on information in the nfs file handle.

It is not clear that this method needs to be exported as (with the exception of nfsd) it is only (indirectly) used by the file system which provides it. Avoiding it would allow more flexibility than a simple 32-bit inode number to identify a particular inode.

The `nfsd` usage could better be replaced by an interface that takes a file handle (or part thereof) and returns an inode.

write_inode

This method gets called on inodes which have been marked dirty with `mark_inode_dirty`. It is called when a sync request is made on the file, or on the file system. It should make sure that any information in the inode is safe on the device.

put_inode

If defined, this method is called whenever the reference count on an inode is decreased. Note that this does not mean that the inode is not in use any more, just that it has one fewer user.

`put_inode` is called **before** the `i_count` field is decreased, so if `put_inode` wants to check if this is the last reference, it should check if `i_count` is 1 or not.

Almost all file systems that define this method use it to do some special handling when the last reference to the inode is released, i.e., when `i_count` is 1 and is about to become zero.

delete_inode

If defined, `delete_inode` is called whenever the reference count on an inode reaches 0, and it is found that the link count (`i_nlink`) is also zero. It is presumed that the file system will deal with this situation by invalidating the inode in the file system and freeing up any resources used.

It could be argued that this, and the previous methods, should be replaced by one method that is called whenever the `i_count` field reaches 0, and then the file system gets to decide if it should do something special with `i_nlink` being 0. The only difficulty that this might cause with current file systems is that ext2 calls `ext2_discard_prealloc` when `put_inode` is called, independently of `i_count`. This would no longer be possible. But is this even desirable? Would it not make more sense to do this only in ext2_release_file (which does it as well).

notify_change

This is called when inode attributes are changed, the argument struct iattr * pointing to the new set of attributes. If the file system does not define this method (i.e., it is NULL) then VFS uses the routine fs/iattr.c:inode_change_ok which implements POSIX standard attributes verification. Then VFS marks the inode as dirty. If the file system implements its own notify_change then it should call mark_inode_dirty(inode) after it has set the attributes. An example of how to implement this method can be seen in fs/ext2/inode.c:ext2_notify_change().

put_super

This is called at the last stages of umount(2) system call, before removing the entry from vfsmntlist. This method is called with super-block lock held. A typical implementation would free file system private resources specific for this mount instance, such as inode bitmaps, block bitmaps, a buffer header containing super-block, and decrement module hold count if the file system is implemented as a dynamically loadable module. For example, fs/bfs/inode.c:bfs_put_super() looks very simple:

```
static void bfs_put_super(struct super_block *s)
{
        brelse(s->su_sbh);
        kfree(s->su_imap);
        kfree(s->su_bmap);
        MOD_DEC_USE_COUNT;
}
```

write_super

Called when VFS decides that the super-block needs to be written to disk. Called from fs/buffer.c:file_fsync, fs/super.c:sync_supers and fs/super.c:do_umount. Obviously not needed for a read-only file system.

statfs

This method is needed to implement statfs(2) system call and is called from fs/open.c:sys_statfs if implemented, otherwise statfs(2) will fail with errno set to ENODEV.

remount_fs

Called when a file system is being remounted, i.e., if the MS_REMOUNT flag is specified with the mount(2) system call. This can be used to change various mount options without unmounting the file system. A common usage is to change a read-only file system into a writable file system.

clear_inode

An optional method, called when VFS clears the inode. This is needed by any file system which attaches `kmalloced` data to the inode structure, as particularly might be the case for file systems using the `generic_ip` field in `struct inode`.

It is currently used by `ntfs` which does attach kalloced data to an inode, and by `fat` which does interesting things to present a pretense of stable inode numbers on a file system which does not support inode numbers.

umount_begin

This method is called early in the unmounting process if the MNT_FORCE flag was given to unmount. The intention is that it should cause any incomplete transaction on the file system to fail quickly rather than block waiting on some external event such as a remote server responding.

Note that calling `umount_begin` will probably not make an active file system become unmountable, but it should allow any processes using that file system to be killable, rather than being in an uninterruptible wait.

Currently, NFS is the only file system which provides `umount_begin`.

PERFORMANCE ISSUES AND OPTIMIZATION STRATEGIES

File system performance is a major component of overall system performance and is heavily dependent on the nature of the application generating the load. To achieve optimal performance, the underlying file system configuration must be balanced to match the application characteristics.

If you're a developer, you might already have a good idea of how your application is reading or writing through the file system; if you're an administrator of an application, however, you might need to spend some time analyzing the application in order to understand the type of I/O profile being presented to the file system.

Once we have a good understanding of the application, we can try to optimize the file system configuration to make the most efficient use of the underlying storage device(s).

The objectives are to:

▼ Reduce the number of I/O's to the underlying device(s) where possible .

■ Group smaller I/O's together into larger I/O's wherever possible.

■ Optimize the seek pattern to reduce the amount of time spent waiting for disk seeks.

▲ Cache as much data as we realistically can, to reduce physical I/Os.

And to make transactions faster, one must consider what can be done to each of a transaction's different parts, in order to increase speed.

A transaction consists of:

▼ Logging start of transaction.

■ Logging data which will be subject to change, before changes are done.

■ Accessing database records from storage.

■ Different operations with the data.

■ Logging data which have been subject to change, after the changes are done.

▲ Logging end of transaction.

One can easily see that quite an amount of I/O is needed, because the database, as well as the logfile, has to be kept on non-volatile storage.

Raw I/O

One recent feature in Linux is the implementation of a "raw" I/O device, one whose accesses are not handled through the caching layer, instead going straight to the low-level device itself. Some applications, such as relational database management systems (Oracle, Sybase, Informix, DB2, and many others) prefer the use of raw devices since they manage their own locking strategies. Additionally, avoiding the file system execution path improves their performance.

A raw device could be used in cases where a sophisticated application wants complete control over how it does data caching, and the overhead of the usual cache is not justified.

A raw device could also be used in data-critical situations where we want to ensure that the data gets written to the disk immediately so that, in the event of a system failure, no data will be lost.

Previous proposals for raw I/O device support were not deemed fit for inclusion, as they required literally doubling the number of device nodes, in order to give every block device a raw device node. Regrettably, this is the implementation that many commercial UNIX's use.

The 2.4 Linux implementation uses a pool of device nodes, which can be associated with any arbitrary block device. Towards this, version 2.4 includes a new object called "kiobuf."

A kiobuf is just an abstract description of an arbitrary bunch of kernel pages, set up during boot-time by the code in init.c, as empty pages in kernel space to be used as buffers. Kiobuf' can be used to describe any sort of buffer at all.

Raw I/O works by creating a kiobuf, and populating it with the physical pages which contain the data buffer that a process is using for I/O.

Once the correct physical pages of memory have been located for the data, the kiobuf is then passed to the I/O layers for reading or writing. The I/O layers don't have to know that the pages concerned happen to belong to a user process: kiobuf hides all that detail from them. All the I/O layers see is a set of physical pages and an I/O request into those pages.

Process Resource Limits

Within the context of processes, limits exist for several system resources which are used by processes when they execute; the system establishes default values and maximum values for each of the resources controlled by these resource limits. These resource limits are practically the only limitation.

For each of the six resource limits defined, there is a rlim_cur (current resource limit), which is the default value, and a rlim_max (maximum resource limit), which is the system-imposed maximum value for the resource.

In Linux 2.4, the default limit value set by the system for open files per process is 1,024.

Each process can only have open, at any given moment, up to rlim_fd_cur files. Remember that, for any process, the total number of open files always contains three additional ones, because every process has three open files as soon as it comes into existence: stdin, stdout, and stderr (standard input, output, and error). These represent the input, output, and error output files for the process.

You can display rlim_fd_cur by using the ulimit(1) or limit(1) command, depending on which shell you're using. Use the ulimit(1) command if you're using sh or bash. Use limit(1) if you're using the C shell (/bin/csh):

```
[root@hatta /root]# ulimit -a
core file size (blocks)   1000000
data seg size (kbytes)    unlimited
file size (blocks)        unlimited
max memory size (kbytes)  unlimited
stack size (kbytes)       8192
cpu time (seconds)        unlimited
max user processes        2048
pipe size (512 bytes)     8
open files                1024
virtual memory (kbytes)   2105343
```

rlim_fd_cur is displayed as "open files," seen here at its default value (in most distributions) of 1024 open files per process.

As root, you can bypass the resource limit check and set the open process limit to, theoretically, 3 billion (signed int data type max value). Obviously, you would never get anywhere near that amount, because you would run out of process virtual address space for the per-process file structure (uf_entry) that you need for every file you open. Fortunately, we never encounter situations which need that many files opened. However, more and more we do see installations where per-process open files go into the thousands, and even tens of thousands.

Keep in mind, also, that the same file can have multiple file control data structures associated with it. If different processes executing on the same system open the same file, each process will have a unique representation of the file, through that file's file descriptor to a file control data structure specific to that process. Thus, each process, as it reads and writes the file, will change the f_offset member of its file control data structure.

Moreover, the behavior differs with file descriptors inherited via the fork() or __ clone() system calls, or when a process issues the dup()system call for duplicating file descriptors. In these scenarios, both the file structure and the f_offset field are shared, thus a read or write by the parent process to a file changes that file's f_offset as seen by the child process in the case of a fork(2), or changes references to the file descriptors returned by dup(2) and dup2(2).

Extent-Based Allocation (General)

Extent-based allocation file systems, such as Veritas' VxFS and IBM's JFS, allocate disk blocks in extents. An extent is a contiguous sequence of multiple blocks allocated as a unit, and described by a triple consisting of logical offset/ length/physical, beginning when the file is first created. The addressing structure is a B+-tree[3] populated with extent descriptors (the triples), rooted in the inode and keyed by logical offset within the file. Note that file system meta-data is written when the file is first created, which differs from block-based allocation. Since initial allocation is sequential, subsequent reads, writes, and seeks are, of course, forced to be sequential; within the first allocated extent of blocks they do not require additional meta-data writes until the next extent is allocated.

This optimizes the disk seek pattern, and the grouping of block writes into clusters allows the file system to issue larger physical disk writes to the storage device, saving the overhead of many small SCSI transfers.

Under block-based allocation, a block address number is required for every logical block in an allocated file, resulting in a lot of meta-data for each file.

In the extent-based allocation method, only the start block number and length is required for each contiguous extent of data blocks. Such a file with only a few very large extents requires only a small amount of meta-data.

In Figure 3-5 you can see how, conceptually, the allocation scheme differs between the two methods, block allocation and extent allocation.

Extent-based file systems provide good performance for sequential file access because of the sequential allocation policy and block clustering into larger writes. For example, if we

---

3   A B-tree is a special kind of balanced m-ary tree that allows us to test for, retrieve, insert, and delete records (leaves) which contain either physical address data or else indexing pointer data. B+-trees have their data pointed to only by the leaf nodes, use virtual keys, and can have a search key value appear more than once. A B+-tree, usually, is built up in such a way that its node size is defined by the page size. Only when the search path has to go along an edge is paging required. Also, data are only stored in the leaves and not in the nodes. Only reference keys, so-called "road maps," are kept in the nodes. Therefore the B+-tree, with more branches possible and hence a flatter branch structure, has been favored.

The B+-tree is the best structure for an efficient search for keys. But the real problems arise with the three different tasks one performs: lookup, insert, delete. In the case of a concurrent deletion and lookup, there is a 50% chance that it might work out or lead to a deadlock. Therefore parallelism is not a good strategy for optimizing performance in an extent-based allocation file system.

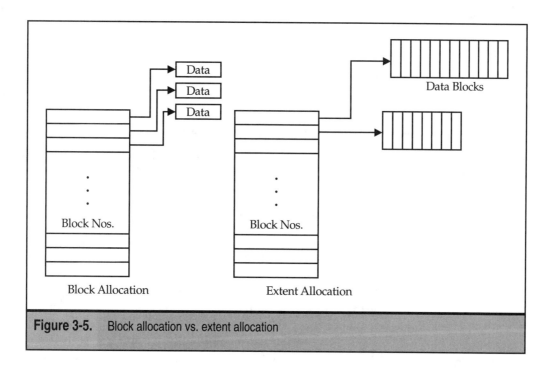

Figure 3-5.   Block allocation vs. extent allocation

want to read sequentially though an extent-based file, we only need to read the start block number and its length. Then, we can continue to read all of the data blocks in that extent. Very little meta-data read overhead is incurred in reading sequentially.

However, extent-based file systems don't provide much advantage when the file system is used for random I/O. If we read a file in a random manner, we need to look up the block address for the desired block for every data block read, similar to what we would do with a block-based file system.

Table 3-1 shows some example file systems and their allocation methods.

Block-Based Allocation (General)

The allocation strategy used by a traditional Unix file system is block-based allocation. When a file is extended, the policy is to allocate, on the fly, a minimal number of blocks (as defined by the file system) to the file. Blocks are allocated from a free block map.

While this policy attempts to conserve storage space, blocks are sometimes allocated in a random order. This can cause excessive disk seeking, and later reads from the file system will result in the disk mechanism seeking to all of the random block locations that were allocated during the extension of the file.

Random block allocation can be avoided by optimizing the block allocation policy so that it attempts to allocate a contiguous (sequential) series of blocks. If large sequential

File System	Allocation Method
Ext2	Block-based, allocator tries to allocate sequential blocks
reiserfs	Extent-based
JFS	Extent-based

Table 3-1.   Various File Systems and Their Allocation Format

allocations can be achieved by using a smarter block allocation policy, disk seeking will be greatly reduced.

However, contiguous file system block allocation will eventually end up with file blocks fragmented across the file system, and file system access will eventually revert back to a random nature.

Also, the block allocation scheme must write information about where each new block is allocated every time the file is extended. If the file is being extended one block at a time, a lot of extra disk I/O will be required to write the file system block control structure information (file system block control structure information is known as *meta-data*).

In the ext2 file system, meta-data is written asynchronously to the storage device, so that operations that change the size of a file do not need to wait for each meta-data operation to complete. This greatly improves speed of updates to files, but increases the risk of inconsistent data if a system crash occurs after changing the file's contents, but before the meta-data was actually written.

The Transaction-Processing or Database Issue of Safety

For managing synchronized access to the same file from multiple processes or threads, file locking interfaces are provided. These will be discussed in my forthcoming book *Linux File Systems*. On a related note: Linux, or any Unix-type OS actually, does not provide kernel-level support for the notion of file records.

In this section, we shall look at the differences between static, journaling, and logging file systems.

All database files have to reside on a file system. The native file system of Linux, ext2fs, fared well for what Linux was three or four years ago. It is, however, not well-poised to handle the challenges of the Linux market today.

For one thing, ext2fs is *static*: it does not keep track of changes to make sure all updates on the disk are done in a safe way. Furthermore, ext2fs is one of the few file systems on any OS to write meta-data asynchronously. While this considerably accelerates file operations, it also means that information about the file, such as creation and change dates, ownership, permissions, etc., are written in a deferred fashion relative to the file contents.

If power goes off after writing the updates to the file, but before actually writing the file header, then there is a problem.

These shortcomings of ext2fs are a major hindrance to a more widespread employment of Linux on database servers. Oracle8i for Linux, for instance, does not support raw I/O devices (although there has been raw I/O support since the 2.2.x kernel).

For some time now, there has been a quest among Linux hackers to come up with a journaling and/or logging file system, to counter the deficiencies of ext2fs.

Advantages of Journaling over Non-Journaling

The journaling file system that will be considered here, JFS, is a key technology for Internet file servers, since it provides fast file system restart times in the event of a system crash. Using database journaling techniques, JFS can restore a file system to a consistent state in a matter of seconds or minutes. In non-journaling file systems, file recovery can take hours or days. Most file server customers cannot tolerate the downtime associated with non-journaling file systems. Only by a technology shift to journaling could these file systems avoid the time-consuming process of examining all of a files system's meta-data to verify/restore the file system to a consistent state.

In a static file system such as ext2fs, there is a map of inode locations. These inodes point to directory blocks, which contain lists of other inodes and each one's associated filename, and to data blocks.

A Linux directory, like any Unix directory, is an association between the file leafnames and inodes numbers. A file's inode number can be found using the "-i" switch to ls.

An inode contains ownership and permission information, along with a pointer to where on the disk the data blocks for a file are. What happens when we change the contents of file "test.file"? Let's assume that the inode for "test.file" lists 4 data blocks.

The data for "test.file" resides at disk locations 3110, 3111, 3506, and 3507. The gaps are there because during the initial allocation of disk blocks, the ones in between 3111 and 3506 were already allocated to some other file(s). We therefore notice that this file is fragmented.

The hard drive will have to seek to the 3110 area on the disk surface, read two blocks, then seek over to the 3506 area and read two blocks to read the entire file.

Let's say you modify the third block. The file system will read the third block, make your changes, and rewrite the third block, still located at 3506.

If you append to the file, you could have blocks allocated anywhere.

There is danger if the power fails. Imagine being in the midst of updating a directory. You've just modified 23 file entries in the fifth block of a giant directory. Just as the disk is in the middle of writing this block, there is a power-outage, and the block is now incomplete, and therefore corrupted.

During reboot, Linux (like all UNIXes) runs a program called fsck (file system check) that steps through the entire file system, validating all entries, and making sure that blocks are allocated and referenced correctly.

It will find this corrupted directory entry and attempt to repair it. However, there is no certainty that fsck will actually manage to repair the damage. Quite often, actually, it does not. Sometimes, in a situation as described above, all the directory entries can be lost.

For large file systems, fsck can take a very long time. On a machine with many gigabytes of files, fsck can run for up to ten or more hours. During this time the system is, of course, not available, and this represents an unacceptable amount of downtime for some installations.

Journaling or logging file systems solves the problem, but introduces new ones. Let's see how and why.

How a Journaling File System Works

A journaling file system (JFS) uses techniques originally developed for databases to log information about operations performed on the file system meta-data as atomic transactions. In the event of a system failure, a file system is restored to a consistent state by replaying the log and applying log records for the appropriate transactions. The recovery time associated with this log-based approach is much faster, since the replay utility need only examine the log records produced by recent file system activity rather than examine all file system meta-data.

A journaling file system such as JFS provides improved structural consistency and recoverability, and much faster restart times (JFS can restore a file system to a consistent state in a matter of seconds or minutes) than non-journaling file systems such as HPFS, ext2fs, and traditional UNIX file systems. These other file systems are subject to corruption in the event of system failure, since a logical write-file operation often takes multiple media I/Os to accomplish and may not be totally reflected on the media at any given time. These file systems rely on restart-time utilities (which in Linux usually means fsck), which examine all of the file system's meta-data, such as directories and disk addressing structures, to detect and repair structural integrity problems. This is a time-consuming and error-prone process which, in the worst case, can lose or misplace data.

Journaling file systems keep track only of inode changes, but not changes to the contents of a file; whereas logging file systems keep track of changes made to both data and inodes. All changes, all appends, and all deletes would be logged to a growing part of the file system known as the log.

In our first example with the "test.file" file, rather than modifying the data in the 3506 block, a logging file system would store a copy of the inodes of both "test.file" and the third block in new locations on the disk.

The in-memory list of inodes would be changed to point "test.file" to the new inode as well. Every once in a while, the file system will checkpoint and update the on-disk list of inodes, as well as freeing the unused parts of files (e.g., the original third block of "test.file").

A logging file system has a dramatically improved write-speed because it's only appending to the same area of the disk, and never really needs to seek around looking for blocks on the disk.

The writing speed is therefore improved and the recovery time is improved (actually, there is no recovery time at all because of its structure).

Logging file systems, when compared to static file systems, have nearly identical read-speed because their file data blocks are still easily seekable. The inode map has the lists of blocks, and those can be read quickly because it is usually memory-mapped.

Thus, logging file systems represent the best of both worlds. The read-time is comparable to that of the static file system. (It is possibly a bit slower due to more fragmentation. The major problem with logging file systems is that they can get fragmented easily.)

The Most Common Form of File System Logging is Meta-Data Logging

When a file system makes changes to its on-disk structure, it uses several disconnected, synchronous writes to make the changes. If an outage occurs halfway through an operation, the state of the file system is unknown, and the whole file system must be checked for consistency.

If one block, say, is appended to the end of a file, the on-disk map that tells the file system where each block for the file is located needs to be read, modified, and rewritten to the disk before the data block is written.

When a failure occurs, the file system must be checked before it is mounted at boot; the file system manager doesn't know if the block map is correct, and it also doesn't know which file was being modified during the crash. This results in a full file system scan.

A meta-data logging file system has a wrap-around, append-only log area on the disk, which it uses to record the state of each disk transaction. Before any on-disk structures are changed, an intent-to-commit record is written to the log. The directory structure is then updated and the log entry is marked complete.

Since every change to the file system structure is in the log, file system consistency can be checked by looking in the log without the need for a full file system scan. At mount time, if an intent-to-commit entry is found but not marked complete, then the file structure for that block is checked and, if necessary, fixed.

Figure 3-6 shows a file's data block (gray) and its inode information (modification times, pointers to data blocks, etc.) in a regular (static) file system, e.g., ext2fs, and what happens when you change the data in that file.

Figure 3-7 shows a similar file in a logging file system, and what happens when it is being modified.

Notice how everything that is changed is appended at the end of the log.

This speeds up things, since the disk doesn't need to seek all over the disk to write to parts of a file. Also it's much safer, because the original data blocks of the file aren't "lost" until the log has successfully written the "new" data blocks. This leads to very stable file systems with nearly no fsck time required after a crash. Such file systems come back online after a crash almost immediately, because only the file system updates after the last checkpoint need to be checked.

All the changes in the log can be reapplied quickly, and the corrupted part of the disk will always be the last change added to the log, which can be thrown away since it will be invalid. The only data lost will be the single change that was lost at power-off. Meta-data

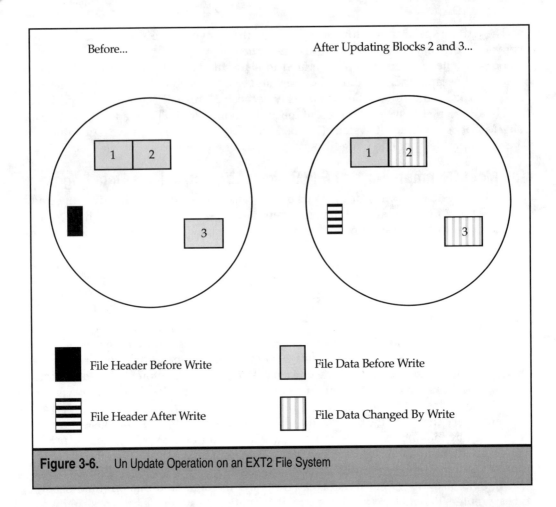

Figure 3-6.   Un Update Operation on an EXT2 File System

logging file systems of 20GB and more typically take 4 or 5 seconds to fsck and repair after a crash. Thus, a meta-data logging file system can make the difference between mounting a heavily populated file system in a few seconds or in ten or more hours without a log.

It should, however, be noted that logging doesn't come free, and there is a significant performance overhead. Logging requires more of the slow synchronous writes, and the most popular implementation of logging, meta-data logging, requires at least three writes per file update, which is significantly more than would be required without logging.

As a result, we should pay attention to what our requirements are: do we want the file system to be fast, or do we need maximum reliability?

Some logging file systems provide an option to put file data into the log together with the meta-data, thus avoiding a second seek and write.

The data is first written to the log, and then replayed into the file system.

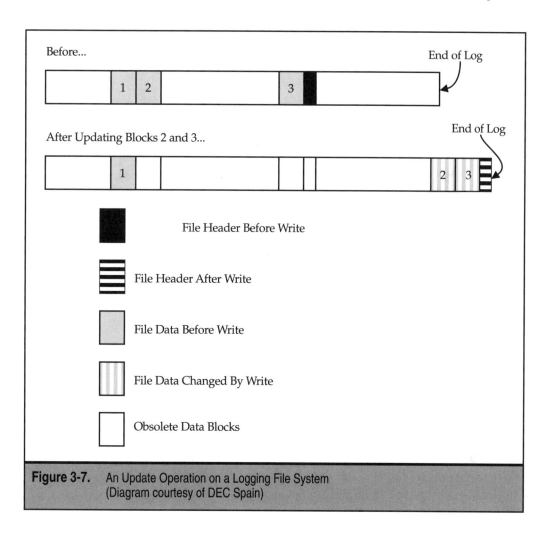

Figure 3-7.   An Update Operation on a Logging File System
(Diagram courtesy of DEC Spain)

This does two things: it ensures data integrity up to, but not including, the last block written; also, it can help performance for small synchronous writes, as in email and news servers, which would otherwise require two or more writes to different parts of the disk for every application write (one for the data and one for the log write).

CHAPTER 4

The Linux VFS

In this chapter we will cover Linux Virtual File System implementation in more detail than in the more generalized third chapter. This is necessary because a true understanding of any Linux file system requires a thorough knowledge of its interface to the kernel. That interface is the VFS.

Linux, as a Unix-type operating system, came very late to VFS. The free BSD operating systems all have had a VFS for a very long time now. Solaris, AIX, and HP-UX all have a very similar VFS. Considering this, it is quite surprising that Linux only very recently got its VFS.

Some people in the Linux community realized this lack, and decided they would create a new VFS layer. After many thousands of coding and testing hours, and following many thousands of e-mails debating design features, with the new version 2.4.0 we finally have a working VFS in Linux. Alexander Viro, a long-time Linux kernel hacker, has been leading the VFS project. Quite strangely, however, at the time of writing this book (January 2001), no written design paper or white paper had been published on VFS and it is, therefore, quite difficult to say more about it than what is readable from the source code. Even the source code is no authoritative information, as there is no declared intention of what the source code is supposed to implement today or in the future. A comparison of the VFS source of Linux to the Solaris 8 and BSD source code shows that there is very little, if any, resemblance. The Solaris 8 and BSD VFS source code are very similar, while Linux seems to have gone, as is often the case, in a completely different direction. Of all the many thousands of lines of Linux kernel source code studied and perused by the author of this book, the VFS implementation might well be the worst part.

As is the nature of software, more of it invariably introduces new bugs and problems. Many of the file systems present in previous versions had problems working with VFS and since nobody wanted to fix them, they were simply discarded.

GENERAL CONCEPTS

In Linux, all files are accessed through the Virtual File System Switch, or VFS. This is a layer of code that implements generic file system actions and vectors requests to the correct specific code to handle the request.

File systems of any type use the VFS to generalize block device access.

The VFS Source Code

As we saw in Chapter 2, "Compiling a Linux Kernel," the source code for the VFS is in the fs/ subdirectory of the Linux kernel source, along with a few other related pieces, such as the buffer cache and code to deal with each executable file format. Each specific file system is kept in a lower subdirectory; for example, the ext2 file system source code is kept in fs/ext2/.

The following table gives the names of the files in the fs/ subdirectory and explains the basic purpose of each one. The middle column, labelled system, is supposed to show to which major subsystem the file is (mainly) dedicated. EXE means that it is used for recognizing and loading executable files. DEV means that it is for device driver support. BUF means buffer cache. VFS means that it is a part of the VFS, and delegates some functionality to file system-specific code. VFS means that this code is completely generic and never delegates part of its operation to specific file system code (that I noticed, anyway), which you shouldn't have to worry about while writing a file system.

Filename	System	Purpose
binfmt_aout.c	EXE	Recognize and execute old-style a.out executables.
binfmt_elf.c	EXE	Recognize and execute new ELF executables.
binfmt_java.c	EXE	Recognize and execute Java apps and applets.
binfmt_script.c	EXE	Recognize and execute #!-style scripts.
block_dev.c	DEV	Generic read(), write(), and fsync() functions for block devices.
buffer.c	BUF	The buffer cache, which caches blocks read from block devices.
dcache.c	VFS	The directory cache, which caches directory name lookups.
devices.c	DEV	Generic device support functions, such as registries.
dquot.c	VFS	Generic disk quota support.
exec.c	VFS	Generic executable support. Calls functions in the binfmt_* files.
fcntl.c	VFS	Fcntl() handling.
fifo.c	VFS	fifo handling.
file_table.c	VFS	Dynamically-extensible list of open files on the system.
file systems.c	VFS	All compiled-in file systems are initialized from here by calling init_*name*_fs().
inode.c	VFS	Dynamically-extensible list of open inodes on the system.
ioctl.c	VFS	First-stage handling for ioctl's; passes handling to the file system or device driver if necessary.
locks.c	VFS	Support for fcntl() locking, flock() locking, and mandatory locking.
namei.c	VFS	Fills in the inode, given a pathname. Implements several name-related system calls.

Filename	System	Purpose
noquot.c	VFS	No quotas: optimization to avoid #ifdef's in dquot.c
open.c	VFS	Lots of system calls including (surprise) open(), close(), and vhangup().
pipe.c	VFS	Pipes.
read_write.c	VFS	Read(), write(), readv(), writev(), lseek().
readdir.c	VFS	Several different interfaces for reading directories.
select.c	VFS	The guts of the select() system call.
stat.c	VFS	Stat() and readlink() support.
super.c	VFS	Super-block support, file system registry, mount()/umount().

How VFS Works

As mentioned before, the Linux Virtual File System is nothing but a layer that intercepts all system calls relating to a file system. As such, it must provide a standard interface (or API, if you prefer) to all file systems. In fact, on a Linux system, there is no difference in commands when listing (i.e., ls) the contents of an ISO 9660 CD-ROM, or a DOS-formatted floppy, or looking at the /boot directory.

In order to achieve that common interface, VFS introduced the concept of the common file model. This model makes a file look the same across file systems to the applications. It is up to the individual file systems, whether ext2, JFS, or whatever, to translate their understanding of a file to the VFS requirement.

In the common file model of VFS, directories are seen as files containing a list of other files and other directories. Some file systems, like FAT, FAT32, and VFAT for example, store the location of each file in the directory tree and in those cases, directories are not normal files. Therefore, these file systems must dynamically build a view of a directory as a file during operations on the file systems. Obviously, such views are not actually stored within the file systems, but exist only as objects in kernel space.

Linux, furthermore, does not actually execute file-related system calls into actual kernel functions. Rather, each read() or ioctl() translates into a pointer to a function specific to each file system handling the file in question.

To do that, the VFS common file model introduced the notion of some common file system control blocks that make each file system correspond to the traditional Unix approach. These control blocks or structures are:

The superblock structure	Information about a mounted file system. This usually matches the file system control block stored on the device.

The inode object	Information about a specific file. Usually this points to a file control block on the device. Each such object has an inode number, which uniquely points to a file in that file system.
The file object	Information about a file currently opened and the process accessing it. This structure is being held in the kernel only and disappears upon closing the file.
The dentry object	Information about the link between a directory's entry and the associated file. Each file system has a different implementation of this link.

The VFS is, as we just saw, not only restricted to creating this common layer. It also tries to maximize file system performance by maintaining a *dentry cache*. This cache provides a way to speed up the lookup of a file's pathname to the inode of the file itself. Statistically, recently accessed files are more likely to be needed again in the near future and the dentry cache greatly accelerates this process.

The VFS also maintains a disk cache. This cache stores in the virtual memory some of the structures normally stored on the disk itself to speed up the usage of this information. In addition to the dentry cache, there is also a *buffer cache* and a *page cache* in Linux. Both were described in the previous chapter.

VFS-handled System Calls

Some of the system calls dealing with files and file systems need to be intercepted by the VFS layer to translate the abstraction to the actual file system-specific handling function call.

In addition to the system calls indicated in the following table, the bind(), connect() ioperm(), ioctl(), pipe(), socket(), and mknod() system calls are also handled by the VFS layer. They will be discussed separately later in this chapter.

System Call	What it does
chroot()	Change root directory.
chmod(), fchdir(), getcwd()	Change current directory.
dup(), dup2(), fcntl()	File descriptor handling.
fdatasync(), fsync(), sync(), msync()	Synchronize buffers.
lseek(), __lseek()	Change file offset.
mount(), umount()	Mount and unmount file systems.
getdents(), readdir(), link(), unlink() rename()	Handle links.
readlink(), symlink()	Handle softlinks.

System Call	What it does
read(), write(), readv(), writev(), sendfile()	File I/O.
pread(), pwrite()	Seek file and handle I/O.
mmap(), munmap()	Map file into memory.
flock()	File locking.
stat(), fstat(), lstat(), access()	Access current file status.
truncate(), ftruncate()	Modify file size.
open(), close(), creat(), umask()	Open and close files.
select(), poll()	Asynchronous I/O handling.
sysfs()	Read general information about file system.
statfs(), fstatfs(), ustat()	Read statistics about the file system.

Dentry Cache

In the previous chapter we saw how the virtual memory manager inside the kernel manages two caches for block devices, the buffer cache and the page cache. One of the caches managed by the VFS layer of Linux is the dentry cache. Looking up a corresponding inode for a filename requires accesses to the device and can—particularly in the case of nested path names—be quite expensive from a performance point of view. It makes sense to manage a cache of recently looked up files and paths and their inode numbers.

This cache is called the dentry cache. It is made up of two main data structures:

▼ A list of dentry objects, either used, unused or in a negative state.

▲ A hash list to quickly find the dentry object of a filename and its directory.

The dentry cache function of Linux is also its inode cache. This is because inodes still in the dentry cache associate with unused dentries and are simply kept on instead of being deleted.

All dentries being flagged as "used" are maintained in a doubly linked list pointed to by the dentry field of the associated inode object. These dentries can at one point or another become "negative," which is when the last hard link to a file is removed. When that happens, the object is moved to the "Least Recently Used" list. The LRU list is a time-sorted, doubly linked list which contains pointers to all the released dentry objects.

When the kernel VM manager determines that the dentry cache has to shrink, it starts by deleting the oldest dentry objects from the LRU list.

The functions in the source code dealing with dentry objects are called dentry operations. They all use the dentry_operations data structure. Its address can be derived from the d_op field.

Some file systems (like NFS) use their own dentry methods. In that case, the above-mentioned files are left empty and VFS uses default functions instead.

The main functions used by the dentry cache are:

dentry cache function	Purpose
d_compare(dir, name1, name2)	It compares the two supplied filenames in the argument. This function is file system-dependent. The FAT file system, f.i., does not distinguish lowercase and capital letters in this comparison.
d_delete(dentry)	After removing the last reference to a dentry, this function will be called.
d_hash(dentry, hash)	It computes a hash value for a particular dentry object. This function is file system-dependent.
d_iput(dentry, ino)	It marks a dentry as "negative" and then moves it to the LRU list.
d_release(dentry)	It frees a dentry object from the list.
d_revalidate(dentry)	It checks whether a particular dentry is still valid before using it for a translation.

File System Mounting

The kernel either registers new file system (mounts them) at boot or during normal operation by means of a mount command. As we saw earlier, mount is one of those commands being executed by the VFS layer.

Each file system must have its own root directory (this is true even for loop-back devices).

Looking at the code in any file system for init_*name*_fs(), you will find that it probably contains about one line of code. For instance, in the ext2fs, it looks like this (from fs/ext2/super.c):

```
int init_ext2_fs(void)
{
        return register_file system(&ext2_fs_type);
}
```

It simply registers the file system with the registry kept in fs/super.c. ext2_fs_type is actually a very simple structure:

```
static struct file_system_type ext2_fs_type = {
        ext2_read_super, "ext2", 1, NULL
};
```

The ext2_read_super entry is a pointer to a function which allows a file system to be mounted. In the above example, "ext2" is the name of the file system type, which is used to determine which file system to use to mount a device. A system administrator usually indicates the file system with the "-t" option in the *mount* command. For example:

```
mount -t jfs /dev/sda1 /disk1
```

indicates the JFS file system. VFS has the capability to detect the file system from the super-block to be mounted, so doing a

```
mount -a /dev/cdrom /mnt
```

will work for most kernels.

But let's come back to the *ext2_fs_type* structure. "1" says that it needs a device to be mounted on (unlike the proc file system or a network file system), and the NULL is required to fill up space that will be used to keep a linked list of file system types in the file system registry, kept in fs/super.c.

It's possible for a file system to support more than one type of file system. For instance, in fs/sysv/inode.c, three possible file system types are supported by one file system, with this code:

```
static struct file_system_type sysv_fs_type[3] = {
        {sysv_read_super, "xenix", 1, NULL},
        {sysv_read_super, "sysv", 1, NULL},
        {sysv_read_super, "coherent", 1, NULL}
};

int init_sysv_fs(void)
{
        int i;
        int ouch;

        for (i = 0; i < 3; i++) {
                if ((ouch = register_file system(&sysv_fs_type[i])) != 0)
                        return ouch;
        }
        return ouch;
}
```

Connecting the File System to a Disk

The kernel and the file system only start working with each other when a device bearing that type of file system is mounted. When a system administrator mounts a device containing an ext2 file system, ext2_read_super() from super.c (which is printed at the end of this chapter) is called. If it succeeds in reading the super-block and is able to mount the file system, it fills in the super_block structure with information that includes a pointer to a structure, called super_operations, which contains pointers to functions that do common operations related to super-blocks; in this case, pointers to functions specific to ext2.

A super-block is the block that defines an entire file system on a device, although not all file systems actually have a super-block (like the FAT file system).

Operations that pertain to the file system as a whole (as opposed to individual files) are considered super-block operations. The `super_operations` structure contains pointers to functions that manipulate inodes, the super-block, and which refer to or change the status of the file system as a whole (`statfs()` and `remount()`).

Because, sadly, kernel development involves a lot of pointers, file system developers can make use of the VFS's ability to correctly resolve pointers for them. All that the programmer for a new file system needs to do is fill in (usually static) structures with pointers to functions, and pass pointers to those structures back to the VFS so it can get at the file system and the files.

For example, the super_operations structure looks like this (from `<linux/fs.h>`) for VFS:

```
struct super_operations {
        void (*read_inode) (struct inode *);
        int (*notify_change) (struct inode *, struct iattr *);
        void (*write_inode) (struct inode *);
        void (*put_inode) (struct inode *);
        void (*put_super) (struct super_block *);
        void (*write_super) (struct super_block *);
        void (*statfs) (struct super_block *, struct statfs *, int);
        int (*remount_fs) (struct super_block *, int *, char *);
};
```

Compare that to the much more elegant declaration for ext2, in fs/ext2/super.c:

```
static struct super_operations ext2_sops = {
        ext2_read_inode,
        NULL,
        ext2_write_inode,
        ext2_put_inode,
        ext2_put_super,
        ext2_write_super,
        ext2_statfs,
        ext2_remount
};
```

You will probably ask yourself what that NULL entry is. Throughout the Linux kernel whenever a certain default action needs to be taken for a function pointer, then a NULL pointer is an easy and elegant way to do that. In the above declaration, notice how simple and clean the syntax is. All the ugly code like `sb->s_op->write_super(sb);` is hidden in the VFS implementation.

The details of how the file system actually reads and writes the blocks, including the super-block, to and from the disk are covered in later chapters of this book. The buffer cache implementation has already been discussed in Chapter 3.

Mounting a file system

When a file system is mounted (which is done by fs/super.c, printed at the end of this chapter for your easy reference) the sequence of events is:

1. `do_umount()`
2. `read_super()`
3. `ext2_read_super()` (in the case of the ext2 file system)

which returns the super-block. That super-block includes a pointer to the structure of pointers to functions that we see in the definition of `ext2_sops` above. It also includes other important data; its definition is printed at the end of this chapter.

Accessing a file

Only once a file system is properly mounted is it possible to access files on it. Two actions are required to do so:

1. Look up the name to find what inode it points to.
2. Access the inode.

When the VFS is looking at a name, it includes a path (see Chapter 3). Unless the filename is absolute, that is, it starts with the "/" character, it is relative to the current directory of the process that made the system call. The kernel then uses file system-specific code to look up files on the file systems specified. It then takes the pathname one component (filename components are separated with / characters) at a time, and looks it up. If it is a directory, the next component is looked up in the directory returned by the previous lookup. Every component which is looked up, whether it is a file or a directory, returns an **inode number** which uniquely identifies it, and by which its contents are accessed.

If the file turns out to be a symbolic link to another file, then the VFS starts over with the new name which is retrieved from the symbolic link. In order to prevent infinite recursion, there's a limit on the **depth** of symlinks; the kernel will only follow a few symlinks in a row before giving up.

The namei() function is used to resolve a name into a single inode number: the open_name() function is included at the end of this chapter for space reasons.

Once the inode number has been obtained, the file can be accessed. The `iget()` function finds and returns the inode specified by an inode number. The `iput()` function is later used to release access to the inode. It is like `malloc()` and `free()`, except that more than one process may hold an inode open at once, and a reference count is maintained to know when it's free and when it's not.

The integer file handle, which is passed back to the application code, is an offset into a file table for that process. That file table slot holds the inode number that was looked up with the `namei()` function until the file is closed or the process terminates. So whenever a process does anything to a "file" using a file handle, it is really manipulating the inode in question.

Inode Operations

As we just saw, accessing a file means finding its inode number. So how does the VFS look up the name in the file system and get an `inode` back?

It starts at the beginning of the pathname and looks up the inode of the first directory in the path. Then it uses that inode to look up the next directory in the path. When it reaches the end, it has found the inode of the file or directory it is trying to look up. But since it needs an `inode` to get going, how *does* it get started with the first lookup?

There is an inode pointer kept in the super-block called `s_mounted` which points at an inode structure for the file system. This inode is allocated when the file system is mounted and de-allocated when the file system is unmounted. Normally, as in the ext2 file system, the `s_mounted` inode is the inode of the root directory of the file system. From there, all the other inodes can be looked up.

Each inode includes a pointer to a structure of pointers to functions. That is the `inode_operations` structure. One of the elements of that structure is called `lookup()`, and it is used to look up another inode on the same file system.

In general, a file system has only one `lookup()` function that is the same in every inode on the file system, but it is possible to have several different `lookup()` functions and assign them as appropriate for the file system. The proc file system does this because different directories in the proc file system have different purposes. The `inode_operations` structure looks like this (defined, like almost everything we are looking at, in `<linux/fs.h>`):

```
struct inode_operations {
        struct file_operations * default_file_ops;
        int (*create) (struct inode *,const char *,int,int,struct inode*);
        int (*lookup) (struct inode *,const char *,int,struct inode **);
        int (*link) (struct inode *,struct inode *,const char *,int);
        int (*unlink) (struct inode *,const char *,int);
        int (*symlink) (struct inode *,const char *,int,const char *);
        int (*mkdir) (struct inode *,const char *,int,int);
        int (*rmdir) (struct inode *,const char *,int);
        int (*mknod) (struct inode *,const char *,int,int,int);
        int (*rename) (struct inode *,const char *,int,struct inode,const char *,int);
        int (*readlink) (struct inode *,char *,int);
        int (*follow_link) (struct inode *,struct inode *,int,int,struct inode **);
        int (*readpage) (struct inode *, struct page *);
        int (*writepage) (struct inode *, struct page *);
        int (*bmap) (struct inode *,int);
        void (*truncate) (struct inode *);
        int (*permission) (struct inode *, int);
        int (*smap) (struct inode *,int);
};
```

Most of these functions map directly to Linux system calls.

In the ext2 file system, directories, files, and symlinks have different `inode_opera-tions`. The file fs/ext2/dir.c contains `ext2_dir_inode_operations`, the file fs/ext2/file.c contains `ext2_file_inode_operations`, and the file fs/ext2/symlink.c contains `ext2_symlink_inode_operations`. All of these files are contained at the end of this chapter.

There are many system calls related to files (and directories) which aren't accounted for in the `inode_operations` structure; those are found in the `file_operations` structure. The `file_operations` structure is the same one used when writing device drivers, and contains operations that work specifically on files, rather than inodes:

```
struct file_operations {
        int (*lseek) (struct inode *, struct file *, off_t, int);
        int (*read) (struct inode *, struct file *, char *, int);
        int (*write) (struct inode *, struct file *, const char *, int);
        int (*readdir) (struct inode *, struct file *, void *, filldir_t);
        int (*select) (struct inode *, struct file *, int, select_table);
        int (*ioctl) (struct inode *, struct file *, unsigned int,nsigned long);
        int (*mmap) (struct inode *, struct file *, struct vm_area_struct );
        int (*open) (struct inode *, struct file *);
        void (*release) (struct inode *, struct file *);
        int (*fsync) (struct inode *, struct file *);
        int (*fasync) (struct inode *, struct file *, int);
        int (*check_media_change) (kdev_t dev);
        int (*revalidate) (kdev_t dev);
};
```

There are also a few functions which aren't directly related to system calls—and where they don't apply, they are simply set to NULL.

Source Files include/linux/fs.h (2.4.3)

```
1 #ifndef _LINUX_FS_H
2 #define _LINUX_FS_H
3
4 /*
5  * This file has definitions for some important file table
6  * structures etc.
7  */
8
9 #include <linux/config.h>
10 #include <linux/linkage.h>
11 #include <linux/limits.h>
12 #include <linux/wait.h>
13 #include <linux/types.h>
14 #include <linux/vfs.h>
15 #include <linux/net.h>
16 #include <linux/kdev_t.h>
17 #include <linux/ioctl.h>
18 #include <linux/list.h>
19 #include <linux/dcache.h>
20 #include <linux/stat.h>
```

```
21 #include <linux/cache.h>
22 #include <linux/stddef.h>
23 #include <linux/string.h>
24
25 #include <asm/atomic.h>
26 #include <asm/bitops.h>
27
28 struct poll_table_struct;
29
30
31 /*
32  * It's silly to have NR_OPEN bigger than NR_FILE, but you can change
33  * the file limit at runtime and only root can increase the per-process
34  * nr_file rlimit, so it's safe to set up a ridiculously high absolute
35  * upper limit on files-per-process.
36  *
37  * Some programs (notably those using select()) may have to be
38  * recompiled to take full advantage of the new limits..
39  */
40
41 /* Fixed constants first: */
42 #undef NR_OPEN
43 #define NR_OPEN (1024*1024)      /* Absolute upper limit on fd num */
44 #define INR_OPEN 1024            /* Initial setting for nfile rlimits */
45
46 #define BLOCK_SIZE_BITS 10
47 #define BLOCK_SIZE (1<<BLOCK_SIZE_BITS)
48
49 /* And dynamically-tunable limits and defaults: */
50 struct files_stat_struct {
51         int nr_files;            /* read only */
52         int nr_free_files;       /* read only */
53         int max_files;           /* tunable */
54 };
55 extern struct files_stat_struct files_stat;
56
57 struct inodes_stat_t {
58         int nr_inodes;
59         int nr_unused;
60         int dummy[5];
61 };
62 extern struct inodes_stat_t inodes_stat;
63
64 extern int max_super_blocks, nr_super_blocks;
65 extern int leases_enable, dir_notify_enable, lease_break_time;
66
67 #define NR_FILE  8192    /* this can well be larger on a larger system */
68 #define NR_RESERVED_FILES 10 /* reserved for root */
69 #define NR_SUPER 256
70
71 #define MAY_EXEC 1
72 #define MAY_WRITE 2
73 #define MAY_READ 4
74
75 #define FMODE_READ 1
76 #define FMODE_WRITE 2
```

```
77
78 #define READ 0
79 #define WRITE 1
80 #define READA 2        /* read-ahead  - don't block if no resources */
81 #define SPECIAL 4      /* For non-blockdevice requests in request queue */
82
83 #define SEL_IN        1
84 #define SEL_OUT       2
85 #define SEL_EX        4
86
87 /* public flags for file_system_type */
88 #define FS_REQUIRES_DEV 1
89 #define FS_NO_DCACHE    2 /* Only dcache the necessary things. */
90 #define FS_NO_PRELIM    4 /* prevent preloading of dentries, even if
91                              * FS_NO_DCACHE is not set.
92                              */
93 #define FS_SINGLE       8 /*
94                              * Filesystem that can have only one superblock;
95                              * kernel-wide vfsmnt is placed in ->kern_mnt by
96                              * kern_mount() which must be called _after_
97                              * register_filesystem().
98                              */
99 #define FS_NOMOUNT      16 /* Never mount from userland */
100 #define FS_LITTER      32 /* Keeps the tree in dcache */
101 #define FS_ODD_RENAME  32768  /* Temporary stuff; will go away as soon
102                                 * as nfs_rename() will be cleaned up
103                                 */
104 /*
105  * These are the fs-independent mount-flags: up to 32 flags are supported
106  */
107 #define MS_RDONLY      1        /* Mount read-only */
108 #define MS_NOSUID      2        /* Ignore suid and sgid bits */
109 #define MS_NODEV       4        /* Disallow access to device special files */
110 #define MS_NOEXEC      8        /* Disallow program execution */
111 #define MS_SYNCHRONOUS 16       /* Writes are synced at once */
112 #define MS_REMOUNT     32       /* Alter flags of a mounted FS */
113 #define MS_MANDLOCK    64       /* Allow mandatory locks on an FS */
114 #define MS_NOATIME     1024     /* Do not update access times. */
115 #define MS_NODIRATIME  2048     /* Do not update directory access times /
116 #define MS_BIND        4096
117
118 /*
119  * Flags that can be altered by MS_REMOUNT
120  */
121 #define MS_RMT_MASK     (MS_RDONLY|MS_NOSUID|MS_NODEV|MS_NOEXEC|\
122 S_SYNCHRONOUS|MS_MANDLOCK|MS_NOATIME|MS_NODIRATIME)
123
124 /*
125  * Magic mount flag number. Has to be or-ed to the flag values.
126  */
127 #define MS_MGC_VAL 0xC0ED0000   /* magic flag number to indicate "new" flags */
128 #define MS_MGC_MSK 0xffff0000   /* magic flag number mask */
129
130 /* Inode flags - they have nothing to superblock flags now */
131
```

```
132 #define S_SYNC            1       /* Writes are synced at once */
133 #define S_NOATIME         2       /* Do not update access times */
134 #define S_QUOTA           4       /* Quota initialized for file */
135 #define S_APPEND          8       /* Append-only file */
136 #define S_IMMUTABLE       16      /* Immutable file */
137 #define S_DEAD            32      /* removed, but still open directory */
138
139 /*
140  * Note that nosuid etc flags are inode-specific: setting some file system
141  * flags just means all the inodes inherit those flags by default. It might be
142  * possible to override it selectively if you really wanted to with some
143  * ioctl() that is not currently implemented.
144  *
145  * Exception: MS_RDONLY is always applied to the entire file system.
146  *
147  * Unfortunately, it is possible to change a filesystems flags with it mounted
148  * with files in use.  This means that all of the inodes will not have their
149  * i_flags updated.  Hence, i_flags no longer inherit the superblock mount
150  * flags, so these have to be checked separately. -- rmk@arm.uk.linux.org
151  */
152 #define __IS_FLG(inode,flg) ((inode)->i_sb->s_flags & (flg))
153
154 #define IS_RDONLY(inode) ((inode)->i_sb->s_flags & MS_RDONLY)
155 #define IS_NOSUID(inode)        __IS_FLG(inode, MS_NOSUID)
156 #define IS_NODEV(inode)         __IS_FLG(inode, MS_NODEV)
157 #define IS_NOEXEC(inode)        __IS_FLG(inode, MS_NOEXEC)
158 #define IS_SYNC(inode)          (__IS_FLG(inode, MS_SYNCHRONOUS) ||
                                     (inode)->i_flags & S_SYNC))
159 #define IS_MANDLOCK(inode)      __IS_FLG(inode, MS_MANDLOCK)
160
161 #define IS_QUOTAINIT(inode)     ((inode)->i_flags & S_QUOTA)
162 #define IS_APPEND(inode)        ((inode)->i_flags & S_APPEND)
163 #define IS_IMMUTABLE(inode)     ((inode)->i_flags & S_IMMUTABLE)
164 #define IS_NOATIME(inode)       (__IS_FLG(inode, MS_NOATIME) || ((inode)-
                                     i_flags & S_NOATIME))
165 #define IS_NODIRATIME(inode)    __IS_FLG(inode, MS_NODIRATIME)
166
167 #define IS_DEADDIR(inode)       ((inode)->i_flags & S_DEAD)
168
169 /* the read-only stuff doesn't really belong here, but any other place is
170    probably as bad and I don't want to create yet another include file. /
171
172 #define BLKROSET    _IO(0x12,93) /* set device read-only (0 = read-write) /
173 #define BLKROGET    _IO(0x12,94) /* get read-only status (0 = read_write) /
174 #define BLKRRPART   _IO(0x12,95) /* re-read partition table */
175 #define BLKGETSIZE  _IO(0x12,96) /* return device size */
176 #define BLKFLSBUF   _IO(0x12,97) /* flush buffer cache */
177 #define BLKRASET    _IO(0x12,98) /* Set read ahead for block device */
178 #define BLKRAGET    _IO(0x12,99) /* get current read ahead setting */
179 #define BLKFRASET   _IO(0x12,100)/* set filesystem (mm/filemap.c) read-head */
180 #define BLKFRAGET   _IO(0x12,101)/* get filesystem (mm/filemap.c) read-head */
181 #define BLKSECTSET  _IO(0x12,102)/* set max sectors per request ll_rw_blk.c) */
182 #define BLKSECTGET  _IO(0x12,103)/* get max sectors per request ll_rw_blk.c) */
```

```
183 #define BLKSSZGET  _IO(0x12,104)/* get block device sector size */
184 #if 0
185 #define BLKPG      _IO(0x12,105)/* See blkpg.h */
186 #define BLKELVGET  _IOR(0x12,106,sizeof(blkelv_ioctl_arg_t))/* elevator set */
187 #define BLKELVSET  _IOW(0x12,107,sizeof(blkelv_ioctl_arg_t))/* elevator set */
188 /* This was here just to show that the number is taken -
189    probably all these _IO(0x12,*) ioctls should be moved to blkpg.h. */
190 #endif
191
192
193 #define BMAP_IOCTL 1            /* obsolete - kept for compatibility */
194 #define FIBMAP     _IO(0x00,1)  /* bmap access */
195 #define FIGETBSZ   _IO(0x00,2)  /* get the block size used for bmap */
196
197 #ifdef __KERNEL__
198
199 #include <asm/semaphore.h>
200 #include <asm/byteorder.h>
201
202 extern void update_atime (struct inode *);
203 #define UPDATE_ATIME(inode) update_atime (inode)
204
205 extern void buffer_init(unsigned long);
206 extern void inode_init(unsigned long);
207
208 /* bh state bits */
209 #define BH_Uptodate    0        /* 1 if the buffer contains valid data */
210 #define BH_Dirty       1        /* 1 if the buffer is dirty */
211 #define BH_Lock        2        /* 1 if the buffer is locked */
212 #define BH_Req         3        /* 0 if the buffer has been invalidated /
213 #define BH_Mapped      4        /* 1 if the buffer has a disk mapping */
214 #define BH_New         5        /* 1 if the buffer is new and not yet written out */
215 #define BH_Protected   6        /* 1 if the buffer is protected */
216
217 /*
218  * Try to keep the most commonly used fields in single cache lines (16
219  * bytes) to improve performance.  This ordering should be
220  * particularly beneficial on 32-bit processors.
221  *
222  * We use the first 16 bytes for the data which is used in searches
223  * over the block hash lists (ie. getblk() and friends).
224  *
225  * The second 16 bytes we use for lru buffer scans, as used by
226  * sync_buffers() and refill_freelist().  -- sct
227  */
228 struct buffer_head {
229         /* First cache line: */
230         struct buffer_head *b_next;     /* Hash queue list */
231         unsigned long b_blocknr;        /* block number */
232         unsigned short b_size;          /* block size */
```

```
233        unsigned short b_list;            /* List that this buffer appears /
234        kdev_t b_dev;                     /* device (B_FREE = free) */
235
236        atomic_t b_count;                 /* users using this block */
237        kdev_t b_rdev;                    /* Real device */
238        unsigned long b_state;            /* buffer state bitmap (see above) */
239        unsigned long b_flushtime;        /* Time when (dirty) buffer should be written */
240
241        struct buffer_head *b_next_free;/* lru/free list linkage */
242        struct buffer_head *b_prev_free;/* doubly linked list of buffers /
243        struct buffer_head *b_this_page;/* circular list of buffers in one page */
244        struct buffer_head *b_reqnext;   /* request queue */
245
246        struct buffer_head **b_pprev;    /* doubly linked list of hash-queue */
247        char * b_data;                    /* pointer to data block */
248        struct page *b_page;              /* the page this bh is mapped to /
249        void (*b_end_io)(struct buffer_head *bh, int uptodate); /* I/O completion */
250        void *b_private;                  /* reserved for b_end_io */
251
252        unsigned long b_rsector;          /* Real buffer location on disk /
253        wait_queue_head_t b_wait;
254
255        struct inode *        b_inode;
256        struct list_head      b_inode_buffers;   /* doubly linked list of
                                             inode dirty buffers */
257 };
258
259 typedef void (bh_end_io_t)(struct buffer_head *bh, int uptodate);
260 void init_buffer(struct buffer_head *, bh_end_io_t *, void *);
261
262 #define __buffer_state(bh, state)        (((bh)->b_state & (1UL << H_##state)) != 0)
263
264 #define buffer_uptodate(bh)        __buffer_state(bh,Uptodate)
265 #define buffer_dirty(bh)           __buffer_state(bh,Dirty)
266 #define buffer_locked(bh)          __buffer_state(bh,Lock)
267 #define buffer_req(bh)              buffer_state(bh,Req)
268 #define buffer_mapped(bh)          __buffer_state(bh,Mapped)
269 #define buffer_new(bh)             __buffer_state(bh,New)
270 #define buffer_protected(bh)       __buffer_state(bh,Protected)
271
272 #define bh_offset(bh)              ((unsigned long)(bh)->b_data & PAGE_MASK)
273
274 extern void set_bh_page(struct buffer_head *bh, struct page *page,unsigned long offset);
275
276 #define touch_buffer(bh)           SetPageReferenced(bh->b_page)
277
278
279 #include <linux/pipe_fs_i.h>
280 #include <linux/minix_fs_i.h>
281 #include <linux/ext2_fs_i.h>
282 #include <linux/hpfs_fs_i.h>
283 #include <linux/ntfs_fs_i.h>
284 #include <linux/msdos_fs_i.h>
285 #include <linux/umsdos_fs_i.h>
286 #include <linux/iso_fs_i.h>
```

```
287 #include <linux/nfs_fs_i.h>
288 #include <linux/sysv_fs_i.h>
289 #include <linux/affs_fs_i.h>
290 #include <linux/ufs_fs_i.h>
291 #include <linux/efs_fs_i.h>
292 #include <linux/coda_fs_i.h>
293 #include <linux/romfs_fs_i.h>
294 #include <linux/shmem_fs.h>
295 #include <linux/smb_fs_i.h>
296 #include <linux/hfs_fs_i.h>
297 #include <linux/adfs_fs_i.h>
298 #include <linux/qnx4_fs_i.h>
299 #include <linux/reiserfs_fs_i.h>
300 #include <linux/bfs_fs_i.h>
301 #include <linux/udf_fs_i.h>
302 #include <linux/ncp_fs_i.h>
303 #include <linux/proc_fs_i.h>
304 #include <linux/usbdev_fs_i.h>
305
306 /*
307  * Attribute flags.   These should be or-ed together to figure out what
308  * has been changed!
309  */
310 #define ATTR_MODE       1
311 #define ATTR_UID        2
312 #define ATTR_GID        4
313 #define ATTR_SIZE       8
314 #define ATTR_ATIME      16
315 #define ATTR_MTIME      32
316 #define ATTR_CTIME      64
317 #define ATTR_ATIME_SET  128
318 #define ATTR_MTIME_SET  256
319 #define ATTR_FORCE      512        /* Not a change, but a change it */
320 #define ATTR_ATTR_FLAG  1024
321
322 /*
323  * This is the Inode Attributes structure, used for notify_change().  It
324  * uses the above definitions as flags, to know which values have changed.
325  * Also, in this manner, a Filesystem can look at only the values it cares
326  * about.  Basically, these are the attributes that the VFS layer can
327  * request to change from the FS layer.
328  *
329  * Derek Atkins <warlord@MIT.EDU> 94-10-20
330  */
331 struct iattr {
332         unsigned int    ia_valid;
333         umode_t         ia_mode;
334         uid_t           ia_uid;
335         gid_t           ia_gid;
336         loff_t          ia_size;
337         time_t          ia_atime;
338         time_t          ia_mtime;
339         time_t          ia_ctime;
340         unsigned int    ia_attr_flags;
341 };
```

```
342
343 /*
344  * This is the inode attributes flag definitions
345  */
346 #define ATTR_FLAG_SYNCRONOUS    1         /* Syncronous write */
347 #define ATTR_FLAG_NOATIME       2         /* Don't update atime */
348 #define ATTR_FLAG_APPEND        4         /* Append-only file */
349 #define ATTR_FLAG_IMMUTABLE     8         /* Immutable file */
350 #define ATTR_FLAG_NODIRATIME    16        /* Don't update atime for directory */
351
352 /*
353  * Includes for diskquotas and mount structures.
354  */
355 #include <linux/quota.h>
356 #include <linux/mount.h>
357
358 /*
359  * oh the beauties of C type declarations.
360  */
361 struct page;
362 struct address_space;
363
364 struct address_space_operations {
365         int (*writepage)(struct page *);
366         int (*readpage)(struct file *, struct page *);
367         int (*sync_page)(struct page *);
368         int (*prepare_write)(struct file *, struct page *, unsigned, unsigned);
369         int (*commit_write)(struct file *, struct page *, unsigned, unsigned);
370         /* Unfortunately this kludge is needed for FIBMAP. Don't use it /
371         int (*bmap)(struct address_space *, long);
372 };
373
374 struct address_space {
375         struct list_head        clean_pages;    /* list of clean pages */
376         struct list_head        dirty_pages;    /* list of dirty pages */
377         struct list_head        locked_pages;   /* list of locked pages /
378         unsigned long           nrpages;        /* number of total pages /
379         struct address_space_operations *a_ops; /* methods */
380         struct inode            *host;          /* owner: inode, block_device */
381         struct vm_area_struct   *i_mmap;        /* list of private mappings */
382         struct vm_area_struct   *i_mmap_shared; /* list of shared mappings */
383         spinlock_t              i_shared_lock;  /* and spinlock protecting it */
384         int                     gfp_mask;       /* how to allocate the pages */
385 };
386
387 struct block_device {
388         struct list_head        bd_hash;
389         atomic_t                bd_count;
390 /*      struct address_space    bd_data; */
391         dev_t                   bd_dev;  /* not a kdev_t - it's a search key */
392         atomic_t                bd_openers;
393         const struct block_device_operations *bd_op;
394         struct semaphore        bd_sem; /* open/close mutex */
395 };
396
397 struct inode {
```

```
398             struct list_head        i_hash;
399             struct list_head        i_list;
400             struct list_head        i_dentry;
401
402             struct list_head        i_dirty_buffers;
403
404             unsigned long           i_ino;
405             atomic_t                i_count;
406             kdev_t                  i_dev;
407             umode_t                 i_mode;
408             nlink_t                 i_nlink;
409             uid_t                   i_uid;
410             gid_t                   i_gid;
411             kdev_t                  i_rdev;
412             loff_t                  i_size;
413             time_t                  i_atime;
414             time_t                  i_mtime;
415             time_t                  i_ctime;
416             unsigned long           i_blksize;
417             unsigned long           i_blocks;
418             unsigned long           i_version;
419             struct semaphore        i_sem;
420             struct semaphore        i_zombie;
421             struct inode_operations *i_op;
422             struct file_operations  *i_fop; /* former ->i_op-default_file_ops */
423             struct super_block      *i_sb;
424             wait_queue_head_t        i_wait;
425             struct file_lock        *i_flock;
426             struct address_space    *i_mapping;
427             struct address_space     i_data;
428             struct dquot            *i_dquot[MAXQUOTAS];
429             struct pipe_inode_info  *i_pipe;
430             struct block_device     *i_bdev;
431
432             unsigned long           i_dnotify_mask; /* Directory notify events */
433             struct dnotify_struct   *i_dnotify; /* for directory notifications */
434
435             unsigned long           i_state;
436
437             unsigned int            i_flags;
438             unsigned char           i_sock;
439
440             atomic_t                i_writecount;
441             unsigned int            i_attr_flags;
442             __u32                   i_generation;
443             union {
444                     struct minix_inode_info         minix_i;
445                     struct ext2_inode_info          ext2_i;
446                     struct hpfs_inode_info          hpfs_i;
447                     struct ntfs_inode_info          ntfs_i;
448                     struct msdos_inode_info         msdos_i;
449                     struct umsdos_inode_info        umsdos_i;
450                     struct iso_inode_info           isofs_i;
451                     struct nfs_inode_info           nfs_i;
452                     struct sysv_inode_info          sysv_i;
453                     struct affs_inode_info          affs_i;
```

```
454                   struct ufs_inode_info            ufs_i;
455                   struct efs_inode_info            efs_i;
456                   struct romfs_inode_info          romfs_i;
457                   struct shmem_inode_info          shmem_i;
458                   struct coda_inode_info           coda_i;
459                   struct smb_inode_info            smbfs_i;
460                   struct hfs_inode_info            hfs_i;
461                   struct adfs_inode_info           adfs_i;
462                   struct qnx4_inode_info           qnx4_i;
463                   struct reiserfs_inode_info       reiserfs_i;
464                   struct bfs_inode_info            bfs_i;
465                   struct udf_inode_info            udf_i;
466                   struct ncp_inode_info            ncpfs_i;
467                   struct proc_inode_info           proc_i;
468                   struct socket                    socket_i;
469                   struct usbdev_inode_info         usbdev_i;
470                   void                             *generic_ip;
471           } u;
472 };
473
474 struct fown_struct {
475           int pid;                    /* pid or -pgrp where SIGIO should be sent*/
476           uid_t uid, euid;            /* uid/euid of process setting the owner */
477           int signum;                 /* posix.1b rt signal to be delivered on IO */
478 };
479
480 struct file {
481           struct list_head         f_list;
482           struct dentry            *f_dentry;
483           struct vfsmount          *f_vfsmnt;
484           struct file_operations   *f_op;
485           atomic_t                 f_count;
486           unsigned int             f_flags;
487           mode_t                   f_mode;
488           loff_t                   f_pos;
489           unsigned long            f_reada, f_ramax, f_raend, f_ralen,_rawin;
490           struct fown_struct       f_owner;
491           unsigned int             f_uid, f_gid;
492           int                      f_error;
493
494           unsigned long            f_version;
495
496           /* needed for tty driver, and maybe others */
497           void                     *private_data;
498 };
499 extern spinlock_t files_lock;
500 #define file_list_lock() spin_lock(&files_lock);
501 #define file_list_unlock() spin_unlock(&files_lock);
502
503 #define get_file(x)     atomic_inc(&(x)->f_count)
504 #define file_count(x)   atomic_read(&(x)->f_count)
```

```
505
506 extern int init_private_file(struct file *, struct dentry *, int);
507
508 #define MAX_NON_LFS       ((1UL<<31) - 1)
509
510 #define FL_POSIX        1
511 #define FL_FLOCK        2
512 #define FL_BROKEN       4          /* broken flock() emulation */
513 #define FL_ACCESS       8          /* for processes suspended by mandatory locking */
514 #define FL_LOCKD        16         /* lock held by rpc.lockd */
515 #define FL_LEASE        32         /* lease held on this file */
516
517 /*
518  * The POSIX file lock owner is determined by
519  * the "struct files_struct" in the thread group
520  * (or NULL for no owner - BSD locks).
521  *
522  * Lockd stuffs a "host" pointer into this.
523  */
524 typedef struct files_struct *fl_owner_t;
525
526 struct file_lock {
527         struct file_lock *fl_next;      /* singly linked list for this inode */
528         struct list_head fl_link;       /* doubly linked list of all blocks */
529         struct list_head fl_block;      /* circular list of blocked processes */
530         fl_owner_t fl_owner;
531         unsigned int fl_pid;
532         wait_queue_head_t fl_wait;
533         struct file *fl_file;
534         unsigned char fl_flags;
535         unsigned char fl_type;
536         loff_t fl_start;
537         loff_t fl_end;
538
539         void (*fl_notify)(struct file_lock *);  /* unblock callback */
540         void (*fl_insert)(struct file_lock *);  /* lock insertion callbac */
541         void (*fl_remove)(struct file_lock *);  /* lock removal callback */
542
543         struct fasync_struct *  fl_fasync; /* for lease break notifications */
544
545         union {
546                 struct nfs_lock_info    nfs_fl;
547         } fl_u;
548 };
549
550 /* The following constant reflects the upper bound of the file/locking space */
551 #ifndef OFFSET_MAX
552 #define INT_LIMIT(x)    (~((x)1 << (sizeof(x)*8 - 1)))
553 #define OFFSET_MAX      INT_LIMIT(loff_t)
554 #define OFFT_OFFSET_MAX INT_LIMIT(off_t)
555 #endif
556
557 extern struct list_head file_lock_list;
558
559 #include <linux/fcntl.h>
560
```

```
561 extern int fcntl_getlk(unsigned int, struct flock *);
562 extern int fcntl_setlk(unsigned int, unsigned int, struct flock *);
563
564 extern int fcntl_getlk64(unsigned int, struct flock64 *);
565 extern int fcntl_setlk64(unsigned int, unsigned int, struct flock64 *);
566
567 /* fs/locks.c */
568 extern void locks_init_lock(struct file_lock *);
569 extern void locks_copy_lock(struct file_lock *, struct file_lock *);
570 extern void locks_remove_posix(struct file *, fl_owner_t);
571 extern void locks_remove_flock(struct file *);
572 extern struct file_lock *posix_test_lock(struct file *, struct file_lock);
573 extern int posix_lock_file(struct file *, struct file_lock *, unsigned nt);
574 extern void posix_block_lock(struct file_lock *, struct file_lock *);
575 extern void posix_unblock_lock(struct file_lock *);
576 extern int __get_lease(struct inode *inode, unsigned int flags);
577 extern time_t lease_get_mtime(struct inode *);
578 extern int lock_may_read(struct inode *, loff_t start, unsigned long
ount);
579 extern int lock_may_write(struct inode *, loff_t start, unsigned long mount);
580
581 struct fasync_struct {
582         int     magic;
583         int     fa_fd;
584         struct  fasync_struct   *fa_next; /* singly linked list */
585         struct  file            *fa_file;
586 };
587
588 #define FASYNC_MAGIC 0x4601
589
590 /* SMP safe fasync helpers: */
591 extern int fasync_helper(int, struct file *, int, struct fasync_struct**);
592 /* can be called from interrupts */
593 extern void kill_fasync(struct fasync_struct **, int, int);
594 /* only for net: no internal synchronization */
595 extern void __kill_fasync(struct fasync_struct *, int, int);
596
597 struct nameidata {
598         struct dentry *dentry;
599         struct vfsmount *mnt;
600         struct qstr last;
601         unsigned int flags;
602         int last_type;
603 };
604
605 #define DQUOT_USR_ENABLED       0x01            /* User diskquotas enabled*/
606 #define DQUOT_GRP_ENABLED       0x02            /* Group diskquotas enabled */
607
608 struct quota_mount_options
609 {
610         unsigned int flags;             /* Flags for diskquotas on this device */
611         struct semaphore dqio_sem;      /* lock device while I/O in progress */
612         struct semaphore dqoff_sem;     /* serialize quota_off() and quota_on()
                                           on device */
```

```
613         struct file *files[MAXQUOTAS];         /* fp's to quotafiles */
614         time_t inode_expire[MAXQUOTAS];        /* expiretime for inode-quota */
615         time_t block_expire[MAXQUOTAS];        /* expiretime for block-quota */
616         char rsquash[MAXQUOTAS];               /* for quotas threat root as any
                                                      other user */
617 };
618
619 /*
620  *       Umount options
621  */
622
623 #define MNT_FORCE       0x00000001    /* Attempt to forcibily umount */
624
625 #include <linux/minix_fs_sb.h>
626 #include <linux/ext2_fs_sb.h>
627 #include <linux/hpfs_fs_sb.h>
628 #include <linux/ntfs_fs_sb.h>
629 #include <linux/msdos_fs_sb.h>
630 #include <linux/iso_fs_sb.h>
631 #include <linux/nfs_fs_sb.h>
632 #include <linux/sysv_fs_sb.h>
633 #include <linux/affs_fs_sb.h>
634 #include <linux/ufs_fs_sb.h>
635 #include <linux/efs_fs_sb.h>
636 #include <linux/romfs_fs_sb.h>
637 #include <linux/smb_fs_sb.h>
638 #include <linux/hfs_fs_sb.h>
639 #include <linux/adfs_fs_sb.h>
640 #include <linux/qnx4_fs_sb.h>
641 #include <linux/reiserfs_fs_sb.h>
642 #include <linux/bfs_fs_sb.h>
643 #include <linux/udf_fs_sb.h>
644 #include <linux/ncp_fs_sb.h>
645 #include <linux/usbdev_fs_sb.h>
646
647 extern struct list_head super_blocks;
648
649 #define sb_entry(list)  list_entry((list), struct super_block, s_list)
650 struct super_block {
651         struct list_head        s_list;        /* Keep this first */
652         kdev_t                  s_dev;
653         unsigned long           s_blocksize;
654         unsigned char           s_blocksize_bits;
655         unsigned char           s_lock;
656         unsigned char           s_dirt;
657         unsigned long long      s_maxbytes;     /* Max file size */
658         struct file_system_type *s_type;
659         struct super_operations *s_op;
660         struct dquot_operations *dq_op;
661         unsigned long           s_flags;
662         unsigned long           s_magic;
663         struct dentry           *s_root;
664         wait_queue_head_t       s_wait;
665
666         struct list_head        s_dirty;        /* dirty inodes */
667         struct list_head        s_files;
```

```
668
669        struct block_device       *s_bdev;
670        struct list_head          s_mounts;        /* vfsmount(s) of this one */
671        struct quota_mount_options s_dquot;        /* Diskquota specific options */
672
673        union {
674                struct minix_sb_info      minix_sb;
675                struct ext2_sb_info       ext2_sb;
676                struct hpfs_sb_info       hpfs_sb;
677                struct ntfs_sb_info       ntfs_sb;
678                struct msdos_sb_info      msdos_sb;
679                struct isofs_sb_info      isofs_sb;
680                struct nfs_sb_info        nfs_sb;
681                struct sysv_sb_info       sysv_sb;
682                struct affs_sb_info       affs_sb;
683                struct ufs_sb_info        ufs_sb;
684                struct efs_sb_info        efs_sb;
685                struct shmem_sb_info      shmem_sb;
686                struct romfs_sb_info      romfs_sb;
687                struct smb_sb_info        smbfs_sb;
688                struct hfs_sb_info        hfs_sb;
689                struct adfs_sb_info       adfs_sb;
690                struct qnx4_sb_info       qnx4_sb;
691                struct reiserfs_sb_info   reiserfs_sb;
692                struct bfs_sb_info        bfs_sb;
693                struct udf_sb_info        udf_sb;
694                struct ncp_sb_info        ncpfs_sb;
695                struct usbdev_sb_info     usbdevfs_sb;
696                void                      *generic_sbp;
697        } u;
698        /*
699         * The next field is for VFS *only*. No filesystems have any business
700         * even looking at it. You had been warned.
701         */
702        struct semaphore s_vfs_rename_sem;        /* Kludge */
703
704        /* The next field is used by knfsd when converting a (inode number based)
705         * file handle into a dentry. As it builds a path in the dcache tree from
706         * the bottom up, there may for a time be a subpath of dentrys which is not
707         * connected to the main tree.  This semaphore ensure that there is only ever
708         * one such free path per filesystem.  Note that unconnected files (or other
709         * non-directories) are allowed, but not unconnected diretories.
710         */
711        struct semaphore s_nfsd_free_path_sem;
712 };
713
714 /*
715  * VFS helper functions..
716  */
717 extern int vfs_create(struct inode *, struct dentry *, int);
718 extern int vfs_mkdir(struct inode *, struct dentry *, int);
719 extern int vfs_mknod(struct inode *, struct dentry *, int, dev_t);
```

```
720 extern int vfs_symlink(struct inode *, struct dentry *, const char *);
721 extern int vfs_link(struct dentry *, struct inode *, struct dentry *);
722 extern int vfs_rmdir(struct inode *, struct dentry *);
723 extern int vfs_unlink(struct inode *, struct dentry *);
724 extern int vfs_rename(struct inode *, struct dentry *, struct inode *,struct dentry *);
725
726 /*
727  * File types
728  */
729 #define DT_UNKNOWN      0
730 #define DT_FIFO         1
731 #define DT_CHR          2
732 #define DT_DIR          4
733 #define DT_BLK          6
734 #define DT_REG          8
735 #define DT_LNK          10
736 #define DT_SOCK         12
737 #define DT_WHT          14
738
739 /*
740  * This is the "filldir" function type, used by readdir() to let
741  * the kernel specify what kind of dirent layout it wants to have.
742  * This allows the kernel to read directories into kernel space or
743  * to have different dirent layouts depending on the binary type.
744  */
745 typedef int (*filldir_t)(void *, const char *, int, off_t, ino_t, unsigned);
746
747 struct block_device_operations {
748         int (*open) (struct inode *, struct file *);
749         int (*release) (struct inode *, struct file *);
750         int (*ioctl) (struct inode *, struct file *, unsigned, unsigned long);
751         int (*check_media_change) (kdev_t);
752         int (*revalidate) (kdev_t);
753 };
754
755 /*
756  * NOTE:
757  * read, write, poll, fsync, readv, writev can be called
758  *   without the big kernel lock held in all filesystems.
759  */
760 struct file_operations {
761         struct module *owner;
762         loff_t (*llseek) (struct file *, loff_t, int);
763         ssize_t (*read) (struct file *, char *, size_t, loff_t *);
764         ssize_t (*write) (struct file *, const char *, size_t, loff_t *);
765         int (*readdir) (struct file *, void *, filldir_t);
766         unsigned int (*poll) (struct file *, struct poll_table_struct *);
767         int (*ioctl) (struct inode *, struct file *, unsigned int, unsigned long);
768         int (*mmap) (struct file *, struct vm_area_struct *);
769         int (*open) (struct inode *, struct file *);
770         int (*flush) (struct file *);
771         int (*release) (struct inode *, struct file *);
772         int (*fsync) (struct file *, struct dentry *, int datasync);
773         int (*fasync) (int, struct file *, int);
```

```
774            int (*lock) (struct file *, int, struct file_lock *);
775            ssize_t (*readv) (struct file *, const struct iovec *, unsigned long, loff_t *);
776            ssize_t (*writev)(struct file *, const struct iovec *, unsigned long, loff_t *);
777 };
778
779 struct inode_operations {
780            int (*create) (struct inode *,struct dentry *,int);
781            struct dentry * (*lookup) (struct inode *,struct dentry *);
782            int (*link) (struct dentry *,struct inode *,struct dentry *);
783            int (*unlink) (struct inode *,struct dentry *);
784            int (*symlink) (struct inode *,struct dentry *,const char *);
785            int (*mkdir) (struct inode *,struct dentry *,int);
786            int (*rmdir) (struct inode *,struct dentry *);
787            int (*mknod) (struct inode *,struct dentry *,int,int);
788            int (*rename) (struct inode *, struct dentry *,
789                              struct inode *, struct dentry *);
790            int (*readlink) (struct dentry *, char *,int);
791            int (*follow_link) (struct dentry *, struct nameidata *);
792            void (*truncate) (struct inode *);
793            int (*permission) (struct inode *, int);
794            int (*revalidate) (struct dentry *);
795            int (*setattr) (struct dentry *, struct iattr *);
796            int (*getattr) (struct dentry *, struct iattr *);
797 };
798
799 /*
800  * NOTE: write_inode, delete_inode, clear_inode, put_inode can be called
801  * without the big kernel lock held in all filesystems.
802  */
803 struct super_operations {
804            void (*read_inode) (struct inode *);
805
806            /* reiserfs kludge.  reiserfs needs 64 bits of information to
807            ** find an inode.  We are using the read_inode2 call to get
808            ** that information.  We don't like this, and are waiting on some
809            ** VFS changes for the real solution.
810            ** iget4 calls read_inode2, iff it is defined
811            */
812            void (*read_inode2) (struct inode *, void *) ;
813            void (*dirty_inode) (struct inode *);
814            void (*write_inode) (struct inode *, int);
815            void (*put_inode) (struct inode *);
816            void (*delete_inode) (struct inode *);
817            void (*put_super) (struct super_block *);
818            void (*write_super) (struct super_block *);
819            void (*write_super_lockfs) (struct super_block *);
820            void (*unlockfs) (struct super_block *);
821            int (*statfs) (struct super_block *, struct statfs *);
822            int (*remount_fs) (struct super_block *, int *, char *);
823            void (*clear_inode) (struct inode *);
824            void (*umount_begin) (struct super_block *);
825 };
826
827 /* Inode state bits.. */
828 #define I_DIRTY_SYNC            1 /* Not dirty enough for O_DATASYNC */
829 #define I_DIRTY_DATASYNC        2 /* Data-related inode changes pending */
```

```
830 #define I_DIRTY_PAGES         4 /* Data-related inode changes pending */
831 #define I_LOCK                 8
832 #define I_FREEING             16
833 #define I_CLEAR               32
834
835 #define I_DIRTY (I_DIRTY_SYNC | I_DIRTY_DATASYNC | I_DIRTY_PAGES)
836
837 extern void __mark_inode_dirty(struct inode *, int);
838 static inline void mark_inode_dirty(struct inode *inode)
839 {
840         __mark_inode_dirty(inode, I_DIRTY);
841 }
842
843 static inline void mark_inode_dirty_sync(struct inode *inode)
844 {
845         __mark_inode_dirty(inode, I_DIRTY_SYNC);
846 }
847
848 static inline void mark_inode_dirty_pages(struct inode *inode)
849 {
850         __mark_inode_dirty(inode, I_DIRTY_PAGES);
851 }
852
853 struct dquot_operations {
854         void (*initialize) (struct inode *, short);
855         void (*drop) (struct inode *);
856         int (*alloc_block) (const struct inode *, unsigned long, char);
857         int (*alloc_inode) (const struct inode *, unsigned long);
858         void (*free_block) (const struct inode *, unsigned long);
859         void (*free_inode) (const struct inode *, unsigned long);
860         int (*transfer) (struct dentry *, struct iattr *);
861 };
862
863 struct file_system_type {
864         const char *name;
865         int fs_flags;
866         struct super_block *(*read_super) (struct super_block *, void *, int);
867         struct module *owner;
868         struct vfsmount *kern_mnt; /* For kernel mount, if it's FS_SINGLE fs */
869         struct file_system_type * next;
870 };
871
872 #define DECLARE_FSTYPE(var,type,read,flags) \
873 struct file_system_type var = { \
874         name:           type, \
875         read_super:     read, \
876         fs_flags:       flags, \
877         owner:          THIS_MODULE, \
878 }
879
880 #define DECLARE_FSTYPE_DEV(var,type,read) \
881         DECLARE_FSTYPE(var,type,read,FS_REQUIRES_DEV)
882
883 /* Alas, no aliases. Too much hassle with bringing module.h everywhere */
884 #define fops_get(fops) \
885         (((fops) && (fops)->owner)        \
```

```
886                          ? ( try_inc_mod_count((fops)->owner) ? (fops) : NULL ) \
887                          : (fops))
888
889 #define fops_put(fops) \
890 do {        \
891         if ((fops) && (fops)->owner) \
892                 __MOD_DEC_USE_COUNT((fops)->owner);        \
893 } while(0)
894
895 extern int register_filesystem(struct file_system_type *);
896 extern int unregister_filesystem(struct file_system_type *);
897 extern struct vfsmount *kern_mount(struct file_system_type *);
898 extern void kern_umount(struct vfsmount *);
899 extern int may_umount(struct vfsmount *);
900 extern long do_mount(char *, char *, char *, unsigned long, void *);
901
902
903 extern int vfs_statfs(struct super_block *, struct statfs *);
904
905 /* Return value for VFS lock functions - tells locks.c to lock conventionally
906  * REALLY kosha for root NFS and nfs_lock
907  */
908 #define LOCK_USE_CLNT 1
909
910 #define FLOCK_VERIFY_READ  1
911 #define FLOCK_VERIFY_WRITE 2
912
913 extern int locks_mandatory_locked(struct inode *);
914 extern int locks_mandatory_area(int, struct inode *, struct file *, loff_t, size_t);
915
916 /*
917  * Candidates for mandatory locking have the setgid bit set
918  * but no group execute bit -  an otherwise meaningless combination.
919  */
920 #define MANDATORY_LOCK(inode) \
921         (IS_MANDLOCK(inode) && ((inode)->i_mode & (S_ISGID | S_IXGRP)) == S_ISGID)
922
923 static inline int locks_verify_locked(struct inode *inode)
924 {
925         if (MANDATORY_LOCK(inode))
926                 return locks_mandatory_locked(inode);
927         return 0;
928 }
929
930 static inline int locks_verify_area(int read_write, struct inode *inode,
931                                     struct file *filp, loff_t offset,
932                                     size_t count)
933 {
934         if (inode->i_flock && MANDATORY_LOCK(inode))
935                 return locks_mandatory_area(read_write, inode, filp,offset, count);
936         return 0;
937 }
938
939 static inline int locks_verify_truncate(struct inode *inode,
940                                     struct file *filp,
941                                     loff_t size)
```

```
942 {
943          if (inode->i_flock && MANDATORY_LOCK(inode))
944                  return locks_mandatory_area(
945                          FLOCK_VERIFY_WRITE, inode, filp,
946                          size < inode->i_size ? size : inode->i_size,
947                          (size < inode->i_size ? inode->i_size - size
948                           : size - inode->i_size)
949                  );
950          return 0;
951 }
952
953 extern inline int get_lease(struct inode *inode, unsigned int mode)
954 {
955          if (inode->i_flock && (inode->i_flock->fl_flags & FL_LEASE))
956                  return __get_lease(inode, mode);
957          return 0;
958 }
959
960 /* fs/open.c */
961
962 asmlinkage long sys_open(const char *, int, int);
963 asmlinkage long sys_close(unsigned int);          /* yes, it's really unsigned */
964 extern int do_truncate(struct dentry *, loff_t start);
965
966 extern struct file *filp_open(const char *, int, int);
967 extern struct file * dentry_open(struct dentry *, struct vfsmount *, int);
968 extern int filp_close(struct file *, fl_owner_t id);
969 extern char * getname(const char *);
970
971 /* fs/dcache.c */
972 extern void vfs_caches_init(unsigned long);
973
974 #define __getname()      kmem_cache_alloc(names_cachep, SLAB_KERNEL)
975 #define putname(name)    kmem_cache_free(names_cachep, (void *)(name))
976
977 enum {BDEV_FILE, BDEV_SWAP, BDEV_FS, BDEV_RAW};
978 extern int register_blkdev(unsigned int, const char *, struct
                               block_device_operations *);
979 extern int unregister_blkdev(unsigned int, const char *);
980 extern struct block_device *bdget(dev_t);
981 extern void bdput(struct block_device *);
982 extern int blkdev_open(struct inode *, struct file *);
983 extern struct file_operations def_blk_fops;
984 extern struct file_operations def_fifo_fops;
985 extern int ioctl_by_bdev(struct block_device *, unsigned, unsigned long);
986 extern int blkdev_get(struct block_device *, mode_t, unsigned, int);
987 extern int blkdev_put(struct block_device *, int);
988
989 /* fs/devices.c */
990 extern const struct block_device_operations *get_blkfops(unsigned int);
991 extern int register_chrdev(unsigned int, const char *, struct file_operations *);
992 extern int unregister_chrdev(unsigned int, const char *);
993 extern int chrdev_open(struct inode *, struct file *);
994 extern const char * bdevname(kdev_t);
995 extern const char * cdevname(kdev_t);
996 extern const char * kdevname(kdev_t);
```

```
997 extern void init_special_inode(struct inode *, umode_t, int);
998
999 /* Invalid inode operations -- fs/bad_inode.c */
1000 extern void make_bad_inode(struct inode *);
1001 extern int is_bad_inode(struct inode *);
1002
1003 extern struct file_operations read_fifo_fops;
1004 extern struct file_operations write_fifo_fops;
1005 extern struct file_operations rdwr_fifo_fops;
1006 extern struct file_operations read_pipe_fops;
1007 extern struct file_operations write_pipe_fops;
1008 extern struct file_operations rdwr_pipe_fops;
1009
1010 extern int fs_may_remount_ro(struct super_block *);
1011
1012 extern int try_to_free_buffers(struct page *, int);
1013 extern void refile_buffer(struct buffer_head * buf);
1014
1015 /* reiserfs_writepage needs this */
1016 extern void set_buffer_async_io(struct buffer_head *bh) ;
1017
1018 #define BUF_CLEAN        0
1019 #define BUF_LOCKED       1              /* Buffers scheduled for write */
1020 #define BUF_DIRTY        2              /* Dirty buffers, not yet scheduled for write */
1021 #define BUF_PROTECTED    3              /* Ramdisk persistent storage */
1022 #define NR_LIST          4
1023
1024 /*
1025  * This is called by bh->b_end_io() handlers when I/O has completed.
1026  */
1027 static inline void mark_buffer_uptodate(struct buffer_head * bh, int on)
1028 {
1029         if (on)
1030                 set_bit(BH_Uptodate, &bh->b_state);
1031         else
1032                 clear_bit(BH_Uptodate, &bh->b_state);
1033 }
1034
1035 #define atomic_set_buffer_clean(bh) test_and_clear_bit(BH_Dirty, &(bh)->b_state)
1036
1037 static inline void __mark_buffer_clean(struct buffer_head *bh)
1038 {
1039         refile_buffer(bh);
1040 }
1041
1042 static inline void mark_buffer_clean(struct buffer_head * bh)
1043 {
1044         if (atomic_set_buffer_clean(bh))
1045                 __mark_buffer_clean(bh);
1046 }
1047
1048 #define atomic_set_buffer_protected(bh) test_and_set_bit(BH_Protected, &(bh)->b_state)
1049
1050 static inline void __mark_buffer_protected(struct buffer_head *bh)
1051 {
1052         refile_buffer(bh);
```

```
1053 }
1054
1055 static inline void mark_buffer_protected(struct buffer_head * bh)
1056 {
1057         if (!atomic_set_buffer_protected(bh))
1058                 __mark_buffer_protected(bh);
1059 }
1060
1061 extern void FASTCALL(__mark_buffer_dirty(struct buffer_head *bh));
1062 extern void FASTCALL(mark_buffer_dirty(struct buffer_head *bh));
1063
1064 #define atomic_set_buffer_dirty(bh) test_and_set_bit(BH_Dirty, &(bh)->b_state)
1065
1066 /*
1067  * If an error happens during the make_request, this function
1068  * has to be recalled. It marks the buffer as clean and not
1069  * uptodate, and it notifys the upper layer about the end
1070  * of the I/O.
1071  */
1072 static inline void buffer_IO_error(struct buffer_head * bh)
1073 {
1074         mark_buffer_clean(bh);
1075         /*
1076          * b_end_io has to clear the BH_Uptodate bitflag in the error case!
1077          */
1078         bh->b_end_io(bh, 0);
1079 }
1080
1081 extern void buffer_insert_inode_queue(struct buffer_head *, struct inode*);
1082 static inline void mark_buffer_dirty_inode(struct buffer_head *bh, struct inode *inode)
1083 {
1084         mark_buffer_dirty(bh);
1085         buffer_insert_inode_queue(bh, inode);
1086 }
1087
1088 extern void balance_dirty(kdev_t);
1089 extern int check_disk_change(kdev_t);
1090 extern int invalidate_inodes(struct super_block *);
1091 extern void invalidate_inode_pages(struct inode *);
1092 extern void invalidate_inode_buffers(struct inode *);
1093 #define invalidate_buffers(dev) __invalidate_buffers((dev), 0)
1094 #define destroy_buffers(dev)    __invalidate_buffers((dev), 1)
1095 extern void __invalidate_buffers(kdev_t dev, int);
1096 extern void sync_inodes(kdev_t);
1097 extern void write_inode_now(struct inode *, int);
1098 extern void sync_dev(kdev_t);
1099 extern int fsync_dev(kdev_t);
1100 extern int fsync_inode_buffers(struct inode *);
1101 extern int osync_inode_buffers(struct inode *);
1102 extern int inode_has_buffers(struct inode *);
1103 extern void filemap_fdatasync(struct address_space *);
1104 extern void filemap_fdatawait(struct address_space *);
1105 extern void sync_supers(kdev_t);
1106 extern int bmap(struct inode *, int);
1107 extern int notify_change(struct dentry *, struct iattr *);
1108 extern int permission(struct inode *, int);
```

```
1109 extern int vfs_permission(struct inode *, int);
1110 extern int get_write_access(struct inode *);
1111 extern int deny_write_access(struct file *);
1112 static inline void put_write_access(struct inode * inode)
1113 {
1114         atomic_dec(&inode->i_writecount);
1115 }
1116 static inline void allow_write_access(struct file *file)
1117 {
1118         if (file)
1119                 atomic_inc(&file->f_dentry->d_inode->i_writecount);
1120 }
1121 extern int do_pipe(int *);
1122
1123 extern int open_namei(const char *, int, int, struct nameidata *);
1124
1125 extern int kernel_read(struct file *, unsigned long, char *, unsigned long);
1126 extern struct file * open_exec(const char *);
1127
1128 /* fs/dcache.c -- generic fs support functions */
1129 extern int is_subdir(struct dentry *, struct dentry *);
1130 extern ino_t find_inode_number(struct dentry *, struct qstr *);
1131
1132 /*
1133  * Kernel pointers have redundant information, so we can use a
1134  * scheme where we can return either an error code or a dentry
1135  * pointer with the same return value.
1136  *
1137  * This should be a per-architecture thing, to allow different
1138  * error and pointer decisions.
1139  */
1140 static inline void *ERR_PTR(long error)
1141 {
1142         return (void *) error;
1143 }
1144
1145 static inline long PTR_ERR(const void *ptr)
1146 {
1147         return (long) ptr;
1148 }
1149
1150 static inline long IS_ERR(const void *ptr)
1151 {
1152         return (unsigned long)ptr > (unsigned long)-1000L;
1153 }
1154
1155 /*
1156  * The bitmask for a lookup event:
1157  *  - follow links at the end
1158  *  - require a directory
1159  *  - ending slashes ok even for nonexistent files
1160  *  - internal "there are more path compnents" flag
1161  */
1162 #define LOOKUP_FOLLOW           (1)
1163 #define LOOKUP_DIRECTORY        (2)
1164 #define LOOKUP_CONTINUE         (4)
```

```
1165 #define LOOKUP_POSITIVE          (8)
1166 #define LOOKUP_PARENT            (16)
1167 #define LOOKUP_NOALT             (32)
1168 /*
1169  * Type of the last component on LOOKUP_PARENT
1170  */
1171 enum {LAST_NORM, LAST_ROOT, LAST_DOT, LAST_DOTDOT, LAST_BIND};
1172
1173 /*
1174  * "descriptor" for what we're up to with a read for sendfile().
1175  * This allows us to use the same read code yet
1176  * have multiple different users of the data that .
1177  * we read from a file.
1178  *
1179  * The simplest case just copies the data to user
1180  * mode.
1181  */
1182 typedef struct {
1183         size_t written;
1184         size_t count;
1185         char * buf;
1186         int error;
1187 } read_descriptor_t;
1188
1189 typedef int (*read_actor_t)(read_descriptor_t *, struct page *, unsigned long,
                                unsigned long);
1190
1191 /* needed for stackable file system support */
1192 extern loff_t default_llseek(struct file *file, loff_t offset, int origin);
1193
1194 extern int __user_walk(const char *, unsigned, struct nameidata *);
1195 extern int path_init(const char *, unsigned, struct nameidata *);
1196 extern int path_walk(const char *, struct nameidata *);
1197 extern void path_release(struct nameidata *);
1198 extern int follow_down(struct vfsmount **, struct dentry **);
1199 extern int follow_up(struct vfsmount **, struct dentry **);
1200 extern struct dentry * lookup_one(const char *, struct dentry *);
1201 extern struct dentry * lookup_hash(struct qstr *, struct dentry *);
1202 #define user_path_walk(name,nd)   __user_walk(name, LOOKUP_FOLLOW|LOOKUP_POSITIVE, nd)
1203 #define user_path_walk_link(name,nd) __user_walk(name, LOOKUP_POSITIVE, nd)
1204
1205 extern void iput(struct inode *);
1206 extern void force_delete(struct inode *);
1207 extern struct inode * igrab(struct inode *);
1208 extern ino_t iunique(struct super_block *, ino_t);
1209
1210 typedef int (*find_inode_t)(struct inode *, unsigned long, void *);
1211 extern struct inode * iget4(struct super_block *, unsigned long, find_inode_t, void *);
1212 static inline struct inode *iget(struct super_block *sb, unsigned long ino)
1213 {
1214         return iget4(sb, ino, NULL, NULL);
1215 }
1216
1217 extern void clear_inode(struct inode *);
1218 extern struct inode * get_empty_inode(void);
1219 static inline struct inode * new_inode(struct super_block *sb)
```

```
1220 {
1221         struct inode *inode = get_empty_inode();
1222         if (inode) {
1223                 inode->i_sb = sb;
1224                 inode->i_dev = sb->s_dev;
1225         }
1226         return inode;
1227 }
1228
1229 extern void insert_inode_hash(struct inode *);
1230 extern void remove_inode_hash(struct inode *);
1231 extern struct file * get_empty_filp(void);
1232 extern void file_move(struct file *f, struct list_head *list);
1233 extern void file_moveto(struct file *new, struct file *old);
1234 extern struct buffer_head * get_hash_table(kdev_t, int, int);
1235 extern struct buffer_head * getblk(kdev_t, int, int);
1236 extern void ll_rw_block(int, int, struct buffer_head * bh[]);
1237 extern void submit_bh(int, struct buffer_head *);
1238 extern int is_read_only(kdev_t);
1239 extern void __brelse(struct buffer_head *);
1240 static inline void brelse(struct buffer_head *buf)
1241 {
1242         if (buf)
1243                 __brelse(buf);
1244 }
1245 extern void __bforget(struct buffer_head *);
1246 static inline void bforget(struct buffer_head *buf)
1247 {
1248         if (buf)
1249                 __bforget(buf);
1250 }
1251 extern void set_blocksize(kdev_t, int);
1252 extern unsigned int get_hardblocksize(kdev_t);
1253 extern struct buffer_head * bread(kdev_t, int, int);
1254 extern void wakeup_bdflush(int wait);
1255
1256 extern int brw_page(int, struct page *, kdev_t, int [], int);
1257
1258 typedef int (get_block_t)(struct inode*,long,struct buffer_head*,int);
1259
1260 /* Generic buffer handling for block filesystems.. */
1261 extern int block_flushpage(struct page *, unsigned long);
1262 extern int block_symlink(struct inode *, const char *, int);
1263 extern int block_write_full_page(struct page*, get_block_t*);
1264 extern int block_read_full_page(struct page*, get_block_t*);
1265 extern int block_prepare_write(struct page*, unsigned, unsigned, get_block_t*);
1266 extern int cont_prepare_write(struct page*, unsigned, unsigned, get_block_t*,
1267                                       unsigned long *);
1268 extern int block_sync_page(struct page *);
1269
1270 int generic_block_bmap(struct address_space *, long, get_block_t *);
1271 int generic_commit_write(struct file *, struct page *, unsigned, unsigned);
1272 int block_truncate_page(struct address_space *, loff_t, get_block_t *);
1273
1274 extern int generic_file_mmap(struct file *, struct vm_area_struct *);
1275 extern ssize_t generic_file_read(struct file *, char *, size_t, loff_t *);
1276 extern ssize_t generic_file_write(struct file *, const char *, size_t, loff_t *);
```

```
1277 extern void do_generic_file_read(struct file *, loff_t *, read_descriptor_t
                                *,read_actor_t);
1278
1279 extern ssize_t generic_read_dir(struct file *, char *, size_t, loff_t *);
1280
1281 extern struct file_operations generic_ro_fops;
1282
1283 extern int vfs_readlink(struct dentry *, char *, int, const char *);
1284 extern int vfs_follow_link(struct nameidata *, const char *);
1285 extern int page_readlink(struct dentry *, char *, int);
1286 extern int page_follow_link(struct dentry *, struct nameidata *);
1287 extern struct inode_operations page_symlink_inode_operations;
1288
1289 extern int vfs_readdir(struct file *, filldir_t, void *);
1290 extern int dcache_readdir(struct file *, void *, filldir_t);
1291
1292 extern struct file_system_type *get_fs_type(const char *name);
1293 extern struct super_block *get_super(kdev_t);
1294 struct super_block *get_empty_super(void);
1295 extern void put_super(kdev_t);
1296 unsigned long generate_cluster(kdev_t, int b[], int);
1297 unsigned long generate_cluster_swab32(kdev_t, int b[], int);
1298 extern kdev_t ROOT_DEV;
1299 extern char root_device_name[];
1300
1301
1302 extern void show_buffers(void);
1303 extern void mount_root(void);
1304
1305 #ifdef CONFIG_BLK_DEV_INITRD
1306 extern kdev_t real_root_dev;
1307 extern int change_root(kdev_t, const char *);
1308 #endif
1309
1310 extern ssize_t char_read(struct file *, char *, size_t, loff_t *);
1311 extern ssize_t block_read(struct file *, char *, size_t, loff_t *);
1312 extern int read_ahead[];
1313
1314 extern ssize_t char_write(struct file *, const char *, size_t, loff_t *);
1315 extern ssize_t block_write(struct file *, const char *, size_t, loff_t *);
1316
1317 extern int file_fsync(struct file *, struct dentry *, int);
1318 extern int generic_buffer_fdatasync(struct inode *inode, unsigned long start_idx,
                                unsigned long end_idx);
1319 extern int generic_osync_inode(struct inode *, int);
1320
1321 extern int inode_change_ok(struct inode *, struct iattr *);
1322 extern void inode_setattr(struct inode *, struct iattr *);
1323
1324 /*
1325  * Common dentry functions for inclusion in the VFS
1326  * or in other stackable file systems.  Some of these
1327  * functions were in linux/fs/ C (VFS) files.
```

```
1328  *
1329  */
1330
1331  /*
1332   * Locking the parent is needed to:
1333   *  - serialize directory operations
1334   *  - make sure the parent doesn't change from
1335   *    under us in the middle of an operation.
1336   *
1337   * NOTE! Right now we'd rather use a "struct inode"
1338   * for this, but as I expect things to move toward
1339   * using dentries instead for most things it is
1340   * probably better to start with the conceptually
1341   * better interface of relying on a path of dentries.
1342   */
1343  static inline struct dentry *lock_parent(struct dentry *dentry)
1344  {
1345          struct dentry *dir = dget(dentry->d_parent);
1346
1347          down(&dir->d_inode->i_sem);
1348          return dir;
1349  }
1350
1351  static inline struct dentry *get_parent(struct dentry *dentry)
1352  {
1353          return dget(dentry->d_parent);
1354  }
1355
1356  static inline void unlock_dir(struct dentry *dir)
1357  {
1358          up(&dir->d_inode->i_sem);
1359          dput(dir);
1360  }
1361
1362  /*
1363   * Whee.. Deadlock country. Happily there are only two VFS
1364   * operations do that this..
1365   */
1366  static inline void double_down(struct semaphore *s1, struct semaphore *s2)
1367  {
1368          if (s1 != s2) {
1369                  if ((unsigned long) s1 < (unsigned long) s2) {
1370                          struct semaphore *tmp = s2;
1371                          s2 = s1; s1 = tmp;
1372                  }
1373                  down(s1);
1374          }
1375          down(s2);
1376  }
1377
1378  /*
1379   * Ewwwwwwww... _triple_ lock. We are guaranteed that the 3rd argument is
1380   * not equal to 1st and not equal to 2nd - the first case (target is parent of
1381   * source) would be already caught, the second is plain impossible (target is
```

```
1382    * its own parent and that case would be caught even earlier). Very messy.
1383    * I _think_ that it works, but no warranties - please, look it through.
1384    * Pox on bloody losers who mandated overwriting rename() for directories...
1385    */
1386
1387   static inline void triple_down(struct semaphore *s1,
1388                                  struct semaphore *s2,
1389                                  struct semaphore *s3)
1390   {
1391          if (s1 != s2) {
1392                  if ((unsigned long) s1 < (unsigned long) s2) {
1393                          if ((unsigned long) s1 < (unsigned long) s3) {
1394                                  struct semaphore *tmp = s3;
1395                                  s3 = s1; s1 = tmp;
1396                          }
1397                          if ((unsigned long) s1 < (unsigned long) s2) {
1398                                  struct semaphore *tmp = s2;
1399                                  s2 = s1; s1 = tmp;
1400                          }
1401                  } else {
1402                          if ((unsigned long) s1 < (unsigned long) s3) {
1403                                  struct semaphore *tmp = s3;
1404                                  s3 = s1; s1 = tmp;
1405                          }
1406                          if ((unsigned long) s2 < (unsigned long) s3) {
1407                                  struct semaphore *tmp = s3;
1408                                  s3 = s2; s2 = tmp;
1409                          }
1410                  }
1411                  down(s1);
1412          } else if ((unsigned long) s2 < (unsigned long) s3) {
1413                  struct semaphore *tmp = s3;
1414                  s3 = s2; s2 = tmp;
1415          }
1416          down(s2);
1417          down(s3);
1418   }
1419
1420   static inline void double_up(struct semaphore *s1, struct semaphore *s2)
1421   {
1422          up(s1);
1423          if (s1 != s2)
1424                  up(s2);
1425   }
1426
1427   static inline void triple_up(struct semaphore *s1,
1428                                struct semaphore *s2,
1429                                struct semaphore *s3)
1430   {
1431          up(s1);
1432          if (s1 != s2)
1433                  up(s2);
1434          up(s3);
1435   }
1436
1437   static inline void double_lock(struct dentry *d1, struct dentry *d2)
```

```
1438 {
1439         double_down(&d1->d_inode->i_sem, &d2->d_inode->i_sem);
1440 }
1441
1442 static inline void double_unlock(struct dentry *d1, struct dentry *d2)
1443 {
1444         double_up(&d1->d_inode->i_sem,&d2->d_inode->i_sem);
1445         dput(d1);
1446         dput(d2);
1447 }
1448
1449 #endif /* __KERNEL__ */
1450
1451 #endif /* _LINUX_FS_H */
1452
```

Source file fs/ext2/super.c (2.4.3)

```
/*
2   *   linux/fs/ext2/super.c
3   *
4   * Copyright (C) 1992, 1993, 1994, 1995
5   * Remy Card (card@masi.ibp.fr)
6   * Laboratoire MASI - Institut Blaise Pascal
7   * Universite Pierre et Marie Curie (Paris VI)
8   *
9   *   from
10  *
11  *   linux/fs/minix/inode.c
12  *
13  *   Copyright (C) 1991, 1992   Linus Torvalds
14  *
15  *   Big-endian to little-endian byte-swapping/bitmaps by
16  *         David S. Miller (davem@caip.rutgers.edu), 1995
17  */
18
19 #include <linux/config.h>
20 #include <linux/module.h>
21 #include <linux/string.h>
22 #include <linux/fs.h>
23 #include <linux/ext2_fs.h>
24 #include <linux/slab.h>
25 #include <linux/init.h>
26 #include <linux/locks.h>
27 #include <asm/uaccess.h>
28
29
30
31 static char error_buf[1024];
32
```

```
33 void ext2_error (struct super_block * sb, const char * function,
34              const char * fmt, ...)
35 {
36        va_list args;
37
38        if (!(sb->s_flags & MS_RDONLY)) {
39                sb->u.ext2_sb.s_mount_state |= EXT2_ERROR_FS;
40                sb->u.ext2_sb.s_es->s_state =
41                        cpu_to_le16(le16_to_cpu(sb->u.ext2_sb.s_es->s_state)
                                | EXT2_ERROR_FS);
42                mark_buffer_dirty(sb->u.ext2_sb.s_sbh);
43                sb->s_dirt = 1;
44        }
45        va_start (args, fmt);
46        vsprintf (error_buf, fmt, args);
47        va_end (args);
48        if (test_opt (sb, ERRORS_PANIC) ||
49            (le16_to_cpu(sb->u.ext2_sb.s_es->s_errors) == EXT2_ERRORS_PANIC&&
50             !test_opt (sb, ERRORS_CONT) && !test_opt (sb, ERRORS_RO)))
51                panic ("EXT2-fs panic (device %s): %s: %s\n",
52                        bdevname(sb->s_dev), function, error_buf);
53        printk (KERN_CRIT "EXT2-fs error (device %s): %s: %s\n",
54                bdevname(sb->s_dev), function, error_buf);
55        if (test_opt (sb, ERRORS_RO) ||
56            (le16_to_cpu(sb->u.ext2_sb.s_es->s_errors) == EXT2_ERRORS_RO &&
57             !test_opt (sb, ERRORS_CONT) && !test_opt (sb, ERRORS_PANIC))) {
58                printk ("Remounting filesystem read-only\n");
59                sb->s_flags |= MS_RDONLY;
60        }
61 }
62
63 NORET_TYPE void ext2_panic (struct super_block * sb, const char * function,
64                        const char * fmt, ...)
65 {
66        va_list args;
67
68        if (!(sb->s_flags & MS_RDONLY)) {
69                sb->u.ext2_sb.s_mount_state |= EXT2_ERROR_FS;
70                sb->u.ext2_sb.s_es->s_state =
71                        cpu_to_le16(le16_to_cpu(sb->u.ext2_sb.s_es
                                >s_state) | EXT2_ERROR_FS);
72                mark_buffer_dirty(sb->u.ext2_sb.s_sbh);
73                sb->s_dirt = 1;
74        }
75        va_start (args, fmt);
76        vsprintf (error_buf, fmt, args);
77        va_end (args);
78        /* this is to prevent panic from syncing this filesystem */
79        if (sb->s_lock)
```

```
80                         sb->s_lock=0;
81              sb->s_flags |= MS_RDONLY;
82              panic ("EXT2-fs panic (device %s): %s: %s\n",
83                      bdevname(sb->s_dev), function, error_buf);
84 }
85
86 void ext2_warning (struct super_block * sb, const char * function,
87                      const char * fmt, ...)
88 {
89          va_list args;
90
91          va_start (args, fmt);
92          vsprintf (error_buf, fmt, args);
93          va_end (args);
94          printk (KERN_WARNING "EXT2-fs warning (device %s): %s: %s\n",
95                  bdevname(sb->s_dev), function, error_buf);
96 }
97
98 void ext2_update_dynamic_rev(struct super_block *sb)
99 {
100         struct ext2_super_block *es = EXT2_SB(sb)->s_es;
101
102         if (le32_to_cpu(es->s_rev_level) > EXT2_GOOD_OLD_REV)
103                 return;
104
105         ext2_warning(sb, __FUNCTION__,
106                         "updating to rev %d because of new feature flag, "
107                         "running e2fsck is recommended",
108                         EXT2_DYNAMIC_REV);
109
110         es->s_first_ino = cpu_to_le32(EXT2_GOOD_OLD_FIRST_INO);
111         es->s_inode_size = cpu_to_le16(EXT2_GOOD_OLD_INODE_SIZE);
112         es->s_rev_level = cpu_to_le32(EXT2_DYNAMIC_REV);
113         /* leave es->s_feature_*compat flags alone */
114         /* es->s_uuid will be set by e2fsck if empty */
115
116         /*
117          * The rest of the superblock fields should be zero, and if not it
118          * means they are likely already in use, so leave them alone.  We
119          * can leave it up to e2fsck to clean up any inconsistencies there.
120          */
121 }
122
123 void ext2_put_super (struct super_block * sb)
124 {
125         int db_count;
126         int i;
127
128         if (!(sb->s_flags & MS_RDONLY)) {
```

```
129                    sb->u.ext2_sb.s_es->s_state = le16_to_cpu(sb-
                       >u.ext2_sb.s_mount_state);
130                    mark_buffer_dirty(sb->u.ext2_sb.s_sbh);
131            }
132        db_count = EXT2_SB(sb)->s_gdb_count;
133        for (i = 0; i < db_count; i++)
134                if (sb->u.ext2_sb.s_group_desc[i])
135                        brelse (sb->u.ext2_sb.s_group_desc[i]);
136        kfree(sb->u.ext2_sb.s_group_desc);
137        for (i = 0; i < EXT2_MAX_GROUP_LOADED; i++)
138                if (sb->u.ext2_sb.s_inode_bitmap[i])
139                        brelse (sb->u.ext2_sb.s_inode_bitmap[i]);
140        for (i = 0; i < EXT2_MAX_GROUP_LOADED; i++)
141                if (sb->u.ext2_sb.s_block_bitmap[i])
142                        brelse (sb->u.ext2_sb.s_block_bitmap[i]);
143        brelse (sb->u.ext2_sb.s_sbh);
144
145        return;
146 }
147
148 static struct super_operations ext2_sops = {
149        read_inode:     ext2_read_inode,
150        write_inode:    ext2_write_inode,
151        put_inode:      ext2_put_inode,
152        delete_inode:   ext2_delete_inode,
153        put_super:      ext2_put_super,
154        write_super:    ext2_write_super,
155        statfs:         ext2_statfs,
156        remount_fs:     ext2_remount,
157 };
158
159 /*
160  * This function has been shamelessly adapted from the msdos fs
161  */
162 static int parse_options (char * options, unsigned long * sb_block,
163                           unsigned short *resuid, unsigned short *resgid,
164                           unsigned long * mount_options)
165 {
166        char * this_char;
167        char * value;
168
169        if (!options)
170                return 1;
171        for (this_char = strtok (options, ",");
172             this_char != NULL;
173             this_char = strtok (NULL, ",")) {
174                if ((value = strchr (this_char, '=')) != NULL)
175                        *value++ = 0;
176                if (!strcmp (this_char, "bsddf"))
```

```
177                         clear_opt (*mount_options, MINIX_DF);
178                 else if (!strcmp (this_char, "nouid32")) {
179                         set_opt (*mount_options, NO_UID32);
180                 }
181                 else if (!strcmp (this_char, "check")) {
182                         if (!value || !*value || !strcmp (value, "none"))
183                                 clear_opt (*mount_options, CHECK);
184                         else
185 #ifdef CONFIG_EXT2_CHECK
186                                 set_opt (*mount_options, CHECK);
187 #else
188                                 printk("EXT2 Check option not supported\n");
189 #endif
190                 }
191                 else if (!strcmp (this_char, "debug"))
192                         set_opt (*mount_options, DEBUG);
193                 else if (!strcmp (this_char, "errors")) {
194                         if (!value || !*value) {
195                                 printk ("EXT2-fs: the errors option requires"
196                                         "an argument\n");
197                                 return 0;
198                         }
199                         if (!strcmp (value, "continue")) {
200                                 clear_opt (*mount_options, ERRORS_RO);
201                                 clear_opt (*mount_options, ERRORS_PANIC);
202                                 set_opt (*mount_options, ERRORS_CONT);
203                         }
204                         else if (!strcmp (value, "remount-ro")) {
205                                 clear_opt (*mount_options, ERRORS_CONT);
206                                 clear_opt (*mount_options, ERRORS_PANIC);
207                                 set_opt (*mount_options, ERRORS_RO);
208                         }
209                         else if (!strcmp (value, "panic")) {
210                                 clear_opt (*mount_options, ERRORS_CONT);
211                                 clear_opt (*mount_options, ERRORS_RO);
212                                 set_opt (*mount_options, ERRORS_PANIC);
213                         }
214                         else {
215                                 printk ("EXT2-fs: Invalid errors option:s\n",
216                                         value);
217                                 return 0;
218                         }
219                 }
220                 else if (!strcmp (this_char, "grpid") ||
221                         !strcmp (this_char, "bsdgroups"))
222                         set_opt (*mount_options, GRPID);
223                 else if (!strcmp (this_char, "minixdf"))
224                         set_opt (*mount_options, MINIX_DF);
225                 else if (!strcmp (this_char, "nocheck"))
```

```
226                         clear_opt (*mount_options, CHECK);
227                 else if (!strcmp (this_char, "nogrpid") ||
228                         !strcmp (this_char, "sysvgroups"))
229                         clear_opt (*mount_options, GRPID);
230                 else if (!strcmp (this_char, "resgid")) {
231                         if (!value || !*value) {
232                                 printk ("EXT2-fs: the resgid option requires"
233                                         "an argument\n");
234                                 return 0;
235                         }
236                         *resgid = simple_strtoul (value, &value, 0);
237                         if (*value) {
238                                 printk ("EXT2-fs: Invalid resgid option:%s\n",
239                                         value);
240                                 return 0;
241                         }
242                 }
243                 else if (!strcmp (this_char, "resuid")) {
244                         if (!value || !*value) {
245                                 printk ("EXT2-fs: the resuid option requires"
246                                         "an argument");
247                                 return 0;
248                         }
249                         *resuid = simple_strtoul (value, &value, 0);
250                         if (*value) {
251                                 printk ("EXT2-fs: Invalid resuid option:%s\n",
252                                         value);
253                                 return 0;
254                         }
255                 }
256                 else if (!strcmp (this_char, "sb")) {
257                         if (!value || !*value) {
258                                 printk ("EXT2-fs: the sb option requires
259                                         "an argument");
260                                 return 0;
261                         }
262                         *sb_block = simple_strtoul (value, &value, 0);
263                         if (*value) {
264                                 printk ("EXT2-fs: Invalid sb option: %s\n",
265                                         value);
266                                 return 0;
267                         }
268                 }
269                 /* Silently ignore the quota options */
270                 else if (!strcmp (this_char, "grpquota")
271                         || !strcmp (this_char, "noquota")
272                         || !strcmp (this_char, "quota")
273                         || !strcmp (this_char, "usrquota"))
274                         /* Don't do anything ;-) */ ;
```

```
275                        else {
276                  printk ("EXT2-fs: Unrecognized mount option %s\n",this_char);
277                          return 0;
278                  }
279          }
280          return 1;
281  }
282
283  static int ext2_setup_super (struct super_block * sb,
284                                  struct ext2_super_block * es,
285                                  int read_only)
286  {
287          int res = 0;
288          if (le32_to_cpu(es->s_rev_level) > EXT2_MAX_SUPP_REV) {
289                  printk ("EXT2-fs warning: revision level too high, "
290                          "forcing read-only mode\n");
291                  res = MS_RDONLY;
292          }
293          if (read_only)
294                  return res;
295          if (!(sb->u.ext2_sb.s_mount_state & EXT2_VALID_FS))
296                  printk ("EXT2-fs warning: mounting unchecked fs, "
297                          "running e2fsck is recommended\n");
298          else if ((sb->u.ext2_sb.s_mount_state & EXT2_ERROR_FS))
299                  printk ("EXT2-fs warning: mounting fs with errors, "
300                          "running e2fsck is recommended\n");
301          else if (( __s16) le16_to_cpu(es->s_max_mnt_count) >= 0 &&
302                  le16_to_cpu(es->s_mnt_count) >=
303                  (unsigned short) (__s16) le16_to_cpu(es->s_max_mnt_count))
304                  printk ("EXT2-fs warning: maximal mount count reached, "
305                          "running e2fsck is recommended\n");
306          else if (le32_to_cpu(es->s_checkinterval) &&
307                  (le32_to_cpu(es->s_lastcheck) +
308                  le32_to_cpu(es->s_checkinterval) <= CURRENT_TIME))
308                  printk ("EXT2-fs warning: checktime reached, "
309                          "running e2fsck is recommended\n");
310          es->s_state = cpu_to_le16(le16_to_cpu(es->s_state)& ~EXT2_VALID_FS);
311          if (!(__s16) le16_to_cpu(es->s_max_mnt_count))
312                  es->s_max_mnt_count = (__s16)
313                          cpu_to_le16(EXT2_DFL_MAX_MNT_COUNT);
313          es->s_mnt_count=cpu_to_le16(le16_to_cpu(es->s_mnt_count) + 1);
314          es->s_mtime = cpu_to_le32(CURRENT_TIME);
315          mark_buffer_dirty(sb->u.ext2_sb.s_sbh);
316          sb->s_dirt = 1;
317          if (test_opt (sb, DEBUG))
318                  printk ("[EXT II FS %s, %s, bs=%lu, fs=%lu, gc=%lu, "
319                          "bpg=%lu, ipg=%lu, mo=%04lx]\n",
320                          EXT2FS_VERSION, EXT2FS_DATE, sb->s_blocksize,
321                          sb->u.ext2_sb.s_frag_size,
```

```
322                              sb->u.ext2_sb.s_groups_count,
323                              EXT2_BLOCKS_PER_GROUP(sb),
324                              EXT2_INODES_PER_GROUP(sb),
325                              sb->u.ext2_sb.s_mount_opt);
326 #ifdef CONFIG_EXT2_CHECK
327         if (test_opt (sb, CHECK)) {
328                 ext2_check_blocks_bitmap (sb);
329                 ext2_check_inodes_bitmap (sb);
330         }
331 #endif
332         return res;
333 }
334
335 static int ext2_check_descriptors (struct super_block * sb)
336 {
337         int i;
338         int desc_block = 0;
339         unsigned long block =
                    le32_to_cpu(sb->u.ext2_sb.s_es->s_first_data_block);
340         struct ext2_group_desc * gdp = NULL;
341
342         ext2_debug ("Checking group descriptors");
343
344         for (i = 0; i < sb->u.ext2_sb.s_groups_count; i++)
345         {
346                 if ((i % EXT2_DESC_PER_BLOCK(sb)) == 0)
347                         gdp = (struct ext2_group_desc *)
                  sb->u.ext2_sb.s_group_desc[desc_block++]->b_data;
348                 if (le32_to_cpu(gdp->bg_block_bitmap) < block ||
349                     le32_to_cpu(gdp->bg_block_bitmap) >= block +
                      EXT2_BLOCKS_PER_GROUP(sb))
350                 {
351                         ext2_error (sb, "ext2_check_descriptors",
352                                     "Block bitmap for group %d"
353                                     " not in group (block %lu)!",
354                                     i, (unsigned long)
                                    le32_to_cpu(gdp->bg_block_bitmap));
355                         return 0;
356                 }
357                 if (le32_to_cpu(gdp->bg_inode_bitmap) < block ||
358                     le32_to_cpu(gdp->bg_inode_bitmap) >= block +
                      EXT2_BLOCKS_PER_GROUP(sb))
359                 {
360                         ext2_error (sb, "ext2_check_descriptors",
361                                     "Inode bitmap for group %d"
362                                     " not in group (block %lu)!",
```

```
363                               i, (unsigned long)
                            le32_to_cpu(gdp->bg_inode_bitmap));
364                         return 0;
365                 }
366                 if (le32_to_cpu(gdp->bg_inode_table) < block ||
367                     le32_to_cpu(gdp->bg_inode_table) +
                        sb->u.ext2_sb.s_itb_per_group >=
368                     block + EXT2_BLOCKS_PER_GROUP(sb))
369                 {
370                         ext2_error (sb, "ext2_check_descriptors",
371                                     "Inode table for group %d"
372                                     " not in group (block %lu)!",
373                                     i, (unsigned long)
                            le32_to_cpu(gdp->bg_inode_table));
374                         return 0;
375                 }
376                 block += EXT2_BLOCKS_PER_GROUP(sb);
377                 gdp++;
378         }
379         return 1;
380 }
381
382 #define log2(n) ffz(~(n))
383
384 struct super_block * ext2_read_super (struct super_block * sb, void * data,
385                                       int silent)
386 {
387         struct buffer_head * bh;
388         struct ext2_super_block * es;
389         unsigned long sb_block = 1;
390         unsigned short resuid = EXT2_DEF_RESUID;
391         unsigned short resgid = EXT2_DEF_RESGID;
392         unsigned long logic_sb_block = 1;
393         unsigned long offset = 0;
394         kdev_t dev = sb->s_dev;
395         int blocksize = BLOCK_SIZE;
396         int hblock;
397         int db_count;
398         int i, j;
399
400         /*
401          * See what the current blocksize for the device is, and
402          * use that as the blocksize.  Otherwise (or if the blocksize
403          * is smaller than the default) use the default.
404          * This is important for devices that have a hardware
405          * sectorsize that is larger than the default.
406          */
407         blocksize = get_hardblocksize(dev);
408         if( blocksize == 0 || blocksize < BLOCK_SIZE )
```

```
409              {
410               blocksize = BLOCK_SIZE;
411              }
412
413        sb->u.ext2_sb.s_mount_opt = 0;
414        if (!parse_options ((char *) data, &sb_block, &resuid, &resgid,
415            &sb->u.ext2_sb.s_mount_opt)) {
416               return NULL;
417        }
418
419        set_blocksize (dev, blocksize);
420
421        /*
422         * If the superblock doesn't start on a sector boundary,
423         * calculate the offset.  FIXME(eric) this doesn't make sense
424         * that we would have to do this.
425         */
426        if (blocksize != BLOCK_SIZE) {
427               logic_sb_block = (sb_block*BLOCK_SIZE) / blocksize;
428               offset = (sb_block*BLOCK_SIZE) % blocksize;
429        }
430
431        if (!(bh = bread (dev, logic_sb_block, blocksize))) {
432               printk ("EXT2-fs: unable to read superblock\n");
433               return NULL;
434        }
435        /*
436         * Note: s_es must be initialized s_es as soon as possible because
437         * some ext2 macro-instructions depend on its value
438         */
439        es = (struct ext2_super_block *) (((char *)bh->b_data) + offset);
440        sb->u.ext2_sb.s_es = es;
441        sb->s_magic = le16_to_cpu(es->s_magic);
442        if (sb->s_magic != EXT2_SUPER_MAGIC) {
443               if (!silent)
444                      printk ("VFS: Can't find an ext2 filesystem on dev "
445                             "%s.\n", bdevname(dev));
446        failed_mount:
447               if (bh)
448                      brelse(bh);
449               return NULL;
450        }
451        if (le32_to_cpu(es->s_rev_level) == EXT2_GOOD_OLD_REV &&
452           (EXT2_HAS_COMPAT_FEATURE(sb, ~0U) ||
453            EXT2_HAS_RO_COMPAT_FEATURE(sb, ~0U) ||
454            EXT2_HAS_INCOMPAT_FEATURE(sb, ~0U)))
455               printk("EXT2-fs warning: feature flags set on rev 0 fs, "
456                      "running e2fsck is recommended\n");
457        /*
```

```
458                 * Check feature flags regardless of the revision level, since we
459                 * previously didn't change the revision level when setting the
flags,
460                 * so there is a chance incompat flags are set on a rev 0
filesystem.
461             */
462             if ((i = EXT2_HAS_INCOMPAT_FEATURE(sb,
~EXT2_FEATURE_INCOMPAT_SUPP))) {
463                     printk("EXT2-fs: %s: couldn't mount because of "
464                         "unsupported optional features (%x).\n",
465                         bdevname(dev), i);
466                     goto failed_mount;
467             }
468             if (!(sb->s_flags & MS_RDONLY) &&
469                 (i = EXT2_HAS_RO_COMPAT_FEATURE(sb,
~EXT2_FEATURE_RO_COMPAT_SUPP))){
470                     printk("EXT2-fs: %s: couldn't mount RDWR because of "
471                         "unsupported optional features (%x).\n",
472                         bdevname(dev), i);
473                     goto failed_mount;
474             }
475             sb->s_blocksize_bits =
476                     le32_to_cpu(EXT2_SB(sb)->s_es->s_log_block_size) + 10;
477             sb->s_blocksize = 1 << sb->s_blocksize_bits;
478             if (sb->s_blocksize != BLOCK_SIZE &&
479                 (sb->s_blocksize == 1024 || sb->s_blocksize == 2048 ||
480                 sb->s_blocksize == 4096)) {
481                     /*
482                      * Make sure the blocksize for the filesystem is larger
483                      * than the hardware sectorsize for the machine.
484                      */
485                     hblock = get_hardblocksize(dev);
486                     if(    (hblock != 0)
487                         && (sb->s_blocksize < hblock) )
488                     {
489                             printk("EXT2-fs: blocksize too small for
device.\n");
490                             goto failed_mount;
491                     }
492
493                     brelse (bh);
494                     set_blocksize (dev, sb->s_blocksize);
495                     logic_sb_block = (sb_block*BLOCK_SIZE) / sb->s_blocksize;
496                     offset = (sb_block*BLOCK_SIZE) % sb->s_blocksize;
```

```
497                     bh = bread (dev, logic_sb_block, sb->s_blocksize);
498                     if(!bh) {
499                             printk("EXT2-fs: Couldn't read superblock on "
500                                     "2nd try.\n");
501                             goto failed_mount;
502                     }
503                     es = (struct ext2_super_block *) (((char *)bh->b_data) +
504                             offset);
504                     sb->u.ext2_sb.s_es = es;
505                     if (es->s_magic != le16_to_cpu(EXT2_SUPER_MAGIC)) {
506                             printk ("EXT2-fs: Magic mismatch, very weird !\n");
507                             goto failed_mount;
508                     }
509             }
510     if (le32_to_cpu(es->s_rev_level) == EXT2_GOOD_OLD_REV) {
511             sb->u.ext2_sb.s_inode_size = EXT2_GOOD_OLD_INODE_SIZE;
512             sb->u.ext2_sb.s_first_ino = EXT2_GOOD_OLD_FIRST_INO;
513     } else {
514             sb->u.ext2_sb.s_inode_size = le16_to_cpu(es->s_inode_size);
515             sb->u.ext2_sb.s_first_ino = le32_to_cpu(es->s_first_ino);
516             if (sb->u.ext2_sb.s_inode_size != EXT2_GOOD_OLD_INODE_SIZE) {
517                     printk ("EXT2-fs: unsupported inode size: %d\n",
518                             sb->u.ext2_sb.s_inode_size);
519                     goto failed_mount;
520             }
521     }
522     sb->u.ext2_sb.s_frag_size = EXT2_MIN_FRAG_SIZE <<
523                             le32_to_cpu(es->s_log_frag_size);
524     if (sb->u.ext2_sb.s_frag_size)
525             sb->u.ext2_sb.s_frags_per_block = sb->s_blocksize /
526                                             sb->u.ext2_sb.s_frag_size;
527     else
528             sb->s_magic = 0;
529     sb->u.ext2_sb.s_blocks_per_group =
                le32_to_cpu(es->s_blocks_per_group);
530     sb->u.ext2_sb.s_frags_per_group =
                le32_to_cpu(es->s_frags_per_group);
531     sb->u.ext2_sb.s_inodes_per_group =
                le32_to_cpu(es->s_inodes_per_group);
532     sb->u.ext2_sb.s_inodes_per_block = sb->s_blocksize /
533                                     EXT2_INODE_SIZE(sb);
534     sb->u.ext2_sb.s_itb_per_group = sb->u.ext2_sb.s_inodes_per_group /
535                                     sb->u.ext2_sb.s_inodes_per_block;
536     sb->u.ext2_sb.s_desc_per_block = sb->s_blocksize /
537                                     sizeof (struct ext2_group_desc);
```

```
538         sb->u.ext2_sb.s_sbh = bh;
539         if (resuid != EXT2_DEF_RESUID)
540                 sb->u.ext2_sb.s_resuid = resuid;
541         else
542                 sb->u.ext2_sb.s_resuid = le16_to_cpu(es->s_def_resuid);
543         if (resgid != EXT2_DEF_RESGID)
544                 sb->u.ext2_sb.s_resgid = resgid;
545         else
546                 sb->u.ext2_sb.s_resgid = le16_to_cpu(es->s_def_resgid);
547         sb->u.ext2_sb.s_mount_state = le16_to_cpu(es->s_state);
548         sb->u.ext2_sb.s_addr_per_block_bits =
549                 log2 (EXT2_ADDR_PER_BLOCK(sb));
550         sb->u.ext2_sb.s_desc_per_block_bits =
551                 log2 (EXT2_DESC_PER_BLOCK(sb));
552         if (sb->s_magic != EXT2_SUPER_MAGIC) {
553                 if (!silent)
554                         printk ("VFS: Can't find an ext2 filesystem on dev "
555                                 "%s.\n",
556                                 bdevname(dev));
557                 goto failed_mount;
558         }
559         if (sb->s_blocksize != bh->b_size) {
560                 if (!silent)
561                         printk ("VFS: Unsupported blocksize on dev "
562                                 "%s.\n", bdevname(dev));
563                 goto failed_mount;
564         }
565
566         if (sb->s_blocksize != sb->u.ext2_sb.s_frag_size) {
567                 printk ("EXT2-fs: fragsize %lu != blocksize %lu
                        (not supported yet)\n",
568                         sb->u.ext2_sb.s_frag_size, sb->s_blocksize);
569                 goto failed_mount;
570         }
571
572         if (sb->u.ext2_sb.s_blocks_per_group > sb->s_blocksize * 8) {
573                 printk ("EXT2-fs: #blocks per group too big: %lu\n",
574                         sb->u.ext2_sb.s_blocks_per_group);
575                 goto failed_mount;
576         }
577         if (sb->u.ext2_sb.s_frags_per_group > sb->s_blocksize * 8) {
578                 printk ("EXT2-fs: #fragments per group too big: %lu\n",
579                         sb->u.ext2_sb.s_frags_per_group);
580                 goto failed_mount;
581         }
582         if (sb->u.ext2_sb.s_inodes_per_group > sb->s_blocksize * 8) {
583                 printk ("EXT2-fs: #inodes per group too big: %lu\n",
584                         sb->u.ext2_sb.s_inodes_per_group);
```

```
585                    goto failed_mount;
586            }
587
588        sb->u.ext2_sb.s_groups_count = (le32_to_cpu(es->s_blocks_count) -
589                                        le32_to_cpu(es->s_first_data_block)+
590                                        EXT2_BLOCKS_PER_GROUP(sb) - 1) /
591                                        EXT2_BLOCKS_PER_GROUP(sb);
592        db_count = (sb->u.ext2_sb.s_groups_count + EXT2_DESC_PER_BLOCK(sb)-1) /
593                    EXT2_DESC_PER_BLOCK(sb);
594        sb->u.ext2_sb.s_group_desc = kmalloc (db_count * sizeof (struct
           buffer_head *), GFP_KERNEL);
595        if (sb->u.ext2_sb.s_group_desc == NULL) {
596                printk ("EXT2-fs: not enough memory\n");
597                goto failed_mount;
598        }
599        for (i = 0; i < db_count; i++) {
600          sb->u.ext2_sb.s_group_desc[i] = bread (dev, logic_sb_block + i + 1,
601                                               sb->s_blocksize);
602                if (!sb->u.ext2_sb.s_group_desc[i]) {
603                        for (j = 0; j < i; j++)
604                                brelse (sb->u.ext2_sb.s_group_desc[j]);
605                        kfree(sb->u.ext2_sb.s_group_desc);
606                        printk ("EXT2-fs: unable to read group descriptors\n");
607                        goto failed_mount;
608                }
609        }
610        if (!ext2_check_descriptors (sb)) {
611                for (j = 0; j < db_count; j++)
612                        brelse (sb->u.ext2_sb.s_group_desc[j]);
613                kfree(sb->u.ext2_sb.s_group_desc);
614                printk ("EXT2-fs: group descriptors corrupted !\n");
615                goto failed_mount;
616        }
617        for (i = 0; i < EXT2_MAX_GROUP_LOADED; i++) {
618                sb->u.ext2_sb.s_inode_bitmap_number[i] = 0;
619                sb->u.ext2_sb.s_inode_bitmap[i] = NULL;
620                sb->u.ext2_sb.s_block_bitmap_number[i] = 0;
621                sb->u.ext2_sb.s_block_bitmap[i] = NULL;
622        }
623        sb->u.ext2_sb.s_loaded_inode_bitmaps = 0;
624        sb->u.ext2_sb.s_loaded_block_bitmaps = 0;
625        sb->u.ext2_sb.s_gdb_count = db_count;
626        /*
627         * set up enough so that it can read an inode
628         */
629        sb->s_op = &ext2_sops;
630        sb->s_root = d_alloc_root(iget(sb, EXT2_ROOT_INO));
631        if (!sb->s_root) {
632                for (i = 0; i < db_count; i++)
```

```
633                             if (sb->u.ext2_sb.s_group_desc[i])
634                                     brelse (sb->u.ext2_sb.s_group_desc[i]);
635                     kfree(sb->u.ext2_sb.s_group_desc);
636                     brelse (bh);
637                     printk ("EXT2-fs: get root inode failed\n");
638                     return NULL;
639             }
640         ext2_setup_super (sb, es, sb->s_flags & MS_RDONLY);
641         return sb;
642 }
643
644 static void ext2_commit_super (struct super_block * sb,
645                                 struct ext2_super_block * es)
646 {
647         es->s_wtime = cpu_to_le32(CURRENT_TIME);
648         mark_buffer_dirty(sb->u.ext2_sb.s_sbh);
649         sb->s_dirt = 0;
650 }
651
652 /*
653  * In the second extended file system, it is not necessary to
654  * write the super block since we use a mapping of the
655  * disk super block in a buffer.
656  *
657  * However, this function is still used to set the fs valid
658  * flags to 0.  We need to set this flag to 0 since the fs
659  * may have been checked while mounted and e2fsck may have
660  * set s_state to EXT2_VALID_FS after some corrections.
661  */
662
663 void ext2_write_super (struct super_block * sb)
664 {
665         struct ext2_super_block * es;
666
667         if (!(sb->s_flags & MS_RDONLY)) {
668                 es = sb->u.ext2_sb.s_es;
669
670                 ext2_debug ("setting valid to 0\n");
671
672                 if (le16_to_cpu(es->s_state) & EXT2_VALID_FS) {
673                         es->s_state = cpu_to_le16(le16_to_cpu(es->s_state) &
674                         ~EXT2_VALID_FS);
674                         es->s_mtime = cpu_to_le32(CURRENT_TIME);
675                 }
676                 ext2_commit_super (sb, es);
677         }
678         sb->s_dirt = 0;
679 }
680
```

```
681 int ext2_remount (struct super_block * sb, int * flags, char * data)
682 {
683         struct ext2_super_block * es;
684         unsigned short resuid = sb->u.ext2_sb.s_resuid;
685         unsigned short resgid = sb->u.ext2_sb.s_resgid;
686         unsigned long new_mount_opt;
687         unsigned long tmp;
688
689         /*
690          * Allow the "check" option to be passed as a remount option.
691          */
692         new_mount_opt = sb->u.ext2_sb.s_mount_opt;
693         if (!parse_options (data, &tmp, &resuid, &resgid,
694                             &new_mount_opt))
695                 return -EINVAL;
696
697         sb->u.ext2_sb.s_mount_opt = new_mount_opt;
698         sb->u.ext2_sb.s_resuid = resuid;
699         sb->u.ext2_sb.s_resgid = resgid;
700         es = sb->u.ext2_sb.s_es;
701         if ((*flags & MS_RDONLY) == (sb->s_flags & MS_RDONLY))
702                 return 0;
703         if (*flags & MS_RDONLY) {
704                 if (le16_to_cpu(es->s_state) & EXT2_VALID_FS ||
705                     !(sb->u.ext2_sb.s_mount_state & EXT2_VALID_FS))
706                         return 0;
707                 /*
708                  * OK, we are remounting a valid rw partition rdonly, so set
709                  * the rdonly flag and then mark the partition as valid again.
710                  */
711                 es->s_state = cpu_to_le16(sb->u.ext2_sb.s_mount_state);
712                 es->s_mtime = cpu_to_le32(CURRENT_TIME);
713                 mark_buffer_dirty(sb->u.ext2_sb.s_sbh);
714                 sb->s_dirt = 1;
715                 ext2_commit_super (sb, es);
716         }
717         else {
718                 int ret;
719                 if ((ret = EXT2_HAS_RO_COMPAT_FEATURE(sb,
720                         ~EXT2_FEATURE_RO_COMPAT_SUPP))) {
721                         printk("EXT2-fs: %s: couldn't remount RDWR because of "
722                                 "unsupported optional features (%x).\n",
723                                 bdevname(sb->s_dev), ret);
724                         return -EROFS;
725                 }
726                 /*
727                  * Mounting a RDONLY partition read-write, so reread and
728                  * store the current valid flag.  (It may have been changed
729                  * by e2fsck since we originally mounted the partition.)
730                  */
```

```
731                     sb->u.ext2_sb.s_mount_state = le16_to_cpu(es->s_state);
732                     if (!ext2_setup_super (sb, es, 0))
733                             sb->s_flags &= ~MS_RDONLY;
734             }
735         return 0;
736 }
737
738 int ext2_statfs (struct super_block * sb, struct statfs * buf)
739 {
740         unsigned long overhead;
741         int i;
742
743         if (test_opt (sb, MINIX_DF))
744                 overhead = 0;
745         else {
746                 /*
747                  * Compute the overhead (FS structures)
748                  */
749
750                 /*
751                  * All of the blocks before first_data_block are
752                  * overhead
753                  */
754                 overhead =
                        le32_to_cpu(sb->u.ext2_sb.s_es->s_first_data_block);
755
756                 /*
757                  * Add the overhead attributed to the superblock and
758                  * block group descriptors.  If the sparse superblocks
759                  * feature is turned on, then not all groups have this.
760                  */
761                 for (i = 0; i < EXT2_SB(sb)->s_groups_count; i++)
762                         overhead += ext2_bg_has_super(sb, i) +
763                                 ext2_bg_num_gdb(sb, i);
764
765                 /*
766                  * Every block group has an inode bitmap, a block
767                  * bitmap, and an inode table.
768                  */
769                 overhead += (sb->u.ext2_sb.s_groups_count *
770                         (2 + sb->u.ext2_sb.s_itb_per_group));
771         }
772
773         buf->f_type = EXT2_SUPER_MAGIC;
774         buf->f_bsize = sb->s_blocksize;
775         buf->f_blocks = le32_to_cpu(sb->u.ext2_sb.s_es->s_blocks_count) -
                        overhead;
776         buf->f_bfree = ext2_count_free_blocks (sb);
```

```
777            buf->f_bavail = buf->f_bfree -
               le32_to_cpu(sb->u.ext2_sb.s_es->s_r_blocks_count);
778            if (buf->f_bfree <le32_to_cpu(sb->u.ext2_sb.s_es->s_r_blocks_count))
779                    buf->f_bavail = 0;
780            buf->f_files = le32_to_cpu(sb->u.ext2_sb.s_es->s_inodes_count);
781            buf->f_ffree = ext2_count_free_inodes (sb);
782            buf->f_namelen = EXT2_NAME_LEN;
783            return 0;
784 }
785
786 static DECLARE_FSTYPE_DEV(ext2_fs_type, "ext2", ext2_read_super);
787
788 static int __init init_ext2_fs(void)
789 {
790            return register_filesystem(&ext2_fs_type);
791 }
792
793 static void __exit exit_ext2_fs(void)
794 {
795            unregister_filesystem(&ext2_fs_type);
796 }
797
798 EXPORT_NO_SYMBOLS;
799
800 module_init(init_ext2_fs)
801 module_exit(exit_ext2_fs)
802
```

Source file fs/ext2/file.c (2.4.3)

```
1 /*
2  *  linux/fs/ext2/file.c
3  *
4  * Copyright (C) 1992, 1993, 1994, 1995
5  * Remy Card (card@masi.ibp.fr)
6  * Laboratoire MASI - Institut Blaise Pascal
7  * Universite Pierre et Marie Curie (Paris VI)
8  *
9  *  from
10  *
11  *  linux/fs/minix/file.c
12  *
13  * Copyright (C) 1991, 1992  Linus Torvalds
14  *
15  * ext2 fs regular file handling primitives
16  *
17  * 64-bit file support on 64-bit platforms by Jakub Jelinek
18  *      (jj@sunsite.ms.mff.cuni.cz)
19  */
20
21 #include <linux/fs.h>
```

```
22 #include <linux/ext2_fs.h>
23 #include <linux/sched.h>
24
25 static loff_t ext2_file_lseek(struct file *, loff_t, int);
26 static int ext2_open_file (struct inode *, struct file *);
27
28 #define EXT2_MAX_SIZE(bits)\
29        (((EXT2_NDIR_BLOCKS + (1LL << (bits - 2)) +\
30          (1LL << (bits - 2)) * (1LL << (bits - 2)) +\
31          (1LL << (bits - 2)) * (1LL << (bits - 2)) * (1LL << (bits - 2)))*\
32          (1LL << bits)) - 1)
33
34 static long long ext2_max_sizes[] = {
35 0, 0, 0, 0, 0, 0, 0, 0, 0, 0,
36 EXT2_MAX_SIZE(10), EXT2_MAX_SIZE(11), EXT2_MAX_SIZE(12), EXT2_MAX_SIZE(13)
37 };
38
39 /*
40  * Make sure the offset never goes beyond the 32-bit mark..
41  */
42 static loff_t ext2_file_lseek(
43        struct file *file,
44        loff_t offset,
45        int origin)
46 {
47        struct inode *inode = file->f_dentry->d_inode;
48
49        switch (origin) {
50                case 2:
51                        offset += inode->i_size;
52                        break;
53                case 1:
54                        offset += file->f_pos;
55        }
56        if (offset<0)
57                return -EINVAL;
58        if (((unsigned long long) offset >> 32) != 0) {
59                if (offset > ext2_max_sizes[EXT2_BLOCK_SIZE_BITS(inode->i_sb)])
60                        return -EINVAL;
61        }
62        if (offset != file->f_pos) {
63                file->f_pos = offset;
64                file->f_reada = 0;
65                file->f_version = ++event;
66        }
67        return offset;
68 }
69
70 /*
71  * Called when an inode is released. Note that this is different
72  * from ext2_file_open: open gets called at every open, but release
73  * gets called only when /all/ the files are closed.
74  */
75 static int ext2_release_file (struct inode * inode, struct file * filp)
76 {
```

```
77              if (filp->f_mode & FMODE_WRITE)
78                      ext2_discard_prealloc (inode);
79          return 0;
80 }
81
82 /*
83  * Called when an inode is about to be open.
84  * We use this to disallow opening RW large files on 32bit systems if
85  * the caller didn't specify O_LARGEFILE.  On 64bit systems we force
86  * on this flag in sys_open.
87  */
88 static int ext2_open_file (struct inode * inode, struct file * filp)
89 {
90          if (!(filp->f_flags & O_LARGEFILE) &&
91              inode->i_size > 0x7FFFFFFFLL)
92                      return -EFBIG;
93          return 0;
94 }
95
96 /*
97  * We have mostly NULL's here: the current defaults are ok for
98  * the ext2 filesystem.
99  */
100 struct file_operations ext2_file_operations = {
101         llseek:         ext2_file_lseek,
102         read:           generic_file_read,
103         write:          generic_file_write,
104         ioctl:          ext2_ioctl,
105         mmap:           generic_file_mmap,
106         open:           ext2_open_file,
107         release:        ext2_release_file,
108         fsync:          ext2_sync_file,
109 };
110
111 struct inode_operations ext2_file_inode_operations = {
112         truncate:       ext2_truncate,
113 };
```

Source Code open_namei() function from fs/namei.c

```
int open_namei(const char * pathname, int flag, int mode, struct nameidata *nd)
940 {
941         int acc_mode, error = 0;
942         struct inode *inode;
943         struct dentry *dentry;
944         struct dentry *dir;
945         int count = 0;
946
947         acc_mode = ACC_MODE(flag);
948
949         /*
950          * The simplest case - just a plain lookup.
951          */
952         if (!(flag & O_CREAT)) {
953                 if (path_init(pathname, lookup_flags(flag), nd))
954                         error = path_walk(pathname, nd);
```

```
955                      if (error)
956                              return error;
957                      dentry = nd->dentry;
958                      goto ok;
959              }
960
961              /*
962               * Create - we need to know the parent.
963               */
964              if (path_init(pathname, LOOKUP_PARENT, nd))
965                      error = path_walk(pathname, nd);
966              if (error)
967                      return error;
968
969              /*
970               * We have the parent and last component. First of all, check
971               * that we are not asked to creat(2) an obvious directory - that
972               * will not do.
973               */
974              error = -EISDIR;
975              if (nd->last_type != LAST_NORM || nd->last.name[nd->last.len])
976                      goto exit;
977
978              dir = nd->dentry;
979              down(&dir->d_inode->i_sem);
980              dentry = lookup_hash(&nd->last, nd->dentry);
981
982 do_last:
983              error = PTR_ERR(dentry);
984              if (IS_ERR(dentry)) {
985                      up(&dir->d_inode->i_sem);
986                      goto exit;
987              }
988
989              /* Negative dentry, just create the file */
990              if (!dentry->d_inode) {
991                      error = vfs_create(dir->d_inode, dentry, mode);
992                      up(&dir->d_inode->i_sem);
993                      dput(nd->dentry);
994                      nd->dentry = dentry;
995                      if (error)
996                              goto exit;
997                      /* Don't check for write permission, don't truncate */
998                      acc_mode = 0;
999                      flag &= ~O_TRUNC;
1000                      goto ok;
1001              }
1002
1003              /*
1004               * It already exists.
1005               */
1006              up(&dir->d_inode->i_sem);
1007
1008              error = -EEXIST;
1009              if (flag & O_EXCL)
1010                      goto exit_dput;
```

```
1011
1012            if (d_mountpoint(dentry)) {
1013                    error = -ELOOP;
1014                    if (flag & O_NOFOLLOW)
1015                            goto exit_dput;
1016                while (__follow_down(&nd->mnt,&dentry) && d_mountpoint(dentry));
1017            }
1018            error = -ENOENT;
1019            if (!dentry->d_inode)
1020                    goto exit_dput;
1021            if (dentry->d_inode->i_op && dentry->d_inode->i_op->follow_link)
1022                    goto do_link;
1023
1024            dput(nd->dentry);
1025            nd->dentry = dentry;
1026            error = -EISDIR;
1027            if (dentry->d_inode && S_ISDIR(dentry->d_inode->i_mode))
1028                    goto exit;
1029 ok:
1030            error = -ENOENT;
1031            inode = dentry->d_inode;
1032            if (!inode)
1033                    goto exit;
1034
1035            error = -ELOOP;
1036            if (S_ISLNK(inode->i_mode))
1037                    goto exit;
1038
1039            error = -EISDIR;
1040            if (S_ISDIR(inode->i_mode) && (flag & FMODE_WRITE))
1041                    goto exit;
1042
1043            error = permission(inode,acc_mode);
1044            if (error)
1045                    goto exit;
1046
1047            /*
1048             * FIFO's, sockets and device files are special: they don't
1049             * actually live on the filesystem itself, and as such you
1050             * can write to them even if the filesystem is read-only.
1051             */
1052            if (S_ISFIFO(inode->i_mode) || S_ISSOCK(inode->i_mode)) {
1053                    flag &= ~O_TRUNC;
1054            } else if (S_ISBLK(inode->i_mode) || S_ISCHR(inode->i_mode)) {
1055                    error = -EACCES;
1056                    if (IS_NODEV(inode))
1057                            goto exit;
1058
1059                    flag &= ~O_TRUNC;
1060            } else {
1061                    error = -EROFS;
1062                    if (IS_RDONLY(inode) && (flag & 2))
1063                            goto exit;
1064            }
```

```
1065            /*
1066             * An append-only file must be opened in append mode for writing.
1067             */
1068            error = -EPERM;
1069            if (IS_APPEND(inode)) {
1070                    if  ((flag & FMODE_WRITE) && !(flag & O_APPEND))
1071                            goto exit;
1072                    if (flag & O_TRUNC)
1073                            goto exit;
1074            }
1075
1076            /*
1077             * Ensure there are no outstanding leases on the file.
1078             */
1079            error = get_lease(inode, flag);
1080            if (error)
1081                    goto exit;
1082
1083            if (flag & O_TRUNC) {
1084                    error = get_write_access(inode);
1085                    if (error)
1086          •                 goto exit;
1087
1088                    /*
1089                 * Refuse to truncate files with mandatory locks held on hem.
1090                     */
1091                    error = locks_verify_locked(inode);
1092                    if (!error) {
1093                            DQUOT_INIT(inode);
1094
1095                            error = do_truncate(dentry, 0);
1096                    }
1097                    put_write_access(inode);
1098                    if (error)
1099                            goto exit;
1100            } else
1101                    if (flag & FMODE_WRITE)
1102                            DQUOT_INIT(inode);
1103
1104            return 0;
1105
1106 exit_dput:
1107            dput(dentry);
1108 exit:
1109            path_release(nd);
1110            return error;
1111
1112 do_link:
1113            error = -ELOOP;
1114            if (flag & O_NOFOLLOW)
1115                    goto exit_dput;
1116            /*
1117             * This is subtle. Instead of calling do_follow_link() we do the
1118             * thing by hands. The reason is that this way we have zero link_count
```

```
1119            * and path_walk() (called from ->follow_link) honoring OOKUP_PARENT.
1120            * After that we have the parent and last component, i.e.
1121            * we are in the same situation as after the first path_walk().
1122            * Well, almost - if the last component is normal we get its copy
1123            * stored in nd->last.name and we will have to putname() it when we
1124            * are done. Procfs-like symlinks just set LAST_BIND.
1125            */
1126           UPDATE_ATIME(dentry->d_inode);
1127           error = dentry->d_inode->i_op->follow_link(dentry, nd);
1128           dput(dentry);
1129           if (error)
1130                   return error;
1131           if (nd->last_type == LAST_BIND) {
1132                   dentry = nd->dentry;
1133                   goto ok;
1134           }
1135           error = -EISDIR;
1136           if (nd->last_type != LAST_NORM)
1137                   goto exit;
1138           if (nd->last.name[nd->last.len]) {
1139                   putname(nd->last.name);
1140                   goto exit;
1141           }
1142           if (count++==32) {
1143                   dentry = nd->dentry;
1144                   putname(nd->last.name);
1145                   goto ok;
1146           }
1147           dir = nd->dentry;
1148           down(&dir->d_inode->i_sem);
1149           dentry = lookup_hash(&nd->last, nd->dentry);
1150           putname(nd->last.name);
1151           goto do_last;
1152 }
```

CHAPTER 5

LVM (Logical Volume Manager)

Nowadays in a Linux server you typically find between three and ten, or even more disks. From a hardware perspective with SCSI channels and separate disk cabinets it's certainly possible to have this many disks.

Managing that many disks and their partitions is not easy. Also, Linux sysadmins have certainly encountered situations where one of the file systems was approaching 100% space occupation and they wished they could just magically extend the partition. Well, with LVM it's not only possible, but it is also quite easy to do so.

The Logical Volume Manager (LVM) is a subsystem for online disk storage management which has become the de facto standard for storage management across UNIX implementations. LVM was initially developed by IBM for its AIX operating system and was subsequently adopted by the OSF (now OpenGroup) for the OSF/1 operating system. The OSF version was then used as a base for the HP-UX and Digital UNIX operating systems. This is why LVMs resemble each other on these platforms. The LVM in Linux is very similar to the HP-UX LVM, with which many sysadmins have had a good experience. The Linux LVM implementation was written, as usual, by hundreds of people all over the Internet. Among the best known developers were people like Andrea Arcangeli, Michael Marxmeier, Andy Bakun, Steve Brueggeman, and others.

LVM completely rethinks the way file systems and volumes are managed. It allows drives to span disks, be resized, and be managed in a more flexible way than can be done using the current partition table schemes.

LINUX LVM INTRODUCTION

The Logical Volume Manager adds an additional layer between the physical devices and the block I/O interface in the kernel. For example, a file system such as ext2 would use a block device provided by LVM instead of using a disk drive directly.

In Figure 5-1 you can see the additional layer in the I/O logic introduced by LVM.

In a traditional system, disk drives are usually partitioned in continuous storage areas ("partitions" or "slices") which are then mapped to block devices. On PC systems this is done by tools like fdisk, which maintain a simple partition table.

For example, a disk drive /dev/sda is partitioned into *n* storage areas, which are associated with /dev/sda1 through /dev/sda*n*, as shown in Figure 5-2.

The shortcomings are clear: A partition is limited in size to the size of the disk drive and resizing a partition requires either rebuilding subsequent partitions or using specialized tools like *GNU Parted*[1] that allow reorganizing your disk without reverting to a backup. This is usually an intrusive operation and quite risky.

By contrast, LVM block devices are not limited by physical constraints, are not necessarily continuous, and can be resized online.

An LVM system organizes storage in volume groups (VG or volg) which consist of one or more physical volumes (PV). LVM block devices are called logical volumes (LV),

---

1   Many a reader will be more familiar with Partition Magic by PowerQuest Corp.

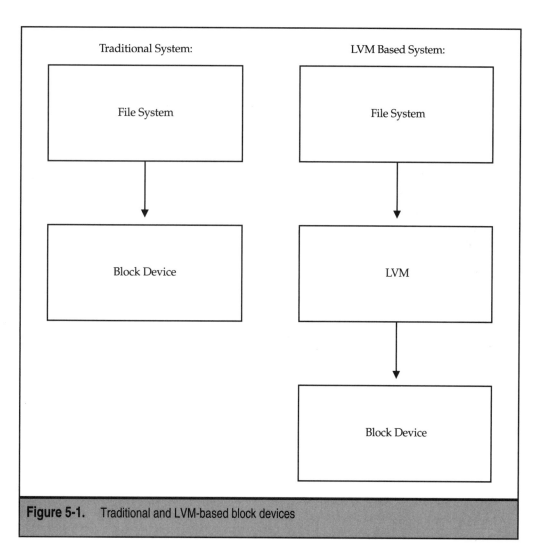

Figure 5-1. Traditional and LVM-based block devices

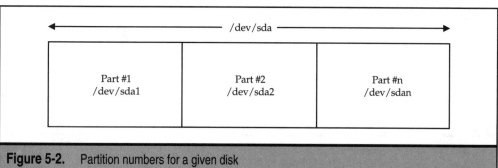

Figure 5-2. Partition numbers for a given disk

which are allocated from a storage pool maintained by LVM. In Figure 5-3 you can see that, under LVM, the disks are not directly controlled by the kernel anymore. Instead it is the LVM layer handling the disks.

There can be more than one volume group in the system. Once created, the volume group, and not the disk, is the basic unit of data storage (think of it as a virtual disk consisting of one or more physical disks).

LVM organizes storage space in several layers: A volume group is a pool which combines the capacity of one or multiple disk drives.

Unlike current partition schemes where disks are divided into fixed-size continuous partitions, LVM allows the user to consider disks, also known as physical volumes, as a pool (or volume) of data storage, consisting of equal-sized extents.

The pool of disk space that is represented by a volume group can be apportioned into virtual partitions, or logical volumes, of various sizes. A logical volume can span a number of physical volumes or represent only a portion of one physical volume. The size of a logical volume is determined by its number of extents. Once created, logical volumes can be used like regular disk partitions—to create a file system or as a swap device.

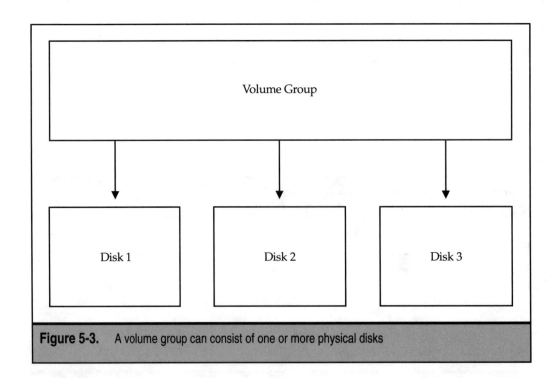

Figure 5-3. A volume group can consist of one or more physical disks

LVM Benefits

What really makes logical volumes different is that they need not be contiguous and can be resized arbitrarily. If a file system created on a logical volume supports resizing, you can enlarge or reduce a file system as needed. In addition, LVM includes a comprehensive administrative framework to manage your disk resources.

LVM works by putting a new layer between the kernel's block (disk) device interface and the actual physical devices on the system. New logical "devices" can be created using parts of one or more physical devices. Simple applications include combining multiple partitions (or whole drives) into single, larger logical drives.

The real attraction of LVM, however, is that it allows the size of logical volumes to be changed on the fly. Any system administrator who experienced the problem of partitions being too small will appreciate the ability to say "make that one bigger" and have it happen. Instead of having to bring down the system, back up everything, repartition, and then restore everything, it is now possible to simply issue an *lvextend* command.

How does LVM work?

The Logical Volume Manager adds an additional layer, a new logical layer, of logical volumes between the physical peripherals and the I/O interface in the kernel. This allows the concatenation of several disks (so-called physical volumes) to form a storage pool or volume group with allocation units called physical extents (PEs). These physical extents are mapped to offsets and blocks on the disk(s) in the volume group. Parts out of the volume group then can be allocated in the form of logical volumes in units called logical extents (LEs). Each logical extent is mapped to a corresponding physical extent of equal size. The logical volumes can then be used through device special files similar to /dev/sd[a-z]* or /dev/hd[a-z]* named /dev/VolumeGroupName/LogicalVolumeName.

The configuration information for each physical volume, the volume group, and the logical volume(s) is stored on each physical volume in an area called the Volume Group Descriptor Area or VGDA. At the time of this writing the VGDA is physically located immediately after the super-block, but this may change in the next release. The configuration information is stored in automatically-created backup files, which are stored in the /etc/lvmtab.d directory.

An LVM driver holds mapping tables between the logical extents of logical volumes and the physical extents of physical volumes. These tables are created, updated, and deleted by super-user LVM commands. The main mapping function of the driver calls for a logical block in a logical volume from functions ll_rw_block() and ll_rw_swap_file() in the file /usr/src/linux/drivers/block/ll_rw_blk.c. The mapping function looks up the corresponding physical block/disk pair in a table. Then it returns this pair to the calling ll_rw_*() function causing a physical I/O request to the disk block(s) to be queued.

A block device in Linux is simply a driver which can take buffer_heads and either fill them with data from a storage device, or else write their data to a storage device. How that read or write works is irrelevant.

In particular, it is perfectly permissible for a device driver to fulfill the I/O request by performing another I/O to a different device, or even to several devices.

Both LVM and the software RAID drivers take advantage of that, implementing I/O to the virtual device by performing one or more I/Os to one or more disks that belong to the logical volume or RAID set.

There is a special optimization used when a single I/O to the LVM or RAID driver results in just a single I/O to an underlying disk. In that case, we don't actually have to create a new I/O operation to send to the underlying device. Rather, the logical device just adds a marker to the buffer_head which is being read or written, to say that the I/O should actually be performed to a different physical device than the logical volume, namely, the block device driver to which the given physical device was mounted at boot-time.

Because the disks and partitions (or volume groups / logical volumes as they are now called) are a virtual representation of the hardware, you can easily extend or shrink the logical volume, even at run-time.

How does LVM work internally to achieve this functionality?

LVM Internals

When creating physical volumes or volume groups (volg) and logical volumes (lvol), the configuration information for each of these logical entities is stored on the corresponding physical volume, and backup of this information is automatically put under the /etc/lvmtab.d directory.

Starting from kernel 2.3.49, the LVM driver is built-in. This driver maintains mapping tables between the volgs and logical volumes and their corresponding physical partitions and drives. These tables are created and maintain LVM commands that only the root may run.

Whenever access to one block on a file system on an LVM-managed lvol is requested, the driver uses these tables to map the block to its real address on the disk. ' It's as simple as that.

How To Use It

Let's assume you have a system with four disks. One is for the operating system and three are for data. LVM knows there are four disks because the kernel sees them at boot-time and maintains a table with a list of them. All you do is create one volume group (volg) for each disk. And then for each file system you need, you continue by creating a separate lvol. You could end up having something like this:

```
/dev/volg01/lvolroot     /  800MB # this is one of the two lvols for the 2GB disk used
    for the OS
/dev/volg01/lvolusr      /usr      1200MB        # and this is the second, for /usr
/dev/volg02/lvolhome     /home   9000MB               #
/dev/volg03/lvoldbf       /ora_data    9000MB  # this might actually be a RAID device
/dev/volg04//lvolidx     /ora_idx
```

Now, assume you are running out of space on, for example, the /home directories and your users just can't delete any of those huge MP3 directories or mpeg movies. What do you do? Since we can't produce disk space magically with Linux yet, you still need to buy another disk. Nowadays, they mostly come in 18GB sizes. So you assign one 4GB partition of the new disk to the /dev/volg02 volume group. Then, using LVM, you go to expand the lvolhome logical volume to the maximum of 13GB (unless you give volg02 more, obviously). Presto! If your server supports hot-swap disk addition, you don't even need to reboot and your /home just got bigger. There are, of course, some caveats.

First, you have to momentarily disconnect the users from the /home directory. The kernel will not allow unmounting the /home file system if there are still open files in it. To momentarily stop all networking (and therefore login) activity on the server, you typically put the machine into single user mode and then just go back to your favorite runlevel'.

Second, with LVM it is easy to just add space whenever needed and your users will just have to get used to having all kinds of junk in the directories that will never be deleted.

Some Command Examples

Assuming you have kernel 2.3.49+ or have patched your existing kernel with the LVM drivers, you can run the following command examples to do some of the things mentioned above.

1. After installing LVM, do an "insmod lvm" or set up kerneld/kmod to load it automatically (see INSTALL).

2. Set up partitions (#1) on both disks with partition type 0x8e.

3. do a "pvcreate /dev/sd[ce]1"
    For testing purposes you can use more than one primary and/or extended partition on a disk. However, don't do that for normal LVM operations for performance reasons. If you have to, don't stripe logical volumes over physical volumes associated to partitions on the same disk.

4. Do a "vgcreate volg02 /dev/sd[ce]1"
    (vgcreate activates the volume group too).

5. Do a "lvcreate -lvoldbf-_lv tvolg02" to get a 100MB linear lvol or a "lvcreate -i2 -I4 -l1000 -nlvoldbf volg02" to get a 1000MB large logical volume with two stripes and stripesize 4KB.

6. Use created LVs as needed. For example, generate a file system in one with "mke2fs /dev/volg02/lvoldbf" and mount it.

Because the Linux LVM follows closely the HP-UX concept, the commands, shown in Table 5-1, are almost identical in name and behavior. So, the commands for physical volume handling all start with pv, those for volume group handling start with vg, and those for logical volumes start with lv.

Command	What It Does
e2fsadm resizing for lvextend, lvreduce, e2fsck and resize2fs	administration wrapper for logical volume including file system
lvchange	change attributes of a logical volume
lvcreate	create a logical volume
lvdisplay	display logical volume config data
lvextend	extend a logical volume in size
lvreduce	reduce a logical volume in size
lvremove	remove a logical volume
lvrename	renames an inactive logical volume
lvscan	find all existing logical volumes
lvmchange	emergency program to change attributes of the LVM
Lvmdiskscan	scan all disks/partitions and multiple devices and list them
lvmsadc	statistic data collector
lvmsar	statistic data reporter
pvchange	change attributes of physical volumes
pvcreate	create a physical volume
pvdata	debug list physical volume group descriptor area
pvdisplay	display physical volume config information
pvmove	move logical extents to a different physical volume
pvscan	find all existing physical volumes
vgcfgbackup	back up all volume group descriptor areas
vgcfgrestore	restore volume group descriptor area(s) to disk(s)
vgchange	activate/deactivate volumr group(s)
vgck	check volume group descriptor area for consistency
vgcreate	create a volume group from physical volume(s)
vgdisplay	display volume group config information
vgexport	export volume group (make it unknown to the system)
vgextend	extend a volume group by one or more physical volumes
vgimport	import a volume group (make it known to the system or another system)
vgmerge	merge two volume groups into one
vgmknodes	create volume group directory with all logical volume specials
vgreduce	reduce a volume group by one or more empty physical volume(s)
vgremove	remove an empty volume group
vgrename	rename an inactive volume group
vgscan	scan for volume groups
vgsplit	split one volume group into two

Table 5-1. LVM Commands

Creating Physical Volumes for LVM

Since LVM requires entire physical volumes to be assigned to volume groups, you must have a few empty partitions ready to be used by LVM. Install the OS on a few partitions and leave a bit of empty space. Use fdisk under Linux to create a number of empty partitions of equal size. You must mark them with fdisk as type 0xFE. We created five 256MB partitions, /dev/hda5 through /dev/hda9.

Registering Physical Volumes

The first task necessary to get LVM running is to register the physical volumes with LVM. This is done with the pvcreate command. Simply run pvcreate /dev/hdxx for each hdxx device you created. In our example, we ran pvcreate /dev/hda5, and so on.

Creating a Volume Group

Next, create a volume group. You can set certain parameters with this command, like physical extent size, but the defaults are probably fine. We'll call the new volume group vg01. Just type vgcreate vg01 /dev/hda5.

When this is done, take a look at the volume group with the vgdisplay command. Type vgdisplay -v vg01. Note that you can create up to 256 LVs, can add up to 256 PVs, and each LV can be up to 255.99GBs! More important, note the Free PE line. This tells you how many physical extents you have to work with when creating LVs. For a 256MB disk, this reads 63 because there is an unused remainder smaller than the 4MB PE size.

Creating a Logical Volume

Next, let's create a logical volume called lv01 in VG vg01. Again, there are some settings that may be changed when creating an LV, but the defaults work fine. The important choice to make is how many logical extents to allocate to this LV. We'll start with four for a total size of 16MB. Just type lvcreate -l4 -nlv01 vg01. You may also specify the size in MBs by using -L instead of -l, and LVM will round off the result to the nearest multiple of the LE size.

Take a look at your LV with the lvdisplay command by typing lvdisplay -v /dev/vg01/lv01. You can ignore the page of logical extents for now, and page up to see the more interesting data.

Adding a Disk to the Volume Group

Next, we'll add /dev/hda6 to the volume group. Just type vgextend vg01 /dev/hda6 and you're done! You can check this out by using vgdisplay -v vg01. Note that there are now a lot more PEs available!

Creating a Striped Logical Volume

Note that LVM created your whole logical volume on one physical volume within the volume group. You can also stripe an LV across two physical volumes with the -i flag in lvcreate. We'll create a new LV, lv02, striped across hda5 and hda6. Type lvcreate -l4

-nlv02 -i2 vg01 /dev/hda5 /dev/hda6. Specifying the PV on the command line tells LVM which PEs to use, while the -i2 command tells it to stripe it across the two volumes.

You now have an LV striped across two PVs.

Moving Data Within a Volume Group

Up to now, PEs and LEs were pretty much interchangable. They are the same size and are mapped automatically by LVM. This does not have to be the case, though. In fact, you can move an entire LV from one PV to another, even while the disk is mounted and in use. This will impact your performance, but it can prove useful.

Let's move lv01 to hda6 from hda5. Type pvmove -n/dev/vg01/lv01 /dev/hda5 /dev/hda6. This will move all LEs used by lv01 mapped to PEs on /dev/hda5 to new PEs on /dev/hda6. Effectively, this migrates data from hda5 to hda6. It takes a while, but when it's done, take a look with lvdisplay -v /dev/vg01/lv01 and notice that it now resides entirely on /dev/hda6.

Removing a Logical Volume from a Volume Group

Let's say we no longer need lv02. We can remove it and place its PEs back in the empty pool for the volume group. First, unmount its file system. Next, deactivate it with lvchange -a n /dev/vg01/lv02. Finally, delete it by typing lvremove /dev/vg01/lv02. Look at the volume group and notice that the PEs are now unused.

Removing a Disk from the Volume Group

You can also remove a disk from a volume group. We aren't using hda5 anymore, so we can remove it from the volume group. Just type vgreduce vg01 /dev/hda5 and it's gone!

Source Code include/linux/lvm.h

Below find the kernel header files with the relevant structures for LVM.

```
/*
2   * include/linux/lvm.h
3   * kernel/lvm.h
4   * tools/lib/lvm.h
5   *
6   * Copyright (C) 1997 - 2000  Heinz Mauelshagen, Sistina Software
7   *
8   * February-November 1997
9   * May-July 1998
10  * January-March,July,September,October,Dezember 1999
11  * January,February,July,November 2000
12  * January 2001
13  *
14  * lvm is free software; you can redistribute it and/or modify
15  * it under the terms of the GNU General Public License as published by
16  * the Free Software Foundation; either version 2, or (at your option)
17  * any later version.
```

```
18  *
19  * lvm is distributed in the hope that it will be useful,
20  * but WITHOUT ANY WARRANTY; without even the implied warranty of
21  * MERCHANTABILITY or FITNESS FOR A PARTICULAR PURPOSE.  See the
22  * GNU General Public License for more details.
23  *
24  * You should have received a copy of the GNU General Public License
25  * along with GNU CC; see the file COPYING.  If not, write to
26  * the Free Software Foundation, 59 Temple Place - Suite 330,
27  * Boston, MA 02111-1307, USA.
28  *
29  */
30
31 /*
32  * Changelog
33  *
34  *    10/10/1997 - beginning of new structure creation
35  *    12/05/1998 - incorporated structures from lvm_v1.h and deleted lvm_v1.h
36  *    07/06/1998 - avoided LVM_KMALLOC_MAX define by using vmalloc/vfree
37  *                 instead of kmalloc/kfree
38  *    01/07/1998 - fixed wrong LVM_MAX_SIZE
39  *    07/07/1998 - extended pe_t structure by ios member (for statistic)
40  *    02/08/1998 - changes for official char/block major numbers
41  *    07/08/1998 - avoided init_module() and cleanup_module() to be static
42  *    29/08/1998 - separated core and disk structure type definitions
43  *    01/09/1998 - merged kernel integration version (mike)
44  *    20/01/1999 - added LVM_PE_DISK_OFFSET macro for use in
45  *                 vg_read_with_pv_and_lv(), pv_move_pe(), pv_show_pe_text()...
46  *    18/02/1999 - added definition of time_disk_t structure for;
47  *                 keeps time stamps on disk for nonatomic writes (future)
48  *    15/03/1999 - corrected LV() and VG() macro definition to use argument
49  *                 instead of minor
50  *    03/07/1999 - define for genhd.c name handling
51  *    23/07/1999 - implemented snapshot part
52  *    08/12/1999 - changed LVM_LV_SIZE_MAX macro to reflect current 1TB limit
53  *    01/01/2000 - extended lv_v2 core structure by wait_queue member
54  *    12/02/2000 - integrated Andrea Arcagnelli's snapshot work
55  *    18/02/2000 - seperated user and kernel space parts by
56  *                 #ifdef them with __KERNEL__
57  *    08/03/2000 - implemented cluster/shared bits for vg_access
58  *    26/06/2000 - implemented snapshot persistency and resizing support
59  *    02/11/2000 - added hash table size member to lv structure
60  *    12/11/2000 - removed unneeded timestamp definitions
61  *    24/12/2000 - removed LVM_TO_{CORE,DISK}*, use cpu_{from, to}_le*
62  *                 instead - Christoph Hellwig
63  *
64  */
65
66
67 #ifndef _LVM_H_INCLUDE
68 #define _LVM_H_INCLUDE
69
```

```
70 #define _LVM_KERNEL_H_VERSION    "LVM 0.9.1_beta2 (18/01/2001)"
71
72 #include <linux/config.h>
73 #include <linux/version.h>
74
75 /*
76  * preprocessor definitions
77  */
78 /* if you like emergency reset code in the driver */
79 #define LVM_TOTAL_RESET
80
81 #ifdef __KERNEL__
82 #undef LVM_HD_NAME /* display nice names in /proc/partitions */
83
84 /* lots of debugging output (see driver source)
85    #define DEBUG_LVM_GET_INFO
86    #define DEBUG
87    #define DEBUG_MAP
88    #define DEBUG_MAP_SIZE
89    #define DEBUG_IOCTL
90    #define DEBUG_READ
91    #define DEBUG_GENDISK
92    #define DEBUG_VG_CREATE
93    #define DEBUG_LVM_BLK_OPEN
94    #define DEBUG_KFREE
95  */
96 #endif                          /* #ifdef __KERNEL__ */
97
98 #include <linux/kdev_t.h>
99 #include <linux/list.h>
100
101 #include <asm/types.h>
102 #include <linux/major.h>
103
104 #ifdef __KERNEL__
105 #include <linux/spinlock.h>
106
107 #include <asm/semaphore.h>
108 #endif                          /* #ifdef __KERNEL__ */
109
110 #include <asm/page.h>
111
112 #if !defined ( LVM_BLK_MAJOR) || !defined ( LVM_CHAR_MAJOR)
113 #error Bad include/linux/major.h - LVM MAJOR undefined
114 #endif
115
116 #ifdef  BLOCK_SIZE
117 #undef  BLOCK_SIZE
118 #endif
119
120 #ifdef CONFIG_ARCH_S390
121 #define BLOCK_SIZE       4096
```

```
122 #else
123 #define BLOCK_SIZE        1024
124 #endif
125
126 #ifndef SECTOR_SIZE
127 #define SECTOR_SIZE       512
128 #endif
129
130 #define LVM_STRUCT_VERSION        1        /* structure version */
131
132 #define LVM_DIR_PREFIX  "/dev/"
133
134 #ifndef min
135 #define min(a,b)  (((a)<(b))?(a):(b))
136 #endif
137 #ifndef max
138 #define max(a,b)  (((a)>(b))?(a):(b))
139 #endif
140
141 /* set the default structure version */
142 #if ( LVM_STRUCT_VERSION == 1)
143 #define pv_t pv_v2_t
144 #define lv_t lv_v4_t
145 #define vg_t vg_v3_t
146 #define pv_disk_t pv_disk_v2_t
147 #define lv_disk_t lv_disk_v3_t
148 #define vg_disk_t vg_disk_v2_t
149 #define lv_block_exception_t lv_block_exception_v1_t
150 #define lv_COW_table_disk_t lv_COW_table_disk_v1_t
151 #endif
152
153
154
155 /*
156  * i/o protocol version
157  *
158  * defined here for the driver and defined separate in the
159  * user land tools/lib/liblvm.h
160  *
161  */
162 #define LVM_DRIVER_IOP_VERSION          10
163
164 #define LVM_NAME        "lvm"
165 #define LVM_GLOBAL      "global"
166 #define LVM_DIR         "lvm"
167 #define LVM_VG_SUBDIR   "VGs"
168 #define LVM_LV_SUBDIR   "LVs"
169 #define LVM_PV_SUBDIR   "PVs"
170
171 /*
172  * VG/LV indexing macros
173  */
```

```
174 /* character minor maps directly to volume group */
175 #define VG_CHR(a) ( a)
176
177 /* block minor indexes into a volume group/logical volume indirection table */
178 #define VG_BLK(a)        ( vg_lv_map[a].vg_number)
179 #define LV_BLK(a)        ( vg_lv_map[a].lv_number)
180
181 /*
182  * absolute limits for VGs, PVs per VG and LVs per VG
183  */
184 #define ABS_MAX_VG       99
185 #define ABS_MAX_PV       256
186 #define ABS_MAX_LV       256     /* caused by 8 bit minor */
187
188 #define MAX_VG  ABS_MAX_VG
189 #define MAX_LV  ABS_MAX_LV
190 #define MAX_PV  ABS_MAX_PV
191
192 #if ( MAX_VG > ABS_MAX_VG)
193 #undef MAX_VG
194 #define MAX_VG ABS_MAX_VG
195 #endif
196
197 #if ( MAX_LV > ABS_MAX_LV)
198 #undef MAX_LV
199 #define MAX_LV ABS_MAX_LV
200 #endif
201
202
203 /*
204  * VGDA: default disk spaces and offsets
205  *
206  *    there's space after the structures for later extensions.
207  *
208  *    offset              what                                 size
209  *    --------------      --------------------------------     ------------
210  *    0                   physical volume structure            ~500 byte
211  *
212  *    1K                  volume group structure               ~200 byte
213  *
214  *    6K                  namelist of physical volumes         128 byte each
215  *
216  *    6k + n * ~300byte n logical volume structures            ~300 byte each
217  *
218  *    + m * 4byte        m physical extent alloc. structs      4 byte each
219  *
220  *    End of disk -       first physical extent                typically 4 megabyte
221  *    PE total *
222  *    PE size
223  *
224  *
225  */
```

```
226
227  /* DONT TOUCH THESE !!! */
228  /* base of PV structure in disk partition */
229  #define LVM_PV_DISK_BASE         0L
230
231  /* size reserved for PV structure on disk */
232  #define LVM_PV_DISK_SIZE         1024L
233
234  /* base of VG structure in disk partition */
235  #define LVM_VG_DISK_BASE         LVM_PV_DISK_SIZE
236
237  /* size reserved for VG structure */
238  #define LVM_VG_DISK_SIZE         ( 9 * 512L)
239
240  /* size reserved for timekeeping */
241  #define LVM_TIMESTAMP_DISK_BASE ( LVM_VG_DISK_BASE +  LVM_VG_DISK_SIZE)
242  #define LVM_TIMESTAMP_DISK_SIZE 512L    /* reserved for timekeeping */
243
244  /* name list of physical volumes on disk */
245  #define LVM_PV_UUIDLIST_DISK_BASE ( LVM_TIMESTAMP_DISK_BASE + \
246                                      LVM_TIMESTAMP_DISK_SIZE)
247
248  /* now for the dynamically calculated parts of the VGDA */
249  #define LVM_LV_DISK_OFFSET(a, b) ( (a)->lv_on_disk.base + \
250                                     sizeof ( lv_disk_t) * b)
251  #define LVM_DISK_SIZE(pv)        ( (pv)->pe_on_disk.base + \
252                                     (pv)->pe_on_disk.size)
253  #define LVM_PE_DISK_OFFSET(pe, pv)     ( pe * pv->pe_size + \
254                                     ( LVM_DISK_SIZE ( pv) / SECTOR_SIZE))
255  #define LVM_PE_ON_DISK_BASE(pv) \
256     { int rest; \
257       pv->pe_on_disk.base = pv->lv_on_disk.base + pv->lv_on_disk.size; \
258       if ( ( rest = pv->pe_on_disk.base % SECTOR_SIZE) != 0) \
259          pv->pe_on_disk.base += ( SECTOR_SIZE - rest); \
260     }
261  /* END default disk spaces and offsets for PVs */
262
263
264  /*
265   * LVM_PE_T_MAX corresponds to:
266   *
267   * 8KB PE size can map a ~512 MB logical volume at the cost of 1MB memory,
268   *
269   * 128MB PE size can map a 8TB logical volume at the same cost of memory.
270   *
271   * Default PE size of 4 MB gives a maximum logical volume size of 256 GB.
272   *
273   * Maximum PE size of 16GB gives a maximum logical volume size of 1024 TB.
274   *
275   * AFAIK, the actual kernels limit this to 1 TB.
276   *
277   * Should be a sufficient spectrum ;*)
```

```
278  */
279
280 /* This is the usable size of pe_disk_t.le_num !!!          v      v */
281 #define LVM_PE_T_MAX               ( ( 1 << ( sizeof ( uint16_t) * 8)) - 2)
282
283 #define LVM_LV_SIZE_MAX(a)        ( ( long long) LVM_PE_T_MAX * (a)->pe_size > (
long long) 1024*1024/SECTOR_SIZE*1024*1024 ? ( long long) 1024*1024/
SECTOR_SIZE*1024*1024 : ( long long) LVM_PE_T_MAX * (a)->pe_size)
284 #define LVM_MIN_PE_SIZE           ( 8192L / SECTOR_SIZE) /* 8 KB in sectors */
285 #define LVM_MAX_PE_SIZE           ( 16L * 1024L * 1024L / SECTOR_SIZE * 1024)      /*
16GB in sectors */
286 #define LVM_DEFAULT_PE_SIZE       ( 4096L * 1024 / SECTOR_SIZE)    /* 4 MB in sectors
*/
287 #define LVM_DEFAULT_STRIPE_SIZE 16L       /* 16 KB  */
288 #define LVM_MIN_STRIPE_SIZE       ( PAGE_SIZE/SECTOR_SIZE)         /* PAGESIZE in
sectors */
289 #define LVM_MAX_STRIPE_SIZE       ( 512L * 1024 / SECTOR_SIZE)    /* 512 KB in
sectors */
290 #define LVM_MAX_STRIPES           128      /* max # of stripes */
291 #define LVM_MAX_SIZE              ( 1024LU * 1024 / SECTOR_SIZE * 1024 * 1024)     /*
1TB[sectors] */
292 #define LVM_MAX_MIRRORS           2        /* future use */
293 #define LVM_MIN_READ_AHEAD        2        /* minimum read ahead sectors */
294 #define LVM_MAX_READ_AHEAD        120      /* maximum read ahead sectors */
295 #define LVM_MAX_LV_IO_TIMEOUT     60       /* seconds I/O timeout (future use) */
296 #define LVM_PARTITION             0xfe     /* LVM partition id */
297 #define LVM_NEW_PARTITION         0x8e     /* new LVM partition id (10/09/1999) */
298 #define LVM_PE_SIZE_PV_SIZE_REL 5          /* max relation PV size and PE
    size */
299
300 #define LVM_SNAPSHOT_MAX_CHUNK    1024     /* 1024 KB */
301 #define LVM_SNAPSHOT_DEF_CHUNK    64       /* 64  KB */
302 #define LVM_SNAPSHOT_MIN_CHUNK    1        /* 1   KB */
303
304 #define UNDEF     -1
305 #define FALSE      0
306 #define TRUE       1
307
308
309 #define LVM_GET_COW_TABLE_CHUNKS_PER_PE(vg, lv) ( \
310         vg->pe_size / lv->lv_chunk_size)
311
312 #define LVM_GET_COW_TABLE_ENTRIES_PER_PE(vg, lv) ( \
313 { \
314         int COW_table_entries_per_PE; \
315         int COW_table_chunks_per_PE; \
316 \
317         COW_table_entries_per_PE = LVM_GET_COW_TABLE_CHUNKS_PER_PE(vg,
lv); \
318         COW_table_chunks_per_PE = ( COW_table_entries_per_PE *
sizeof(lv_COW_table_disk_t) / SECTOR_SIZE + lv->lv_chunk_size - 1) /
lv->lv_chunk_size; \
```

```
319             COW_table_entries_per_PE - COW_table_chunks_per_PE;})
320
321
322 /*
323  * ioctls
324  */
325 /* volume group */
326 #define VG_CREATE              _IOW ( 0xfe, 0x00, 1)
327 #define VG_REMOVE              _IOW ( 0xfe, 0x01, 1)
328
329 #define VG_EXTEND              _IOW ( 0xfe, 0x03, 1)
330 #define VG_REDUCE              _IOW ( 0xfe, 0x04, 1)
331
332 #define VG_STATUS              _IOWR ( 0xfe, 0x05, 1)
333 #define VG_STATUS_GET_COUNT    _IOWR ( 0xfe, 0x06, 1)
334 #define VG_STATUS_GET_NAMELIST _IOWR ( 0xfe, 0x07, 1)
335
336 #define VG_SET_EXTENDABLE      _IOW ( 0xfe, 0x08, 1)
337 #define VG_RENAME              _IOW ( 0xfe, 0x09, 1)
338
339
340 /* logical volume */
341 #define LV_CREATE              _IOW ( 0xfe, 0x20, 1)
342 #define LV_REMOVE              _IOW ( 0xfe, 0x21, 1)
343
344 #define LV_ACTIVATE            _IO ( 0xfe, 0x22)
345 #define LV_DEACTIVATE          _IO ( 0xfe, 0x23)
346
347 #define LV_EXTEND              _IOW ( 0xfe, 0x24, 1)
348 #define LV_REDUCE              _IOW ( 0xfe, 0x25, 1)
349
350 #define LV_STATUS_BYNAME       _IOWR ( 0xfe, 0x26, 1)
351 #define LV_STATUS_BYINDEX      _IOWR ( 0xfe, 0x27, 1)
352
353 #define LV_SET_ACCESS          _IOW ( 0xfe, 0x28, 1)
354 #define LV_SET_ALLOCATION      _IOW ( 0xfe, 0x29, 1)
355 #define LV_SET_STATUS          _IOW ( 0xfe, 0x2a, 1)
356
357 #define LE_REMAP               _IOW ( 0xfe, 0x2b, 1)
358
359 #define LV_SNAPSHOT_USE_RATE   _IOWR ( 0xfe, 0x2c, 1)
360
361 #define LV_STATUS_BYDEV        _IOWR ( 0xfe, 0x2e, 1)
362
363 #define LV_RENAME              _IOW ( 0xfe, 0x2f, 1)
364
365 #define LV_BMAP                _IOWR ( 0xfe, 0x30, 1)
366
367
368 /* physical volume */
369 #define PV_STATUS              _IOWR ( 0xfe, 0x40, 1)
```

```
370 #define PV_CHANGE              _IOWR ( 0xfe, 0x41, 1)
371 #define PV_FLUSH               _IOW ( 0xfe, 0x42, 1)
372
373 /* physical extent */
374 #define PE_LOCK_UNLOCK         _IOW ( 0xfe, 0x50, 1)
375
376 /* i/o protocol version */
377 #define LVM_GET_IOP_VERSION    _IOR ( 0xfe, 0x98, 1)
378
379 #ifdef LVM_TOTAL_RESET
380 /* special reset function for testing purposes */
381 #define LVM_RESET              _IO ( 0xfe, 0x99)
382 #endif
383
384 /* lock the logical volume manager */
385 #define LVM_LOCK_LVM           _IO ( 0xfe, 0x100)
386 /* END ioctls */
387
388
389 /*
390  * Status flags
391  */
392 /* volume group */
393 #define VG_ACTIVE         0x01      /* vg_status */
394 #define VG_EXPORTED       0x02      /*      "     */
395 #define VG_EXTENDABLE     0x04      /*      "     */
396
397 #define VG_READ           0x01      /* vg_access */
398 #define VG_WRITE          0x02      /*      "     */
399 #define VG_CLUSTERED      0x04      /*      "     */
400 #define VG_SHARED         0x08      /*      "     */
401
402 /* logical volume */
403 #define LV_ACTIVE         0x01      /* lv_status */
404 #define LV_SPINDOWN       0x02      /*      "     */
405
406 #define LV_READ           0x01      /* lv_access */
407 #define LV_WRITE          0x02      /*      "     */
408 #define LV_SNAPSHOT       0x04      /*      "     */
409 #define LV_SNAPSHOT_ORG   0x08      /*      "     */
410
411 #define LV_BADBLOCK_ON    0x01      /* lv_badblock */
412
413 #define LV_STRICT         0x01      /* lv_allocation */
414 #define LV_CONTIGUOUS     0x02      /*       "        */
415
416 /* physical volume */
417 #define PV_ACTIVE         0x01      /* pv_status */
418 #define PV_ALLOCATABLE    0x02      /* pv_allocatable */
419
420
421 /*
```

```
422   * Structure definitions core/disk follow
423   *
424   * conditional conversion takes place on big endian architectures
425   * in functions * pv_copy_*(), vg_copy_*() and lv_copy_*()
426   *
427   */
428
429  #define NAME_LEN                 128     /* don't change!!! */
430  #define UUID_LEN                 32      /* don't change!!! */
431
432  /* copy on write tables in disk format */
433  typedef struct {
434          uint64_t pv_org_number;
435          uint64_t pv_org_rsector;
436          uint64_t pv_snap_number;
437          uint64_t pv_snap_rsector;
438  } lv_COW_table_disk_v1_t;
439
440  /* remap physical sector/rdev pairs including hash */
441  typedef struct {
442          struct list_head hash;
443          ulong rsector_org;
444          kdev_t rdev_org;
445          ulong rsector_new;
446          kdev_t rdev_new;
447  } lv_block_exception_v1_t;
448
449  /* disk stored pe information */
450  typedef struct {
451          uint16_t lv_num;
452          uint16_t le_num;
453  } pe_disk_t;
454
455  /* disk stored PV, VG, LV and PE size and offset information */
456  typedef struct {
457          uint32_t base;
458          uint32_t size;
459  } lvm_disk_data_t;
460
461
462  /*
463   * Structure Physical Volume (PV) Version 1
464   */
465
466  /* core */
467  typedef struct {
468          char id[2];             /* Identifier */
469          unsigned short version; /* HM lvm version */
470          lvm_disk_data_t pv_on_disk;
471          lvm_disk_data_t vg_on_disk;
472          lvm_disk_data_t pv_namelist_on_disk;
473          lvm_disk_data_t lv_on_disk;
```

```
474          lvm_disk_data_t pe_on_disk;
475          char pv_name[NAME_LEN];
476          char vg_name[NAME_LEN];
477          char system_id[NAME_LEN];       /* for vgexport/vgimport */
478          kdev_t pv_dev;
479          uint pv_number;
480          uint pv_status;
481          uint pv_allocatable;
482          uint pv_size;              /* HM */
483          uint lv_cur;
484          uint pe_size;
485          uint pe_total;
486          uint pe_allocated;
487          uint pe_stale;             /* for future use */
488          pe_disk_t *pe;             /* HM */
489          struct inode *inode;       /* HM */
490 } pv_v1_t;
491
492 /* core */
493 typedef struct {
494          char id[2];                   /* Identifier */
495          unsigned short version; /* HM lvm version */
496          lvm_disk_data_t pv_on_disk;
497          lvm_disk_data_t vg_on_disk;
498          lvm_disk_data_t pv_uuidlist_on_disk;
499          lvm_disk_data_t lv_on_disk;
500          lvm_disk_data_t pe_on_disk;
501          char pv_name[NAME_LEN];
502          char vg_name[NAME_LEN];
503          char system_id[NAME_LEN];       /* for vgexport/vgimport */
504          kdev_t pv_dev;
505          uint pv_number;
506          uint pv_status;
507          uint pv_allocatable;
508          uint pv_size;              /* HM */
509          uint lv_cur;
510          uint pe_size;
511          uint pe_total;
512          uint pe_allocated;
513          uint pe_stale;             /* for future use */
514          pe_disk_t *pe;             /* HM */
515          struct inode *inode;       /* HM */
516          char pv_uuid[UUID_LEN+1];
517 } pv_v2_t;
518
519
520 /* disk */
521 typedef struct {
522          uint8_t id[2];                /* Identifier */
523          uint16_t version;                    /* HM lvm version */
524          lvm_disk_data_t pv_on_disk;
525          lvm_disk_data_t vg_on_disk;
```

```
526          lvm_disk_data_t pv_namelist_on_disk;
527          lvm_disk_data_t lv_on_disk;
528          lvm_disk_data_t pe_on_disk;
529          uint8_t pv_name[NAME_LEN];
530          uint8_t vg_name[NAME_LEN];
531          uint8_t system_id[NAME_LEN];     /* for vgexport/vgimport */
532          uint32_t pv_major;
533          uint32_t pv_number;
534          uint32_t pv_status;
535          uint32_t pv_allocatable;
536          uint32_t pv_size;                /* HM */
537          uint32_t lv_cur;
538          uint32_t pe_size;
539          uint32_t pe_total;
540          uint32_t pe_allocated;
541 } pv_disk_v1_t;
542
543 /* disk */
544 typedef struct {
545          uint8_t id[2];              /* Identifier */
546          uint16_t version;                /* HM lvm version */
547          lvm_disk_data_t pv_on_disk;
548          lvm_disk_data_t vg_on_disk;
549          lvm_disk_data_t pv_uuidlist_on_disk;
550          lvm_disk_data_t lv_on_disk;
551          lvm_disk_data_t pe_on_disk;
552          uint8_t pv_uuid[NAME_LEN];
553          uint8_t vg_name[NAME_LEN];
554          uint8_t system_id[NAME_LEN];     /* for vgexport/vgimport */
555          uint32_t pv_major;
556          uint32_t pv_number;
557          uint32_t pv_status;
558          uint32_t pv_allocatable;
559          uint32_t pv_size;                /* HM */
560          uint32_t lv_cur;
561          uint32_t pe_size;
562          uint32_t pe_total;
563          uint32_t pe_allocated;
564 } pv_disk_v2_t;
565
566
567 /*
568  * Structures for Logical Volume (LV)
569  */
570
571 /* core PE information */
572 typedef struct {
573          kdev_t dev;
574          ulong pe;                   /* to be changed if > 2TB */
575          ulong reads;
576          ulong writes;
577 } pe_t;
```

```
578
579 typedef struct {
580         char lv_name[NAME_LEN];
581         kdev_t old_dev;
582         kdev_t new_dev;
583         ulong old_pe;
584         ulong new_pe;
585 } le_remap_req_t;
586
587 typedef struct lv_bmap {
588         ulong lv_block;
589         dev_t lv_dev;
590 } lv_bmap_t;
591
592 /*
593  * Structure Logical Volume (LV) Version 3
594  */
595
596 /* core */
597 typedef struct lv_v4 {
598         char lv_name[NAME_LEN];
599         char vg_name[NAME_LEN];
600         uint lv_access;
601         uint lv_status;
602         uint lv_open;             /* HM */
603         kdev_t lv_dev;            /* HM */
604         uint lv_number;           /* HM */
605         uint lv_mirror_copies;    /* for future use */
606         uint lv_recovery;         /*          "        */
607         uint lv_schedule;         /*          "        */
608         uint lv_size;
609         pe_t *lv_current_pe;      /* HM */
610         uint lv_current_le;       /* for future use */
611         uint lv_allocated_le;
612         uint lv_stripes;
613         uint lv_stripesize;
614         uint lv_badblock;         /* for future use */
615         uint lv_allocation;
616         uint lv_io_timeout;       /* for future use */
617         uint lv_read_ahead;
618
619         /* delta to version 1 starts here */
620         struct lv_v4 *lv_snapshot_org;
621         struct lv_v4 *lv_snapshot_prev;
622         struct lv_v4 *lv_snapshot_next;
623         lv_block_exception_t *lv_block_exception;
624         uint lv_remap_ptr;
625         uint lv_remap_end;
626         uint lv_chunk_size;
627         uint lv_snapshot_minor;
628 #ifdef __KERNEL__
629         struct kiobuf *lv_iobuf;
```

```
630          struct semaphore lv_snapshot_sem;
631          struct list_head *lv_snapshot_hash_table;
632          ulong lv_snapshot_hash_table_size;
633          ulong lv_snapshot_hash_mask;
634          struct page *lv_COW_table_page;
635          wait_queue_head_t lv_snapshot_wait;
636          int     lv_snapshot_use_rate;
637          void    *vg;
638
639          uint lv_allocated_snapshot_le;
640 #else
641          char dummy[200];
642 #endif
643 } lv_v4_t;
644
645 /* disk */
646 typedef struct {
647          uint8_t lv_name[NAME_LEN];
648          uint8_t vg_name[NAME_LEN];
649          uint32_t lv_access;
650          uint32_t lv_status;
651          uint32_t lv_open;               /* HM */
652          uint32_t lv_dev;                /* HM */
653          uint32_t lv_number;     /* HM */
654          uint32_t lv_mirror_copies;      /* for future use */
655          uint32_t lv_recovery;   /*        "        */
656          uint32_t lv_schedule;   /*        "        */
657          uint32_t lv_size;
658          uint32_t lv_snapshot_minor;/* minor number of original */
659          uint16_t lv_chunk_size; /* chunk size of snapshot */
660          uint16_t dummy;
661          uint32_t lv_allocated_le;
662          uint32_t lv_stripes;
663          uint32_t lv_stripesize;
664          uint32_t lv_badblock;   /* for future use */
665          uint32_t lv_allocation;
666          uint32_t lv_io_timeout; /* for future use */
667          uint32_t lv_read_ahead; /* HM */
668 } lv_disk_v3_t;
669
670 /*
671  * Structure Volume Group (VG) Version 1
672  */
673
674 /* core */
675 typedef struct {
676          char vg_name[NAME_LEN]; /* volume group name */
677          uint vg_number;         /* volume group number */
678          uint vg_access;         /* read/write */
679          uint vg_status;         /* active or not */
680          uint lv_max;            /* maximum logical volumes */
681          uint lv_cur;            /* current logical volumes */
```

```
682         uint lv_open;              /* open    logical volumes */
683         uint pv_max;               /* maximum physical volumes */
684         uint pv_cur;               /* current physical volumes FU */
685         uint pv_act;               /* active physical volumes */
686         uint dummy;                /* was obsolete max_pe_per_pv */
687         uint vgda;                 /* volume group descriptor arrays FU */
688         uint pe_size;              /* physical extent size in sectors */
689         uint pe_total;             /* total of physical extents */
690         uint pe_allocated;         /* allocated physical extents */
691         uint pvg_total;            /* physical volume groups FU */
692         struct proc_dir_entry *proc;
693         pv_t *pv[ABS_MAX_PV + 1];       /* physical volume struct pointers */
694         lv_t *lv[ABS_MAX_LV + 1];       /* logical  volume struct pointers */
695 } vg_v1_t;
696
697 typedef struct {
698         char vg_name[NAME_LEN]; /* volume group name */
699         uint vg_number;            /* volume group number */
700         uint vg_access;            /* read/write */
701         uint vg_status;            /* active or not */
702         uint lv_max;               /* maximum logical volumes */
703         uint lv_cur;               /* current logical volumes */
704         uint lv_open;              /* open    logical volumes */
705         uint pv_max;               /* maximum physical volumes */
706         uint pv_cur;               /* current physical volumes FU */
707         uint pv_act;               /* active physical volumes */
708         uint dummy;                /* was obsolete max_pe_per_pv */
709         uint vgda;                 /* volume group descriptor arrays FU */
710         uint pe_size;              /* physical extent size in sectors */
711         uint pe_total;             /* total of physical extents */
712         uint pe_allocated;         /* allocated physical extents */
713         uint pvg_total;            /* physical volume groups FU */
714         struct proc_dir_entry *proc;
715         pv_t *pv[ABS_MAX_PV + 1];       /* physical volume struct pointers */
716         lv_t *lv[ABS_MAX_LV + 1];       /* logical  volume struct pointers */
717         char vg_uuid[UUID_LEN+1];       /* volume group UUID */
718 #ifdef __KERNEL__
719         struct proc_dir_entry *vg_dir_pde;
720         struct proc_dir_entry *lv_subdir_pde;
721         struct proc_dir_entry *pv_subdir_pde;
722 #else
723         char dummy1[200];
724 #endif
725 } vg_v3_t;
726
727
728 /* disk */
729 typedef struct {
730         uint8_t vg_name[NAME_LEN];      /* volume group name */
731         uint32_t vg_number;     /* volume group number */
732         uint32_t vg_access;     /* read/write */
733         uint32_t vg_status;     /* active or not */
```

```
734         uint32_t lv_max;                 /* maximum logical volumes */
735         uint32_t lv_cur;                 /* current logical volumes */
736         uint32_t lv_open;                /* open    logical volumes */
737         uint32_t pv_max;                 /* maximum physical volumes */
738         uint32_t pv_cur;                 /* current physical volumes FU */
739         uint32_t pv_act;                 /* active physical volumes */
740         uint32_t dummy;
741         uint32_t vgda;          /* volume group descriptor arrays FU */
742         uint32_t pe_size;                /* physical extent size in sectors */
743         uint32_t pe_total;               /* total of physical extents */
744         uint32_t pe_allocated;  /* allocated physical extents */
745         uint32_t pvg_total;     /* physical volume groups FU */
746 } vg_disk_v1_t;
747
748 typedef struct {
749         uint8_t vg_uuid[UUID_LEN];       /* volume group UUID */
750         uint8_t vg_name_dummy[NAME_LEN-UUID_LEN];      /* rest of v1 VG name */
751         uint32_t vg_number;     /* volume group number */
752         uint32_t vg_access;     /* read/write */
753         uint32_t vg_status;     /* active or not */
754         uint32_t lv_max;                 /* maximum logical volumes */
755         uint32_t lv_cur;                 /* current logical volumes */
756         uint32_t lv_open;                /* open    logical volumes */
757         uint32_t pv_max;                 /* maximum physical volumes */
758         uint32_t pv_cur;                 /* current physical volumes FU */
759         uint32_t pv_act;                 /* active physical volumes */
760         uint32_t dummy;
761         uint32_t vgda;          /* volume group descriptor arrays FU */
762         uint32_t pe_size;                /* physical extent size in sectors */
763         uint32_t pe_total;               /* total of physical extents */
764         uint32_t pe_allocated;  /* allocated physical extents */
765         uint32_t pvg_total;     /* physical volume groups FU */
766 } vg_disk_v2_t;
767
768
769 /*
770  * Request structures for ioctls
771  */
772
773 /* Request structure PV_STATUS_BY_NAME... */
774 typedef struct {
775         char pv_name[NAME_LEN];
776         pv_t *pv;
777 } pv_status_req_t, pv_change_req_t;
778
779 /* Request structure PV_FLUSH */
780 typedef struct {
781         char pv_name[NAME_LEN];
782         kdev_t pv_dev;
783 } pv_flush_req_t;
784
785
```

```
786 /* Request structure PE_MOVE */
787 typedef struct {
788         enum {
789                 LOCK_PE, UNLOCK_PE
790         } lock;
791         struct {
792                 kdev_t lv_dev;
793                 kdev_t pv_dev;
794                 ulong pv_offset;
795         } data;
796 } pe_lock_req_t;
797
798
799 /* Request structure LV_STATUS_BYNAME */
800 typedef struct {
801         char lv_name[NAME_LEN];
802         lv_t *lv;
803 } lv_status_byname_req_t, lv_req_t;
804
805 /* Request structure LV_STATUS_BYINDEX */
806 typedef struct {
807         ulong lv_index;
808         lv_t *lv;
809         /* Transfer size because user space and kernel space differ */
810         ushort size;
811 } lv_status_byindex_req_t;
812
813 /* Request structure LV_STATUS_BYDEV... */
814 typedef struct {
815         dev_t dev;
816         pv_t *lv;
817 } lv_status_bydev_req_t;
818
819
820 /* Request structure LV_SNAPSHOT_USE_RATE */
821 typedef struct {
822         int     block;
823         int     rate;
824 } lv_snapshot_use_rate_req_t;
825
826 #endif                            /* #ifndef _LVM_H_INCLUDE */
827
```

CHAPTER 6

RAID with Linux

Today, quite a lot of the data under the control of file systems for Linux is stored on RAID disk devices. It is therefore imperative to gain a thourough understanding of how Linux manages RAID devices.

Since the technical implementation of RAID is not at issue in this book, we will instead concentrate on how to properly use RAID. This chapter shows how easy it actually is to install and configure Redundant Array of Inexpensive/Independent Disks (RAID) technology with the current breed of Linux kernels (2.4.0 at the time of this book).

There are three ways to do RAID on Intel PC hardware. The most common is the PCI SCSI RAID controller. The problem with these, under Linux, is that many are high-end and require an NDA to get the programming information. These NDAs are prohibitive to free software because the source code cannot be released.

The next most common way to do RAID under Linux is through the use of a SCSI-to-SCSI RAID controller. This requires a supported SCSI controller (of which there are many). On that controller's bus is the RAID controller, which simply looks like one or more drives (depending on how you set up the array in the controller). The RAID controller then has its own SCSI bus(es) that are connected to the physical drives that comprise the array(s).

You can use any supported block device (IDE disks, supported SCSI, etc.) to set up a RAID array. All RAID operations are handled by kernel threads. These will be available in full form from the 2.2 Linux kernel. Software RAID is a set of kernel modules together with management utilities that implement RAID purely in software, and require no extraordinary hardware. The Linux RAID subsystem is implemented as a layer in the kernel that sits above the low-level disk drivers (for IDE, SCSI, and Paraport drives) and the block-device interface. The file system, whether it's ext2fs, DOS-FAT, or another, sits above the block-device interface. Software RAID, by its very nature, tends to be more flexible than a hardware solution. The downside is that it requires more CPU cycles and power to run well than a comparable hardware system. Of course, the cost can't be beat! Software RAID has one further important distinguishing feature: it operates on a partition-by-partition basis, where a number of individual disk partitions are ganged together to create a RAID partition. This is in contrast to most hardware RAID solutions, which gang together entire disk drives into an array. With hardware, the fact that there is a RAID array is transparent to the operating system, which tends to simplify management. With software, there are far more configuration options and choices, which tends to complicate matters.

PCI CONTROLLERS

There are two PCI SCSI RAID controllers that are now available and supported under Linux: the DPT and the ICP-Vortex. Linux developers are also working on support for the Mylex cards, but that hasn't been completed yet.

The DPT has been supported for a few years now, but the problem is that it requires DOS or SCO to run its configuration utility. There have been promises to port it to Linux, but that has yet to happen. DPT does support Linux by providing the necessary information, but the actual work is being done mostly by Michael Neuffer. Unfortunately he hasn't yet had time to port the StorageManager to Linux, but he thinks he will have time to do it in the foreseeable future. The DPT does have some nice features including multiple channel controllers and caching. There is an audible alarm on the card as well as driver notification available to an external process. There is no monitoring software, but a simple program to monitor the RAID array and e-mail an administrator would be easy to write.

The ICP-Vortex is fully supported by Linux and doesn't require any other OS for its configuration. All ICP-Vortex configuration happens at the BIOS level of the card. There is a Linux daemon that will alert the system administrator if there are problems with any of the disks in the array. ICP has several models available ranging from cards that can do only RAID 0 and 1 to multi-channel RAID 5 cards (and even Fiber Channel). The RAID 0/1 card can be upgraded via software to full RAID 5 capability if you later find the need for RAID 5. All cards have the ability to add cache via a 72 pin SIMM socket (both EDO and standard 50ns SIMMs work fine).

The ICP-Vortex is only supported as of version 2.0.33, but the company appears very dedicated to supporting Linux. They wrote and maintain their own Linux driver and are becoming very active in the Linux community (they will be exhibiting at LinuxExpo in 2001).

SCSI-TO-SCSI CONTROLLERS

The SCSI-to-SCSI solutions vary wildly. There are solutions from many companies including Mylex, CMD, and others. These solutions are usually external or require a full height slot in the case of the controller. The actual administration is done via an LCD panel with buttons on the front and/or via a terminal emulator and a serial port. Some models have only one and some have both. You set up your array on the controller itself and then the controller presents the array to the OS as one logical drive (or more if that's how you set it up). The biggest drawback to these types of controllers is that they are usually quite expensive.

The CMD controllers are the only ones I know of that offer Linux software to do the administration. They have several models available including one that is a dual redundant hot swappable controller. If one of your controllers fails you can replace it without bringing your server down at all! CMD controllers can also be upgraded to multiple channels with expansion cards.

Many companies produce SCSI-to-SCSI solutions. My own personal experience is only with the Mylex. The server for Food for the Hungry International runs Linux on a Mylex DAC-960 SU RAID controller and has performed extremely well (their server was built by Linux Hardware Solutions). They have been very happy with the performance and ease of use of their RAID solution.

SOFTWARE RAID

The final solution is kernel software RAID. RAID 0 and 1 was introduced quite some time ago in the kernel, but now patches are available for the 2.0.x kernel that allow RAID 0-5. This will be a standard option in the 2.2 kernel.

Software RAID has been proven to have the advantage of speed over all the hardware options that have been tested. It also has the advantage of allowing the use of any supported block device. That means that you can mix things like IDE and SCSI in one array, which is completely impossible with existing hardware solutions (I doubt you would want to, but it may at least be helpful in situations where you have lost a drive and the only available replacement is an IDE one). The main disadvantage appears to be that a server may need those CPU cycles for functions other than calculating RAID parity.

The biggest advantage of software RAID is price. Hardware RAID controllers seem to range in price from about $500 to $5,000. For many systems, most likely it will be sufficient to use a single $200 supported SCSI controller (non-RAID) and simply use the kernel's software RAID across multiple disks on that controller. People on a really tight budget might even want to go with RAID 5 across four similar IDE disks using the IDE controller built into today's motherboards. With 9GB UDMA IDE drive prices at about $400, this is becoming a very interesting option. You can get about 27GB of RAID 5 protected space for a grand total of $1600 if you already have a machine available with two free IDE controllers.

Software RAID does have one current problem, though, and that is the ability to do full RAID for the root file system. This can be overcome by using a boot floppy or a small non-RAID boot partition from which to boot your system. I don't consider this a real obstacle, though. Any server should have a floppy drive available anyway, and given that they are cheap and easy to replace should one of them die, they make perfect boot media for this application. You can even keep extra copies of your boot floppy around if you are worried about it. Once the 2.2 kernel is available (and stable), we hope to have RAID support at install time that allows you to set up a system using a boot floppy, small boot partition, or perhaps some other form of removable media (Zip drive, CD-ROM, etc.).

Some RAID devices may be configured in a variety of ways for redundancy, eliminating the possibility of a single point of failure. The configuration can be set up through the hardware platform, operating system, storage-management software, or through special drivers. In the case of Linux it is done through drivers.

You can use RAID in mixed configuration to provide enhanced reliability and/or performance. Since Linux 2.2.x the RAID drivers are delivered with all standard distributions.

While there are different levels of RAID technology, the following are the most relevant to performance and reliability/availability:

RAID 0   Where availability isn't the primary concern, the disks may configured as RAID 0, which is nonredundant striping of files across disks to spread I/O among them.

RAID 1   RAID level 1 is the first level that offers protection. This level allows
              you to use two or more disks to "mirror" each other and thus data is
              reproduced in whole across more than one disk. If one disk fails,
              then the RAID system being used will simply ignore the failed disk
              and use only operable disks. RAID 1 space usage for two disks
              would be the same as the size of one of the disks (if they were the
              same size; otherwise the available space is exactly the same amount
              as the smaller of the two disks). RAID 1 performance for reads
              should be good because the RAID system can balance reading
              between all disks in the array. Write performance is poor, however,
              since all writes must occur on all disks. That's fine for many systems
              (especially file server type systems) since they are heavily read
              oriented (often as high as 95% of the time, in fact).

RAID 0+1   Combines the one-to-one mirroring of RAID 1 with the striping of
              RAID 0, therefore this technology is both fast and increases
              availability

RAID 3   Provides redundancy by storing parity information on a single disk
              in the array. This parity information can help to recover the data on
              other disks should they fail. RAID 3 saves on disk storage compared
              to RAID 1, but it is not used very often because the parity disk can
              become a performance bottleneck.

RAID 5   Uses parity data for redundancy similar to RAID 3, but stripes the
              parity data aross all of the disks, similar to the way in which the
              actual data is striped. This alleviates the bottleneck on the parity
              disk. RAID 5 is very often used. RAID level 5 is the best compromise
              in terms of both data availability and performance. RAID 5 allows
              you to create an array of at least three disks. The amount of space is
              usually calculated by the sum total of the amount of disks minus one.
              For example, the amount of usable space when using four 9GB disks
              would be three times 9GB, or 27GB. There may be a little extra
              overhead as well, but this is close. With RAID 5, data is stored in a
              striped format across all disks. What is a little different is that parity
              information is also striped along with the data. So, if any disk has
              lost its contents, it can be re-created using the data that is still
              available plus the parity. Since striping is used, performance is
              generally good. Read performance is good since reads are balanced
              across disks. Write performance is slightly slower than normal due to
              the parity generation and extra data to write. Performance does drop
              considerably when the array loses a disk, though, as some data will
              have to be re-created by reading several disks and generating the
              data based on the data and parity information. The pay-off is that all
              the data *is* still available, even though an entire disk may have died.

There are additional levels of RAID, including RAID 6, which adds dual parity data, and RAID 7 and RAID 8, which add performance enhancements to the characteristics of RAID 5.

In server environments with databases and online transaction processing (OLTP), most often you find RAID 0+1 and RAID 5 mixed configurations. In Linux, the configuration is actually very easy. There are only two files that need to be edited to implement RAID under Linux: /etc/raidtab and /etc/rc.d/rc.local. The concept is that Linux provides a special driver, /dev/md0, to access separate disk partitions as a logical RAID unit. The beauty of it is these partitions under RAID do not actually need to be different disks. Most of you will only have one disk on your Linux server. The good news is that you can still implement the things you will learn in this chapter.

The steps to go through to set up RAID are listed here:

▼ Configure the /dev/md0 driver.

■ Initialize the partitions under RAID and tell /etc/raidtab about them.

■ Automate RAID activation in /etc/rc.d/rc.local.

▲ Mount the RAID drive under a mountpoint.

Striping

If performance is the reason for your use of RAID, then you should implement RAID 0 (striping). In order to make sure that even people with just one hard disk dedicated to RAID can play along, I will just use spare partitions /dev/sda3 and /dev/sda4 (which means we are using a SCSI disk here, otherwise we would have /dev/hda3 and /dev/hda4). Obviously, in a production environment it doesn't make any sense to put different RAID partitions on the same disk or controller.

RAID 0 Configuration

To configure RAID 0, first you must tell /etc/raidtab about the partitions or drives that you want to put under RAID 0.

Your /etc/raidtab must look like this:

```
raiddev dev/md0
    raid-level       0
    nr-raid-disks    2
    nr-spare-disks      0
    chunk/size      4
    persistent-superblock      1
    device              /dev/sda3
    raid-disk       0
    device              /dev/sda4
    raid-disk       1
```

Once you have correctly created the above file, you need to format your new RAID disks (remember, RAID 0 will distribute your data among several disks to increase performance. Of course, in this example there will be no performance gain, because both partitions are on the same physical disk.).

To format a RAID disk you do the following (as root, obviously):

```
mkraid /dev/md0
```

Then, make a new ext2f file system on that new logical drive by typing:

```
mkfs -t ext2 /dev/md0
```

Finally, you need to add a line to your /etc/rc.d/rc.local file to automatically activate the RAID drivers at boot-time. The line looks like this:

```
raidstart /dev/md0
```

Now, assuming you want to mount the new RAID logical driver under /opt2, you would also add (after the previous line) the following line in the same above file:

```
mount /dev/md0 /opt2
```

Why are we not putting this line where it usually belongs, in /etc/fstab? For a very good reason, actually. The Linux kernel would try to mount it before it had the chance to execute raidstart /dev/md0 and would therefore fail.

Now, to start the RAID and mount it without rebooting the system and to let it go through /etc/rc.d/rc.local, just do:

```
raidstart /dev/md0
mount /dev/md0 /opt2
```

RAID 1 Configuration

If you want RAID level 1, just edit your /etc/raidtab like this:

```
raiddev /dev/md0
    raid-level      1
    nr-raid-disks      2
    nr-spare-disks     0
    chunk-size      4
    persistent-superblock 1
    device      /dev/sda3
    raid-disk 0
    device /dev/sda4
    raid/disk 1
```

Get the picture? It is all in the RAID-level directive. Now again, mkraid /dev/md0, then mkfs -t ext2 /dev/md0 and then start the RAID with raidstart /dev/md0 and mount it wherever you wish. I think RAID 5 with a hot spare disk is a very worthwhile investment for the safety of data. Besides all the post-configuration programs to execute, here is the appropriate /etc/raidtab:

```
raiddev /dev/md0
    raid-level        5
    nr-raid-disks     7
    nr-spare-disks    1
    parity-algorithm       left-symmetric
    chunk-size        32
     device              /dev/sda1
    raid-disk       0
    device              /dev/sdb1
    raid-disk       1
    device              /dev/sdc3
    raid-disk       2
    device              /dev/sdd4
    raid-disk       3
    device              /dev/sde1
    raid-disk       4
    device              /dev/sdf1
    raid-disk       5
    device              /dev/sdg1
    raid-disk       6
    # here come the spare-disk
    device              /dev/sdh1
    spare-disk      0
```

LIMITS OF RAID

RAID is good and fun, but there are certain limits to it as well, as there are with all good things in life.

Do not, I repeat, do not put the system directories (especially /boot and /usr) under any kind of software RAID. At boot, Linux still doesn't have much notion of RAID and it will fail to properly initialize. RAID is only recommended for data disks. Programs and system files do not belong on RAID devices. Bad things will happen when trying to play with the all-important /boot /sbin and /usr directories.

You can do mirroring over striping, but not the reverse. That is, you can put a stripe over several disks and then build a mirror on top of this. However, you cannot stripe a mirror, although it is certainly a desirable thing.

You can set up one-half of a RAID 1 mirror now with the one disk that you have and then later drop it to a new disk when you get it. I do not recommend this though, as it is quite difficult to copy the contents of one disk to the other and then pair them up. To do that, first one needs to back up the data on a tape or a third disk and then restore it again after adding the second mirror disk.

Another way to do it is to define the second RAID 1 as /dev/null and later put a real disk as the second disk in /etc/raidtab.

What is the difference between RAID 1 and RAID 5 for a two-disk configuration (i.e., the difference between a RAID 1 array built out of two disks, and a RAID 5 array built out of two disks)?

There is no difference in storage capacity, nor can disks be added to either array to increase capacity (see below for details). RAID 1 offers a performance advantage for read I/Os: the RAID 1 driver uses distributed-read technology to simultaneously read two sectors, one from each drive, thus doubling read performance.

The RAID 5 driver, although it contains many optimizations, does not currently realize the parity disk is actually a mirrored copy of the data disk. Thus, it serializes data reads.

RECOVERING FROM RAID DEVICE FAILURE

Some of the RAID algorithms do guard against multiple disk failures, but these are not currently implemented for Linux. However, the Linux software RAID can guard against multiple disk failures by layering an array on top of an array. For example, nine disks can be used to create three RAID 5 arrays.

These three arrays can in turn be hooked together into a single RAID 5 array on top. In fact, this kind of a configuration will guard against a three-disk failure. Note that a large amount of disk space is "wasted" on the redundancy information. In an unclean shutdown, the partitions might be in one of the following states:

▼   The in-memory disk cache was in sync with the RAID set when the unclean shutdown occurred; no data was lost.

■   The in-memory disk cache was newer than the RAID set contents when the crash occurred; this results in a corrupted file system and potential data loss. This state can be further divided to the following two states:

    ■   Linux was writing data when the unclean shutdown occurred.

    ■   Linux was not writing data when the crash occurred.

Suppose we were using a RAID 1 array. In 2A above, it might be that before the crash, a small number of data blocks were successfully written to only some of the mirrors, so that on the next reboot, the mirrors will no longer contain the same data. If we were to ignore the mirror differences, the RAID driver's read-balancing code might choose to read the data blocks from any of the mirrors, which would result in inconsistent behavior.

If a RAID partition hasn't been unmounted cleanly, fsck runs and fixes the file system by itself most of the time. There is also a ckraid -fix command to fix or recover RAID partitions. The best is to put this command on /etc/rc.local and run it at every system boot.

This can be done by adding lines like the following to /etc/rc.d/rc.local:

```
mdadd /dev/md0 /dev/sda1 /dev/sdc1 || {
ckraid --fix /etc/raid.usr.conf
mdadd /dev/md0 /dev/hda1 /dev/hdc1
}
```

or

```
mdrun -p1 /dev/md0
if [ $? -gt 0 ] ; then
ckraid --fix /etc/raid1.conf
mdrun -p1 /dev/md0
fi
```

By default, ckraid -fix will choose the first operational mirror and update the other mirrors with its contents. However, depending on the exact timing of the crash, the data on another mirror might be more recent, and we might want to use it as the source mirror instead.

Case A

You have a RAID 1 (mirroring) set up, and lost power while there was disk activity. Solution: the redundancy of RAID levels is designed to protect against a disk failure, not against a power failure. There are several ways to recover from this situation.

Use the RAID tools, which can be used to sync the RAID arrays. They do not fix file system damage; after the RAID arrays are sync'ed, then the file-system still has to be fixed with fsck.

RAID arrays can be checked with ckraid /etc/raid1.conf (for RAID 1, otherwise use /etc/raid5.conf, etc.) Calling ckraid /etc/raid1.conf -fix will pick one of the disks in the array (usually the first), and use that as the master copy, and copy its blocks to the others in the mirror. To designate which of the disks should be used as the master, you can use the - force-source flag: for example, ckraid /etc/raid1.conf -fix -force-source /dev/hdc3. The ckraid command can be safely run without the -fix option to verify the inactive RAID array without making any changes. When you are comfortable with the proposed changes, supply the -fix option.

Instead of the above, you can instead run ckraid /etc/raid1.conf -fix -force-source /dev/hdc3, which should be a bit faster.

In any case, the above steps will only sync up the RAID arrays. The file system probably needs fixing as well. For this, fsck needs to be run on the active, unmounted md device.

With a three-disk RAID 1 array, there are more possibilities, such as using two disks to "vote" a majority answer. Tools to automate this do not currently exist.

Case B

You have a RAID 4 or a RAID 5 (parity) setup, and lost power while there was disk activity.

Solution: the redundancy of RAID levels is designed to protect against a disk failure, not against a power failure. Since the disks in a RAID 4 or RAID 5 array do not contain a file system that fsck can read, there are fewer repair options. You cannot use fsck to do preliminary checking and/or repair; you must use ckraid first.

The ckraid command can be safely run without the -fix option to verify the inactive RAID array without making any changes. When you are comfortable with the proposed changes, supply the -fix option.

If you wish, you can try designating one of the disks as a "failed disk." Do this with the -suggest-failed-disk-mask flag.

Only one bit should be set in the flag: RAID 5 cannot recover two failed disks. The mask is a binary bit mask, thus:

```
0x1 == first disk
0x2 == second disk
0x4 == third disk
0x8 == fourth disk, etc.
```

Alternately, you can choose to modify the parity sectors by using the suggest-fix-parity flag. This will recompute the parity from the other sectors.

The flags -suggest-failed-dsk-mask and -suggest-fix-parity can be safely used for verification. No changes are made if the -fix flag is not specified. Thus, you can experiment with different possible repair schemes.

```
/*
+    md_k.h : kernel internal structure of the Linux MD driver
+          Copyright (C) 1996-98 Ingo Molnar, Gadi Oxman
+
+    This program is free software; you can redistribute it and/or modify
+    it under the terms of the GNU General Public License as published by
+    the Free Software Foundation; either version 2, or (at your option)
+    any later version.
+
+    You should have received a copy of the GNU General Public License
+    (for example /usr/src/linux/COPYING); if not, write to the Free
+    Software Foundation, Inc., 675 Mass Ave, Cambridge, MA 02139, USA.
+*/
+
+#ifndef _MD_K_H
+#define _MD_K_H
+
+#define MD_RESERVED        0UL
+#define LINEAR             1UL
+#define STRIPED            2UL
```

```
+#define RAID0              STRIPED
+#define RAID1              3UL
+#define RAID5              4UL
+#define TRANSLUCENT        5UL
+#define HSM                6UL
+#define MAX_PERSONALITY    7UL
+
+extern inline int pers_to_level (int pers)
+{
+    switch (pers) {
+        case HSM:          return -3;
+        case TRANSLUCENT:    return -2;
+        case LINEAR:         return -1;
+        case RAID0:         return 0;
+        case RAID1:         return 1;
+        case RAID5:         return 5;
+    }
+    panic("pers_to_level()");
+}
+
+extern inline int level_to_pers (int level)
+{
+    switch (level) {
+        case -3: return HSM;
+        case -2: return TRANSLUCENT;
+        case -1: return LINEAR;
+        case 0: return RAID0;
+        case 1: return RAID1;
+        case 4:
+        case 5: return RAID5;
+    }
+    return MD_RESERVED;
+}
+
+typedef struct mddev_s mddev_t;
+typedef struct mdk_rdev_s mdk_rdev_t;
+
+#if (MINORBITS != 8)
+#error MD doesnt handle bigger kdev yet
+#endif
+
+#define MAX_REAL     12           /* Max number of disks per md dev */
+#define MAX_MD_DEVS  (1<<MINORBITS)    /* Max number of md dev */
+
+/*
+ * Maps a kdev to an mddev/subdev. How 'data' is handled is up to
+ * the personality. (eg. HSM uses this to identify individual LVs)
+ */
+typedef struct dev_mapping_s {
```

```
+    mddev_t *mddev;
+    void *data;
+} dev_mapping_t;
+
+extern dev_mapping_t mddev_map [MAX_MD_DEVS];
+
+extern inline mddev_t * kdev_to_mddev (kdev_t dev)
+{
+        return mddev_map[MINOR(dev)].mddev;
+}
+
+/*
+ * options passed in raidrun:
+ */
+
+#define MAX_CHUNK_SIZE (4096*1024)
+
+/*
+ * default readahead
+ */
+#define MD_READAHEAD    (256 * 512)
+
+extern inline int disk_faulty(mdp_disk_t * d)
+{
+    return d->state & (1 << MD_DISK_FAULTY);
+}
+
+extern inline int disk_active(mdp_disk_t * d)
+{
+    return d->state & (1 << MD_DISK_ACTIVE);
+}
+
+extern inline int disk_sync(mdp_disk_t * d)
+{
+    return d->state & (1 << MD_DISK_SYNC);
+}
+
+extern inline int disk_spare(mdp_disk_t * d)
+{
+    return !disk_sync(d) && !disk_active(d) && !disk_faulty(d);
+}
+
+extern inline int disk_removed(mdp_disk_t * d)
+{
+    return d->state & (1 << MD_DISK_REMOVED);
+}
+
+extern inline void mark_disk_faulty(mdp_disk_t * d)
+{
```

```
+       d->state |= (1 << MD_DISK_FAULTY);
+}
+
+extern inline void mark_disk_active(mdp_disk_t * d)
+{
+       d->state |= (1 << MD_DISK_ACTIVE);
+}
+
+extern inline void mark_disk_sync(mdp_disk_t * d)
+{
+       d->state |= (1 << MD_DISK_SYNC);
+}
+
+extern inline void mark_disk_spare(mdp_disk_t * d)
+{
+       d->state = 0;
+}
+
+extern inline void mark_disk_removed(mdp_disk_t * d)
+{
+       d->state = (1 << MD_DISK_FAULTY) | (1 << MD_DISK_REMOVED);
+}
+
+extern inline void mark_disk_inactive(mdp_disk_t * d)
+{
+       d->state &= ~(1 << MD_DISK_ACTIVE);
+}
+
+extern inline void mark_disk_nonsync(mdp_disk_t * d)
+{
+       d->state &= ~(1 << MD_DISK_SYNC);
+}
+
+/*
+ * MD's 'extended' device
+ */
+struct mdk_rdev_s
+{
+       struct md_list_head same_set;    /* RAID devices within the same set */
+       struct md_list_head all;    /* all RAID devices */
+       struct md_list_head pending;    /* undetected RAID devices */
+
+       kdev_t dev;                 /* Device number */
+       kdev_t old_dev;                 /*  "" when it was last imported */
+       int size;              /* Device size (in blocks) */
+       mddev_t *mddev;              /* RAID array if running */
+       unsigned long last_events;    /* IO event timestamp */
+
+       struct inode *inode;        /* Lock inode */
```

```
+    struct file filp;          /* Lock file */
+
+    mdp_super_t *sb;
+    int sb_offset;
+
+    int faulty;                /* if faulty do not issue IO requests */
+    int desc_nr;               /* descriptor index in the superblock */
+};
+
+
+/*
+ * disk operations in a working array:
+ */
+#define DISKOP_SPARE_INACTIVE    0
+#define DISKOP_SPARE_WRITE       1
+#define DISKOP_SPARE_ACTIVE      2
+#define DISKOP_HOT_REMOVE_DISK   3
+#define DISKOP_HOT_ADD_DISK      4
+
+typedef struct mdk_personality_s mdk_personality_t;
+
+struct mddev_s
+{
+    void                *private;
+    mdk_personality_t        *pers;
+    int               __minor;
+    mdp_super_t             *sb;
+    int               nb_dev;
+    struct md_list_head          disks;
+    int               sb_dirty;
+    mdu_param_t             param;
+    int             ro;
+    unsigned int           curr_resync;
+    unsigned long            resync_start;
+    char               *name;
+    int               recovery_running;
+    struct semaphore         reconfig_sem;
+    struct semaphore         recovery_sem;
+    struct semaphore         resync_sem;
+    struct md_list_head        all_mddevs;
+    request_queue_t           queue;
+};
+
+struct mdk_personality_s
+{
+    char *name;
+    int (*map)(mddev_t *mddev, kdev_t dev, kdev_t *rdev,
+        unsigned long *rsector, unsigned long size);
+    int (*make_request)(mddev_t *mddev, int rw, struct buffer_head * bh);
```

```
+    void (*end_request)(struct buffer_head * bh, int uptodate);
+    int (*run)(mddev_t *mddev);
+    int (*stop)(mddev_t *mddev);
+    int (*status)(char *page, mddev_t *mddev);
+    int (*ioctl)(struct inode *inode, struct file *file,
+        unsigned int cmd, unsigned long arg);
+    int max_invalid_dev;
+    int (*error_handler)(mddev_t *mddev, kdev_t dev);
+
+/*
+ * Some personalities (RAID-1, RAID-5) can have disks hot-added and
+ * hot-removed. Hot removal is different from failure. (failure marks
+ * a disk inactive, but the disk is still part of the array) The interface
+ * to such operations is the 'pers->diskop()' function, can be NULL.
+ *
+ * the diskop function can change the pointer pointing to the incoming
+ * descriptor, but must do so very carefully. (currently only
+ * SPARE_ACTIVE expects such a change)
+ */
+    int (*diskop) (mddev_t *mddev, mdp_disk_t **descriptor, int state);
+
+    int (*stop_resync)(mddev_t *mddev);
+    int (*restart_resync)(mddev_t *mddev);
+};
+
+
+/*
+ * Currently we index md_array directly, based on the minor
+ * number. This will have to change to dynamic allocation
+ * once we start supporting partitioning of md devices.
+ */
+extern inline int mdidx (mddev_t * mddev)
+{
+    return mddev->__minor;
+}
+
+extern inline kdev_t mddev_to_kdev(mddev_t * mddev)
+{
+    return MKDEV(MD_MAJOR, mdidx(mddev));
+}
+
+extern mdk_rdev_t * find_rdev(mddev_t * mddev, kdev_t dev);
+extern mdk_rdev_t * find_rdev_nr(mddev_t *mddev, int nr);
+
+/*
+ * iterates through some rdev ringlist. It's safe to remove the
+ * current 'rdev'. Dont touch 'tmp' though.
+ */
+#define ITERATE_RDEV_GENERIC(head,field,rdev,tmp)                \
```

```
+                                              \
+    for (tmp = head.next;                       \
+        rdev = md_list_entry(tmp, mdk_rdev_t, field),      \
+            tmp = tmp->next, tmp->prev != &head       \
+        ; )
+/*
+ * iterates through the 'same array disks' ringlist
+ */
+#define ITERATE_RDEV(mddev,rdev,tmp)                 \
+    ITERATE_RDEV_GENERIC((mddev)->disks,same_set,rdev,tmp)
+
+/*
+ * Same as above, but assumes that the device has rdev->desc_nr numbered
+ * from 0 to mddev->nb_dev, and iterates through rdevs in ascending order.
+ */
+#define ITERATE_RDEV_ORDERED(mddev,rdev,i)               \
+    for (i = 0; rdev = find_rdev_nr(mddev, i), i < mddev->nb_dev; i++)
+
+
+/*
+ * Iterates through all 'RAID managed disks'
+ */
+#define ITERATE_RDEV_ALL(rdev,tmp)                    \
+    ITERATE_RDEV_GENERIC(all_raid_disks,all,rdev,tmp)
+
+/*
+ * Iterates through 'pending RAID disks'
+ */
+#define ITERATE_RDEV_PENDING(rdev,tmp)                  \
+    ITERATE_RDEV_GENERIC(pending_raid_disks,pending,rdev,tmp)
+
+/*
+ * iterates through all used mddevs in the system.
+ */
+#define ITERATE_MDDEV(mddev,tmp)                    \
+                                              \
+    for (tmp = all_mddevs.next;                    \
+        mddev = md_list_entry(tmp, mddev_t, all_mddevs),   \
+            tmp = tmp->next, tmp->prev != &all_mddevs   \
+        ; )
+
+extern inline int lock_mddev (mddev_t * mddev)
+{
+    return down_interruptible(&mddev->reconfig_sem);
+}
+
+extern inline void unlock_mddev (mddev_t * mddev)
+{
+    up(&mddev->reconfig_sem);
```

```
+}
+
+#define xchg_values(x,y) do { __typeof__(x) __tmp = x; \
+               x = y; y = __tmp; } while (0)
+
+typedef struct mdk_thread_s {
+    void            (*run) (void *data);
+    void            *data;
+    md_wait_queue_head_t    wqueue;
+    unsigned long           flags;
+    struct semaphore    *sem;
+    struct task_struct    *tsk;
+    const char          *name;
+} mdk_thread_t;
+
+#define THREAD_WAKEUP  0
+
+#define MAX_DISKNAME_LEN 32
+
+typedef struct dev_name_s {
+    struct md_list_head list;
+    kdev_t dev;
+    char name [MAX_DISKNAME_LEN];
+} dev_name_t;
+
+#endif _MD_K_H
+
```

CHAPTER 7

The Second Extended File System (ext2)

This chapter looks in detail at the Second Extended File System, ext2fs, the most widely used Linux file system. This major rewrite of the Extended File System was written by Rémy Card, Theodore Ts'o, and Stephen Tweedie, and originally released in January 1993. Currently, it is the predominant file system in use by Linux. There are also implementations available for NetBSD, FreeBSD, the GNU HURD, Windows 95/98/NT, OS/2, and RISC OS. Ext2fs was designed and implemented to fix problems present in the first Extended File System and to provide a powerful file system, which implements Unix file semantics and offers advanced features.

NEW FEATURES

Of course, the designers also wanted ext2fs to have excellent performance. They wanted a very robust file system in order to reduce the risk of data loss in intensive use and last, but not least, ext2fs had to include a provision for extensions to allow users to benefit from new features without reformatting their file system.

Standard ext2fs Features

The ext2fs supports standard Unix file types: regular files, directories, device special files, and symbolic links.

Ext2fs is able to manage file systems created on really big partitions. While the original kernel code restricted the maximum file system size to 2GB, recent work in the VFS layer has raised this limit to 4TB. Therefore, it is now possible to use big disks without the necessity to create many partitions.

Ext2fs provides the facility to use long filenames of up to 255 characters and uses variable length directory entries. The filename limit could be extended to 1012 if necessary.

Ext2fs reserves up to five percent of its blocks for the super-user (root). This allows administrators to easily recover from situations where user processes fill up file systems.

Advanced ext2fs Features

In addition to the standard Unix features, ext2fs supports a number of extensions which are not usually present in Unix file systems.

File attributes allow users to modify the kernel behavior when acting on a set of files. A user can set attributes on a file or on a directory. In the latter case, new files created in the directory inherit these attributes.

BSD or System V Release 4 semantics can be selected at mount time. A mount option allows administrators to choose the file creation semantics. On a file system mounted with BSD semantics, files are created with the same group id as their parent directory. System V semantics are a bit more complex. If a directory has the setgid bit set, new files inherit the group id of the directory and subdirectories inherit the group id and the setgid bit. Otherwise, files and subdirectories are created with the primary group id of the calling process.

BSD-like synchronous updates can be used in ext2fs. A mount option allows administrators to request that meta-data (inodes, bitmap blocks, indirect blocks, and directory blocks) be written synchronously on the disk when they are modified. This can be useful in maintaining strict meta-data consistency, but can lead to poor performance. In reality, this feature is not generally used since, in addition to the performance loss associated with using synchronous updates of the meta-data, it can cause corruption in the user data, which will not be flagged by the file system checker.

Ext2fs allows administrators to choose the logical block size when creating the file system. Block sizes can typically be 1024, 2048, and 4096 bytes. Using big block sizes can speed up I/O since fewer I/O requests, and thus fewer disk head seeks, need to be done to access a file. On the other hand, big blocks waste more disk space and on average, the last block allocated to a file is only half-full, so as blocks get bigger, more space is wasted. In addition, most of the advantages of larger block sizes are obtained by ext2 file system's preallocation techniques.

Lastly, ext2fs implements fast symbolic links (symlinks). A fast symbolic link does not use any data blocks on the file system. The target name is not stored in a data block but in the inode itself. This policy can save some disk space because no data block needs to be allocated, and speeds up link operations as there is no need to read a data block when accessing such a link. Of course, the space available in the inode is limited so not every link can be implemented as a fast symbolic link. The maximum size of the target name in a fast symbolic link is 60 characters. We plan to extend this scheme to small files in the near future.

Symbolic links are also file system objects with inodes. They deserve special mention because the data for them is stored within the inode itself if the symlink is less than 60 bytes long. It uses the fields that would normally be used to store the pointers to blocks to store the data. This is a worthwhile optimization to make as it does not then take up a block.

Directories

A directory is a file system object and has an inode, just like a file. It is a specially formatted file containing records that associate each name with an inode number. Later revisions of the file system also encode the object type, e.g., file, directory, symlink, device, fifo, socket in the directory entry for the purpose of speed. The current implementation of ext2 uses a linked list in directories and a planned enhancement will use B-trees instead. The current implementation never shrinks directories once they have grown to accommodate more files.

Character and block special devices never have data blocks assigned to them. Instead, their device number is stored in the inode, again reusing the fields which would be used to point to the blocks.

Ext2fs keeps track of the file system state. A special field in the super-block is used by the kernel code to indicate the status of the file system. When a file system is mounted in read/write mode, its state is set to "Not Clean." When it is unmounted or remounted in read-only mode, its state is reset to "Clean." At boot-time, the file system checker uses this information to decide if a file system must be checked. The kernel code also records errors in this field. When an inconsistency is detected by the kernel code, the file system is marked as "Erroneous." The file system checker tests this to force a check of the file system regardless of its apparently clean state.

Skipping file system checks may sometimes be dangerous, so ext2fs provides two ways to force checks at regular intervals. A mount counter is maintained in the super-block. Each time the file system is mounted in read/write mode, this counter is incremented. When it reaches a maximum value (also recorded in the super-block), the file system checker forces the check even if the file system is "clean." A last check time and a maximum check interval are also maintained in the super-block. These two fields allow administrators to request periodic checks. When the maximum check interval has been reached, the checker ignores the file system state and forces a file system check.

Ext2fs also offers tools to tune file system behavior. The `tune2fs` program can be used to modify the following:

▼ Error behavior. When an inconsistency is detected by the kernel code, the file system is marked as "Erroneous" and one of the following three actions can be taken: continue normal execution, remount the file system in read-only mode to avoid corrupting the file system, make the kernel panic and reboot to run the file system checker.

■ The maximum mount count.

■ The maximum check interval.

▲ The number of logical blocks reserved for the super-user.

Mount options can also be used to change the kernel error behavior.

An attribute allows users to request secure deletion on files. When such a file is deleted, random data is written in the disk blocks previously allocated to the file. This prevents hackers or those with malicious intent from using a disk editor to gain access to the previous content of the file.

Finally, new types of files inspired by the 4.4 BSD file system have recently been added to ext2fs. Immutable files can only be read; they cannot be written to or deleted. These files can be used to protect sensitive configuration files. Append-only files can be opened in write mode, but data is always appended at the end of the file. Like immutable files, they cannot be deleted or renamed. This is especially useful for log files which can only grow in size.

Blocks

The space in the device or file is split up into blocks. These are a fixed size of 1024, 2048, or 4096 bytes. The size is decided when the file system is created. Smaller blocks mean less wasted space per file, but require slightly more accounting overhead.

Blocks are clustered into block groups in order to reduce fragmentation and minimize the amount of head seeking when reading a large amount of consecutive data. Each block group has a descriptor and the array of descriptors is stored immediately after the super-block. Two blocks at the start of each group are reserved for the block usage bitmap and the inode usage bitmap that show which blocks and inodes are used.

Since each bitmap fits in a block, this means that the maximum size of a block group is eight times the size of a block. The first (non-reserved) blocks in the block group are designated as the inode table for the block and the remainder are the data blocks. The block allocation algorithm attempts to allocate data blocks in the same block group as the inode that contains them.

Reserved Space

Ext2 has a mechanism for reserving a certain number of blocks for a particular user (normally the super-user), which is intended to allow the system to continue functioning even if a user fills up all the available space. It also keeps the file system from filling up entirely, which helps combat fragmentation.

File System Check

At boot-time, most systems run a consistency check (e2fsck) on their file systems. The ext2 file system super-block contains several fields that indicate whether fsck should actually run since checking the file system at boot can take a long time if it is large. Fsck will run if the file system was not unmounted without errors, if the maximum mount count has been exceeded, or if the maximum time between checks has been exceeded.

Inodes

The inode (index node) is the fundamental concept in the ext2 file system. Each object in the file system is represented by an inode. The inode structure contains pointers to the file system blocks that contain the data held in the object and all of the meta-data about an object except its name. The meta-data includes the permissions, owner, group, flags, size, number of blocks used, access time, change time, modification time, deletion time, number of links, fragments, version (for NFS), and ACLs.

There are several reserved fields currently unused in the inode structure and several that are overloaded. One field is used for the directory ACL if the inode is a directory and for the top 32 bits of the file size if the inode is a regular file. The translator field is unused under Linux, but is used by the HURD to reference the inode of a program that will be used to interpret this object. The HURD also has larger permissions, and owner and group fields, so it uses some of the other unused fields to store the extra bits.

There are pointers to the first 12 blocks that contain the file's data in the inode. There is a pointer to an indirect block that contains pointers to the next set of blocks, a pointer to a double-indirect block containing pointers to indirect blocks, and a pointer to a triple-indirect block which contains pointers to double-indirect blocks.

The flags field contains some ext2-specific flags that aren't catered for by the standard chmod flags. These flags can be listed with lsattr and changed with the chattr command. There are flags for secure deletion, undeletable, compression, synchronous updates, immutability, append-only, dumpable, no-atime, and B-tree directories. Not all of these are supported yet.

The Super-Block

The super-block contains all the information about the configuration of the filing system. It is stored in block 1 of the file system (numbering from 0) and is essential to mounting. Since it is so important, backup copies of the super-block are stored in block groups throughout the file system. The first revision of ext2 stores a copy at the start of every block group. Later revisions can store a copy in only some block groups so as to reduce the amount of redundancy on large file systems. The specific groups are 0, 1 and powers of 3, 5, and 7.

The super-block contains such information as how many inodes and blocks are in the file system, how many of them are unused, how many inodes and blocks are in a block group, when the file system was mounted, when it was modified, what version of the file system it is (see the Revisions section), and which OS created it.

If the revision of the file system is recent, then there are extra fields, such as volume name, a unique identifier, the inode size, and support for compression, block preallocation, and the necessity of creating fewer backup super-blocks.

All fields in the super-block (as in all other ext2 structures) are stored on the disk in little endian format, so a file system is portable between machines and there is no need to know what machine it was created on.

Revisions

The revisioning mechanism used in ext2 is sophisticated. It is not supported by version 0 (EXT2_GOOD_OLD_REV) of ext2 but was introduced in version 1. There are three 32-bit fields, one for compatible features, one for read-only compatible features, and one for incompatible features.

Physical Structure

The physical structure of ext2 file systems has been strongly influenced by the layout of the BSD file system. An ext2 file system is made up of block groups, which are analogous to BSD FFS's cylinder groups. However, block groups are not tied to the physical layout of the blocks on the disk, since modern drives tend to be optimized for sequential access and hide their physical geometry from the operating system.

The physical structure of a file system is represented in this table:

Boot Sector	Block Group 1	Block Group 2	Block Group N

Each block group contains a redundant copy of crucial file system control information (super-block and the file system descriptors) and also contains a part of the file system (a block bitmap, an inode bitmap, a piece of the inode table, and data blocks). The structure of a block group is represented in this table:

Super-Block	FS descriptions	Block Bitmap	Inode Bitmap	Indode Table	Data Blocks

Using block groups has a big advantage in terms of reliability. Since the control structures are replicated in each block group, it is easy to recover from a file system where the super-block has been corrupted. This structure also produces good performance. By reducing the distance between the inode table and the data blocks, it is possible to reduce the disk head seeks during I/O on files.

In ext2fs, directories are managed as linked lists of variable length entries. Each entry contains the inode number, the entry length, the filename, and its length. By using variable length entries, it is possible to implement long filenames without wasting disk space in directories. The structure of a directory entry is shown in this table:

inode number	entry length	name length	filename

As an example, this table represents the structure of a directory containing three files: `file1`, `long_file_name`, and `f2`:

i1	16	05	file1
i2	40	14	long_file_name
i3	12	02	f2

Performance Optimizations

The ext2fs kernel code contains many performance optimizations, which tend to improve I/O speed when reading and writing files.

Ext2fs takes advantage of the buffer cache management by performing read-aheads. When a block has to be read, the kernel code requests the I/O on several contiguous blocks. This means that it tries to ensure that the next block to read will already be loaded into the buffer cache. Read-aheads are normally performed during sequential reads on files and ext2fs extends them to directory reads, either as explicit reads (`readdir(2)` calls) or implicit reads (`namei` kernel directory lookup).

Ext2fs also contains many allocation optimizations. Block groups are used to cluster related inodes and data and the kernel code always tries to allocate data blocks for a file in the same group as its inode. This is intended to reduce the disk head seeks made when the kernel reads an inode and its data blocks.

When writing data to a file, ext2fs preallocates up to eight adjacent blocks. Preallocation hit rates are around 75% even on very full file systems. This preallocation achieves good write performances under heavy load. It also allows contiguous blocks to be allocated to files, thus speeding up future sequential reads.

These two allocation optimizations produce a very good locality of:

▼ Related files through block groups.

▲ Related blocks through the 8-bits clustering of block allocations.

Meta-Data

It is often claimed that the ext2 implementation of writing asynchronous meta-data is faster than the FFS synchronous meta-data scheme, but less reliable. Both methods are equally resolvable by their respective fsck programs.

There are three ways of making meta-data writes synchronous:

▼ Per file if you have the source: use the O_SYNC argument to open( ).

■ Per file if you don't have the source: use chattr +S.

▲ Per file system: mount -o sync.

The first and last methods are not ext2-specific but do force the meta-data to be written synchronously.

The Ext2fs Library

The libext2fs library was developed to allow user mode programs to manipulate the control structures of an ext2 file system. This library provides routines which can be used to examine and modify the data of an ext2 file system by accessing the file system directly through the physical device.

The ext2fs library allows maximum code reuse through the use of software abstraction techniques. For example, several different iterators are provided. A program can simply pass in a function to `ext2fs_block_interate()`, which will be called for each block in an inode. Another iterator function allows an user-provided function to be called for each file in a directory.

Many of the ext2fs utilities (`mke2fs`, `e2fsck`, `tune2fs`, `dumpe2fs`, and `debugfs`) use the ext2fs library. This greatly simplifies the maintenance of these utilities, since any changes to reflect new features in the ext2 file system format need only be made in one place—in the ext2fs library. This code reuse also results in smaller binaries, since the ext2fs library can be built as a shared library image.

Because the interfaces of the ext2fs library are so abstract and general, new programs that require direct access to the ext2fs file system can be written very easily. For example, the ext2fs library was used during the port of the 4.4BSD dump and restore of backup utilities. Very few changes were needed to adapt these tools to Linux and only a few file system-dependent functions had to be replaced by calls to the ext2fs library.

The ext2fs library provides access to several classes of operations. The first are the file system-oriented operations. A program can open and close a file system, read and write the bitmaps, and create a new file system on the disk. Functions are also available to manipulate the file system's bad blocks list.

The second class of operations affects directories. A caller of the ext2fs library can create and expand directories, as well as add and remove directory entries. Functions are also provided to resolve a pathname to an inode number, and to determine a pathname of an inode when given its inode number.

With the final class of operations it is possible to scan the inode table, read and write inodes, and scan through all of the blocks in an inode. Allocation and deallocation routines are also available and allow user mode programs to allocate and free blocks and inodes.

The Ext2fs Tools

Powerful management tools have been developed for ext2fs. These utilities are used to create, modify, and correct any inconsistencies in ext2 file systems. The mke2fs program is used to initialize a partition to contain an empty ext2 file system.

The tune2fs program is used to modify the file system parameters. As explained in the section on advanced ext2fs features, it can change the error behavior, the maximum mount count, the maximum check interval, and the number of logical blocks reserved for the super-user.

However, the most interesting tool is probably the file system checker. e2fsck is intended to repair file system inconsistencies after an unclean shutdown of the system. The original version of e2fsck was based on Linus Torvald's fsck program for the Minix file system. The current version of e2fsck was rewritten from scratch using the ext2fs library, is much faster, and can correct more file system inconsistencies than the original version. The e2fsck program is designed to run as quickly as possible. Since file system checkers tend to be disk-bound, this was done by optimizing the algorithms used by e2fsck so that file system structures are not repeatedly accessed from the disk. In addition, the order in which inodes and directories are checked is sorted by block number to reduce the amount of time in disk seeks.

In pass 1, e2fsck iterates over all of the inodes in the file system and performs checks over each inode as an unconnected object in the file system. These checks do not require any cross-checks to other file system objects. Examples of checks include making sure the file mode is legal, and that all of the blocks in the inode are valid block numbers. During pass 1, bitmaps are compiled indicating which blocks and inodes are in use.

If e2fsck notices data blocks which are claimed by more than one inode, it invokes passes 1B through 1D to resolve these conflicts, either by cloning the shared blocks so that each inode has its own copy of the shared block, or by deallocating one or more of the inodes.

Pass 1 takes the longest time to execute, since all of the inodes have to be read into memory and checked. To reduce the I/O time in future passes, critical file system information is cached in memory. The most important example of this technique is the location on disk of all of the directory blocks on the file system. This obviates the need to re-read the directory inodes structures during pass 2 to obtain this information.

Pass 2 checks directories as unconnected objects. Since directory entries do not span disk blocks, each directory block can be checked individually without reference to other directory blocks. This allows e2fsck to sort all of the directory blocks by block number, and check directory blocks in ascending order, thus decreasing disk seek time. The directory blocks are checked to make sure that the directory entries are valid, and contain references to inode numbers which are in use (as determined by pass 1).

For the first directory block in each directory inode, the '.' and '..' entries are checked to make sure they exist, and that the inode number for the '.' entry matches the current directory. (The inode number for the '..' entry is not checked until pass 3.)

Pass 2 also caches information concerning the parent directory in which each directory is linked. If a directory is referenced by more than one directory, the second reference of the directory is treated as an illegal hard link, and is removed.

Note that at the end of pass 2, nearly all of the disk I/O which e2fsck needs to perform is complete. Information required by passes 3, 4, and 5 are cached in memory; hence, the remaining passes of e2fsck are largely CPU-bound, and take less than five to ten percent of the total running time.

In pass 3, the directory connectivity is checked. e2fsck traces the path of each directory back to the root, using information that was cached during pass 2. At this time, the '..' entry for each directory is also checked to make sure it is valid. Any directories which cannot be traced back to the root are linked to the /lost+found directory.

In pass 4, e2fsck checks the reference counts for all inodes by iterating over all the inodes and comparing the link counts (which were cached in pass 1) against internal counters computed during passes 2 and 3. During this pass, any undeleted files with a zero link count are also linked to the /lost+found directory.

Finally, in pass 5, e2fsck checks the validity of the file system summary information. It compares the block and inode bitmaps that were constructed during the previous passes against the actual bitmaps on the file system, and corrects the on-disk copies if necessary.

The file system debugger is another useful tool. debugfs is a powerful program that can be used to examine and change the state of a file system. Basically, it provides an interactive interface to the ext2fs library. Commands typed by the user are translated into calls to the library routines. debugfs can be used to examine the internal structures of a file system, manually repair a corrupted file system, or create test cases for e2fsck. Unfortunately, this program can be dangerous if it is used by people who do not know what they are doing as it is very easy to destroy a file system with this tool. For this reason, the default is that debugfs opens file sytems for read-only access. The user must explicitly specify the -w flag in order to use debugfs to open a file system for read/write access.

The Second Extended File system was devised as an extensible and powerful file system for Linux. It is the most successful file system so far in the Linux community and is the basis for all of the currently shipping Linux distributions.

The ext2 file system, like many of the file systems, is built on the premise that the data held in files is kept in data blocks. These data blocks are all of the same length and, although that length can vary between different ext2 file systems, the block size of a particular ext2 file system is set when it is created (using mke2fs). Every file's size is rounded up to an integral number of blocks. If the block size is 1024 bytes, then a file of 1025 bytes will occupy two 1024-byte blocks. Unfortunately this means that on average half a block is wasted per file. Usually in computing CPU usage the trade-off is for memory and disk space utilization. In this case Linux, along with most operating systems, trades off relatively inefficient disk usage in order to reduce the workload on the CPU. Not all of the blocks in the file system hold data, some are used to contain the information that describes the structure of the file system. Ext2 defines the file system topology by describing each file in the system with an inode data structure. An inode describes which blocks the data within a file occupies, as well as the access rights of the file, the file's modification times, and the type of the file. Every file in the ext2 file system is described by a single inode and each inode has a single unique identifying number. The inodes for the file system are all kept together in inode tables. Ext2 directories are simply special files (themselves described by inodes) that contain pointers to the inodes of their directory entries.

Figure 7-1 shows the layout of the ext2 file system as occupying a series of blocks in a block structured device. As far as each file system is concerned, block devices are just a series of blocks which can be read and written. A file system does not need to know where on the physical media a block should be put, that is the job of the device's driver. Whenever a file system needs to read information or data from the block device in which it is contained, it requests that its supporting device driver read an integral number of blocks. The ext2 file system divides the logical partition that it occupies into block groups. Each group duplicates information critical to the integrity of the file system as well as holding real files and directories as blocks of information and data. This duplication is neccessary should a disaster occur and the file system needs to be recovered. The following subsections describe the contents of each block group in more detail.

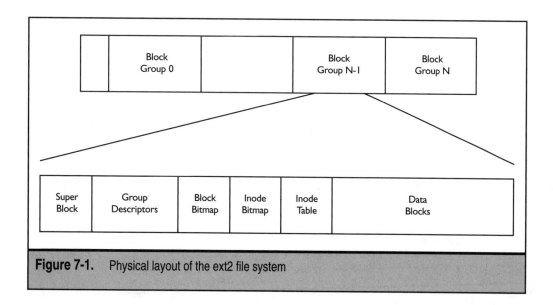

Figure 7-1.   Physical layout of the ext2 file system

The Inode in ext2fs

The inode is the basic building block of the ext2 file system with every file and directory in the file system described by one inode. The ext2 inodes for each block group are kept in the inode table together with a bitmap that allows the system to keep track of allocated and unallocated inodes. Figure 7-1 shows the format of an ext2 inode. An inode contains the fields described in the following sections.

Mode

The mode holds two pieces of information: what the inode describes and the permissions that users have to it. For ext2, an inode can describe a file, directory, symbolic link, block device, character device, or FIFO.

Owner Information

This field contains the user and group identifiers of the owners of the file or directory. This allows the file system to allow the right accesses.

Size

The size of the file in bytes.

Timestamps

The time that the inode was created and the last time it was modified.

Datablocks

Pointers to the blocks that contain the data that the inode is describing. The first 12 are pointers to the physical blocks containing the data described by the inode and the last three pointers contain more and more levels of indirection. For example, the double-indirect blocks pointer points at a block of pointers that point to blocks of pointers to data blocks. This means that files less than or equal to 12 data blocks in length are accessed faster than larger files.

Note also that ext2 inodes can describe special device files, which are not real files but handles that programs can use to access devices. All of the device files in /dev are there to allow programs to access Linux's devices. For example the mount program takes the device file that it wishes to mount as an argument.

The ext2fs Super-block

The super-block contains a description of the basic size and shape of the file system. The information within it allows the file system manager to use and maintain the file system. Usually only the super-block in block group 0 is read when the file system is mounted but each block group contains a duplicate copy in case of file system corruption. The super-block contains the following information:

Magic Number

This allows the mounting software to check that it is indeed the super-block for an ext2 file system. For the current version of ext2 this is *0xEF53*.

Revision Level

The major and minor revision levels allow the mounting code to determine whether or not the file system supports features that are only available in particular revisions of the file system. There are also feature compatibility fields which help the mounting code to determine what new features can be used safely on this file system.

Mount Count and Maximum Mount Count

Together these allow the system to determine if the file system should be fully checked. The mount count is incremented each time the file system is mounted and when it equals the maximum mount count, the warning message "maximum mount count reached, running e2fsck is recommended" is displayed.

Block Group Number

The block group number that holds a copy of the super-block.

Block Size

The size of the block for the file system in bytes, e.g., 1024 bytes.

Blocks per Group

The number of blocks in a group. Like the block size, this is fixed when the file system is created.

Free Blocks

The number of free blocks in the file system.

Free Inodes

The number of free inodes in the file system.

First Inode

This is the number of the first inode in the file system. The first inode in an ext2 root file system would be the directory entry for the '/' directory.

The ext2 Group Descriptor

Each block group has a data structure describing it. Like the super-block, all the group descriptors for all of the block groups are duplicated in each block group in case of file system corruption.

Each group descriptor contains the following information:

Blocks Bitmap

The block number of the block allocation bitmap for the block group. This is used during block allocation and deallocation.

Inode Bitmap

The block number of the inode allocation bitmap for the block group. This is used during inode allocation and deallocation.

Inode Table

The block number of the starting block for the inode table for this block group. Each inode is represented by the ext2 inode data structure described below.

Free Blocks Count, Free Inodes Count, Used Directory Count

The group descriptors are placed one after another and together they make up the group descriptor table. Each block group contains the entire table of group descriptors following its copy of the super-block. Only the first copy (in block group 0) is actually used by the ext2 file system. The other copies are there, like the copies of the super-block, in case the main copy is corrupted.

In the ext2 file system directories are special files used to create and hold access paths to the files in the file system.

A directory file is a list of directory entries, each containing the following information.

Inode

The inode for the directory entry. This is an index into the array of inodes held in the inode table of the block group. For example, the directory entry for the file called "file" has a reference to inode number i1.

Name Length

The length of the directory entry in bytes.

Name

The name of the directory entry.

The first two entries for every directory are always the standard "." and ".." entries meaning "this directory" and "the parent directory," respectively.

Changing the Size of a File in an ext2 File System

A common problem with file systems is their tendency to fragment. The blocks that hold the file's data get spread all over the file system making sequential access to the data blocks of a file more and more inefficient the further apart the data blocks are. The ext2 file system tries to overcome this problem by allocating new blocks for a file physically close to its current data blocks or at least in the same block group. Only when this fails does it allocate data blocks in another lock group.

Whenever a process attempts to write data into a file, the Linux file system checks to see if the data has gone off the end of the file's last allocated block. If it has, then it must allocate a new data block for the file. Until the allocation is complete, the process cannot run; it must wait for the file system to allocate a new data block and write the rest of the data to it before it can continue. The first thing that the ext2 block allocation routines do is to lock the ext2 super-block for the file system. Allocating and deallocating changes fields within the super-block and the Linux file system cannot allow more than one process to do this at the same time. If another process needs to allocate more data blocks, then it will have to wait until the process has finished. Processes waiting for the super-block are suspended and unable to run until control of the super-block is relinquished by its current user. Access to the super-block is granted on a first come, first served basis and once a process has control of the super-block then it keeps control until it has finished. Having locked the super-block, the process checks that there are enough free blocks left in the file system. If there are not enough free blocks, then the attempt to allocate more will fail and the process will relinquish control of this file system's super-block. If there are enough free blocks, the process tries to allocate one.

If the ext2 file system has been built to preallocate data blocks then it may be able to use one of them. The preallocated blocks do not actually exist, they are just reserved within the allocated block bitmap. The VFS inode representing the file that we are trying to allocate a new data block for has two ext2-specific fields, `prealloc_block` and `prealloc_count`, which are the block number of the first preallocated data block and the number of them, respectively. If there are no preallocated blocks or block preallocation is not enabled, the ext2 file system must allocate a new block. The ext2 file system first looks to see if the next data block in the file is free. Logically, this is the most efficient block to allocate as it makes sequential accesses much quicker. If this block is not free, then the search widens and it looks for a data block within 64 blocks of the ideal block. This block, although not ideal, is at least fairly close and within the same block group of the other data blocks belonging to the file.

If the next block is not free, the process starts looking in all of the other block groups in turn until it finds some free blocks. The block allocation code looks for a cluster of eight free data blocks somewhere in one of the block groups. If it cannot find eight together, it will settle for less. If block preallocation is wanted and enabled it will update `prealloc_block` and `prealloc_count` accordingly.

Wherever it finds the free blocks, the block allocation code updates the block group's block bitmap and allocates a data buffer in the buffer cache. That data buffer is uniquely identified by the file system's supporting device identifier and the block number of the allocated block. The data in the buffer is zeroed and the buffer is marked as "dirty" to show that its contents have not been written to the physical disk. Finally, the super-block itself is marked as "dirty" to show that it has been changed and it is unlocked. If there are any processes waiting for the super-block, the first one in the queue is allowed to run again and will gain exclusive control of the super-block for its file operations. The process's data is written to the new data block and, if that data block is filled, the entire process is repeated and another data block allocated.

In this section, the layout of a super-block is described. Here is the official structure of an ext2fs super-block [include/linux/ext2_fs.h]:

```
struct ext2_super_block {
  unsigned long   s_inodes_count;
  unsigned long   s_blocks_count;
  unsigned long   s_r_blocks_count;
  unsigned long   s_free_blocks_count;
  unsigned long   s_free_inodes_count;
  unsigned long   s_first_data_block;
  unsigned long   s_log_block_size;
  long            s_log_frag_size;
  unsigned long   s_blocks_per_group;
  unsigned long   s_frags_per_group;
  unsigned long   s_inodes_per_group;
  unsigned long   s_mtime;
  unsigned long   s_wtime;
  unsigned short  s_mnt_count;
  short           s_max_mnt_count;
  unsigned short  s_magic;
  unsigned short  s_state;
  unsigned short  s_errors;
  unsigned short  s_pad;
  unsigned long   s_lastcheck;
  unsigned long   s_checkinterval;
  unsigned long   s_reserved[238];
};
```

Here are some explanations:

s_inodes_count	The total number of inodes on the fs.
s_blocks_count	The total number of blocks on the fs.
s_r_blocks_count	The total number of blocks reserved for the exclusive use of the super-user.
s_free_blocks_count	The total number of free blocks on the fs.
s_free_inodes_count	The total number of free inodes on the fs.
s_first_data_block	The position on the fs of the first data block. Usually, this is block number 1 for fs containing 1024 bytes blocks and is number 0 for other fs.

s_log_block_size	Used to compute the logical block size in bytes. The logical block size is in fact 1024 << s_log_block_size.
s_log_frag_size	Used to compute the logical fragment size. The logical fragment size is in fact 1024 << s_log_frag_size if s_log_frag_size is positive, and 1024 >> -s_log_frag_size if s_log_frag_size is negative.
s_blocks_per_group	The total number of blocks contained in a group.
s_frags_per_group	The total number of fragments contained in a group.
s_inodes_per_group	The total number of inodes contained in a group.
s_mtime	The time at which the last mount of the fs was performed.
s_wtime	The time at which the last write of the super-block on the fs was performed.
s_mnt_count	The number of time the fs has been mounted in read/write mode without having been checked.
s_max_mnt_count	The maximum number of times the fs may be mounted in read/write mode before a check must be done.
s_magic	A magic number that permits the identification of the file system. It is 0xEF53 for a normal ext2fs and 0xEF51 for versions of ext2fs prior to 0.2b.
s_state	The state of the file system. It contains an or'ed value of EXT2_VALID_FS (0x0001) which means unmounted cleanly; and EXT2_ERROR_FS (0x0002) which means errors detected by the kernel code.
s_errors	Indicates what operation to perform when an error occurs.
s_pad	Unused.
s_lastcheck	The time of the last check performed on the fs.
s_checkinterval	The maximum possible time between checks on the fs.
s_reserved	Unused.

Times are measured in seconds since 00:00:00 GMT, January 1, 1970.

Once the super-block is read in memory, the ext2fs kernel code calculates some other information and keeps them in another structure. This structure has the following layout:

```
struct ext2_sb_info {
    unsigned long s_frag_size;
    unsigned long s_frags_per_block;
    unsigned long s_inodes_per_block;
```

```
    unsigned long s_frags_per_group;
    unsigned long s_blocks_per_group;
    unsigned long s_inodes_per_group;
    unsigned long s_itb_per_group;
    unsigned long s_desc_per_block;
    unsigned long s_groups_count;
    struct buffer_head * s_sbh;
    struct ext2_super_block * s_es;
    struct buffer_head * s_group_desc[EXT2_MAX_GROUP_DESC];
    unsigned short s_loaded_inode_bitmaps;
    unsigned short s_loaded_block_bitmaps;
    unsigned long s_inode_bitmap_number[EXT2_MAX_GROUP_LOADED];
    struct buffer_head * s_inode_bitmap[EXT2_MAX_GROUP_LOADED];
    unsigned long s_block_bitmap_number[EXT2_MAX_GROUP_LOADED];
    struct buffer_head * s_block_bitmap[EXT2_MAX_GROUP_LOADED];
    int s_rename_lock;
    struct wait_queue * s_rename_wait;
    unsigned long   s_mount_opt;
    unsigned short s_mount_state;
};
```

Here are some explanations:

s_frag_size	Fragment size in bytes.
s_frags_per_block	Number of fragments in a block.
s_inodes_per_block	Number of inodes in a block of the inode table.
s_frags_per_group	Number of fragments in a group.
s_blocks_per_group	Number of blocks in a group.
s_inodes_per_group	Number of inodes in a group.
s_itb_per_group	Number of inode table blocks per group.
s_desc_per_block	Number of group descriptors per block.
s_groups_count	Number of groups.
s_sbh	The buffer containing the disk super-block in memory.
s_es	Pointer to the super-block in the buffer.
s_group_desc	Pointers to the buffers containing the group descriptors.
s_loaded_inode_bitmaps	Number of inodes bitmap cache entries used.
s_loaded_block_bitmaps	Number of blocks bitmap cache entries used.
s_inode_bitmap_number	Indicates to which group the inodes bitmap in the buffers belong.

s_inode_bitmap	Inode bitmap cache.
s_block_bitmap_number	Indicates to which group the blocks bitmap in the buffers belong.
s_block_bitmap	Block bitmap cache.
s_rename_lock	Lock used to avoid two simultaneous rename operations on a fs.
s_rename_wait	Wait queue used to wait for the completion of a rename operation in progress.
s_mount_opt	The mounting options specified by the administrator.
s_mount_state	Most of those values are computed from the super-block on disk.

Linux ext2fs manager caches access to the inodes and blocks bitmaps. This cache is a list of buffers ordered from the most recently used to the least recently used buffer. Managers should use the same kind of bitmap caching or other similar method of improving access time to disk.

Group Descriptors

On disk, the group descriptors immediately follow the super-block and each descriptor has the following layout:

```
struct ext2_group_desc
{
  unsigned long  bg_block_bitmap;
  unsigned long  bg_inode_bitmap;
  unsigned long  bg_inode_table;
  unsigned short bg_free_blocks_count;
  unsigned short bg_free_inodes_count;
  unsigned short bg_used_dirs_count;
  unsigned short bg_pad;
  unsigned long  bg_reserved[3];
};
```

Here are some explanations:

bg_block_bitmap	Points to the blocks bitmap block for the group.
bg_inode_bitmap	Points to the inodes bitmap block for the group.
bg_inode_table	Points to the inodes table first block.
bg_free_blocks_count	Number of free blocks in the group.
bg_free_inodes_count	Number of free inodes in the group.

bg_used_dirs_count	Number of inodes allocated to directories in the group.
bg_pad	Padding.

The information in a group descriptor pertains only to the group it is actually describing.

Bitmaps

The ext2 file system uses bitmaps to keep track of allocated blocks and inodes.

The blocks bitmap of each group refers to blocks ranging from the first block to the last block in the group. To access the bit of a precise block, first look for the group to which the block belongs and then look for the bit of the block in the blocks bitmap contained in the group. It it very important to note that the blocks bitmap refers, in fact, to fragments, the smallest allocation unit supported by the file system. Since the block size is always a multiple of fragment size, when the file system manager allocates a block, it actually allocates a multiple number of fragments. This use of the blocks bitmap permits the file system manager to allocate and deallocate space on a fragment basis.

The inode bitmap of each group refers to inodes ranging from the first to the last inode of the group. To access the bit of a precise inode, first look for the group to which the inode belongs and then look for the bit of the inode in the inode bitmap contained in the group. To obtain the inode information from the inode table, the process is the same as for fragments, except that the final search is in the inode table of the group instead of the inode bitmap.

Inodes

An inode uniquely describes a file. Here's what an inode looks like on disk:

```
struct ext2_inode {
  unsigned short  i_mode;
  unsigned short  i_uid;
  unsigned long   i_size;
  unsigned long   i_atime;
  unsigned long   i_ctime;
  unsigned long   i_mtime;
  unsigned long   i_dtime;
  unsigned short  i_gid;
  unsigned short  i_links_count;
  unsigned long   i_blocks;
  unsigned long   i_flags;
  unsigned long   i_reserved1;
  unsigned long   i_block[EXT2_N_BLOCKS];
  unsigned long   i_version;
  unsigned long   i_file_acl;
```

```
    unsigned long  i_dir_acl;
    unsigned long  i_faddr;
    unsigned char  i_frag;
    unsigned char  i_fsize;
    unsigned short i_pad1;
    unsigned long  i_reserved2[2];
};
```

Here are some explanations:

i_mode	Type of file (character, block, link, etc.) and access rights on the file.
i_uid	Uid of the owner of the file.
i_size	Logical size in bytes.
i_atime	Last time the file was accessed.
i_ctime	Last time the inode information of the file was changed.
i_mtime	Last time the file content was modified.
i_dtime	When the file was deleted.
i_gid	Gid of the file.
i_links_count	Number of links pointing to this file.
i_blocks	Number of blocks allocated to the file counted in 512-byte units.
i_flags	Flags (see below).
i_reserved1	Reserved.
i_block	Pointers to blocks (see below).
i_version	Version of the file (used by NFS).
i_file_acl	Control access list of the file (not used yet).
i_dir_acl	Control access list of the directory (not used yet).
i_faddr	Block where the fragment of the file resides.
i_frag	Number of the fragment in the block.
i_size	Size of the fragment.
i_pad1	Padding.
i_reserved2	Reserved.

As you can see, the inode contains EXT2_N_BLOCKS (15 in ext2fs 0.5) pointers to blocks. Of these pointers, the first EXT2_NDIR_BLOCKS (12) are direct pointers to data. The following entry points to a block of pointers to data (indirect). The entry following that points to a block of pointers to blocks of pointers to data (double indirection).

The next entry in line points to a block of pointers to a block of pointers to a block of pointers to data (triple indirection).

The inode flags may take one or more of the following or'ed values:

EXT2_SECRM_FL 0x0001

Secure Deletion. This usually means that when this flag is set and we delete the file, random data is written in the blocks previously allocated to the file.

EXT2_UNRM_FL 0x0002

Undelete. When this flag is set and the file is being deleted, the file system code must store enough information to ensure the undeletion of the file (to a certain extent).

EXT2_COMPR_FL 0x0004

Compress File. The content of the file is compressed, the file system code must use compression/decompression algorithms when accessing the data of this file.

EXT2_SYNC_FL 0x0008

Synchronous Updates. The disk representation of this file must be kept in sync with its in-core representation. Asynchronous I/O on this kind of file is not possible. The synchronous updates only apply to the inode itself and to the indirect blocks. Data blocks are always written asynchronously on the disk.

Some inodes have a special meaning:

EXT2_BAD_INO 1	A file containing the list of bad blocks on the file system.
EXT2_ROOT_INO 2	The root directory of the file system.
EXT2_ACL_IDX_INO 3	ACL inode.
EXT2_ACL_DATA_INO 4	ACL inode.
EXT2_BOOT_LOADER_INO 5	The file containing the boot loader. (Not used yet.)
EXT2_UNDEL_DIR_INO 6	The undelete directory of the system.
EXT2_FIRST_INO 11	This is the first inode that does not have a special meaning.

Directories

Directories are special files that are used to create access paths to the files on disk. It is very important to understand that an inode may have many access paths. Since the directories are essential parts of the file system, they have a specific structure. A directory file is a list of entries of the following format:

```
struct ext2_dir_entry {
  unsigned long   inode;
  unsigned short  rec_len;
  unsigned short  name_len;
  char            name[EXT2_NAME_LEN];
};
```

Here are some explanations:

inode   Points to the inode of the file.

rec_len   Length of the entry record.

name_len   Length of the filename.

name   Name of the file. This name may have a maximum length of
            EXT2_NAME_LEN bytes (255 bytes as of version 0.5).

There is such an entry in the directory file for each file in the directory. Since ext2fs is a Unix file system, the first two entries in the directory are file "." and ".." which point to the current directory and the parent directory, respectively.

Allocation algorithms

Following are the allocation algorithms that ext2 file system managers **must** use. Nowadays, many users use more than one operating system on the same computer. If more than one operating system uses the same ext2 partition, it has to use the same allocation algorithms. If done otherwise, what will happen is that one file system manager will undo the work of the other file system manager. It is useless to have a manager that uses highly efficient allocation algorithms if the other one does not bother with allocation and uses quick and dirty algorithms.

Here are the rules used to allocate new inodes:

▼   The inode for a new file is allocated in the same group of the inode of its parent directory.

▲   Inodes are allocated equally among groups.

Here are the rules used to allocate new blocks:

▼   A new block is allocated in the same group as its inode.

▲   Allocate consecutive sequences of blocks.

Of course, sometimes it may be impossible to abide by those rules. In that case, the manager may allocate the block or inode anywhere.

Error Handling

This section describes how a standard ext2 file system handles errors. The super-block contains two parameters controlling the way errors are handled.

The first is the s_mount_opt member of the super-block structure in memory. Its value is computed from the options specified when the fs is mounted. Its error handling related values are:

`EXT2_MOUNT_ERRORS_CONT`	Continue even if an error occurs.
`EXT2_MOUNT_ERRORS_RO`	Remount the file system read-only.
`EXT2_MOUNT_ERRORS_PANIC`	The kernel panics on error.

The second parameter is the s_errors member of the super-block structure on disk. It may take one of the following values:

`EXT2_ERRORS_CONTINUE`	Continue even if an error occurs.
`EXT2_ERRORS_RO`	Remount the file system read only.
`EXT2_ERRORS_PANIC`	In which case the kernel simply panics.
`EXT2_ERRORS_DEFAULT`	Use the default behavior (as of 0.5a EXT2_ERRORS_CONTINUE).

s_mount_opt has precedence on s_errors.
The following is a list of options:

`bsddf`	(*)Makes 'df' act like BSD.
`minixdfMakes`	'df' act like Minix.
`check=none,nocheck`	Perform no checks upon the file system.
`check=normal`	(*)Perform normal checks on the file system.
`check=strict`	Perform extra checks on the file system.
`debug`	For developers only.
`errors=continue`	(*)Keep going on a file system error.
`errors=remount-ro`	Remount the file system read-only on an error.
`errors=panic`	Panic and halt the machine if an error occurs.
`grpid, bsdgroups`	Give objects the same group ID as their parent.
`nogrpid, sysvgroups`	(*)New objects have the group ID of their creator.
`resuid=n`	The user that may use the reserved blocks.

resgid=n   The group that may use the reserved blocks.

sb=n   Use alternate super-block at this location.

grpquota,noquota,quota, usrquota   Quota options are silently ignored by ext2.

SOURCE CODE INCLUDE/LINUX/EXT2_FS.H

```
1  /*
2   *  linux/include/linux/ext2_fs.h
3   *
4   * Copyright (C) 1992, 1993, 1994, 1995
5   * Remy Card (card@masi.ibp.fr)
6   * Laboratoire MASI - Institut Blaise Pascal
7   * Universite Pierre et Marie Curie (Paris VI)
8   *
9   *  from
10  *
11  *  linux/include/linux/minix_fs.h
12  *
13  *  Copyright (C) 1991, 1992  Linus Torvalds
14  */
15
16 #ifndef _LINUX_EXT2_FS_H
17 #define _LINUX_EXT2_FS_H
18
19 #include <linux/types.h>
20 /*
21  * The second extended filesystem constants/structures
22  */
23
24
25 /*
26  * Define EXT2FS_DEBUG to produce debug messages
27  */
28 #undef EXT2FS_DEBUG
29
30 /*
31  * Define EXT2_PREALLOCATE to preallocate data blocks for expanding files
32  */
33 #define EXT2_PREALLOCATE
34 #define EXT2_DEFAULT_PREALLOC_BLOCKS    8
35
36 /*
37  * The second extended file system version
38  */
39 #define EXT2FS_DATE             "95/08/09"
40 #define EXT2FS_VERSION          "0.5b"
41
42 /*
```

```
43   * Debug code
44   */
45  #ifdef EXT2FS_DEBUG
46  #      define ext2_debug(f, a...)      { \
47                                          printk ("EXT2-fs DEBUG (%s,
d): %s:", \
48                                              __FILE__, __LINE__,_FUNCTION__); \
49                                          printk (f, ## a); \
50                                          }
51  #else
52  #      define ext2_debug(f, a...)      /**/
53  #endif
54
55  /*
56   * Special inodes numbers
57   */
58  #define EXT2_BAD_INO              1      /* Bad blocks inode */
59  #define EXT2_ROOT_INO             2      /* Root inode */
60  #define EXT2_ACL_IDX_INO          3      /* ACL inode */
61  #define EXT2_ACL_DATA_INO         4      /* ACL inode */
62  #define EXT2_BOOT_LOADER_INO      5      /* Boot loader inode */
63  #define EXT2_UNDEL_DIR_INO        6      /* Undelete directory inode */
64
65  /* First non-reserved inode for old ext2 filesystems */
66  #define EXT2_GOOD_OLD_FIRST_INO 11
67
68  /*
69   * The second extended file system magic number
70   */
71  #define EXT2_SUPER_MAGIC          0xEF53
72
73  /*
74   * Maximal count of links to a file
75   */
76  #define EXT2_LINK_MAX             32000
77
78  /*
79   * Macro-instructions used to manage several block sizes
80   */
81  #define EXT2_MIN_BLOCK_SIZE            1024
82  #define EXT2_MAX_BLOCK_SIZE            4096
83  #define EXT2_MIN_BLOCK_LOG_SIZE         10
84  #ifdef __KERNEL__
85  # define EXT2_BLOCK_SIZE(s)            ((s)->s_blocksize)
86  #else
87  # define EXT2_BLOCK_SIZE(s)            (EXT2_MIN_BLOCK_SIZE << (s)-
                                            s_log_block_size)
88  #endif
89  #define EXT2_ACLE_PER_BLOCK(s)         (EXT2_BLOCK_SIZE(s) / sizeof struct
                                            ext2_acl_entry))
```

```
90 #define EXT2_ADDR_PER_BLOCK(s)            (EXT2_BLOCK_SIZE(s) / sizeof (__u32))
91 #ifdef __KERNEL__
92 # define EXT2_BLOCK_SIZE_BITS(s)       ((s)->s_blocksize_bits)
93 #else
94 # define EXT2_BLOCK_SIZE_BITS(s)       ((s)->s_log_block_size + 10)
95 #endif
96 #ifdef __KERNEL__
97 #define EXT2_ADDR_PER_BLOCK_BITS(s)    ((s)->u.ext2_sb.s_addr_per_block_bits)
98 #define EXT2_INODE_SIZE(s)             ((s)->u.ext2_sb.s_inode_size)
99 #define EXT2_FIRST_INO(s)              ((s)->u.ext2_sb.s_first_ino)
100 #else
101 #define EXT2_INODE_SIZE(s)        (((s)->s_rev_level == EXT2_GOOD_OLD_REV) ? \
102                                   EXT2_GOOD_OLD_INODE_SIZE : \
103                                   (s)->s_inode_size)
104 #define EXT2_FIRST_INO(s)         (((s)->s_rev_level == EXT2_GOOD_OLD_REV) ? \
105                                   EXT2_GOOD_OLD_FIRST_INO : \
106                                   (s)->s_first_ino)
107 #endif
108
109 /*
110  * Macro-instructions used to manage fragments
111  */
112 #define EXT2_MIN_FRAG_SIZE            1024
113 #define EXT2_MAX_FRAG_SIZE            4096
114 #define EXT2_MIN_FRAG_LOG_SIZE         10
115 #ifdef __KERNEL__
116 # define EXT2_FRAG_SIZE(s)            ((s)->u.ext2_sb.s_frag_size)
117 # define EXT2_FRAGS_PER_BLOCK(s)      ((s)->u.ext2_sb.s_frags_per_block)
118 #else
119 # define EXT2_FRAG_SIZE(s)            (EXT2_MIN_FRAG_SIZE <<
                                          (s)->s_log_frag_size)
120 # define EXT2_FRAGS_PER_BLOCK(s)      (EXT2_BLOCK_SIZE(s) /
                                          EXT2_FRAG_SIZE(s))
121 #endif
122
123 /*
124  * ACL structures
125  */
126 struct ext2_acl_header  /* Header of Access Control Lists */
127 {
128         __u32   aclh_size;
129         __u32   aclh_file_count;
130         __u32   aclh_acle_count;
131         __u32   aclh_first_acle;
132 };
133
134 struct ext2_acl_entry   /* Access Control List Entry */
135 {
136         __u32   acle_size;
137         __u16   acle_perms;       /* Access permissions */
138         __u16   acle_type;        /* Type of entry */
139         __u16   acle_tag;         /* User or group identity */
```

```
140            __u16  acle_pad1;
141            __u32  acle_next;        /* Pointer on next entry for the */
142                                     /* same inode or on next free entry */
143 };
144
145 /*
146  * Structure of a blocks group descriptor
147  */
148 struct ext2_group_desc
149 {
150            __u32  bg_block_bitmap;        /* Blocks bitmap block */
151            __u32  bg_inode_bitmap;        /* Inodes bitmap block */
152            __u32  bg_inode_table;         /* Inodes table block */
153            __u16  bg_free_blocks_count;   /* Free blocks count */
154            __u16  bg_free_inodes_count;   /* Free inodes count */
155            __u16  bg_used_dirs_count;     /* Directories count */
156            __u16  bg_pad;
157            __u32  bg_reserved[3];
158 };
159
160 /*
161  * Macro-instructions used to manage group descriptors
162  */
163 #ifdef __KERNEL__
164 # define EXT2_BLOCKS_PER_GROUP(s)      ((s)->u.ext2_sb.s_blocks_per_group)
165 # define EXT2_DESC_PER_BLOCK(s)        ((s)->u.ext2_sb.s_desc_per_block)
166 # define EXT2_INODES_PER_GROUP(s)      ((s)->u.ext2_sb.s_inodes_per_group)
167 # define EXT2_DESC_PER_BLOCK_BITS(s)   ((s)->u.ext2_sb.s_desc_per_block_bits)
168 #else
169 # define EXT2_BLOCKS_PER_GROUP(s)      ((s)->s_blocks_per_group)
170 # define EXT2_DESC_PER_BLOCK(s)        (EXT2_BLOCK_SIZE(s) / sizeof
(struct ext2_group_desc))
171 # define EXT2_INODES_PER_GROUP(s)      ((s)->s_inodes_per_group)
172 #endif
173
174 /*
175  * Constants relative to the data blocks
176  */
177 #define EXT2_NDIR_BLOCKS           12
178 #define EXT2_IND_BLOCK             EXT2_NDIR_BLOCKS
179 #define EXT2_DIND_BLOCK            (EXT2_IND_BLOCK + 1)
180 #define EXT2_TIND_BLOCK            (EXT2_DIND_BLOCK + 1)
181 #define EXT2_N_BLOCKS             (EXT2_TIND_BLOCK + 1)
182
183 /*
184  * Inode flags
185  */
186 #define EXT2_SECRM_FL              0x00000001 /* Secure deletion
/
187 #define EXT2_UNRM_FL               0x00000002 /* Undelete */
188 #define EXT2_COMPR_FL              0x00000004 /* Compress file */
189 #define EXT2_SYNC_FL               0x00000008 /* Synchronous updates */
```

```
190 #define EXT2_IMMUTABLE_FL              0x00000010 /* Immutable file */
191 #define EXT2_APPEND_FL                 0x00000020 /* writes to file may only
append */
192 #define EXT2_NODUMP_FL                 0x00000040 /* do not dump file */
193 #define EXT2_NOATIME_FL                0x00000080 /* do not update atime */
194 /* Reserved for compression usage... */
195 #define EXT2_DIRTY_FL                  0x00000100
196 #define EXT2_COMPRBLK_FL               0x00000200 /* One or more compressed
clusters */
197 #define EXT2_NOCOMP_FL                 0x00000400 /* Don't compress */
198 #define EXT2_ECOMPR_FL                 0x00000800 /* Compression error */
199 /* End compression flags --- maybe not all used */
200 #define EXT2_BTREE_FL                  0x00001000 /* btree format dir */
201 #define EXT2_RESERVED_FL               0x80000000 /* reserved for ext2 lib */
202
203 #define EXT2_FL_USER_VISIBLE           0x00001FFF /* User visible flags */
204 #define EXT2_FL_USER_MODIFIABLE        0x000000FF /* User modifiable flags */
205
206 /*
207  * ioctl commands
208  */
209 #define EXT2_IOC_GETFLAGS              _IOR('f', 1, long)
210 #define EXT2_IOC_SETFLAGS              _IOW('f', 2, long)
211 #define EXT2_IOC_GETVERSION            _IOR('v', 1, long)
212 #define EXT2_IOC_SETVERSION            _IOW('v', 2, long)
213
214 /*
215  * Structure of an inode on the disk
216  */
217 struct ext2_inode {
218         __u16   i_mode;         /* File mode */
219         __u16   i_uid;          /* Low 16 bits of Owner Uid */
220         __u32   i_size;         /* Size in bytes */
221         __u32   i_atime;        /* Access time */
222         __u32   i_ctime;        /* Creation time */
223         __u32   i_mtime;        /* Modification time */
224         __u32   i_dtime;        /* Deletion Time */
225         __u16   i_gid;          /* Low 16 bits of Group Id */
226         __u16   i_links_count;  /* Links count */
227         __u32   i_blocks;       /* Blocks count */
228         __u32   i_flags;        /* File flags */
229         union {
230                 struct {
231                         __u32  l_i_reserved1;
232                 } linux1;
233                 struct {
234                         __u32  h_i_translator;
235                 } hurd1;
236                 struct {
237                         __u32  m_i_reserved1;
238                 } masix1;
239         } osd1;                         /* OS dependent 1 */
```

```
240            __u32   i_block[EXT2_N_BLOCKS];/* Pointers to blocks */
241            __u32   i_generation;   /* File version (for NFS) */
242            __u32   i_file_acl;     /* File ACL */
243            __u32   i_dir_acl;      /* Directory ACL */
244            __u32   i_faddr;        /* Fragment address */
245        union {
246                struct {
247                        __u8    l_i_frag;       /* Fragment number */
248                        __u8    l_i_fsize;      /* Fragment size */
249                        __u16   i_pad1;
250                        __u16   l_i_uid_high;   /* these 2 fields   /
251                        __u16   l_i_gid_high;   /* were reserved2[0]*/
252                        __u32   l_i_reserved2;
253                } linux2;
254                struct {
255                        __u8    h_i_frag;       /* Fragment number */
256                        __u8    h_i_fsize;      /* Fragment size */
257                        __u16   h_i_mode_high;
258                        __u16   h_i_uid_high;
259                        __u16   h_i_gid_high;
260                        __u32   h_i_author;
261                } hurd2;
262                struct {
263                        __u8    m_i_frag;       /* Fragment number */
264                        __u8    m_i_fsize;      /* Fragment size */
265                        __u16   m_pad1;
266                        __u32   m_i_reserved2[2];
267                } masix2;
268        } osd2;                              /* OS dependent 2 */
269 };
270
271 #define i_size_high     i_dir_acl
272
273 #if defined(__KERNEL__) || defined(__linux__)
274 #define i_reserved1     osd1.linux1.l_i_reserved1
275 #define i_frag          osd2.linux2.l_i_frag
276 #define i_fsize         osd2.linux2.l_i_fsize
277 #define i_uid_low       i_uid
278 #define i_gid_low       i_gid
279 #define i_uid_high      osd2.linux2.l_i_uid_high
280 #define i_gid_high      osd2.linux2.l_i_gid_high
281 #define i_reserved2     osd2.linux2.l_i_reserved2
282 #endif
283
284 #ifdef  __hurd__
285 #define i_translator    osd1.hurd1.h_i_translator
286 #define i_frag          osd2.hurd2.h_i_frag;
287 #define i_fsize         osd2.hurd2.h_i_fsize;
288 #define i_uid_high      osd2.hurd2.h_i_uid_high
289 #define i_gid_high      osd2.hurd2.h_i_gid_high
290 #define i_author        osd2.hurd2.h_i_author
291 #endif
```

```
292
293 #ifdef  __masix__
294 #define i_reserved1      osd1.masix1.m_i_reserved1
295 #define i_frag           osd2.masix2.m_i_frag
296 #define i_fsize          osd2.masix2.m_i_fsize
297 #define i_reserved2      osd2.masix2.m_i_reserved2
298 #endif
299
300 /*
301  * File system states
302  */
303 #define EXT2_VALID_FS            0x0001  /* Unmounted cleanly */
304 #define EXT2_ERROR_FS            0x0002  /* Errors detected */
305
306 /*
307  * Mount flags
308  */
309 #define EXT2_MOUNT_CHECK         0x0001 /* Do mount-time checks */
310 #define EXT2_MOUNT_GRPID         0x0004 /* Create files with
                                            directory's group */
311 #define EXT2_MOUNT_DEBUG         0x0008 /* Some debugging messages */
312 #define EXT2_MOUNT_ERRORS_CONT   0x0010  /* Continue on errors */
313 #define EXT2_MOUNT_ERRORS_RO     0x0020 /* Remount fs ro on errors */
314 #define EXT2_MOUNT_ERRORS_PANIC  0x0040 /* Panic on errors */
315 #define EXT2_MOUNT_MINIX_DF      0x0080 /* Mimics the Minix statfs */
316 #define EXT2_MOUNT_NO_UID32      0x0200 /* Disable 32-bit UIDs */
317
318 #define clear_opt(o, opt)        o &= ~EXT2_MOUNT_##opt
319 #define set_opt(o, opt)          o |= EXT2_MOUNT_##opt
320 #define test_opt(sb, opt)        ((sb)->u.ext2_sb.s_mount_opt & \
321                                  EXT2_MOUNT_##opt)
322 /*
323  * Maximal mount counts between two filesystem checks
324  */
325 #define EXT2_DFL_MAX_MNT_COUNT   20     /* Allow 20 mounts */
326 #define EXT2_DFL_CHECKINTERVAL   0      /* Don't use interval check */
327
328 /*
329  * Behaviour when detecting errors
330  */
331 #define EXT2_ERRORS_CONTINUE     1      /* Continue execution */
332 #define EXT2_ERRORS_RO           2      /* Remount fs read-only */
333 #define EXT2_ERRORS_PANIC        3      /* Panic */
334 #define EXT2_ERRORS_DEFAULT      EXT2_ERRORS_CONTINUE
335
336 /*
337  * Structure of the super block
338  */
339 struct ext2_super_block {
340         __u32  s_inodes_count;        /* Inodes count */
341         __u32  s_blocks_count;        /* Blocks count */
342         __u32  s_r_blocks_count;      /* Reserved blocks count */
```

```
343         __u32   s_free_blocks_count;    /* Free blocks count */
344         __u32   s_free_inodes_count;    /* Free inodes count */
345         __u32   s_first_data_block;     /* First Data Block */
346         __u32   s_log_block_size;       /* Block size */
347         __s32   s_log_frag_size;        /* Fragment size */
348         __u32   s_blocks_per_group;     /* # Blocks per group */
349         __u32   s_frags_per_group;      /* # Fragments per group */
350         __u32   s_inodes_per_group;     /* # Inodes per group */
351         __u32   s_mtime;                /* Mount time */
352         __u32   s_wtime;                /* Write time */
353         __u16   s_mnt_count;            /* Mount count */
354         __s16   s_max_mnt_count;        /* Maximal mount count */
355         __u16   s_magic;                /* Magic signature */
356         __u16   s_state;                /* File system state */
357         __u16   s_errors;               /* Behaviour when detecting errors */
358         __u16   s_minor_rev_level;      /* minor revision level */
359         __u32   s_lastcheck;            /* time of last check */
360         __u32   s_checkinterval;        /* max. time between checks */
361         __u32   s_creator_os;           /* OS */
362         __u32   s_rev_level;            /* Revision level */
363         __u16   s_def_resuid;           /* Default uid for reserved blocks */
364         __u16   s_def_resgid;           /* Default gid for reserved blocks */
365         /*
366          * These fields are for EXT2_DYNAMIC_REV superblocks only.
367          *
368          * Note: the difference between the compatible feature set and
369          * the incompatible feature set is that if there is a bit set
370          * in the incompatible feature set that the kernel doesn't
371          * know about, it should refuse to mount the filesystem.
372          *
373          * e2fsck's requirements are more strict; if it doesn't know
374          * about a feature in either the compatible or incompatible
375          * feature set, it must abort and not try to meddle with
376          * things it doesn't understand...
377          */
378         __u32   s_first_ino;            /* First non-reserved inode */
379         __u16   s_inode_size;           /* size of inode structure */
380         __u16   s_block_group_nr;       /* block group # of this superblock */
381         __u32   s_feature_compat;       /* compatible feature set */
382         __u32   s_feature_incompat;     /* incompatible feature set */
383         __u32   s_feature_ro_compat;    /* readonly-compatible feature set */
384         __u8    s_uuid[16];             /* 128-bit uuid for volume */
385         char    s_volume_name[16];      /* volume name */
386         char    s_last_mounted[64];     /* directory where last mounted */
387         __u32   s_algorithm_usage_bitmap; /* For compression */
388         /*
389          * Performance hints.  Directory preallocation should only
390          * happen if the EXT2_COMPAT_PREALLOC flag is on.
391          */
392         __u8    s_prealloc_blocks;      /* Nr of blocks to try to preallocate*/
393         __u8    s_prealloc_dir_blocks;  /* Nr to preallocate for dirs */
394         __u16   s_padding1;
```

```
395          __u32    s_reserved[204];          /* Padding to the end of the block */
396 };
397
398 #ifdef __KERNEL__
399 #define EXT2_SB(sb)      (&((sb)->u.ext2_sb))
400 #else
401 /* Assume that user mode programs are passing in an ext2fs superblock, not
402  * a kernel struct super_block.  This will allow us to call the feature-test
403  * macros from user land. */
404 #define EXT2_SB(sb)      (sb)
405 #endif
406
407 /*
408  * Codes for operating systems
409  */
410 #define EXT2_OS_LINUX            0
411 #define EXT2_OS_HURD             1
412 #define EXT2_OS_MASIX            2
413 #define EXT2_OS_FREEBSD          3
414 #define EXT2_OS_LITES            4
415
416 /*
417  * Revision levels
418  */
419 #define EXT2_GOOD_OLD_REV        0        /* The good old (original) format */
420 #define EXT2_DYNAMIC_REV         1        /* V2 format w/ dynamic inode sizes */
421
422 #define EXT2_CURRENT_REV         EXT2_GOOD_OLD_REV
423 #define EXT2_MAX_SUPP_REV        EXT2_DYNAMIC_REV
424
425 #define EXT2_GOOD_OLD_INODE_SIZE 128
426
427 /*
428  * Feature set definitions
429  */
430
431 #define EXT2_HAS_COMPAT_FEATURE(sb,mask)                        \
432         ( EXT2_SB(sb)->s_es->s_feature_compat & cpu_to_le32(mask) )
433 #define EXT2_HAS_RO_COMPAT_FEATURE(sb,mask)                     \
434         ( EXT2_SB(sb)->s_es->s_feature_ro_compat & cpu_to_le32(mask) )
435 #define EXT2_HAS_INCOMPAT_FEATURE(sb,mask)                      \
436         ( EXT2_SB(sb)->s_es->s_feature_incompat & cpu_to_le32(mask) )
437 #define EXT2_SET_COMPAT_FEATURE(sb,mask)                        \
438         EXT2_SB(sb)->s_es->s_feature_compat |= cpu_to_le32(mask)
439 #define EXT2_SET_RO_COMPAT_FEATURE(sb,mask)                     \
440         EXT2_SB(sb)->s_es->s_feature_ro_compat |= cpu_to_le32(mask)
441 #define EXT2_SET_INCOMPAT_FEATURE(sb,mask)                      \
442         EXT2_SB(sb)->s_es->s_feature_incompat |= cpu_to_le32(mask)
443 #define EXT2_CLEAR_COMPAT_FEATURE(sb,mask)                      \
444         EXT2_SB(sb)->s_es->s_feature_compat &= ~cpu_to_le32(mask)
445 #define EXT2_CLEAR_RO_COMPAT_FEATURE(sb,mask)                   \
446         EXT2_SB(sb)->s_es->s_feature_ro_compat &= ~cpu_to_le32(mask)
```

```
447 #define EXT2_CLEAR_INCOMPAT_FEATURE(sb,mask)                         \
448         EXT2_SB(sb)->s_es->s_feature_incompat &= ~cpu_to_le32(mask)
449
450 #define EXT2_FEATURE_COMPAT_DIR_PREALLOC        0x0001
451
452 #define EXT2_FEATURE_RO_COMPAT_SPARSE_SUPER     0x0001
453 #define EXT2_FEATURE_RO_COMPAT_LARGE_FILE       0x0002
454 #define EXT2_FEATURE_RO_COMPAT_BTREE_DIR        0x0004
455
456 #define EXT2_FEATURE_INCOMPAT_COMPRESSION       0x0001
457 #define EXT2_FEATURE_INCOMPAT_FILETYPE          0x0002
458
459 #define EXT2_FEATURE_COMPAT_SUPP        0
460 #define EXT2_FEATURE_INCOMPAT_SUPP      EXT2_FEATURE_INCOMPAT_FILETYPE
461 #define EXT2_FEATURE_RO_COMPAT_SUPP     (EXT2_FEATURE_RO_COMPAT_SPARSE_SUPER| \
462
XT2_FEATURE_RO_COMPAT_LARGE_FILE| \
463                                         EXT2_FEATURE_RO_COMPAT_BTREE_DIR)
464
465 /*
466  * Default values for user and/or group using reserved blocks
467  */
468 #define EXT2_DEF_RESUID         0
469 #define EXT2_DEF_RESGID         0
470
471 /*
472  * Structure of a directory entry
473  */
474 #define EXT2_NAME_LEN 255
475
476 struct ext2_dir_entry {
477         __u32   inode;                  /* Inode number */
478         __u16   rec_len;                /* Directory entry length */
479         __u16   name_len;               /* Name length */
480         char    name[EXT2_NAME_LEN];    /* File name */
481 };
482
483 /*
484  * The new version of the directory entry.  Since EXT2 structures are
485  * stored in intel byte order, and the name_len field could never be
486  * bigger than 255 chars, it's safe to reclaim the extra byte for the
487  * file_type field.
488  */
489 struct ext2_dir_entry_2 {
490         __u32   inode;                  /* Inode number */
491         __u16   rec_len;                /* Directory entry length */
492         __u8    name_len;               /* Name length */
493         __u8    file_type;
494         char    name[EXT2_NAME_LEN];    /* File name */
495 };
496
497 /*
```

```
498  * Ext2 directory file types.  Only the low 3 bits are used.  The
499  * other bits are reserved for now.
500  */
501 #define EXT2_FT_UNKNOWN          0
502 #define EXT2_FT_REG_FILE         1
503 #define EXT2_FT_DIR              2
504 #define EXT2_FT_CHRDEV           3
505 #define EXT2_FT_BLKDEV           4
506 #define EXT2_FT_FIFO             5
507 #define EXT2_FT_SOCK             6
508 #define EXT2_FT_SYMLINK          7
509
510 #define EXT2_FT_MAX              8
511
512 /*
513  * EXT2_DIR_PAD defines the directory entries boundaries
514  *
515  * NOTE: It must be a multiple of 4
516  */
517 #define EXT2_DIR_PAD                    4
518 #define EXT2_DIR_ROUND                  (EXT2_DIR_PAD - 1)
519 #define EXT2_DIR_REC_LEN(name_len)      (((name_len) + 8 + EXT2_DIR_ROUND) & \
520                                         ~EXT2_DIR_ROUND)
521
522 #ifdef __KERNEL__
523 /*
524  * Function prototypes
525  */
526
527 /*
528  * Ok, these declarations are also in <linux/kernel.h> but none of the
529  * ext2 source programs needs to include it so they are duplicated here.
530  */
531 # define NORET_TYPE     /**/
532 # define ATTRIB_NORET   __attribute__((noreturn))
533 # define NORET_AND      noreturn,
534
535 /* acl.c */
536 extern int ext2_permission (struct inode *, int);
537
538 /* balloc.c */
539 extern int ext2_bg_has_super(struct super_block *sb, int group);
540 extern unsigned long ext2_bg_num_gdb(struct super_block *sb, int group);
541 extern int ext2_new_block (const struct inode *, unsigned long,
542                           __u32 *, __u32 *, int *);
543 extern void ext2_free_blocks (const struct inode *, unsigned long,
544                               unsigned long);
545 extern unsigned long ext2_count_free_blocks (struct super_block *);
546 extern void ext2_check_blocks_bitmap (struct super_block *);
547 extern struct ext2_group_desc * ext2_get_group_desc(struct super_block * sb,
548                                               unsigned int block_group,
549                                               struct buffer_head ** bh);
```

```
550
551 /* bitmap.c */
552 extern unsigned long ext2_count_free (struct buffer_head *, unsigned);
553
554 /* dir.c */
555 extern int ext2_check_dir_entry (const char *, struct inode *,
556                                   struct ext2_dir_entry_2 *, struct buffer_head *,
557                                   unsigned long);
558
559 /* file.c */
560 extern int ext2_read (struct inode *, struct file *, char *, int);
561 extern int ext2_write (struct inode *, struct file *, char *, int);
562
563 /* fsync.c */
564 extern int ext2_sync_file (struct file *, struct dentry *, int);
565 extern int ext2_fsync_inode (struct inode *, int);
566
567 /* ialloc.c */
568 extern struct inode * ext2_new_inode (const struct inode *, int);
569 extern void ext2_free_inode (struct inode *);
570 extern unsigned long ext2_count_free_inodes (struct super_block *);
571 extern void ext2_check_inodes_bitmap (struct super_block *);
572
573 /* inode.c */
574
575 extern struct buffer_head * ext2_getblk (struct inode *, long, int,
int *);
576 extern struct buffer_head * ext2_bread (struct inode *, int, int, int *);
577
578 extern void ext2_read_inode (struct inode *);
579 extern void ext2_write_inode (struct inode *, int);
580 extern void ext2_put_inode (struct inode *);
581 extern void ext2_delete_inode (struct inode *);
582 extern int ext2_sync_inode (struct inode *);
583 extern void ext2_discard_prealloc (struct inode *);
584
585 /* ioctl.c */
586 extern int ext2_ioctl (struct inode *, struct file *, unsigned int,
587                        unsigned long);
588
589 /* namei.c */
590 extern struct inode_operations ext2_dir_inode_operations;
591
592 /* super.c */
593 extern void ext2_error (struct super_block *, const char *, const char *, ...)
594         __attribute__ ((format (printf, 3, 4)));
595 extern NORET_TYPE void ext2_panic (struct super_block *, const char *,
596                                    const char *, ...)
597         __attribute__ ((NORET_AND format (printf, 3, 4)));
598 extern void ext2_warning (struct super_block *, const char *, const char *, ...)
599         __attribute__ ((format (printf, 3, 4)));
600 extern void ext2_update_dynamic_rev (struct super_block *sb);
```

```
601 extern void ext2_put_super (struct super_block *);
602 extern void ext2_write_super (struct super_block *);
603 extern int ext2_remount (struct super_block *, int *, char *);
604 extern struct super_block * ext2_read_super (struct super_block *,void
*,int);
605 extern int ext2_statfs (struct super_block *, struct statfs *);
606
607 /* truncate.c */
608 extern void ext2_truncate (struct inode *);
609
610 /*
611  * Inodes and files operations
612  */
613
614 /* dir.c */
615 extern struct file_operations ext2_dir_operations;
616
617 /* file.c */
618 extern struct inode_operations ext2_file_inode_operations;
619 extern struct file_operations ext2_file_operations;
620
621 /* symlink.c */
622 extern struct inode_operations ext2_fast_symlink_inode_operations;
623
624 extern struct address_space_operations ext2_aops;
625
626 #endif  /* __KERNEL__ */
627
628 #endif  /* _LINUX_EXT2_FS_H */
629
```

CHAPTER 8

IBM's JFS Journaling File System for Linux

Journaling and/or logging file systems eliminate the consistency problems of simpler file systems such as ext2fs, but introduce the issue of speed. As we shall see, they introduce the concept of transactions to be updated in the file system and, similar to database management systems, use a log to store the update event before actually committing the update to the file(s). Once the commit is successful, the log intent entry is marked as executed, and this additional operation slows down overall file system performance. Certain journaling/logging file systems are faster than others. In this chapter we look at the JFS implementation.

JFS provides the super-block and file operation system calls required by the Linux Virtual File System layer. JFS, a log-based, byte-level file system, is both robust and scalable. While tailored primarily for the high throughput and reliability requirements of transaction-oriented, high performance servers (from single processor systems to advanced multi-processor and clustered systems), JFS is also applicable to client configurations where performance and reliability are desired.

IBM's journaling file system, JFS, was made available to the public in February 2000 (see, http://www-4.ibm.com/software/developer/library/jfs.html).

THE MAIN JFS DATA STRUCTURES AND ALGORITHMS

A detailed study of the JFS code reveals an examplary elegance of implementation. The data structures are self-evident and reduced to the most simple form. The variable name space is used intelligently and the functions are beautifully crafted. Let's analyze these structures and algorithms.

Super-blocks: Primary Aggregate Super-block and Secondary Aggregate Super-block

The super-blocks contain aggregate-wide information such as the size of the aggregate, size of allocation groups, aggregate block size, etc. The secondary aggregate super-block is a direct copy of the primary aggregate super-block and is used if the primary aggregate super-block is corrupted. These super-blocks are at fixed locations, which allows JFS to always find them without depending on any other information. The super-block structure is defined in linux\include\linux\JFS\JFS_superblock.h, struct JFS_superblock.

Inodes

A JFS on-disk inode is 512 bytes and contains four basic sets of information:

▼ The first set describes the POSIX attributes of the JFS object.

■ The second set describes additional attributes for the JFS object. These attributes include information necessary for VFS support, information specific to the OS environment, and the header for the B+-tree.

- ■ The third set either contains the extent allocation descriptors of the root of the B+-tree, or will contain inline data.

- ▲ The fourth set contains extended attributes, more inline data, or additional extent allocation descriptors.

The definition of the on-disk inode structure is defined in linux\include\JFS\ JFS_dinode.h, struct dinode.

Standard Administrative Utilities

JFS provides standard administration utilities for creating and maintaining the file system.

1. Create a file system. This utility provides the JFS-specific portion of the mkfs command, initializing a JFS file system on a specified drive. The utility operates at a low level and assumes that any creation/initialization of the volume on which the file system is to reside is handled outside of the utility at a higher level. The user can provide information, such as block size, during mkfs, which will change the characteristics of the file system.

2. Check/recover a file system: This utility provides the JFS-specific portion of the fsck command. It checks the file system for consistency, and repairs problems it discovers. It replays the log and applies committed changes to the file system meta-data. If the file system is declared clean as a result of the log replay, no further action is taken. If the file system is not deemed clean, indicating that the log was not replayed completely and correctly for some reason, or that the file system could not be restored to a consistent state simply by replaying the log, then a full pass of the file system is performed.

In performing a full integrity check, the check/repair utility's primary goal is to achieve a reliable file system state to prevent future file system corruption or failures. Its secondary goal is that of preserving data in the face of corruption. This means the utility may throw away data in the interest of achieving file system consistency. Specifically, data is discarded when the utility does not have the information needed to restore a structurally inconsistent file or directory to a consistent state without making assumptions. In the case of an inconsistent file or directory, the entire file or directory is discarded with no attempt to save any portion. Any files or sub-directories orphaned by the deletion of a corrupted directory are placed in the lost+found directory located at the root of the file system.

An important consideration for a file system check/repair utility is the amount of virtual memory it requires. Typically, the memory required by these utilities is dependent on file system size, since the bulk of the required virtual memory is used to track the allocation state of the individual blocks in the file system. As file systems grow larger, the number of blocks increases and so does the amount of virtual memory needed to track these blocks.

The design of the JFS check/repair utility differs from the ordinary Linux fsck in that its virtual memory requirements are dictated by the number of files and directories within the file system, rather than the file system's number of blocks. The virtual memory requirements for the JFS check/repair utility are on the order of 32 bytes per file or directory, or approximately 32MB for a file system that contains one million files and directories, regardless of the file system size. Like all other file systems, the JFS utility needs to track block allocation states, but avoids using virtual memory to do so, by using a small reserved work area located within the actual file system.

How JFS Is Set up at Boot Time

At boot time the file system create utility, mkfs, creates an aggregate that is wholly contained within each logical volume (partition) that is mounted. An aggregate is an array of disk blocks allocated according to a specific format. The aggregate includes:

▼ A super-block, which identifies the partition as a JFS aggregate.

▲ An allocation map, which describes the allocation state of each data block within the aggregate.

Block Allocation Map

The Block Allocation Map is used to track the allocated or freed disk blocks for an entire aggregate. Since all of the filesets[1] within an aggregate share the same pool of disk blocks, this allocation map is used by all of the filesets within an aggregate when allocating or freeing disk blocks.

The Block Allocation Map is itself a file which is described by aggregate inode 2. When the aggregate is initially created, the data blocks for the map to cover the aggregate space are allocated. The map may grow or shrink dynamically as the aggregate is expanded or shrunk.

The map contains three types of pages: bmap control, dmap control, and dmap pages. Each page of the map is 4K in length.

Each dmap page contains a single bit to represent each aggregate block. The nth bit represents the allocation status of the nth logical aggregate block. This is defined by struct dmap_t, in linux\include\linux\JFS\JFS_dmap.h file. Each dmap page covers 8K of aggregate blocks.

Since the Block Allocation Map may have many dmap pages, they are managed through the dmap control pages. Dmap pages improve the performance of finding large extents of free blocks. The size of the aggregate will determine how many of these pages and how many levels are needed.

---

1   The fileset(s) are the mountable entity or entities, analogous to an ext2fs file system. A fileset manages files and directories. Files and directories are represented persistently by inodes. Each inode describes the attributes of the file or directory and serves as the starting point for finding the file or directory's data on disk. JFS also uses inodes to represent other file system objects, such as the map that describes the allocation state and location on disk of each inode in the fileset.

If not all of the levels are needed, then the Block Map Inode will be a sparse file with holes for the first page of each of the unused levels.

JFS employs a commit strategy to ensure that the control data is reliably updated. "Reliable update" means that a consistent JFS structure and resource allocation state is maintained in the face of system failures.

In order to ensure that the Block Allocation Map is in a consistent state, JFS maintains two maps in the dmap structure: the working map and the persistent map. The working map records the current allocation state. The persistent map records the committed allocation state, as found on disk or described by records within the JFS log or committed JFS transactions.

When an aggregate block is freed, the permanent map is updated first and when an aggregate block is allocated, the working map is updated first. A bit of zero represents a free resource and a value of one represents an allocated resource.

The dmap control pages of the Block Allocation Map "contain" a tree similar to the tree in a dmap structure, except the leaf level contains 1024 elements. The dmap control page is defined by struct dmapctl_t which can be found in the linux\include\linux\JFS\JFS_dmap.h.

At the top of the Block Allocation Map is a map control structure, struct dbmap_t. This structure contains summary information which speeds up the finding of Allocation Groups (AG) which have higher than average free space. The structure can be found in the linux\include\linux\JFS\JFS_dmap.h.

The Block Allocation Map is not journaled: it can be repaired during recovery time by logredo, or reconstructed by fsck.

Inode Allocation Map

The Inode Allocation Map solves the forward lookup problem.

The aggregate and each fileset maintains Inode Allocation Map, which is a dynamic array of Inode Allocation Groups (IAG). The IAG is the data for the Inode Allocation Map. For the aggregate, the inodes mapped by the Inode Allocation Map are also known as the Aggregate Inode Table. For a fileset, the inodes mapped by the Inode Allocation Map are also known as the File Inode Table.

Each IAG is 4K in size and describes 128 physical inode extents on the disk. Since each inode extent contains 32 inodes, each IAG describes 4096 inodes. An IAG can exist anywhere in the aggregate. All of the inode extents for an IAG exist in one allocation group. The IAG is then tied to that AG until all of its inode extents are freed. At that point an inode extent could be allocated for it in any AG, and then the IAG would be tied to that AG. The IAG is defined by the iag_t structure which can be found in the the file linux\include\linux\JFS\JFS_imap.h.

The first 4K page of the Inode Allocation Map is a control page, which contains summary information for the Inode Allocation Map. The definition for the dinomap_t structure can be found in the linux\include\linux\JFS\JFS_imap.h file.

Abstractly, the Inode Allocation Map is a dynamically extensible array of the IAG structures: struct iag inode_allocation_map [1..N]. Physically, the Inode Allocation Map is itself a file within the aggregate. The aggregate Inode Allocation Map is described by the aggregate self-node.

The fileset Inode Allocation Map is described by fileset_inode. Its pages are allocated and freed as necessary under standard B+-tree indexing. The key for the B+-tree is the byte offset of the IAG page.

AG Free Inode List

The AG Free Inode List solves the reverse lookup problem.

In order to reduce the overhead of extending or truncating the aggregate, JFS will set a maximum number of Allocation Groups allowed per aggregate. Therefore, there will be a fixed number of AG Free Inode List headers. The header for the list is in the control page of the Inode Allocation Map. The nth entry is the header for a doubly-linked list of all Inode Allocation Map entries (IAGs) with free inodes contained in the nth AG.

The IAG number is used as the index in the list. A-1 indicates the end of the list. Each IAG control section contains forward and backward pointers for the list. The definition for describing the AG Free Inode List is in struct dinomap_t, in the linux\include\linux\JFS\JFS_imap.h file.

IAG Free List

The IAG Free List solves the problem of the free inode number lookup. It allows JFS to find the IAG without any corresponding allocated inode extents. The definition for describing the IAG Free list is in struct inomap_t, in the linux\include\linux\JFS\JFS_dinode.h file.

Fileset Allocation Map Inodes

The Fileset Allocation Map Inodes in the Aggregate Inode Table are a special type of inode. Since they represent the fileset, they are the "super-inode" for the fileset. Instead of the normal inode data, they contain some fileset-specific information in the top half of the inode. They also track the location of the Fileset Inode Allocation Map in its B+-tree. The structure is defined by struct dinode_t in the linux\include\linux\JFS\JFS_dinode.h file.

Every JFS object is represented by an inode. Inodes contain the object-specific information such as time stamps, file type (regular vs. directory), etc. They also "contain" a B+-tree to record the allocation of the extents.

Note specifically that all JFS meta-data structures (except for the super-block) are represented as "files." By using the inode structure for this data, the data format (on-disk layout) becomes inherently extensible.

Directories map user-specified names to the inodes allocated for files and directories, and form the traditional name hierarchy. Files contain user data, and there are no restrictions or formats implied in the data. That is, user data is treated by JFS as an uninterpreted byte stream. Extent-based addressing structures rooted in the inode are used for mapping file data to disk blocks. A "file" is allocated in sequences of extents. Together, the aggregate's super-block and disk allocation map, file descriptor and inode map, inodes, directories, and addressing structures comprise the JFS control structures, i.e., its meta-data.

Design Features that Distinguish JFS from Other File Systems

JFS was designed to have journaling fully integrated from the start, rather than as an addition to an existing file system. In addition, a number of other features in JFS distinguish it from other file systems.

▼ Internal JFS (potential) limits

JFS is a full 64-bit file system. All of the appropriate file system structure fields are 64 bits in size. This allows JFS to support both large files and large partitions.

▼ Removable media

JFS will not support diskettes as an underlying file system device.

▼ File system size

The minimum file system (fileset) size supported by JFS is 16MB. The maximum file system size is a function of the file system (fileset) block size and the maximum number of blocks supported by the file system meta-data structures. JFS will support a maximum file system size of 512TB (with block size of 512 bytes) to 4PB (with block size of 4KB).

▼ File size

The maximum file size is the largest file size that VFS framework supports. For example, if the framework only supports 32-bits, then this limits the file size.

▼ JFS extensively uses B+-trees as extent-based addressing structures. Some of the areas where JFS uses B+-trees are in the allocation of extents. A file is represented by an inode containing the root of the B+-tree which describes the extent containing user data. An extent is a sequence of contiguous aggregate blocks allocated to a JFS object as a unit. Each extent is wholly contained within a single aggregate.

There are two values needed to define an extent: its length and its address. The length is measured in units of aggregate block size. JFS uses a 24-bit value to represent the length of an extent, so an extent can range in size from 1 to $(2^{24}-1)$ aggregate blocks. The address is the address of the first block of the extent, in units of the aggregate blocks (it is the block offset from the beginning of the aggregate). An extent may span multiple Allocation Groups. These extents are indexed in a B+-tree for optimum performance of inserting new extents, locating particular extents, etc.

With a 512 byte aggregate block size (the smallest allowable), the maximum extent is $512 * (2^{24}-1)$ bytes long (slightly under 8GB). With a 4096-byte aggregate block size (the largest allowable), the maximum extent is $4096 * (2^{24}-1)$ bytes long (slightly under 64GB). These limits only apply to a single extent. In no way do they have any limiting effects on overall file size.

An extent-based file system combined with a user-specified aggregate block size does not allow JFS to have separate support for internal fragmentation. The user can configure the aggregate with a small aggregate block size (e.g., 512 bytes) to minimize internal fragmentation for aggregates with a large number of small size files.

In general, the allocation policy for JFS tries to maximize contiguous allocation by allocating a minimum contiguous allocation, i.e., allocating a minimum number of extents with each extent as large and contiguous as possible. This allows for large I/O transfers, resulting in improved performance.

A B+-tree sorted by name is used to improve the ability to locate a specific directory entry.

JFS uses extent-based addressing structures, along with aggressive block allocation policies, to produce compact, efficient, and scalable structures for mapping logical offsets within files to physical addresses on disk. An extent, as mentioned earlier, is a sequence of contiguous blocks allocated to a file as a unit and is described by a triple, consisting of logical offset/ length/physical. The addressing structure is a B+-tree, populated with extent descriptors (triples), rooted in the inode, and keyed by logical offset within the file.

JFS's Further Extensive Use of B+-Trees

This section describes the B+-tree data structure used for file layout. B+-trees were selected to increase the performance of reading and writing extents, the most common operations JFS will have to do. B+-trees also provide an efficient append or insert of an extent in a file.

Less commonly, JFS will need to traverse an entire B+-tree when removing a file to ensure that JFS will remove the blocks used for the B+-tree as well as the file data. The B+-tree is also efficient for traversal.

An extent allocation descriptor (xad structure) describes the extent and adds two more fields needed for representing files: an offset, describing the logical byte address the extent represents, and a flags field. The extent allocation descriptor structure is defined in linux\include\JFS\JFS_xtree.h, struct xad.

There is one generic B+-tree index structure for all index objects in JFS except for directories. The data being indexed will depend on the object. The B+-tree is keyed by the offset of xad of data being described by the tree.The entries are sorted by the offsets of the xad structures. An xad structure is an entry in a node of a B+-tree.

Once the eight xad structures in the inode are filled, an attempt will be made to use the last "quadrant" of the inode for more xad structures. If the INLINEEA bit is set in the di_mode field of the inode, then the last quadrant of the inode is available. Once all of the available xad structures in the inodes are used, the B+-tree must be split.

The bottom of the second section of a disk inode contains a data descriptor which tells what is stored in the second half of the inode. The second half could contain in-line data for the file if it is small enough. If the file data won't fit in the in-line data space for the inode, it will be contained in extents, and the inode will contain the root node of the B+-tree. The header will indicate how many xads are in use and how many are available.

Generally, the inode will contain eight xad structures for the root of the B+-tree. If there are eight or fewer extents for the file, then these xad structures are also a leaf node of the B+-tree, and will describe the extents. Otherwise, the xad structures in the inode will point to either the leaves or internal nodes of the B+-tree.

Leaf Nodes

JFS allocates 4KB of disk space for a *leaf node* of the B+-tree. A leaf node is an array of xad entries with a header. The header points to the first free xad entry in the node, and all xad entries following that one are not allocated. The eight xad entries are copied from the inode to the leaf node, and the header is initialized to point to the ninth entry as the first free entry. Then JFS will update the root of the B+-tree into the inode's first xad structure, which will point to the newly allocated leaf node.

The offset for this new xad structure will be the offset of the first entry in the leaf node. The header in the inode will be updated to indicate that now only one xad is being used for the B+-tree. The header also needs to be updated to indicate that the inode now contains the pure root of the B+-tree.

As new extents are added to the file, they will continue to be added to the same leaf node in order until the node is filled. At that point, a new 4KB of disk space will be allocated for another leaf node and the second xad structure from the inode will be set to point to this newly allocated node. This will continue until all eight xad structures in the inode are filled, at which time another split of the B+-tree will occur. This split will create internal nodes of the B+-tree which are used purely to route the searches of the tree.

Internal Nodes

JFS allocates 4KB of disk space for an *internal node* of the B+-tree. An internal node looks the same as a leaf node. As with leaf nodes, the eight xad entries are copied from the inode to the internal node, the header is initialized to point to the ninth and then JFS will update the root of the B+-tree by making the inode's first xad structure point to the newly allocated internal inode.

The header in the inode will be updated to indicate that only one xad is being used for the B+-tree. The file linux\include\linux\JFS\JFS_xtree.h describes the header for the root of the B+-tree in struct xtpage_t. The file linux\include\linux\JFS\JFS_btree.h is the header for an internal node or a leaf node in struct btpage_t.

Variable Block Size

JFS supports block sizes of 512, 1024, 2048, and 4096 bytes on a per-file system basis, allowing users to optimize space utilization based on their application environment. Smaller block sizes reduce the amount of internal fragmentation within files and directories and are more space efficient. However, small blocks can increase path length, since block allocation activities may occur more often than if a large block size were used. The default block size is 4096 bytes since performance, rather than space utilization, is generally the primary consideration for server systems.

JFS dynamically allocates space for disk inodes as required, freeing the space when it is no longer needed. This support avoids the traditional approach of reserving a fixed amount of space for disk inodes at the time of file system creation, thus eliminating the need for users to estimate the maximum number of files and directories that a file system will contain. Additionally, this support decouples disk inodes from fixed disk locations.

Directory Organization

Two different directory organizations are provided with JFS. The first organization is used for small directories and stores the directory contents within the directory's inode. This eliminates the need for separate directory block I/O as well as the need to allocate separate storage. Up to eight entries may be stored in-line within the inode, excluding the self(.) and parent(..) directory entries, which are stored in separate areas.

The second organization is used for larger directories and represents each directory as a B+-tree keyed on name. A Linux directory, like any Unix directory, is an association between the file leafnames and inode numbers. A file's inode number can be found using the "-i" switch to ls. This organization provides faster directory lookup, insertion, and deletion capabilities when compared to traditional unsorted directory organizations.

JFS's Support for both Sparse[2] and Dense Files

JFS supports both sparse and dense files, on a per-file system basis.

Sparse files allow data to be written to random locations within a file without instantiating previously unwritten intervening file blocks. The file size reported is the highest byte that has been written to, but the actual allocation of any given block in the file does not occur until a write operation is performed on that block. For example, suppose a new file is created in a file system designated for sparse files. An application writes a block of data to block 100 in the file. JFS will report the size of this file as 100 blocks, although only one block of disk space has been allocated to it. If the application next reads block 50 of the file, JFS will return a block of zero-filled bytes. Suppose the application then writes a block of data to block 50 of the file. JFS will still report the size of this file as 100 blocks, and now two blocks of disk space have been allocated to it. Sparse files are of

---

2   We store all indexes in memory to achieve the best query performance. In this case, a sparse index on S.B is not as good as a dense index, because not all keys appear in the sparse index, and we may have to fetch a data block for each R.B value, even if it is not in the sparse index on S.B.

interest to applications that require a large logical space but only use a (small) subset of this space.

For dense files, disk resources are allocated to cover the file size. In the above example, the first write would cause 100 blocks of disk space to be allocated to the file. A read operation on any block that has been implicitly written to will return a block of zero-filled bytes, just as in the case of the sparse file.

AGGREGATES AND FILESETS

In JFS parlance there is a notion of aggregates and file sets. In this section we will understand what they are.

Files

A file is represented by an inode containing the root of a B+-tree, which describes the extents containing user data.

The B+-tree is indexed by the offset of the extents.

Directory

In JFS a directory is a journaled meta-data file.

A Linux directory, like any Unix directory, is an association between the file leafnames and inode numbers. A file's inode number can be found using the "-i" switch to ls.

A directory is composed of directory entries which indicate the objects contained in the directory. A directory entry links a name to an inode number. The specified inode describes the object with the specified name. In order to improve the ability to locate a specific directory entry, a B+-tree sorted by name is used.

The directory inode's di_size field represents just the leaf pages of the directory B+-tree. When the leaf node of the directory is contained within the inode, the di_size field's value is 256. A directory will not contain specific entries for self (".") and parent (".."). Instead, these will be represented in the inode itself. Self is the directory's own inode number. Parent will be a special field in the inode, idotdot, struct dtroot_t, in the linux\include\linux\JFS\JFS_dtree.h file.

The directory inode will contain the root of its B+-tree in a similar manner to a normal file. However, this B+-tree will be keyed by name. The leaf nodes of a directory B+-tree will contain the directory entry and will be keyed from the complete name of the entry.

The directory B+-tree will use suffix compression for the last internal nodes of the B+-tree. The rest of the internal nodes will use the same compressed suffix. Suffix compression truncates the name to just enough characters to distinguish the current entry from the previous entry.

Logs

JFS logs are maintained in each aggregate and are used to record information about operations on meta-data. The log has a format that is set by the file system creation utility. A single log may be used simultaneously by multiple mounted filesets within the aggregate.

Several aspects of log-based recovery are of interest. First, JFS only logs operations on meta-data, so replaying the log only restores the consistency of structural relationships and resource allocation states within the file system. It does not log file data or recover the data to a consistent state. Consequently, some file data may be lost or stale after recovery, therefore customers with a critical need for data consistency should use synchronous I/O.

Logging is not particularly effective in the face of media errors. Specifically, an I/O error during the write to disk of the log or meta-data means that a time-consuming and potentially intrusive full integrity check is required after a system crash to restore the file system to a consistent state. This implies that bad block relocation is a key feature of any storage manager or device residing below JFS.

JFS logging semantics are such that, when a file system operation involving changes to meta-data (e.g., unlink()) returns a successful return code, the effects of the operation have been committed to the file system and will be seen even if the system crashes. For example, once a file has been successfully removed, it remains removed and will not reappear if the system crashes and is restarted.

This logging style introduces a synchronous write to the log disk into each inode or VFS (virtual file system) operation that modifies meta-data. (For the database mavens, this is a redo-only, physical after-image, write-ahead logging protocol using a no-steal buffer policy.) In terms of performance, this compares well with many non-journaling file systems that rely upon multiple synchronous meta-data writes for consistency. However, there is a performance disadvantage when compared to other journaling file systems, such as Veritas VxFS and Transarc Episode, which use different logging styles and lazily write log data to disk. In the server environment, where multiple concurrent operations are performed, this performance cost is reduced by group commit, which combines multiple synchronous write operations into a single write operation. The logging style of JFS has been improved over time and now provides asynchronous logging, which increases performance of the file system.

The File Structure and Access Control

If files are to be shared among various users in a way which can be flexibly controlled, various forms of safeguards are desirable. These include the following:

▼ Safety from someone masquerading as another person.

■ Safety from accidents or maliciousness by someone who is specifically permitted controlled access.

■ Safety from accidents or maliciousness by someone who is specifically denied access.

- ■ Safety from self-inflicted accidents.

- ■ Total privacy, if needed, with access only by one user or set of users.

- ■ Safety from hardware or system software failures.

- ■ Security of system safeguards themselves from tampering by non-authorized users.

- ▲ Safeguard against the overzealous application of other safeguards.

In later chapters of this book we shall analyze how these safeguards are implemented as a general concept in Linux and in individual file systems available for it.

CHAPTER 9

ReiserFS for Linux

One of the earliest journaling file systems for Linux was ReiserFS. This project was started by a remarkable person, Hans Reiser, a young Ph.D. in computer science. Hans Reiser is a harsh critic of mediocrity in operating system design and software design in general. As a strong believer in the thorough implementation of excellent design, he felt compelled to start his project as proof of his ideas about file systems. The result, ReiserFS, is remarkable most of all for its scientific and intellectual approach to design and programming. However, its biggest shortcoming is its poor interaction with other Linux kernel components (like NFS, for instance). Still, ReiserFS has now been in use for a few years and many users are quite satisfied with it, for example, the mp3.com Web site. The SuSE distribution was ReiserFS's earliest adopter and has been supporting it since release 6.2 of SuSE Linux.

The main goal of ReiserFS is to provide reasonably fast recovery after a crash, and to have transactional file system meta-data updates. ReiserFS is fast, especially for small files and also for directories with many files in them. One of the future goals is to have write-ahead logging at least as fast as the original file system with preserve lists turned on. In this chapter we will get to know the details of the ReiserFS design and concepts as well as more practical issues, such as installation, administration, etc.

THE FILE SYSTEM NAME SPACE

One of ReiserFS's central concepts is the unified name space. Ideally, Hans Reiser would like to create a file system composed of objects that are both "files" and directories.

In this example, bmoshe is a user, bmoshe/mail is an inbox, bmoshe/mail/Message-ID/20000615091245.A2500@moshebar.com is an e-mail, and bmoshe/mail/Message-ID/20000615091245.A2500@moshebar.com/to might be the To: field of the header of that e-mail. Combined with groupings, I should be able to look for:

    mail/[from/Avivit phones]

to find all of Avivit's e-mails on phones.

Such a unified and closed name space potentially has a big impact on the ease of programming, especially object-oriented (OO) programming. As you can see from the line below, every object can naturally be thought of as its own NamingContext, with its fields/accessor and mutator methods as the subnames. So, to paraphrase the above example:

    moshe.getMailBox().getMessageByID("20000615091245.A2500@moshebar.com")

Those familiar with the Plan 9 and Inferno operating systems might find similarities, and rightly so. A unified name space, such as that proposed by Hans Reiser, is nothing but an "everything-is-a-file" concept, turned upside down.

There are, however, still some conceptual anomalies in his proposed abstraction of a file system. First of all, the problem with relying on attributes is that they break closure, since attributes are not objects. In fact, they are not even object fields (although they may be exposures of such fields).

Unifying Reiser's groupings and orderings may prove a difficult task. As Reiser puts it, hypersemantics attempts "to pick a manageably few columns which cover all possible needs. Generalization, aggregation, classification, and membership correspond to the is-a, has-property, is-an-instance-of, and is-a-member-of columns, respectively." The problem, Reiser pointed out, is that you must know the relationship in order to be able to search for it. Using Reiser's example, you can't find Santa Claus without reindeer, unless you know how to decompose the propulsion-provider-for relationship into the above canonical relationships.

So, as you can see, name space unification and closure still remain to be explored. As such, using ReiserFS for a production system might prove reliable and efficient, but you will still be using a proof-of-concept file system or a research-and-development tool, and not a product by any means.

Let's now explore some more of ReiserFS's technical design concepts.

BLOCK ALIGNMENTS OF FILE BOUNDARIES

ReiserFS aligns file boundaries with blocks on the disk. It does so for a number of reasons: to minimize the number of blocks a file is spread across (which is especially beneficial for multiple block files when locality of reference across files is poor); to avoid wasting disk and buffer space in storing every less-than-fully-packed block; to not waste I/O bandwidth with every access to a less-than-fully-packed block when locality of reference is present; to decrease the average number of block fetches required to access every file in a directory; and it results in simpler code.

The simpler code of block aligning file systems follows from not needing to create a layering to distinguish the units of the disk controller and buffering algorithms from the units of space allocation, and also from not having to optimize the packing of nodes, as is done in balanced tree algorithms.

Hans Reiser tried from the beginning to aggregate small files in a way so as to avoid wasting disk space. The simplest solution was to aggregate all small files in a directory, into either a file or the directory. But any aggregation into a file or directory wastes part of the last block in the aggregation. What does one do if there are only a few small files in a directory—aggregate them into the parent of the directory? What if there are only a few small files in a directory at first, and then there are many small files—how does the OS decide what level to aggregate them at, and when to take them back from a parent of a directory and store them directly in the directory?

Of course, this problem is closely related to the balancing of nodes in a balanced tree. The balanced tree approach, by using an ordering of files which are then dynamically aggregated into nodes at a lower level, rather than a static aggregation or grouping, avoids this set of questions.

In the ReiserFS approach, both files and filenames are stored in a balanced tree. This, along with small files, directory entries, inodes, and the tail ends of large files causes everything to be more efficiently packed as a result of relaxing the requirements of block alignment, and eliminating the use of a fixed space allocation for inodes.

The body of large files is stored in unformatted nodes that are attached to the tree but are isolated from the effects of possible shifting by the balancing algorithms. Neither NTFS nor XFS aggregate files: they block align files, although they do store small files in the statically allocated block address fields of inodes if they are small enough to fit there.

Semantics (files), packing (blocks/nodes), caching (read-ahead sizes, etc.), and the hardware interfaces of disks (sectors) and paging (pages) all have different granularity issues associated with them. Understand that the optimal granularity of these often differs, and abstracting them into separate layers in which the granularity of one layer does not unintentionally impact other layers can improve space/time performance. ReiserFS innovates in that its semantic layer often conveys an un-granulated ordering to the other layers rather than one granulated by file boundaries. While reading the algorithms of ReiserFS's code, the reader is encouraged to note the areas in which ReiserFS needs to go further.

BALANCED TREES AND LARGE FILE I/O

It is quite complex to understand the interplay between I/O efficiency and block size for larger files, and space does not allow a systematic review of traditional approaches. ReiserFS has the following architectural weaknesses that stem directly from the overhead of repacking to save space and increase block size:

▼ When the tail (files less than 4K are all tail) of a file grows large enough to occupy an entire node by itself, it is removed from the formatted node(s) it resides in, and converted into an unformatted node.

■ A tail that is smaller than one node may be spread across two nodes, which requires more I/O to read if the locality of reference is poor.

■ Aggregating multiple tails into one node introduces the separation of the file body from tail, which reduces read performance. For ReiserFS files near to the node in size the effect can be significant.

▲ When you add one byte to a file or tail that is not the last item in a formatted node, then on average half of the whole node is shifted in memory. If any of your applications perform I/O in such a way that they generate many small unbuffered writes, ReiserFS will make you pay a high price for not being able to buffer the I/O.

Most applications that create substantial file system load employ effective I/O buffering, often simply as a result of using the I/O functions in the standard C libraries.

By avoiding accesses in small blocks/extents, ReiserFS improves I/O efficiency. Extent-based file systems such as VFS, and write-clustering systems such as ext2fs, are not so effective in applying these techniques that they choose to use 512-byte blocks rather than

1K blocks as their defaults. Ext2fs reports a 20 percent speed-up when 4K rather than 1K blocks are used, but the authors of ext2fs advise the use of 1K blocks to avoid wasting space.

There are a number of worthwhile large file optimizations that have not been added to either ext2fs or ReiserFS, and both file systems are somewhat primitive in this regard, ReiserFS being the more primitive of the two. Large files simply were not my research focus, and this being a small research project, I did not implement the many well-known techniques for enhancing large file I/O. The buffering algorithms are probably more crucial than any other component in large file I/O, and partly out of a desire for a fair comparison of the approaches, I have not modified these. No significant optimizations for large files have been devised in ReiserFS, beyond increasing the block size. Except for the size of the blocks, there is not a large inherent difference between:

▼   The cost of adding a pointer to an unformatted node to a tree plus writing the node.

▲   Adding an address field to an inode plus writing the block. It is likely that, except for block size, the primary determinants of high performance large file access are orthogonal to the decision of whether to use balanced tree algorithms for small and medium sized files.

For large files there is an advantage to not having the tree more balanced than the tree formed by an inode which points to a triple indirect block. There is performance overhead due to the memory bandwidth cost of balancing nodes for small files.

Serialization and Consistency

The issue of ensuring recoverability with minimal serialization and data displacement inevitably dominate high performance design. Let's define the two extremes in serialization so that the reason for this can be made clear. Consider the relative speed of a set of I/Os in which every block request in the set is fed to the elevator algorithms[1] of the kernel and serially to the disk drive firmware, each request awaiting the completion of the previous request. Now consider the other extreme, in which all block requests are fed to the elevator algorithms together, so that they are all sorted and performed close to their sorted order. The un-serialized extreme may be an order of magnitude faster due to the cost of rotations and seeks. Unnecessarily serializing I/O prevents the elevator algorithm from doing its job of placing all of the I/O's in their layout sequence rather than chronological sequence. Most high performance design centers around making I/O's in the order they are laid out on disk, and in the order that the I/O's will want to be issued.

ReiserFS employs a new scheme called `preserve lists` for ensuring recoverability, which avoids overwriting old meta-data by writing the meta-data nearby.

---

1   The elevator algorithms within the kernel schedule I/O operations to and from the disk(s).

Tree Definitions

Balanced trees are designed with a set of keys assumed to be defined by the application, and the purpose of the tree design is to optimize searching with these keys. In ReiserFS, the purpose of the tree is to optimize the reference locality and space-efficient packing of objects, and the keys are defined according to that algorithm. Keys are used in place of inode numbers in the file system, thus substituting the mapping of keys to a node location (the internal nodes) rather than a mapping of an inode number to a file location. Keys are longer than inode numbers, but fewer of them need to be cached when more than one file is stored in a node.

ReiserFS trees require that a filename be resolved one component at a time. It is an interesting topic for future research whether this is necessary or optimal. It is a more complex issue than one might realize. Directory at a time lookup accomplishes a form of compression, makes mounting other name spaces and file system extensions simpler, makes security simpler, and makes future enhanced semantics simpler. Since small files typically lead to large directories, it is fortunate that, as a natural consequence of our use of tree algorithms, our directory mechanisms are much more effective for very large directories than most other file systems. The tree has three node types: internal nodes, formatted nodes, and unformatted nodes. The contents of internal and formatted nodes are sorted in the order of their keys. (Unformatted nodes contain no keys.)

Internal nodes consist of pointers to subtrees separated by their delimiting keys. The key that precedes a pointer to a subtree is a duplicate of the first key in the first formatted node of that subtree. Internal nodes exist solely to allow a determination of which formatted node contains the item corresponding to a key. ReiserFS starts at the root node, examines its contents and can determine which subtree contains the item corresponding to the desired key. From the root node ReiserFS descends into the tree, branching at each node, until it reaches the formatted node containing the desired item.

The first (bottom) level of the tree consists of unformatted nodes, the second level consists of formatted nodes, and all levels above consist of internal nodes. The highest level contains the root node. The number of levels is increased as needed by adding a new root node at the top of the tree.

All paths from the root of the tree to all formatted leaves are equal in length. The paths to unformatted leaves are also equal in length but are one node longer than paths to formatted leaves. This equality in path length, and the high fanout it provides, is vital to high performance.

Formatted nodes consist of items, of which are four types: direct, indirect, directory, and stat data items. All items contain a unique key that is used to sort and find the item. Direct items contain the tails of files, which are the last part of the file (the last file_size modulo FS block size of a file). Indirect items consist of pointers to unformatted nodes. All but the tail of the file is contained in the unformatted nodes. Directory items contain the key of the first directory entry in the item followed by a number of directory entries.

A file consists of a set of indirect items followed by a set of up to two direct items, with the two direct items representing an example of a tail split across two nodes. If a tail is larger than the maximum size of a file that can fit into a formatted node, but is smaller than the unformatted node size (4K), then it is stored in an unformatted node, and a pointer to it, plus a count of the space used, is stored in an indirect item.

Directories consist of a set of directory items, which, in turn, consist of a set of directory entries. Directory entries contain the filename and the key of the file which is named. There is never more than one item of the same item type from the same object stored in a single node (there is no reason one would want to use two separate items rather than combining). The first item of a file or directory contains its stat data.

When performing balancing, and when analyzing the packing of the node and its two neighbors, ReiserFS ensures that the three nodes cannot be compressed into two nodes.

Ordering Within the Tree

Some key definition decisions depend on usage patterns, and this means that someday one will select from several key definitions when creating the file system. For example, consider the decision of whether to pack all directory entries together at the front of the file system, or to pack the entries near the files they name. For large file usage patterns one should pack all directory items together, since systems with such usage patterns are effective in caching the entries for all directories. For small files the name should be near the file. Similarly, for large files the stat data should be stored separately from the body, either with the other stat data from the same directory, or with the directory entry.

It is feasible to pack an object completely independently of its semantics using these algorithms, and there may be applications for which a packing different than that determined by object names is more appropriate.

The Structure of a Key

Each file item has a key with a structure: locality_id, object_id, offset, and uniqueness. The locality_id is, by default, the object_id of the parent directory. The object_id is the unique id of the file, and is set to the first unused object_id when the object is created. This can result in successive object creations in a directory being adjacently packed, which is advantageous for many usage patterns. For files, the offset is within the logical object of the first byte of the item. In version 0.2 all directory entries had their own individual keys stored with them and each were distinct items. In the current version, ReiserFS stores one key in the item that is the key of the first entry, and computes each entry's key as needed from this one key. For directories, the offset key component is the first four bytes of the filename; you may think of this as a lexicographic rather than numeric offset. For directory items, the uniqueness field differentiates identical filename entries in the first four bytes. For all items it indicates the item type and for the leftmost item in a buffer, it indicates whether the preceding item in the tree is of the same type and object. Placing this information in the key is useful when analyzing balancing conditions, but increases key length for non-directory items, and is a questionable architectural feature.

Every file has a unique object_id, but this cannot be used for finding the object, only keys are used for that. Object_ids merely ensure that keys are unique. If you never use the ReiserFS features that change an object's key then it is immutable, otherwise it is mutable. (This feature aids support for NFS daemons, etc.) Developers spent some time debating whether the use of mutable keys for identifying an object had deleterious long-term architectural consequences. In the end, Hans Reiser decided it was acceptable if there was a requirement that any object recording a key should possess a method for updating the copy of itself.

This is the architectural price of avoiding having to cache a map of the object_id to a location that might have very poor locality of reference due to object_ids not changing with object semantics. ReiserFS packs an object with the packing locality of the directory it was first created in unless the key is explicitly changed. It remains packed there even if it is unlinked from the directory. It will not move it from the locality where it was created without an explicit request, unlike some other file systems which store all multiple link files together and pay the cost of moving them from their original locations when a second link occurs. A file linked with multiple directories should at least get the locality reference benefits of one of those directories.

In summary, this approach first places files from the same directory together, and then places directory entries from the same directory together, with the stat data for the directory. Note that there is no interleaving of objects from different directories in the ordering, and that all directory entries from the same directory are contiguous. This does not actually pack the files of small directories with common parents together, and does not employ the full partial ordering in determining the linear ordering. It merely uses parent directory information. The appropriate place for employing full tree structure knowledge is in the implementation of an FS cleaner, not in the dynamic algorithms.

The balancing of nodes in the tree happens according to the following ordered priorities:

1. Minimize the number of nodes used.
2. Minimize the number of nodes affected by the balancing operation.
3. Minimize the number of uncached nodes affected by the balancing operation.
4. If shifting to another formatted node is necessary, maximize the bytes shifted by priority.
5. Is based on the assumption that the location of an insertion of bytes into the tree is an indication of the likely future location of an insertion, and that policy 4 will, on average, reduce the number of formatted nodes affected by future balance operations.

There are also more subtle effects. If you randomly place nodes next to each other, and have a choice between those nodes being somewhat efficiently packed or packed to an extreme—either well or poorly packed—you are more likely to be able to combine more of the nodes if you choose the policy of extremism. Extremism is a virtue in space-efficient node packing. The maximum shift policy is not applied to internal nodes, as extremism is not a virtue in time-efficient internal node balancing.

BUFFERING AND THE PRESERVE LIST

Version 0.2 of ReiserFS implemented a system of write ordering that tracked all shifting of items in the tree. It ensured that no node that an item had been shifted from was written before the node that had received the item was written. This is necessary as it will prevent a system crash causing the loss of an item that might not be recently created. This tracking approach worked, and the overhead it imposed was not measurable by our benchmarks. When, in the next version, we changed to partially shifting items and increased the number of item types, this code grew out of control in its complexity. I decided to replace it with a scheme that was far simpler to code and was also more effective in typical usage patterns. This scheme is as follows.

If an item is shifted from a node, change the block that its buffer will be written to. Change it to the nearest free block to the old block's left neighbor, and rather than freeing it, place the old block number on a "preserve list.'. (Saying nearest is slightly simplistic, in that the blocknr assignment function moves from the left neighbor in the direction of increasing block numbers.) When a "moment of consistency" is achieved, free all of the blocks on the preserve list. A moment of consistency occurs when there are no nodes in memory into which objects have been shifted. If disk space runs out, force a moment of consistency to occur. This is sufficient to ensure that the file system is recoverable. Note that during the large file benchmarks, the preserve list was freed several times in the middle of the benchmark. The percentage of buffers preserved is small in practice except during deletes, and you can arrange for moments of consistency to occur as frequently as necessary.

This approach may not be better than the Soft Updates approach of BSD or by ReiserFS in version 0.2. However, those tracking orders of writes are more complex than this approach for balanced trees, which partially shifts items. ReiserFS might shift back to the old algorithm in the future, however, as preserve lists substantially hamper performance for files in the 1-10K size range.

ReiserFS Structures

The ReiserFS tree has a maximum tree height, called Max_Height = N (current default value for N = 5). The tree resides in the disk blocks. Each disk block that belongs to the ReiserFS tree has a block head.

Everything in the file system is stored as a set of items. Each item has its item_head. The item_head contains the key of the item, its free space (for indirect items), and specifies the location of the item itself within the block.

The disk block containing the internal node of the tree is the place for keys and pointers to disk blocks and looks like this:

Block_Head	Key 0	Key 1	Key 2	--	Key N	Pointer 0	Pointer 1	Pointer 2	--	Pointer N	Pointer N+1	........Free Space........

Within the tree, each leaf—each with n items and their corresponding headers, has a corresponding disk block with the following:

Block_Head	IHead	IHead	IHead	--	IHead	Pointer	........Free	Item	--	Item	Item	Item
	0	1	2		N	0	Space........	N		2	1	0

There are also disk blocks containing an unformatted node of the above-mentioned tree. These kinds of disk blocks contain data and thus look structurally empty from the outside (although they may contain data):

....

The maximum number of objects in a ReiserFS namespace (including files and directories) are calculated this way:

$2^{32}-4$

which equals the maximum number of 4,294,967,292.

Internal Node Structures   In the following table, you can find the structure of the inode block as stored on disk. The ReiserFS inode is just one node of the ReiserFS tree, storing keys and pointers to disks data blocks:

Block_Head	Key	Key	Key	--	Key	Pointer	Pointer	Pointer	--	Pointer	Pointer	........Free
	0	1	2		N	0	1	2		N	N+1	Space........

Here you get the description of the *key* structure; notice how all variable are 32bit in size:

Field Name	Type	Size (in bytes)	Description
k_dir_id	__u32	4	ID of the parent directory
k_object_id	__u32	4	ID of the object (also it is the number of inode)
k_offset	__u32	4	Offset from beginning of the object to the current byte of the object
k_uniqueness	__u32	4	Type of the item (Stat Data = 0, direct = -1, InDirect = -2, Directory = 500)
	total	16	(6) 8 bytes for internal nodes; (22) 24 bytes for leaf nodes

Finally, here is the disk_child structure, which is the actual pointer to the disk block:

Field Name	Type	Size (in bytes)	Description
dc_block_number	unsigned long	4	Disk child's block number.
dc_size	unsigned short	2	Disk child's used space.
	total	6	(6) 8 bytes

Leaf Node Structures   Now, we continue analyzing the disk block, which is a node of the ReiserFS tree and stores items and their headers, as shown in the following table. There are four types of items: stat data item, directory item, indirect item, and direct item, which are in this case self-explanatory.

Block_Head	IHead 0	IHead 1	IHead 2	- -	IHead N	Pointer 0	........Free Space........	Item N	- -	Item 2	Item 1	Item 0

Again, we go through the individual objects, starting with the block_head structure in the disk block:

Field Name	Type	Size (in bytes)	Description
blk_level	unsigned short	2	Level of block in the tree (1-leaf; 2,3, 4,...-internal
blk_nr_item	unsigned short	2	Number of keys in an Internal block, or number of items in a leaf block.
blk_free_space	unsigned short	2	Block free space in bytes
blk_right_delim_key	struct key	16	Right delimiting key for this block (for Leaf nodes only)
total		**22**	**(22) 24 bytes for leaf nodes**

Each item head contains various variables that allow the item to know its exact position in the item tree and get some information about the space used, as well as free space left in the item.

Field Name	Type	Size (in bytes)	Description
ih_key	struct key	16	Key to search the item. All item headers is sorted by this key
u.ih_free_space u.ih_entry_count	__u16	2	Free space in the last unformatted node for an indirect item; 0xFFFF for a sirect item; 0xFFFF for a stat data item. The number of directory entries for a directory item.
ih_item_len	__u16	2	Total size of the item body
ih_item_location	__u16	2	An offset to the item body within the block
ih_reserved	__u16	2	Used by reiserfsck
	total	24	**24 bytes**
sd_mode	__u16	2	File type, permissions
sd_nlink	__u16	2	Number of hard links
sd_uid	__u16	2	Owner id

Field Name	Type	Size (in bytes)	Description
sd_gid	__u16	2	Group id
sd_size	__u32	4	File size
sd_atime	__u32	4	Time of last access
sd_mtime	__u32	4	Time file was last modified
sd_ctime	__u32	4	Time inode (stat data) was last changed (except changes to sd_atime and sd_mtime)
sd_rdev	__u32	4	Device
sd_first_direct_byte	__u32	4	Offset from the beginning of the file to the first byte of direct item of the file. (-1) for directory (1) for small files (file has direct items only) (>1) for big files (file has indirect and direct items) (-1) for big files (file has indirect, but has not direct item)
total		**32**	**32 bytes**

The directory object just contains filenames, which can be either small files or big files:

deHead 0	deHead 1	deHead 2	—	deHead N	**filename N**	—	**filename 2**	**filename 1**	**filename 0**

The small file is called the *direct item*, because it is addressable by just one pointer:

.......................Small File Body........................

Bigger files (those that require more than one disk block), need some pointer acrobatics to find all the subsequent blocks, and are therefore called *indirect items*:

unfPointer 0	unfPointer 1	unfPointer 2	—	unfPointer N

This needs some explanation. The unfPointer is a pointer (32bits) to an unformatted block containing the body of a big file. In the following table you see how the pointers find that unformatted block:

Field Name	Type	Size (in bytes)	Description
deh_offset	__u32	4	Third component of the directory entry key (all reiserfs_de_head sorted by this value)
deh_dir_id	__u32	4	Object_id of the parent directory of the object, that is referenced by directory entry

Field Name	Type	Size (in bytes)	Description
deh_objectid	__u32	4	Object_id of the object that is referenced by directory entry
deh_location	__u16	2	Offset of name in the whole item
deh_state	__u16	2	1) Entry contains stat data (for future) 2) Entry is hidden (unlinked)
total		**16**	**16 bytes**

Filename here represents the name of the file (array of bytes of variable length). The maximum length of filename = blocksize - 64 (for a 4K blocksize, the maximum name length is 4032 bytes).

USING THE TREE TO OPTIMIZE LAYOUT OF FILES

There are four levels at which layout optimization is performed:

▼ The mapping of logical block numbers to physical locations on disk.

■ The assigning of nodes to logical block numbers.

■ The ordering of objects within the tree.

▲ The balancing of the objects across the nodes they are packed into.

Physical Layout

The mapping of logical block numbers to physical locations on the disk is performed by the disk drive manufacturer for SCSI, and by the device driver for IDE drives. There can, of course, be a higher level of software like LVM, discussed in a previous chapter, which abstracts that mapping further. The logical block number to physical location mapping by the drive manufacturer is usually done using cylinders. The ReiserFS developers found that minimizing the distance in logical blocks of semantically adjacent nodes without tracking cylinder boundaries accomplishes an excellent approximation of optimizing according to actual cylinder boundaries. That simplicity also makes for a more elegant implementation.

Node Layout

When ReiserFS places nodes of the tree on the disk, it searches for the first empty block in the bitmap of used block numbers, which it finds by starting at the location of the left neighbour of the node in the tree ordering, and then moves in the direction it last moved in.

This was found, by experimentation, to be better than the following alternatives for the benchmarks:

1. Taking the first non-zero entry in the bitmap.

2. Taking the entry after the last one that was assigned in the direction last moved in (this was three percent faster for writes and 10-20% slower for subsequent reads).

3. Starting at the left neighbor and moving in the direction of the right neighbor. When changing block numbers for the purpose of avoiding the overwriting of sending nodes before shifted items reach the disk in their new recipient node (see description of preserve lists), the benchmarks employed were approximately ten percent faster than when starting the search from the left neighbor rather than the node's current block number, even though it adds significant overhead to determine the left neighbor (the current implementation risks I/O to read the parent of the left neighbor).

It used to be that ReiserFS could reverse direction when the end of the disk drive was reached. The developers checked to see if it made a difference which direction one moves in when allocating blocks to a file, and found it made a significant difference to always allocate in the increasing block number direction. This may be due to matching disk spin direction by allocating increasing block numbers.

Write-Ahead Logging

Most meta-data operations involve more than one block, and meta-data will usually be corrupted if only some of the blocks involved in an operation get updated. With write-ahead logging, blocks are written to a log before they are allowed to hit their real locations. After a crash, the log is replayed to bring the file system back to a consistent state. This replay is much faster than an fsck, and its time is bounded by the size of the log area instead of the size of the file system.

ReiserFS Journaling Features

Journaling requires some kind of logging and the serialization of that locking. That is why a journaled file system is necessarily slower than a nonlogging counterpart. Therefore, journaling requires some kind of fundamental operation to perform that logging and serialization. Let's look at what these are in ReiserFS.

Transactions Each transaction in the journal consists of a description block, followed by a number of data blocks and a commit block. The description and commit blocks contain a sequential list of the real disk locations for each log block. The log must preserve the order of updates, so if a writer logs blocks A, B, C, and D, and then A again, they will be ordered in the log as B, C, D, A.

While a block is in an uncommitted transaction, it must remain clean, and must have a reference count of at least one. Once a transaction has all its log blocks on disk, the real buffers are dirtied and released.

Batched Transactions I allow multiple transactions to be combined into a single atomic unit. So if transaction one logs blocks A, B, C and transaction two logs blocks A, C, and D, the resulting joined transaction would write a description block, then blocks B, A, C, and D, and then a commit block. This allows fewer total blocks to be written to the log, but increases the chance of file system changes being undone by a crash. There are a number of tuning parameters to control how and when transactions are batched together. Take a look at the tuning section for the details.

Asynchronous Commits This is an extension of the batched transactions. I allow a transaction to end without flushing all of its log blocks to disk. This adds a great deal of complexity, but makes it possible for operations to return faster, and release any locks they might hold. Bdflush takes care of forcing old asynchronous log blocks to disk.

New Blocks Can Die in the Cache If a block is allocated and then freed before being written to disk, or logged and then freed before its transaction is completed, the block is never written to the log or its real disk location. This is inherent in many file systems, but took a little work to get right in ReiserFS.

Selective Flushing This is actually more of a requirement than a feature. Many blocks (bitmaps, super-blocks, etc) tend to get logged over and over again. When a block is in an uncommitted transaction, it can't be dirtied, and can't be sent to disk. But before a log area can be reused, any transactions contained in it must have all their blocks flushed to their real locations.

Even if a multiply logged block could be flushed somehow, it has changed in relation to all the other blocks in the older transaction, and the meta-data could be corrupted after a crash. Instead of trying to flush blocks that will also be in future transactions, I force the future transaction's log blocks to disk. After a crash, log replay should make everything consistent.

This means that frequently logged blocks might only get written once per transaction to the log, and then once to their real location on file system unmount.

Data Block Logging Data blocks are logged when they are part of a direct to indirect item conversion. These conversions are done when small files grow beyond what can fit in a direct item, and on the mmap of files that contain direct items. Since the conversion is sometimes done to old data, I want to make sure the data won't be lost after a crash.

The problem is that once a block is in the log, you must continue logging it while there is any chance log replay will overwrite the block after a crash. So, mark_buffer_dirty is never called directly. Instead, a journal call exists to only log a block if it is in the current transaction, or in a transaction that might be replayed.

This is a performance hit on average size files with tails enabled, because many of the data blocks will be logged. Possible solutions include implementing packing on file close or mounting without tails enabled. The ReiserFS team will probably be looking into these and other ideas over the next few months.

Tuning

The size of the log area has the biggest effect on your performance. Make it too small, and you will have to flush blocks to their real locations too frequently. Make it too large and your replay times will be much too long.

How do you find the right size? Well, in beta1, you need to try many different ones until your benchmark gets as fast as it's going to get. Beta2 will have a mount option to add informational statements while flushing the real blocks. These should make tuning much easier.

The max transaction size, max batch size, and various time limits for how old things can get are also very important. It will be a while before I really have the chance to explore these.

ReiserFS Drops

Consider dividing a file or directory into drops, with each drop having a separate key, and no two drops from one file or directory occupying the same node without being compressed into one drop. The key for each drop is set to the key for the object (file or directory) plus the offset of the drop within the object. For directories the offset is lexicographic and by filename, for files it is numeric and in bytes. In the course of several file system versions, we have experimented with and implemented solid, liquid, and air drops. Solid drops were never shifted, and drops would only solidify when they occupied the entirety of a formatted node. Liquid drops are shifted in such a way that any liquid drop which spans a node fully occupies the space in its node. Like a physical liquid it is shiftable, but not compressible. Air drops merely meet the balancing condition of the tree.

ReiserFS 0.2 implemented solid drops for all but the tail of files. If a file was at least one node in size it would align the start of the file with the start of a node, block-aligning the file. This block alignment of the start of multi-drop files was a design error that wasted space. Even if the locality of reference is so poor as to make one not want to read parts of semantically adjacent files, if the nodes are near to each other then the cost of reading an extra block is thoroughly dwarfed by the cost of the seek and rotation to reach the first node of the file. As a result the block alignment saves little time, though the cost is significant space for 4-20K files.

ReiserFS with block alignment of multi-drop files and no indirect items experienced the following rather interesting behavior that was partially responsible for making it only 88% space-efficient for files that averaged 13K (the Linux kernel) in size. When the tail of a larger than 4K file was followed in the tree ordering by another file larger than 4K, since the drop before was solid and aligned, and the drop afterwards was solid and aligned, no matter what size the tail was, it occupied an entire node.

In the current version we place all but the tail of large files into a level of the tree reserved for full unformatted nodes, and create indirect items in the formatted nodes which point to the unformatted nodes. This is known in the database literature as the approach. This extra level added to the tree comes at the cost of making the tree less balanced (I consider the unformatted nodes pointed to as part of the tree) and increasing the maximum depth of the tree by one. For medium-sized files, the use of indirect items increases the cost of caching pointers by mixing data with them. The reduction in fanout often causes the read algorithms to fetch only one node at a time, as one waits to read the uncached indirect item before reading the node with the file data. There are more parents per file read with the use of indirect items than with internal nodes, as a direct result of reduced fanout due to mixing tails and indirect items in the node. The most serious flaw is that these reads of various nodes, necessary to the reading of the file, have additional rotations and seeks compared to drops. With my initial drop approach they are usually sequential in their disk layout, even the tail, and the internal node parent points to all of them in such a way that all of them that are contained by that parent or another internal node in cache can be requested at once in one sequential read. Non-sequential reads of nodes are more costly than sequential reads, and this single consideration dominates effective read optimization.

Unformatted nodes make file system recovery faster and less robust, in that one reads their indirect item instead of inserting it into the recovered tree, and one cannot read it to confirm that its contents are from the file that an indirect item says they are from. In this, they make ReiserFS similar to an inode-based system without logging.

A moderately better solution would have simply eliminated the requirement for placement of the start of multi-node files at the start of nodes, rather than introducing BLOBs, and have depended on the use of a file system cleaner to optimally pack the 80% of files that don't move frequently, using algorithms that move even solid drops. Yet that still leaves the problem of formatted nodes not being efficient for mmap() purposes (one must copy them before writing rather than merely modifying their page table entries, and memory bandwidth is expensive even if the CPU is cheap).

For this reason I have the following plan for the next version. I will have three trees: one tree maps keys to unformatted nodes, one tree maps keys to formatted nodes, and one tree maps keys to directory entries and stat data. This would seem to mean that to read a file and first access the directory entry and stat data, the unformatted node, and then the tail, one must hop long distances across the disk, going first to one tree and then the other. It took me two years to realize that it could be made to work. My plan is to interleave the nodes of the three trees according to the following algorithm:

Block numbers are assigned to nodes when the nodes are created, or preserved, and someday will be assigned when the cleaner runs. The choice of block number is based on first determining what other node it should be placed near, and then finding the nearest free block in the elevator's current direction. Currently we use the left neighbor of the node in the tree as the node it should be placed near.

The new scheme will continue to first determine the node it should be placed near, and then start the search for an empty block from that spot, but it will use a more complicated determination of what node to place it near. This new method will cause all nodes from the same packing locality to be near each other, will cause all directory entries and stat data to be grouped together within that packing locality, and will interleave formatted and unformatted nodes from the same packing locality. Pseudo-code is best for describing this.

```
/* for use by reiserfs_get_new_blocknrs when determining where in the bitmap to
start the search for a free block, and for use by read-ahead algorithm when
there are not enough nodes to the right and in the same packing locality for
packing locality reading ahead purposes */
get_logical_layout_left_neighbors_blocknr(key of current node)
{
/* Based on examination of current node key and type, find the virtual neighbor of that
node. */
    If body node
        if first body node of file
            if (node in tail tree whose key is less but is in same packing locality exists)
                return blocknr of such node with largest key
              else
                find node with largest key less than key of current node in stat_data tree
                    return its blocknr
          else
              return blocknr of node in body tree with largest key less than key
                  of current node
      else
          if tail node
           if (node in body tree belonging to same file as first tail of current node exists)
                  return its blocknr
          else if (node in tail tree with lesser delimiting key but same packing
                  locality exists)
                    return blocknr of such node with largest delimiting key
            else
                  return blocknr of node with largest key less than key of current node in
stat_data tree
      else /* is stat_data tree node */
          if stat_data node with lesser key from same packing locality exists
              return blocknr of such node with largest key
          else /* no node from same packing locality with lesser key exists */
}
/* for use by packing locality read-ahead */
get_logical_layout_right_neighbors_blocknr(key of current node)
{
    right-handed version of get_logical_layout_left_neighbors_blocknr logic
}
```

Code Complexity

I thought it appropriate to mention some of the notable effects of simple design decisions on our implementation's code length. When we changed our balancing algorithms to shift parts of items rather than only whole items, so as to pack nodes tighter, this had an impact on code complexity. Another multiplicative determinant of balancing code complexity was the number of item types. Introducing indirect items doubled this, and changing directory items from liquid drops to air drops also increased it. Storing stat data in the first direct or indirect item of the file complicated the code for processing those items more than if I had made stat data its own item type.

When one finds oneself with an NxN coding complexity issue, it usually indicates the need for adding a layer of abstraction. The NxN effect of the number of items on balancing code complexity is an instance of that design principle, and we will address it in the next major rewrite. The balancing code will employ a set of item operations which all item types must support. The balancing code will then invoke those operations without needing to understand any more of the meaning of an item's type than it determines which item-specific item operation handler is called. Adding a new item type, e.g., a compressed item, will then merely require writing a set of item operations for that item rather than requiring a modicication of most parts of the balancing code as it does now.

We now feel that the function to determine what resources are needed to perform a balancing operation, fix_nodes(), might as well be written to decide what operations will be performed during balancing since it pretty much has to do so anyway. That way, the function that performs the balancing with the nodes locked, do_balance(), can be gutted of most of its complexity.

INSTALLING AND CONFIGURING REISERFS ON A LINUX KERNEL

The ReiserFS file system is quite easy to install. From Linux kernel 2.4.3, Linus Torvalds included ReiserFS in the standard Linux source. This means for newer kernels you don't need to do anything to the kernel source; it is ready to be compiled with ReiserFS turned on. For older kernels there is a somewhat tedious procedure to follow to obtain a patch from the www.namesys.com Web site and then apply the patch to the standard Linux source code.

Linux-2.2.X Kernels

For Linux-2.2.X kernels, follow these steps:

1. Get the latest ReiserFS patch from one of our mirrors.
   Suppose you get linux-2.2.19-reiserfs-3.5.32-patch.bz2,
   put it somewhere, for example: /usr/src/2.2.19/

2. Get the kernel sources of 2.2.19 on http://www.kernel.org.
   Put it somewhere, for example: /usr/src/2.2.19/linux.
   Now if you perform "ls" in /usr/src/2.2.19/,
   the result will look like:
   # ls
   linux linux-2.2.19-reiserfs-3.5.32-patch.bz2

3. Apply ReiserFS patch to it:
    # cd /usr/src/2.2.19
    # bzcat linux-2.2.19-reiserfs-3.5.32-patch.bz2 | patch -p0

4. Compile the linux-kernel, set ReiserFS support:
    # cd /usr/src/2.2.19/linux
    # make mrproper; make menuconfig

5. Set ReiserFS support here. You might need to turn on experimental features, depending on the exact kernel you are using:
    # make dep; make bzImage

6. When configuring, say y or n on ReiserFS support question. Read our Configuration Web page. If you set ReiserFS as a module, please also do the following:
    # make modules
    # make modules_install

    If you upgrade ReiserFS sometime later, don't think that you only have to recompile the module. It is a nice theory, but not a reality, mainly because interfaces to the file system are rapidly changing all of the time.

    Bugs due to recompiling only the module tend to be completely cryptic, and the developers know it is because you didn't recompile the whole because somebody else already made that error.

    The kernel image will be in:
    /usr/src/2.2.19/linux/arch/i386/boot/bzImage

7. Compile and install the ReiserFS utils:
    # cd /usr/src/2.2.19/linux/fs/reiserfs/utils
    # make; make install

8. Copy a new Linux kernel image with ReiserFS support to its proper place: (it is "/boot" directory usually.)

9. Change the /etc/lilo.conf file, so that you can boot with new kernel. Perform lilo command, please use lilo-21.6 or newer:
    Lilo-21.6-or-newer

10. Boot with the built kernel, mkreiserfs spare partition, and mount it:
    # mkreiserfs /dev/xxxx
    # mount /dev/xxxx /mount-point-dir
    or
    # mount -t reiserfs /dev/xxxx /mount-point-dir

11. Have fun.

Linux-2.4.0 to 2.4.2

ReiserFS code is inside Linux kernel from Linux 2.4.1-pre4.

1. Get Linux 2.4.2: http://www.kernel.org.
2. Get the latest ReiserFS-3.6.x patch.
3. Apply it:
   # zcat linux-2.4.2-reiserfs-20010327-full.patch.gz | patch -p0
4. Compile the kernel (as previously described, and turn on experimental features).
5. Get the ReiserFS utils: reiserfsprogs.
6. Untar in any dir, then compile and install rReiserFS utils:
   # tar -xzvf reiserfsprogs-3.x.0i-1.tar.gz
   # cd reiserfsprogs-3.x.0i-1
   # ./configure
   # make; make install
7. Boot with the built kernel, mkreiserfs spare partition.

Configuration   There are compile-time options that affect ReiserFS functionality. You can set them up during the configuration stage of a Linux kernel build:

```
make config
make menuconfig
make xconfig
```

Turn on the ReiserFS option in the kernel configurator. This will build the ReiserFS external module.

Build ReiserFS. It will be either built into the kernel or as a stand-alone kernel module.

Option	Description
CONFIG REISERFS CHECK	If you set this to yes during the kernel configuration, then ReiserFS will perform every check possible of its internal consistency throughout its operation. It will also go substantially slower. Use of this option allows our team to check for consistency when debugging without fear of its effect on end-users. If you are on the verge of sending in a bug report, say yes and you might get a useful error message. Almost everyone should say no.

Option	Description
<u>CONFIG REISERFS RAW</u>	Setting this to yes will enable a set of ioctls that provide raw interface to ReiserFS tree, bypassing directories, and automatically removing aged files. This is an experimental feature designed for squid cache directories. See **Documentation/filesystems/reiserfs_raw.txt**. This was designed specifically to use ReiserFS as a back-end for the Squid. The general idea is that it is possible to bypass all file system overhead and address the ReiserFS internal tree directly. This is not in the stock kernels.
<u>USE INODE GENERATION COUNTER</u>	Use s_inode_generation field in the 3.6 super-block to keep track of inode generations. If not defined, use global event counter for this purpose (as do ext2 and most other file systems). The behavior of inode generations is important for NFS. This variable is unavailable through kernel configuration procedures, edit include/linux/reiserfs_fs.h manually.
<u>REISERFS HANDLE BADBLOCKS</u>	Enable ioctl for manipulating the bitmap. This can be used as crude form of bad block handling, but a real solution is underway. This variable is unavailable through kernel configuration procedures, edit include/linux/reiserfs_fs.h manually. Then, take a look at the available mount options.

CHAPTER 10

XFS

One of the most promising new journaling file systems for Linux is the SGI-sponsored XFS file system. XFS first existed under the Irix operating system and was ported in 2000 and 2001 to Linux by a team of developers both within sgi and outside of sgi. XFS was introduced by them—named Silicon Graphics Inc. as a replacement for the non-journaling EFS file system for their Irix 5.3 operating system. In the early '90s, Silicon Graphics recognized that the market for storage was about to explode and that their powerful servers would need to be able to access and serve data quickly, efficiently, and securely.

Among the high-level goals for the design and development of XFS were the following:

▼   It must be useable in scientific file and computer servers, in commercial data processing servers, and in digital media servers.

■   XFS must support high availability by recovering quickly from failures and by keeping its disk-based data in a consistent state at all times.

■   It must have efficient support for very large files, i.e., 64-bit size. There must be little or no performance penalty to access blocks in different areas of the file. Some disk space penalty (for indices, for example) is allowed to increase performance. Linear searches through the file system data structures to get to blocks at the end of a large file are unacceptable.

■   There must be efficient support for sparse files. Arbitrary holes must be supported —these are areas of the file which have never been written and which read back as zeroes. The representation must be disk space-efficient as well as CPU time-efficient in its retrieval of old data and insertion of new data. There is no requirement to detect blocks of zeroes being written in order to replace them with holes (nor is it forbidden).

■   It must have efficient support for very small files, under 1KB or so. A normal root or usr file system has many such files, as does a file system which contains program sources. Most symbolic links also fit into this category.

■   It must have efficient support for large directories, both for searches and for insertions and deletions. This implies some kind of index scheme to avoid linear searches through a long directory. The time to recover from failure does not increase with the size of the file system. The time is allowed to increase with the level of activity in the file system at the time of the failure. The recovery scheme must not scan all inodes, or all directories, to ensure consistency. This implies that consistency is guaranteed by use of a log, since the alternative (synchronous behavior as in MS-DOS) is unacceptably slow. Recovery never backs out changes that were committed after returning successfully to the user. Some operations must be synchronous, at least as far as the log writes are concerned. Certainly this includes file creation and deletion, and does not include ordinary (buffered) writes.

- ■ It should support ACLs and other POSIX 1003.6 functionality. This includes some form of support for Mandatory Access Controls, Information Labeling, and auditing.

- ▲ It should also support multiple logical block sizes, ranging from the disk sector size up to sizes of 64KB or 256KB. The block size is set at file system creation time. It is the minimum unit of allocation in the file system (except for inodes, which can be smaller).

With these goals in mind the original developers, under the guidance of SGI programmer Doug Doucette and others, produced a remarkably fast and efficient—as well as extremely extensible—file system that is being ported to Linux 2.4.x. XFS is very scalable, using btrees extensively to support large and/or sparse files, and extremely large directories.

At the time of writing this book, XFS is already in a stable beta version running both under the older 2.2.1x and the newer 2.4.x kernels. As of version 2.4.4, XFS is already part of the standard Linux kernel source code and one of the options during kernel configuration.

THE XFS IMPLEMENTATION

Like all other file systems under Linux, XFS is implemented under VFS and therefore everything in the VFS chapter also applies to XFS.

The XFS file system is a journaled file system. This means that updates to file system meta-data (inodes, directories, bitmaps, etc.) are written to a serial log area on disk before the original disk blocks are updated in place. In the event of a crash, such operations can be redone or undone, using data present in the log to restore the file system to a consistent state. This implementation technique replaces the use of a file system check and repair program (fsck) before mounting file systems that were active when a system crash occurred.

XFS uses the Linux Logical Volume Manager which is described in the LVM chapter of this book. For readers planning to use XFS on top of LVM, keep in mind that the current XFS cvs tree (as of May 2001 and also the XFS 1.0 previews) already contains the lvm beta6 code and some tweaks for XFS. Currently it is recommended to stay with this version instead of the current LVM version (beta7) because there are some logistical problems around beta7. There is one caveat however: mounting snapshots of LVM containing the XFS file system does not work due to the journaling nature of the file system (but a fix for this is on the To Do list).

XFS is a 64-bit file system. In order to support the access of 64- bit files from 32-bit applications, new interfaces must be defined which take 64-bit parameters. These interfaces must be cleanly supported in the kernel (which at present are still not in Linux), without the information of whether an application is 64 or 32-bit filtering down below the system call level.

The file system-related calls are implemented here: read, write, open, ioctl, etc., for all file system types. The operations are then vectored out to different routines for each file system type through the VFS interfaces. Both 32-bit and 64-bit interfaces are supported by the underlying OS and hardware. The semantics of 32-bit applications operating natively on files longer than 232 bytes are defined later in this chapter.

The main components of XFS are listed here:

▼ Log Manager—Serially logs all meta-data changes to a separate area of the disk space.

■ Buffer Cache Manager.

■ Lock Manager—Implements locking on user files (fcntl and flock calls).

■ Space Manager—Manages the allocation of disk space within a file system.

■ Attribute Manager—Implements file system attribute operations.

■ System Call and VFS Interface

▲ Name Space Manager—Implements file system naming operations, translating pathnames into file references.

Log Manager

All changes to file system meta-data (inodes, directories, bitmaps, etc.) are serially logged to a separate area of the disk space. There is a separate log for each file system. The log allows fast reconstruction of a consistent and correct file system (recovery) if a crash intervenes before the meta-data blocks are written to disk. The log space is allocated independently from the file system space for safety; this separation is managed by the underlying volume manager. The Log Manager utilizes information provided by the Space Manager to control the sequencing of write operations from the buffer cache, since specific log writes must be sequenced before or after data operations for correctness if there is a crash.

The Space and Name Manager subsystems send logging requests to the Log Manager. Each request may fill a partial log block or multiple blocks of the log. The log is implemented as a circular sequential list that wraps when writes reach the end. Each log entry contains a log sequence number, so that the end of the log may be found by looking for the highest sequence number.

After a crash, the log must be recovered before the file system can be used. Operations which are recorded and are complete in the log but are not yet stored in the data area of the file system are redone so that the file system data reflects a correct and consistent state. The Log Manager's role in this is to identify the log records and to call other pieces of the file system to perform recovery operations. Log operations are blocked together to get higher throughput on the log portion of the volume. The block is called a log record. Typically, log records are written asynchronously; the Log Manager can be directed by higher levels of the system to force writing of the current log record as soon as possible. A given log write cannot be started until the previous one finishes.

Buffer Cache Manager

The buffer cache is a cache of disk blocks for the various file systems local to a machine (node). Read requests may be satisfied from the buffer cache; write requests may write into the cache. Cache entries are flushed when new entries are needed, in an order which takes into account frequency (or freshness) of use and file system semantics. File system meta-data as well as file data is stored in the buffer cache. User requests may bypass the cache by setting flags (O_DIRECT); otherwise all file system I/O goes through the cache.

The current buffer cache interfaces will be extended in two ways. First, 64-bit versions of the interfaces will be added to support XFS's 64-bit file sizes. Second, a transaction mechanism will be provided to allow buffer cache clients to collect and modify buffers during an operation, send the changed buffers to the Log Manager, and release all the buffers after successful logging. In future distributed systems, a buffer cache will hold data for file systems remote to a machine.

Lock Manager

The Lock Manager uses advanced algorithms to shorten the length of time locks are held. At the same time, the lock manager design is prepared for distributed file system (DFS) operation, allowing file system objects to be locked among many nodes in a cluster.

Space Manager

The Space Manager manages the allocation of disk space within a file system. It is responsible for mapping a file (a sequence of bytes) into a sequence of disk blocks. The internal structure of the file system—allocation (cylinder) groups, inodes, and free space management—is controlled by the Space Manager, as well as the mapping function.

The space layout choices in the design are influenced by the requirement to support very large files and file systems efficiently, including the possibility of sparse 64-bit files. The Space Manager is also responsible for optimizing the layout of blocks in a file to avoid seeking during sequential processing, and keeping related files (those in the same directory) close to each other on the disks.

Each file system is divided into log, meta-data, data, and real-time sub-volumes. Normally, the data sub-volume and the real-time sub-volume do not exist. If the data sub-volume exists, then ordinary user data is stored in it, otherwise it is stored in the meta-data sub-volume. Data blocks for real-time files are stored in the real-time sub-volume if it exists, otherwise in the data sub-volume if that exists, and if not, in the meta-data sub-volume. All file system data is stored in the log and meta-data sub-volumes.

The Space Manager divides each file system meta-data and data sub-volume into a number of allocation groups. When the data sub-volume exists, the allocation group contains blocks from both the meta-data and data sub-volumes. Each allocation group has a collection of inodes, data blocks and data structures to control their allocation. The blocks containing inodes are allocated dynamically from the data block pool, to permit more efficient use of disk space. Knowledge of the location of the sequence of inode blocks for an allocation group is kept the same way as it is for ordinary files (in a B-tree). Free blocks in an allocation group are kept track of via one of two schemes. The first scheme uses a bitmap and a set of counters organized by the starting bitmap block and the log2 size of the free extent. The second scheme uses a pair of B-trees, one indexed by the size of the free extent (and secondarily by the starting block), the other indexed by the starting block of the free extent. The scheme to be used will be chosen after both methods have been prototyped and their performance analyzed. The real-time sub-volume is divided into a number of fixed-size extents. The size is chosen at mkfs time; it is expected to be large, at least 1MB. The size does not have to be a power of two, just a multiple of the file system block size. It should be the ideal I/O size for that volume configuration, or a multiple of it. A single extent in the meta-data sub-volume contains an allocation bitmap for the real-time sub-volume extents and another extent contains summary information per bitmap block (number of free extents). This alternate method of allocation is chosen for the real-time sub-volume due to the improved performance that is possible because of the fixed-size extents.

Storage for files is represented in one of three ways, depending on the size and contiguity of the file. For small files, the data in the file is stored in the inode. For medium files, the inode contains pointers to extents containing the file data. For large files, the inode contains the root block of a B-tree indexed by logical position in the file, where the records point to disk extents containing the file data. This storage structure allows for large fragmented and sparse files to be implemented efficiently, at the cost of some overhead to manage the B-tree indices.

An active file system may be extended by adding more space to the underlying volume. This operation is supported online by the Space Manager, which receives a request to expand the file system, and updates on-disk and in-memory structures to implement it. In a future implementation it may be required to support splitting the control of space management in a single file system over multiple nodes of the system. The first implementation will not take this into account.

Attribute Manager

The Attribute Manager implements file system attribute operations, i.e., storing and retrieving arbitrary user-defined attributes associated with objects in the name space. Arbitrary attributes are name and value pairs where the name is a printable string and the value is a small string of arbitrary bytes. Attributes may be controlled either by user applications or by the kernel. Certain attributes are pre-defined by the system and may be accessed using both existing UNIX interfaces and the new attribute access system calls, for example, file access and modification times.

An attribute is stored internally by attaching it to the inode of the referenced object. The Attribute Manager manages the attribute structures that are associated with inodes.

However, it does not manage those fields handled by the Name Space Manager such as file permissions and timestamps.

No storage for arbitrary attributes is allocated when an object is created, and any attributes that exist when an object is destroyed are also destroyed. Attributes are not shared between inodes.

Access control lists are handled as a special case as they can be shared between inodes. This means that all objects in a file system that have certain attributes or attribute values can be located quickly. Some system utility programs will be modified to know about attributes, for example, cp will copy selected attributes of a file when it copies the file. The system backup utility will back up and restore the attributes of an object when that object is backed up or restored. Standard NFS does not support attributes beyond the traditional UNIX set, so these attributes will not be visible in any way to a client accessing an XFS file system via standard NFS.

Name Space Manager

The Name Space Manager implements file system naming operations and translates pathnames into file references. A file is internally identified by its file system and its inode number. The inode is the on-disk structure which holds information about a file; the inode number is the label (or index) of the inode within the particular file system. Files are also identified by a numeric value unique to the file, called the file unique id. File systems may be identified either by a "magic cookie," typically a memory address of the root inode, or by a file system unique id. File system unique id's are assigned when the file system is created and are associated uniquely with that file system until the file system is destroyed. An additional temporary unique id, the file system I/O unique id, is created whenever a file system is mounted, and is valid only for the duration of the mount.

The Name Space Manager manages the directory structures and the contents of the inode that are unrelated to space management, such as file permissions and timestamps. Requests from other systems via NFS come into the system with a file handle which the Name Space Manager uses to find the inode. The file handle includes enough information to deduce the file system, the inode, and which version of the file is meant (inodes may be reused). Requests from other nodes in a distributed XFS file system would enter with a file system unique id and inode number, and a file unique id, and be validated at this level to see that the two forms of identification match. The Name Space Manager may have a cache to speed up naming operations. The details of the name translation are hidden from the callers.

The current design of the Name Space Manager's mount semantics have a file system node called a mount point which replaces the empty-directory mount points of the current file system. The mount point node contains a file system unique id. When a mount point which refers to a remote file system is encountered during a naming operation, a message is sent to the remote machine that is managing the file system with that file system unique id, along with the naming request, to complete the operation.

It is possible that alternate or extended naming schemes may be implemented in user mode by allowing the entity at the other end of the message queue to be a program. This will not be implemented in the first release of the system.

Administration of XFS File Systems

XFS administration includes the utilities needed to create and maintain volumes and file systems. It also includes programmatic interfaces for volume control, file system control (mount, unmount, etc.), backup and restore, hierarchical file systems, etc. In the future, administration support will be expanded to allow remote access to volumes and file systems for mounting, backup, and other functions. Graphical interfaces will be provided by the system administration group in MSD for the new tools that need it, i.e., volume administration.

XFS STRUCTURES AND METHODS

This section of the chapter describes the creation, manipulation, and destruction of in-core inodes in XFS.

Inode Data Structure

The XFS in-core inode structure is defined as:

```
typedef struct xfs_inode {
struct xfs_ihash *i_hash; /* pointer to hash header */
struct xfs_inode *i_next; /* inode hash link forw */
struct xfs_inode **i_prevp; /* ptr to prev i_next */
 struct xfs_mount *i_mount; /* fs mount struct ptr */
 struct xfs_inode *i_mnext; /* next inode in mount's list */
 struct xfs_inode **i_mprevp; /* ptr to prev i_mnext */
 struct vnode *i_vnode; /* ptr to associated vnode */
 dev_t i_dev; /* dev containing this inode */
xfs_ino_t i_ino; /* inode number (agno/agino) */
 xfs_agblock_t i_bno; /* ag block # of inode */
int i_index; /* which inode in block */
xfs_trans_t *i_transp; /* ptr to owning transaction */
xfs_inode_log_item_t i_item; /* logging information */
mrlock_t i_lock; /* inode lock */
sema_t i_flock; /* inode flush lock */
 unsigned int i_pincount; /* # of times inode is pinned */
 sema_t i_pinsema; /* inode pin sema */
 ushort i_flags; /* misc state */
 ulong i_vcode; /* version code token (RFS) */
ulong i_mapcnt; /* count of mapped pages */
```

```
ulong i_update_core; /* inode timestamp dirty flag */
size_t i_bytes; /* bytes in i_u1 */
union {xfs_bmbt_rec_t *iu_extents; /* linear map of file extents */
char *iu_data; /* inline file data */ }
 i_u1; xfs_btree_block_t *i_broot; /* file's in-core b-tree root */
size_t i_broot_bytes; /* bytes allocated for root */
union {xfs_bmbt_rec_t iu_inline_ext[2]; /* very small file extents */
char iu_inline_data[32]; /* very small file data */ dev_t iu_rdev; /*
dev number if special */ xfs_uuid_t iu_uuid; /* mount point value */ }
 i_u2; ushort i_abytes; /* bytes in i_u3 */
union {xfs_bmbt_rec_t *iu_aextents; /* map of attribute extents */ char
*iu_adata; /* inline attribute data */ }
 i_u3; xs_dinode_core_t i_d; /* most of the on-disk inode */ }
 xfs_inode_t;
```

Inode Life Cycle

We now follow the life cycle of an in-core inode from the time it is read in from the disk until the time the in-core structure is returned to the kernel heap.

Step 1

Allocate an in-core inode. The user of in-core inodes first needs to get one via a call to xfs_iget() or xfs_trans_iget(). The caller specifies the inode number of the desired inode and whether the inode should be locked exclusively or shared, and the function returns a pointer to the initialized in-core inode. This is usually done as part of file lookup. The inode is returned locked with the reference count of the inode's vnode incremented. Others may have references to the same inode, and the inode lock is used to synchronize accesses to the structure.

Step 2

Look at the inode. Once a process gets a hold of an inode it looks at it. If the process intends to modify the inode it should be locked exclusively, but if it is only reading the inode it should be locked shared. Actually, since inodes are usually found by the lookupname() routine, their user usually gets the inode/vnode with a reference, but without a lock. The user then explicitly locks the inode with a call to xfs_ilock(). Once the inode is locked, the process holding it can read any of its fields. The inode can only be modified, however, if it has been brought into the context of a transaction.

Step 3

Modifying the inode. If the inode is to be modified it must be locked exclusively. If the caller did not obtain the inode with a call to xfs_trans_iget(), which is just like xfs_iget() except that it takes a transaction pointer, then it should be locked exclusively with a call to xfs_ilock() and added to the transaction with a call to xfs_trans_ijoin(). Once this is done, the inode can be modified. When all changes to the inode have been made, the transaction mechanism needs to be told what within the inode has been changed and therefore needs to be logged.

Step 4

Logging the inode changes. The changes made to an inode can be logged as part of a transaction using the xfs_trans_log_in-ode() function. This function takes flags indicating which parts of the inode have been modified and therefore need to be logged. The flags are all defined in xfs_inode_item.h and will be described in more detail further on in this chapter.

Step 5

Releasing the inode. Once a process is through looking at or modifying an inode, the inode needs to be unlocked and released. If the inode was not used as part of a transaction, then the process can simply call xfs_iput() which will unlock the inode and release the reference to the inode's vnode. If the inode is being used as part of a transaction, then when the process calls xfs_trans_commit(), the inode will be unlocked and its reference released. If the process wants to hold on to the inode even after the commit, then it needs to call xfs_trans_ihold() before committing the transaction. This tells the transaction code not to unlock or release the inode when the transaction commits.

Step 6

Writing back inode changes. When an inode is modified as part of a transaction, the dirty inode structure will remain in memory and the changes will be written into the on-disk log. At some point the inode will be written back to its on-disk home by either bdflush() calling xfs_sync() or by the inode structure being reclaimed for use as another inode. In either case, all modifications to the inode will, at this point, be written back to the disk and the on-disk log copy will no longer be needed for file system recovery.

Step 7

Destroying the inode structure. As mentioned above, the inode structure may at some point be recycled for use as another inode. This is the end of the in-core inode's life cycle as its memory is freed and reused for something else.

Inode Allocation

In-core inodes are allocated by calls to xfs_iget(). The function prototype for xfs_iget() is:

xfs_inode_t*xfs_iget(xfs_mount_t *mp, xfs_trans_t *tp, xfs_ino_t ino, uint flags).

The caller gives a pointer to the file system's mount structure, a transaction pointer if executing within a transaction, the inode number of the desired inode, and flags indicating whether the inode should be locked in shared or exclusive mode. The function returns a pointer to the in-core version of the desired inode. The inode is returned to the caller locked in the requested mode. The fields of the inode will be filled in according to the format of the on-disk inode. If the inode is in LOCAL format, meaning that the file's data fits entirely within the on-disk inode, then i_u1.iu_data will point to an in-memory array containing the contents of the file and i_bytes will contain the number of bytes in the array. This array will either be the i_u2.iu_inline_dataarray if the file data is less than or equal to 32 bytes or it will be an array allocated from the kernel heap. If the file is of length 0, then i_u1.iu_data will be NULL and i_bytes will be 0. If the inode is in EXTENTS format, meaning that the file's data will not fit in the on-disk inode but the extent descriptors for the inode will, then i_u1.iu_extents will point to an in-memory array containing the extent descriptors of the file and i_bytes will contain the number of bytes in the array. This array will be either the i_u1.iu_inline_ext array if there are only one or two extents or it will be an array allocated from the kernel heap. If the file is of length 0, then i_u1.iu_extents will be NULL and i_bytes will be 0. The XFS_IEXTENTS flag will be set in i_flags. This flag indicates that all of the file's extent descriptors have been read in and are in the i_u1.iu_extents array.

If the inode is in B-tree format, meaning that the file has too many extent descriptors to fit into the on-disk inode, then i_broot will point to an in-memory array containing the file's extent b-tree root and i_broot_bytes that will contain the number of bytes in the array. If the XFS_IEXTENTS flag is set in i_flags, then i_u1.iu_extents will point to an array containing all of the extents of the file as in the case above. If the flag is not set, then the extents have not yet been read in and should be read in with a call to xfs_ireadindir() if they are needed. Reading in all of the extents for files with a large number of extents ensures that simple stat()s of the file can be done efficiently. The returned inode will be hashed into a per file system in-core inode hash table. We are switching from the traditional single hash table for all file systems to per file system hash tables to improve the scalability of the system. Calls to xfs_iget() first look for the desired inode in this hash table before bringing in the inode from disk. An in-core inode is only removed from the hash table when it is recycled. The inode will also be placed on a list attached to the file system's mount structure. This list is used for traversal of all the in-core inodes in routines such as xfs_sync().

Inode In-line Data/Extents/B-tree Root

This section describes the management of the iu_data, iu_extents, and i_broot fields. These fields point to arrays whose size must change as the size of the file changes.

iu_data

As described in the section on inode allocation, this field points to an array containing the in-line data of an inode in LOCAL format. When the size of a file in this format changes, the process changing the size should call xfs_idata_realloc() to resize the in-core array. This function takes the delta in the number of bytes needed. If the delta is positive, then more memory will be allocated for the array, and if it is negative the array will be made smaller. If the size goes to 0 then iu_data will be made NULL. If the size will become greater than will fit in the on-disk inode, then it is the responsibility of the process changing the size to perform a transaction to change the inode from LOCAL to EXTENTS format. As a part of that transaction the in-line data should be logged, the iu_data array should be freed with a call to xfs_idata_realloc(), and an array for the inode's extents should be allocated in iu_extents with a call to xfs_iext_realloc().

iu_extents

When an inode is in EXTENTS or BTREE format, this field points to an array containing all of the extent descriptors for that inode. If the file is in EXTENTS format, then this array is guaranteed to be there unless the file is of length 0. If the file is in BTREE format, then this array is read in when it is first needed and its presence is signified by the XFS_IEXTENTS flag in the inode's i_flags field. When the number of extents in the file changes, the process changing the number of extents should call xfs_iext_realloc() to resize the in-core array. This function takes the delta in the number of extents needed and allocates and frees memory for the array as needed. If the number of extents goes to 0 then iu_extents will be set to NULL. If the number of extents exceeds a threshold which is yet to be determined, then the array will stop growing and the block mapping code will have slower access through its B-tree in the buffer cache. The iu_extents array contains all of the extents of the inode sorted by file offset. It will be used by the block mapping code to quickly find the location of file disk blocks. This will be done by binary search of the array, possibly enhanced with a single entry cache for improving the efficiency of sequential access lookups.

iu_broot

When an inode is in BTREE format, this field points to an in-core copy of the on-disk inode's B-tree root. Like the other arrays mentioned above, this array only takes enough memory to hold the used portion of the B-tree root and must be resized dynamically as the root grows and shrinks.This is done by calls to xfs_iroot_realloc(), which takes the change in the number of B-tree records needed. This routine understands the format of the B-tree root, and it moves existing information within the root as appropriate when the size changes. This means that when the size of the root increases by some number of records, the pointers for the records are shifted towards the end of the data structure, and when the size shrinks the pointers are moved forward.

When the number of records in the B-tree root goes to 0, the data structure is not freed because it still contains the B-tree block header. If this is no longer needed, the process should call xfs_iroot_free() to release the memory used to contain the root. This should only be done if the inode is no longer in BTREE format.

i_bytes and i_broot_bytes

These two counters track the used bytes in the arrays pointed to by the corresponding iu_data/iu_extents and i_broot fields. For now the arrays are exactly the size needed, except when using the iu_inline_data/iu_inline_ext array. This implies that we must call kmem_-realloc() or something similar each time one of the xfs_i***_realloc() routines is called. We could keep more memory than we are currently using in an attempt to reduce the number of kmem calls, but this is currently being traded in favor of better memory utilization. If this turns out to be a high overhead decision in terms of cpu cycles, we can pretty easily change it.

Inode locking

As mentioned above, inodes can be locked in either shared or exclusive mode. This means we can have multiple readers of the same inode simultaneously, which should allow multiple readers and non-allocating writers of the file to work in parallel. Simultaneous file access is especially important for async I/O and for directories. Our async I/O implementation is based on threads, so allowing multiple threads to access the file at the same time can increase the pipeline of I/O requests to high throughput devices, such as large, striped volumes. Directories are read doing path searches far more often than they are written, so allowing parallel access to popular directories should increase our pathname resolution performance. This has been a significant bottleneck in other file systems, so this is good progress. The inode lock will need to be held exclusively for anything updating the contents of the inode. The contents include all fields which are contained in the on-disk inode, and others as needed.

Inode Transactions and Logging

Almost all changes to an inode that will be reflected in the on-disk inode must be done within the context of a transaction and must logged within that transaction. The only exceptions to this may be the access, change, and modify times on the inode which are discussed in the next section. Once an inode has been modified, the transaction mechanism should be notified of the change with a call to xfs_trans_log_inode(). This function takes a set of flags indicating which parts of the inode have been changed. The flags are:

▼ XFS_ILOG_META   This should be specified if any of the fields in the i_d sub-structure have been modified.

■ XFS_ILOG_DATA   This should be specified if the inline data of the inode has been changed.

■ XFS_ILOG_EXT   This should be specified if the iu_extents array has been modified and the file is in EXTENTS format.

■ XFS_ILOG_BROOT   This should be specified if the file is in BTREE format and the contents of the i_broot array have been modified.

▲ XFS_ILOG_DEV   This should be specified if the i_u2.iu_rdev field has been modified. These flags tell the transaction code which parts of the inode need to be logged when the current transaction commits. Each specified section is logged in its entirety, so specifying XFS_ILOG_- META will log the entire xfs_dinode_core structure embedded in the in-core inode, and specifying

XFS_ILOG_BROOT will log the entire B-tree root. We will not be logging little, tiny pieces of the inode, because the overhead for tracking such pieces is as high as the overhead for copying them into the log.

When a transaction manipulating an inode commits, the inode is unlocked and the reference to the inode is released. In order to prevent dirty inodes from being reclaimed, which could become a performance problem if they are reclaimed while they are still pinned by a transaction, when a clean inode is logged an additional reference to the inode will be taken by the transaction code. This reference will be released when the inode is flushed back to disk to clean it.

Inode Flushing

Dirty inodes are flushed to disk either by calls to the bdflush daemon or by the transaction management code when an inode's log image is too far back in the log. The inode must be locked in shared mode to prevent other processes from modifying the inode but will still allow other processes to look at the inode while it is being written to disk. Since multiple processes could attempt to flush the inode simultaneously, the i_flock will be used to synchronize the flushing of an inode. This is necessary both for performance and for correctness. For performance we don't want to do unnecessary work. For correctness we must make sure that the one reference on the inode taken by the transaction management code is not used or released by multiple processes. Once the reference is released, it will be possible for the inode to be recycled. Thus only one process can assume that the reference will protect it.

The routine to perform the actual flushing of the inode is xfs_iflush(). This routine will obtain the buffer for the disk block of the inode from the buffer cache, copy the inode into that buffer, and write the buffer back to the disk synchronously, asynchronously, or as delayed write. If the inode is pinned in memory (because it is a part of a transaction which has not yet been committed to disk) this routine will sleep until it is unpinned. When the inode is not pinned, the routine will attach the function xfs_iflush_done() and the inode's log item to the buffer's b_iodone function and the b_fsprivate pointer. This routine will be executed when the write completes. Its purpose is to remove the inode from the file system's Active Item List (AIL), mark the inode clean, and release the reference to the inode taken by the transaction code. Finally, the inode will be marked clean, unlocked, and the buffer write initiated.

Since the buffer is unlocked in xfs_iflush(), it is possible for the inode to be dirtied again before the write completes and xfs_iflush_done() executes. In this case the inode may even be moved forward in the AIL, meaning that the flush being completed by xfs_iflush_done() does not have the right to remove the inode from the AIL. In order to coordinate this, xfs_iflush_done() will do the following:

▼ First look at the inode's LSN without obtaining the AIL lock (which protects this field). If it has changed then the inode has moved or is moving in the AIL and we should not bother with it.

- If the value has not changed then get the AIL lock and if the value has still not changed then remove the inode from the AIL.
- Next, release the inode's i_flock.
- Finally, release the reference to the inode.

Once the reference is released, we can no longer manipulate or look at the inode. Note that we are not doing anything special with the inode reference where the inode is re-dirtied while the disk write is taking place. Since the inode will be marked clean in xfs_i-flush() before releasing the lock, any process modifying the inode during the write will obtain another reference for the transaction code. This allows us to drop just the one that we are using.

Inode Recycling

At some point a call to xfs_reclaim() will want to recycle an inode which is not being referenced. The inode is guaranteed to have no references at this point, so we know that it is not dirty. All we need to do is flush any dirty file data associated with the inode, remove the inode from the mount structure's list of in-core inodes, and free all memory associated with the inode.

THE XFS SUPER-BLOCK STRUCTURES AND METHODS

The super-block is a centralized resource which is modified by most transactions. This means that it has a high potential for becoming a bottleneck. This is because once a transaction modifies a resource, that resource cannot be made visible to other transactions until the first is committed. If a resource such as the super-block is accessed by many transactions and each holds the resource for a significant period of time, the transactions will become bottlenecked waiting for access to the resource. To prevent this problem, in XFS the super-block will be modified through routines designed to minimize the amount of time the super-block is kept locked.

The reason the super-block is modified so much is that it contains counters of the total number of inodes, the total number of free inodes, and the total number of free blocks in the file system. These counters will be modified most of the time, so it is updates to them that will be optimized. This is consistent with the general rule of optimizing for the common case. While updates to the super-block counters are the most common, other fields of the super-block will need to be modified within transactions occasionally. The interfaces for this uncommon path must work with those for the fast path without breaking anything. All of this must also be coordinated with access to the in-core copy of the super-block.

The Super-block Buffer

Instead of being kept in a common buffer cache buffer accessed through the normal getblk()/bread() path, the XFS super-block will be kept in a buffer private to the file system. This way the buffer cache code, such as that in bdflush(), will never interact with the super-block buffer. This means, of course, that we are entirely responsible for making sure that the super-block is flushed to disk when necessary. Since the xfs_sync() routine will be called periodically anyway, flushing the superblock from there when necessary should be more than enough.

The super-block buffer will simply be pointed to by a pointer kept in the mount structure. Access to the buffer will be through the xfs_getsb() and xfs_trans_getsb() routines described in detail below. These routines are responsible for properly synchronizing access to the super-block buffer. The buffer will only be read in from disk at mount time, and from then on the buffer will be kept in sync with the on-disk copy of the super-block. This ensures that accesses to the super-block are never delayed to do I/O because another resource forced the buffer to be recycled.

In order to minimize the amount of time the super-block buffer is kept locked during a transaction, the super-block will not actually be locked and changed until just before the transaction commits. This will ensure that the buffer is not held locked while waiting for other resources to be read in from disk or released by other transactions. This works fine for the counters which are modified in the common case, as their updates consist of amounts to add or subtract from counters rather than absolute numbers. These updates can be delayed until the end of the transaction without violating the correctness of the transactions. The user of a transaction will indicate that a change needs to be applied to a super-block counter with a call to xfs_trans_mod_sb(). This routine will be responsible for recording the requested change and making sure that it is applied to the super-block as part of the transaction.

When fields of the super-block other than the counters need to be modified, the super-block buffer can be accessed just as any other buffer except that it must be obtained with a call to xfs_trans_getsb() rather than xfs_trans_getblk() / xfs_trans_bread(). Calls to xfs_trans_log_buf() using the super-block buffer will work fine and can even be intermixed with the use of xfs_trans_mod_sb().

The in-core super-block can be used to look up static information about the file system as well as system summary information. The super-block buffer should only be accessed when something is being changed. The fields in the in-core super-block which do change are protected by the m_sb_lock spin lock in the mount structure. This lock can be used to ensure that what is being looked at is consistent. The code that modifies the in-core super-block, after the transaction which modified the super-block commits, uses this lock to protect its updates.

Super-block Management Interfaces

The call xfs_trans_mod_sb() xfs_trans_mod_sb() is used to apply changes to the counters in the super-block without immediately locking the super-block buffer. The prototype for the function is:

    void xfs_trans_mod_sb(xfs_trans_t *tp, uint field, int delta);

The field argument specifies to which counters the number passed in the delta parameter should be added. To subtract a negative value from a given counter should be passed in delta. The valid values for the field parameter are:

▼ XFS_SB_ICOUNT   Apply the delta to the sb_icount field.

■ XFS_SB_IFREE   Apply the delta to the sb_ifree field.

■ XFS_SB_FDBLOCKS   Apply the delta to the sb_fdblocks field.

▲ XFS_SB_FREXTENTS   Apply the delta to the sb_frextents field.

When xfs_trans_commit() is called, the super-block buffer will be locked by the transaction and all specified deltas will be applied to it. The deltas are cumulative, so the same field may be specified in multiple calls to xfs_trans_mod_sb() within a given transaction. Once the transaction commits, the deltas will also be applied to the in-core copy of the super-block.

The call xfs_trans_getsb() xfs_trans_getsb() is used to lock the super-block buffer within a transaction. This should only be used when the transaction needs to modify fields in the super-block other than those that can be modified by xfs_trans_mod_sb(). The results of this function are just like those of xfs_trans_-bread(), but it is only used to obtain the super-block. The function prototype is:

    buf_t *xfs_trans_getsb(xfs_trans_t *tp);

The buffer can be released with a call to xfs_trans_brelse(). No special call is necessary.

The call xfs_getsb() xfs_getsb() is just like xfs_trans_getsb() except that it can be used outside of a transaction. It returns a pointer to the locked super-block buffer. This buffer should never be modified, however, as the super-block can only be updated within transactions. Most of the time the information needed should also be available from the in-core super-block, so use of this function is discouraged. The prototype for the function is:

    buf_t *xfs_getsb(xfs_mount_t *mp);

xfs_mod_incore_sb() xfs_mod_incore_sb() is used to modify the in-core copy of the super-block. Its prototype is:

    int xfs_mod_incore_sb(xfs_mount_t *mp, uint field, int delta);

The field parameter indicates which super-block field is applied to the given delta. This routine takes care of acquiring the spin lock protecting the in-core super-block.

It currently only supports updates to the fields available through xfs_trans_mod_sb() specified above, but this can be expanded as necessary.

This routine enforces the assumption that the counters in the super-block never go below zero. If a delta is specified that would cause such a condition, then the delta will not be applied and the routine will return EINVAL.

The call xfs_mod_incore_sb_batch() xfs_mod_incore_sb_batch() is used to apply multiple deltas to multiple fields in the super-block. It takes an array of xfs_mod_sb_t structures, each of which specify a field and a delta for that field. By allowing the caller to specify multiple deltas to be applied to the super-block, this routine allows multiple updates to be atomically applied and reduces the locking overhead necessary for multiple calls to xfs_mod_incore_sb(). The prototype for the function and the xfs_mod_sb_t definition is:

```
typedef struct xfs_mod_sb {
uint msb_field; /* the field to which to apply msb_delta */
int msb_delta; /* the amount to add to the specified field */
 xfs_mod_sb_t;
int xfs_mod_incore_sb_batch(xfs_mount_t *mp, xfs_mod_sb_t *msb, uint nmsb);
```

Like xfs_mod_incore_sb(), this routine handles the locking that protects the super-block and enforces the restriction that no counter in the super-block may go below zero. If any of the specified deltas would cause such a condition, then none of the deltas will be applied and the function will return EINVAL.

On-Disk Structures

The space layout choices in the design of XFS were influenced by the requirements to support very large files and file systems efficiently. The space manager, described at the beginning of this chapter, is responsible for optimizing the layout of blocks in a file, determining rate guarantee information for each file, and keeping related files close to each other on the disks.

The internal details of space management are hidden from the users and from the Name Manager layer, except that users are allowed to determine whether a file is sufficiently contiguous and, if not, to have the file's space be reallocated so that it is more contiguous.

All exported interfaces are call-based, not message-based. Control and administration messages may come from another node but will be handled by the system call and administration layer and turned into a local call.

Structures on Disk

The super-block is the root of all file system information. It is located at the beginning of the file system (offset 0, which is why it conflicts with LILO under Linux); this is a departure from the historical behavior of UNIX file systems, which typically start at offset 512.

To avoid confusion between XFS and other Linux file systems, offset 512 of an XFS file system must contain a value other than the magic number value of other file system's super-blocks. The super-block contains enough information to find all the other pieces of the file system. There is an in-core copy of it which is part of the information belonging to a mounted file system.

The following fields are the most important in the super-block:

▼ XFS magic number

■ XFS version

■ File system unique id

■ Last name file system mounted as

■ Logical block size (lbsz, in bytes, 29 .. 216)

■ Unreliable extent size (in lbsz)

■ Physical sector size (bytes)

■ Inode size (bytes, 27 .. 211) and information about how the space in the inode is divided up, such as a minimum size for each of the data and attribute areas of the inode.

■ Data block allocation mechanism, choice of bitmap or B-tree, and others

■ Small files allocated in inodes, or not

■ Allocation group size (in lbsz)

■ Total file system data sub-volume size (in lbsz)

■ Total file system unreliable sub-volume size (in extents)

■ Logical block number of bitmap for unreliable sub-volume extents

■ Logical block number of summary information for unreliable sub-volume bitmap

■ Total number of allocated and free inodes

■ Total number of free data sub-volume blocks

▲ Total number of blocks allocated as data and as metadata in the data sub-volume

The only fields which change during normal operation are the statistical fields, containing information used by df.

Changes to this information must be logged, to keep the file system consistent, if the information is trusted across reboots. Alternatively, the information could be computed at mount time, and never written to disk at all (except possibly at unmount time). This would avoid the overhead of logging changes to the super-block at the cost of scanning all the allocation structures of the file system at mount time. The current plan is to avoid the mount-time scan, and log the super-block changes. The file system size and total fields also change when the file system is re-sized dynamically; these changes must be logged.

Allocation Group Header

Each file system data sub-volume is divided into allocation groups of the same size (except possibly the last). The size is chosen at the time the file system is created. The size will be in the range of 16MB to 1GB, with the default size being the total file system size divided by eight. Subject to the overriding minimum allocation group size, there shall be a minimum of eight allocation groups. There may also be some rounding done to the allocation group size; these details are still to be figured out.

The primary reason to divide a file system into allocation groups is to promote parallelism in space allocation in the file system. Locking on allocation information can be done separately per allocation group, which allows improved performance, especially in a multiprocessor. The allocation groups are a uniform size to make it easier to find them in the event of an unreadable block. If the allocation groups were of a variable size, then either each one would have to be readable to figure out where the next one was, or there would need to be an index containing all the allocation group addresses. Each allocation group is composed of the following: a super-block (only the first one gets values updated after file system creation time) at location zero bytes; an allocation group header (fit into the first logical block along with the super-block data); and data pointed at by the allocation group header. All the "pointers" in the file system meta-data are 64-bit logical block numbers, with exceptions noted below being 32-bit block numbers relative to the start of the allocation group. The following fields are present in the allocation group header:

▼   Allocation group header magic number (for checking).

■   Allocation group header version number.

■   Allocation group sequence number (for checking), starting from zero.

■   If the bitmap allocation scheme is used, the location (relative block number) and size (lbsz) of the free block bitmap and summary information.

■   If the two B-tree allocation scheme is used, the location (relative block number) of each of the B-tree roots. We might choose to fit one or both roots into the allocation group header's logical block.

▲   Location (relative block number) of the "inode" which contains the inode table; this might instead be stored next to the allocation group.

The number of free and allocated blocks and inodes could be maintained per allocation group. For accuracy the changes would need to be logged, implying extra log activity not otherwise needed to log the allocation group header. Instead, this information will be present only in the super-block, which is sufficient for df purposes.

Data Block Freelist

There are two basic schemes under consideration for data block allocation. In both cases, the designs do not keep any information in kernel memory, just in buffers. That is, all information is read from and written to disk, and all changes are logged. This makes the designs scale better with respect to memory usage than designs which eat up memory per allocation group.

In the first scheme, a bitmap covers all the logical blocks in the allocation group, including the header information and the bitmap itself. The bitmap is a single extent of logical blocks taken from inside the allocation group's blocks. The bitmap moves only if the file system is extended (for the old last allocation group of the file system) or shrunk (for the new last allocation group of the file system). Bits in the bitmap are set for free blocks, clear for allocated blocks. To avoid having to scan the entire bitmap to find free extents of a given size, additional information is stored. For each block of the bitmap, for each possible extent size in the allocation group that is a power of two (2KB), we keep a count of the number of free extents of sizes 2KB to 2KB+1-1, starting in the block. The "blocks" are file system logical blocks. This information occupies a variable amount of space depending on the allocation group and logical block size of the file system. The worst case for 512-byte blocks and 1GB allocation groups is 21KB. For 4KB blocks and 1GB allocation groups the size of the information is 288 bytes (assuming that 4KB is taken as the bitmap block size). Each count entry is 16 bits. The information is ordered so that all entries related to a given size are together. These entries are searched to find a bitmap block that must describe a free extent large enough to satisfy the request. Then the bitmap block is searched to find the starting location; the search must be successful. A slight alteration of this scheme restricts each count to cover only free sections inside a single bitmap block. One scheme will be chosen depending on performance. In the second scheme, the allocation information is kept in a pair of B-trees. Both B-trees contain as data the pairs (starting free block, free block count) for all the free extents in the allocation group. One B-tree is indexed by the starting free block, the other by the free block count and secondarily by the starting free block, to make the keys unique. Block allocations first search one B-tree and then update both B-trees in the buffer cache and log the changes. Once the log entry is made, the B-tree buffers can be released to be written to disk when practical. Assuming that the buffer cache implements basically an LRU scheme for meta-data, this means that only blocks which are actually being referenced will be in memory.

Inode Table

The XFS designers felt that the traditional approach (as in UFS, the UNIX File System of Solaris) of statically allocating the inodes was contrary to the basic design goals of XFS. Therefore, XFS uses a scheme where the inodes are allocated on-demand, in small groups. This implies either that the inodes are stored in a single variable-sized extent, or that there is a high-level index pointing to chunks of inodes. The single-extent scheme is simple but prone to failure of allocation if the file system is fragmented, so we will ignore it.

An index scheme could work in one of two general ways: either with fixed-size chunks of inodes and a single-extent index, or with a B-tree (or a sequence of extent pointers) for the inode "file" as is done for regular files. We have chosen the latter method. Each allocation group header contains the root of a B-tree representing the inode space and an inode number. The B-tree represents a "file" which contains all the inode space for the allocation group, and the inode number refers to the first inode in the inode free list for the allocation group. Inodes on the inode free list are linked together by inode number through a field in the inode. The "file" containing the inodes is extended when necessary, with pre-allocation when possible. As is done for any other file, an attempt will be made to extend the inode table contiguously. Note, however, that sequential access to the inode table is rare, so its performance is not that important. The real reason for keeping the number of extents of the inode table small is to keep the B-tree representing it flatter. The B-tree entries contain the low 32 bits of the inode number for the first inode in the inode extent, the number of inodes in the extent (always a multiple of the number of inodes in a block), and the relative (to the allocation group header) disk block number of the start of the extent. The B-tree is indexed by the inode number field. This is different from the B-tree used for the bmap function only in the units and the sizes of the fields; the algorithms are the same.

The issue of having an inode bitmap versus having a freelist are really an independent dimension in the comparison of inode management schemes. In the bitmap case, allocation and freeing both require changing the inode and the bitmap word. In the freelist case, allocation and freeing both require changing the allocation group header and the inode. The freelist case may require less overall storage, since the freelist pointers are stored in the inodes. Theoretically, the freelist case allows less parallelism than the bitmap case, since the bitmap is broken into pieces which could be locked independently. In practice, this does not appear to be a significant restriction, since inode allocations can proceed in parallel in each allocation group. The bitmap case allows for allocating inodes near each other more easily. However, it's not clear how important this is.

By using a bitmap scheme instead of a freelist, the most likely design is to scatter inode-sized chunks of the free inode bitmap at the appropriate interval through the inode "file." For instance, if the inode size is 256 bytes, then at 256 * 8 = 2048 inode intervals, the data at that offset in the inode "file" would be a piece of bitmap instead of an inode. Thus, to find a free inode "near" an allocated one, calculate and read the appropriate bitmap block, and look near the allocated inode's bit position.

Another possible design is to have an independent set of extents for the bitmap. Then the whole set of issues about dealing with arbitrary sized bitmaps arises; it might be practical to restrict the bitmap to be a small number of extents, either fixed or variable sized. In any case, more disk I/O is required to manipulate the bitmap unless it's trivial to find the right bitmap block. The other disadvantage of an unadorned bitmap versus a freelist is that it's harder to find a free inode in the normal case when most inodes are allocated.

Inode Numbers

Inodes contain the information defining each file, directory, etc., in the file system. Each inode is named by its inode number, or inumber. In traditional UNIX file systems, inodes are numbered sequentially through the entire file system. In such file systems, there are the same number of inodes in each allocation, or cylinder group, and so there is no difficulty in locating a particular inode. In XFS, there is a variable number of inodes in each allocation group, and so having the traditional numbering scheme would mean that there would be great difficulty in translating an inumber to an inode disk address. The inode number in XFS is divided into two bitfields. The more significant bitfield is the allocation group number, the less significant is the inode number within the allocation group. For the moment, the two bitfields are each 32 bits, and the inumber is thus a 64-bit integer. The difficulty with dividing up a 32-bit integer into an allocation group number and an inode number is the possibility of making a file system so large that one or the other would run out of space in the bitfield. Since we want this file system design to be good for ten years or so, we will choose to spend this space in the disk format.

Data and Attribute Block Representation

The mapping from the address spaces of a file to disk blocks in the volume is implemented either by a B-tree or by a set of extent descriptors. For the B-tree, the information in each node of the tree is starting file offset [in logical blocks], starting volume block number, length of extent[in logical blocks]. The B-tree is keyed on the starting file offset field. The root block of the B-tree is stored in the inode, which means that the root block is a different size than the other blocks of the B-tree, which are of the logical block size of the file system.

The B-tree is composed of (potentially) multiple levels. At each level except the root level there are multiple blocks. Each non-leaf block contains keys (the starting file offset values) and pointers to other blocks; each leaf node contains only nodes (as above). The keys and pointers alternate logically in each block. When a pointer lies between two keys, the data (starting file offsets) in the block pointed to by the pointer lies between the two keys' values. Each block has K keys and K+1 pointers. When a block becomes full and an insertion is necessary, one of two operations is performed. First, a rotation is attempted. A rotation attempts to move overflow nodes to both neighboring blocks. If they are full, then the block is split: half of the information is moved to a new block, and the parent block points to two blocks instead of one. Alternatively, two blocks can be split producing three new blocks. This keeps the tree bushier. The procedure is followed recursively until the root is reached or there is room for the new information in the parent block. Deletion operations do essentially the opposite if the remaining blocks are not full enough. Search operations find the nearest lower or equal block number in the tree, then check to see if the block requested exists.

For the extent descriptor case, we have a pair of arrays: one of extent sizes (lbsz, 32 bits) and one of pointers to extents (64-bit volume block numbers). If there is a hole in the file, it is represented by a zero extent pointer. This scheme can be used for all files with a small number of extents. The scheme requires a linear search through the array to find

a particular block, since the file offset information is implied by the cumulative sizes. As an alternative, the file offset (another 64 bits) can be stored as well, and we can leave out the zero-pointers for holes in files. This means that a binary search was possible. On the other hand, fewer descriptors fit for the normal case where the files do not have holes. This information is stored in the inode directly. To compress this information down to 128 bits the information can be stored, for example, as 21 bits for the size, 52 bits for the volume block number, and 55 bits for the file block number.

The extent descriptor method is used unless that representation does not fit in the inode. The unreliable sub-volume is divided into a number of fixed-size pieces. The size is a multiple of the file system block size, and is set at mkfs time and stored in the superblock. The size is relatively large, 1MB or so. Free space in this sub-volume can therefore be represented by a simple bitmap. The bitmap must be reliable and thus is stored in the data sub-volume; the superblock points to it. In order to speed allocation further, a count is kept per bitmap block of the number of bits set. This set of counts is saved as an extent in the data sub-volume and also pointed to by the super-block.

File System Structure

For each mounted file system there is an in-core (allocated) structure containing or pointing to information pertaining to the file system, the VFS structure. This structure includes a field vfs_data which is private data for the file system implementation. This field points to a structure (xfs_mount for XFS, mount for EFS) which contains some per-file system information. Included in the xfs_mount structure will be the following information:

▼ Pointer back to the VFS structure.

■ Vnode pointer for the block device for the data region of the volume.

■ vvnode pointer for the block device for the log region of the volume.

■ Inode pointer to the in-core root inode of the file system.

■ Pointer to the list of in-core inodes for the file system.

■ Some fields for quotas; in EFS there are flags, an inode pointer, and a size.

■ Some statistics for our own use in tuning the implementation.

■ A copy of the super-block structure.

▲ An array of short structures, one per allocation group.

Buffering vs. Allocation

The critical data structures where there is some question about in-core (allocated) versus buffered are inodes and data and inode allocation bitmaps (or alternate data structures). For inodes, there is certainly a precedent for caching them in-core, into a fixed-size pool of in-core inode structures. The in-core inodes contain an on-disk inode as well as pointers and other information. The allocation strategy for this inode pool must be examined.

The next question for inodes is whether the B-tree representing the file's on-disk structure is pulled into memory or pulled on-demand into buffers. To allow support of very large files, this will need to use buffers. The free data block bitmaps (or B-trees) are potentially very large, indicating the use of buffers to reference them. We do not believe we can afford to copy these into allocated memory for large file systems. The inode allocation structures, while not as large, can be buffered as well without a substantial loss in performance. This assumption must be checked against the real implementation, though.

XFS Availability and Release Caveats

SGI XFS Pre-release 0.9 is available as a patch against Linux-2.4.0. It is also available as a set of RPMs and as a Modified Red Hat® 7.0 Installer which works with existing Red Hat 7.0 installation media to install a Red Hat 7.0 system with XFS on root, or any other partition, right out of the box.

Before installing the XFS file system for Linux, you should look over the XFS for Linux Pre-release 0.9 Caveats for a list of limitations, requirements, and special instructions for this release.

WORKING WITH XFS

In order to make XFS work for your Linux workstation or, better yet, server, you need to recreate partition and file systems for it. A direct migration from an ext2 file system is not possible. The three necessary steps for working with XFS are partitioning, formatting, and mounting.

Partitioning

You will need a partition on which to create your new XFS file system. This partition could be from a new disk, unpartitioned space on an existing disk, or you could overwrite an existing partition. In general, use the `fdisk` command to create or set the partition to "Linux Native (83)," and follow the instructions below to make an XFS file system on that partition.

Creating an XFS File System

You can create a new XFS file system in the same manner as you would any other Linux file system with the command:

```
mkfs -t xfs /dev/<devfile>
```

where `/dev/<devfile>` is the partition where you wish to create the file system. Note that this will destroy any file system currently on that partition.

For example, to create a file system on the third partition of your second SCSI drive, you would use the command:

```
mkfs -t xfs /dev/sdb3
```

One important option that you may need is "-f" which will force the creation of a new file system, if a file system already exists on that partition. Again, note that this will destroy all data currently on that partition:

```
mkfs -t xfs -f /dev/<devfile>
```

You may achieve better performance by increasing the logfile size from the default of 1200 blocks to, say, 8000 blocks. You can do this by creating the file system with the command:

```
mkfs -t xfs -l internal,size=8000b -d name=/dev/<devfile>
```

Other options are available for XFS file system creation.

Mounting an XFS filesystem

You can then mount the new file system with the command:

```
mount -t xfs /dev/<devfile> /<mount_pt>
```

where /dev/<devfile> is the device containing the file system, and /<mount_pt> is the mount point for the file system. Since XFS is a journaling file system, before it mounts the file system, it will check the transaction log for any unfinished transactions, and bring the file system up to date.

APPENDIX A

The Software-RAID HOWTO

Jakob OEstergaard (jakob@ostenfeld.dk)v. 0.90.7,
January 19, 2000

This HOWTO describes how to use Software RAID under Linux. It addresses a specific version of the Software RAID layer, namely the 0.90 RAID layer made by Ingo Molnar and others. This is the RAID layer that will be standard in Linux 2.4, and it is the version that is also used by Linux 2.2 kernels shipped from some vendors. The 0.90 RAID support is available as patches to Linux 2.0 and Linux 2.2, and is by many considered far more stable that the older RAID support already in those kernels.

TABLE OF CONTENTS

1. Introduction
    1.1 Disclaimer
    1.2 Requirements

2. Why RAID?
    2.1 Technicalities
    2.2 Terms
    2.3 The RAID levels
      2.3.1 Spare disks
    2.4 Swapping on RAID

3. Hardware issues
    3.1 IDE Configuration
    3.2 Hot Swap
      3.2.1 Hot-swapping IDE drives
      3.2.2 Hot-swapping SCSI drives
      3.2.3 Hot-swapping with SCA

4. RAID setup
    4.1 General setup
    4.2 Linear mode
    4.3 RAID-0
    4.4 RAID-1
    4.5 RAID-4
    4.6 RAID-5
    4.7 The Persistent Superblock
    4.8 Chunk sizes
      4.8.1 RAID-0
      4.8.2 RAID-1

4.8.3 RAID-4
4.8.4 RAID-5
4.9 Options for mke2fs
4.10 Autodetection
4.11 Booting on RAID
4.12 Root filesystem on RAID
4.12.1 Method 1
4.12.2 Method 2
4.13 Making the system boot on RAID
4.13.1 Booting with RAID as module
4.14 Pitfalls

5. Testing

5.1 Simulating a drive failure
5.2 Simulating data corruption

6. Reconstruction

6.1 Recovery from a multiple disk failure

7. Performance

7.1 RAID-0
7.2 RAID-0 with TCQ
7.3 RAID-5
7.4 RAID-10

8. Credits

1. Introduction

For a description of the older RAID layer, the one which is standard in 2.0 and 2.2 kernels, see the excellent HOWTO from Linas Vepstas (linas@linas.org) available from the Linux Documentation Project at linuxdoc.org.

The home site for this HOWTO is http://ostenfeld.dk/~jakob/Software-RAID.HOWTO/, where updated versions appear first. The HOWTO is written by Jakob OEstergaard based on a large number of e-mails between the author and Ingo Molnar (mingo@chiara.csoma.elte.hu), one of the RAID developers, the linux-raid mailing list (linux- raid@vger.rutgers.edu), and various other people.

The reason this HOWTO was written, even though a Software-RAID HOWTO already exists, is that the old HOWTO describes the old-style Software RAID found in the standard 2.0 and 2.2 kernels. This HOWTO describes the use of the new-style RAID that has been developed more recently. The new-style RAID has a lot of features not present in old-style RAID.

If you want to use the new-style RAID with 2.0 or 2.2 kernels, you should get a patch for your kernel, either from ftp://ftp.[your-country-code].kernel.org/pub/linux/daemons/raid/alpha, or more recently from http://people.redhat.com/mingo/ The standard 2.2 kernel does not have direct support for the new-style RAID described in this HOWTO. Therefore these patches are needed. The old-style RAID support in standard 2.0 and 2.2 kernels is buggy and lacks several important features present in the new-style RAID software.

As of this writing, the new-style RAID support is being merged into the 2.3 development kernels, and will therefore (most likely) be present in the 2.4 Linux kernel when that one comes out. But until then, the stable kernels must be patched manually.

You might want to use the -ac kernel releases done by Alan Cox, for RAID support in 2.2. Some of those contain the new-style RAID, and that will save you from patching the kernel yourself.

Some of the information in this HOWTO may seem trivial, if you know RAID all ready. Just skip those parts.

1.1. Disclaimer

The mandatory disclaimer:

Although RAID seems stable for me, and stable for many other people, it may not work for you. If you lose all your data, your job, get hit by a truck, whatever, it's not my fault, nor the developers'. Be aware, that you use the RAID software and this information at your own risk! There is no guarantee whatsoever, that any of the software, or this information, is in any way correct, nor suited for any use whatsoever. Back up all your data before experimenting with this. Better safe than sorry.

That said, I must also say that I haven't had a single stability problem with Software RAID, I use it on quite a few machines with no problems whatsoever, and I haven't seen other people having problems with random crashes or instability caused by RAID.

1.2. Requirements

This HOWTO assumes you are using a late 2.2.x or 2.0.x kernel with a matching raid0145 patch and the 0.90 version of the raidtools, or that you are using a late 2.3 kernel (version > 2.3.46) or eventually 2.4. Both the patches and the tools can be found at ftp://ftp.fi.kernel.org/pub/linux/daemons/raid/alpha, and in some cases at http://people.redhat.com/mingo/. The RAID patch, the raidtools package, and the kernel should all match as close as possible. At times it can be necessary to use older kernels if raid patches are not available for the latest kernel.

2. Why RAID?

There can be many good reasons for using RAID. A few are: the ability to combine several physical disks into one larger "virtual" device, performance improvements, and redundancy.

2.1. Technicalities

Linux RAID can work on most block devices. It doesn't matter whether you use IDE or SCSI devices, or a mixture. Some people have also used the Network Block Device (NBD) with more or less success.

Be sure that the bus(ses) to the drives are fast enough. You shouldn't have 14 UW-SCSI drives on one UW bus, if each drive can give 10MB/s and the bus can only sustain 40MB/s. Also, you should only have one device per IDE bus. Running disks as master/slave is horrible for performance. IDE is really bad at accessing more that one drive per bus. Of Course, all newer motherboards have two IDE busses, so you can set up two disks in RAID without buying more controllers.

The RAID layer has absolutely nothing to do with the filesystem layer. You can put any filesystem on a RAID device, just like any other block device.

2.2. Terms

The word "RAID" means "Linux Software RAID." This HOWTO does not treat any aspects of Hardware RAID.

When describing setups, it is useful to refer to the number of disks and their sizes. At all times the letter N is used to denote the number of active disks in the array (not counting spare-disks). The letter S is the size of the smallest drive in the array, unless otherwise mentioned. The letter P is used as the performance of one disk in the array, in MB/s. When used, we assume that the disks are equally fast, which may not always be true.

Note that the words "device" and "disk" are supposed to mean about the same thing. Usually the devices that are used to build a RAID device are partitions on disks, not necessarily entire disks. But combining several partitions on one disk usually does not make sense, so the words devices and disks just mean "partitions on different disks."

2.3. The RAID levels

Here's a short description of what is supported in the Linux RAID patches. Some of this information is absolutely basic RAID info, but I've added a few notices about what's special in the Linux implementation of the levels. Just skip this section if you know RAID. Then come back when you are having problems.

The current RAID patches for Linux support the following levels:

▼   Linear mode

■   Two or more disks are combined into one physical device. The disks are "appended" to each other, so writing to the RAID device will fill up disk 0 first, then disk 1 and so on. The disks do not have to be of the same size. In fact, size doesn't matter at all here.

■ There is no redundancy in this level. If one disk crashes you will most probably lose all your data. You can however be lucky to recover some data, since the filesystem will just be missing one large consecutive chunk of data.

■ The read and write performance will not increase for single reads/writes. But if several users use the device, you may be lucky that one user effectively is using the first disk, and the other user is accessing files which happen to reside on the second disk. If that happens, you will see a performance gain.

■ RAID-0

■ Also called "stripe" mode. Like linear mode, except that reads and writes are done in parallel to the devices. The devices should have approximately the same size. Since all access is done in parallel, the devices fill up equally. If one device is much larger than the other devices, that extra space is still utilized in the RAID device, but you will be accessing this larger disk alone during writes in the high end of your RAID device. This of course hurts performance.

■ Like linear, there's no redundancy in this level either. Unlike linear mode, you will not be able to rescue any data if a drive fails. If you remove a drive from a RAID-0 set, the RAID device will not just miss one consecutive block of data, it will be filled with small holes all over the device. e2fsck will probably not be able to recover much from such a device.

■ The read and write performance will increase, because reads and writes are done in parallel on the devices. This is usually the main reason for running RAID-0. If the busses to the disks are fast enough, you can get very close to N*P MB/sec.

■ RAID-1

■ This is the first mode which actually has redundancy. RAID-1 can be used on two or more disks with zero or more spare-disks. This mode maintains an exact mirror of the information on one disk on the other disk(s). Of Course, the disks must be of equal size. If one disk is larger than another, your RAID device will be the size of the smallest disk.

■ If up to N-1 disks are removed (or crashes), all data are still intact. If there are spare disks available, and if the system (e.g., SCSI drivers or IDE chipset etc.) survived the crash, reconstruction of the mirror will immediately begin on one of the spare disks, after detection of the drive fault.

■ Write performance is slightly worse than on a single device, because identical copies of the data written must be sent to every disk in the array. Read performance is usually pretty bad because of an oversimplified read-balancing strategy in the RAID code. However, there has been implemented a much improved read-balancing strategy, which might be available for the Linux-2.2

RAID patches (ask on the linux-kernel list), and which will most likely be in the standard 2.4 kernel RAID support.

- RAID-4

- This RAID level is not used very often. It can be used on three or more disks. Instead of completely mirroring the information, it keeps parity information on one drive, and writes data to the other disks in a RAID-0 like way. Because one disks is reserved for parity information, the size of the array will be (N-1)*S, where S is the size of the smallest drive in the array. As in RAID-1, the disks should either be of equal size, or you will just have to accept that the S in the (N-1)*S formula above will be the size of the smallest drive in the array.

- If one drive fails, the parity information can be used to reconstruct all data. If two drives fail, all data is lost.

- The reason this level is not more frequently used, is because the parity information is kept on one drive. This information must be updated every time one of the other disks is written to. Thus, the parity disk will become a bottleneck, if it is not a lot faster than the other disks. However, if you just happen to have a lot of slow disks and a very fast one, this RAID level can be very useful.

- RAID-5

- This is perhaps the most useful RAID mode when one wishes to combine a larger number of physical disks, and still maintain some redundancy. RAID-5 can be used on three or more disks, with zero or more spare-disks. The resulting RAID-5 device size will be (N-1)*S, just like RAID-4. The big difference between RAID-5 and -4 is that the parity information is distributed evenly among the participating drives, avoiding the bottleneck problem in RAID-4.

- If one of the disks fail, all data are still intact, thanks to the parity information. If spare disks are available, reconstruction will begin immediately after the device failure. If two disks fail simultaneously, all data is lost. RAID-5 can survive one disk failure, but not two or more.

▲ Both read and write performance usually increase, but it's hard to predict how much.

2.3.1. Spare disks   Spare disks are disks that do not take part in the RAID set until one of the active disks fail. When a device failure is detected, that device is marked as "bad" and reconstruction is immediately started on the first spare-disk available.

Thus, spare disks add nice extra safety especially to RAID-5 systems that perhaps are hard to get to (physically). One can allow the system to run for some time, with a faulty device, since all redundancy is preserved by means of the spare disk.

You cannot be sure that your system will survive a disk crash. The RAID layer should handle device failures just fine, but SCSI drivers could be broken on error handling, or the IDE chipset could lock up, or a lot of other things could happen.

2.4. Swapping on RAID

There's no reason to use RAID for swap performance reasons. The kernel itself can stripe swapping on several devices, if you just give them the same priority in the fstab file.

A nice fstab looks like:

```
/dev/sda2          swap              swap      defaults,pri=1   0 0
/dev/sdb2          swap              swap      defaults,pri=1   0 0
/dev/sdc2          swap              swap      defaults,pri=1   0 0
/dev/sdd2          swap              swap      defaults,pri=1   0 0
/dev/sde2          swap              swap      defaults,pri=1   0 0
/dev/sdf2          swap              swap      defaults,pri=1   0 0
/dev/sdg2          swap              swap      defaults,pri=1   0 0
```

This setup lets the machine swap in parallel on seven SCSI devices. No need for RAID, since this has been a kernel feature for a long time.

Another reason to use RAID for swap is high availability. If you set up a system to boot on e.g., a RAID-1 device, the system should be able to survive a disk crash. But if the system has been swapping on the now faulty device, you will for sure be going down. Swapping on the RAID-1 device would solve this problem.

There has been a lot of discussion about whether swap was stable on RAID devices. This is a continuing debate, because it depends highly on other aspects of the kernel as well. As of this writing, it seems that swapping on RAID should be perfectly stable, except for when the array is reconstructing (e.g., after a new disk is inserted into a degraded array). When 2.4 comes out this is an issue that will most likely get addressed fairly quickly, but until then, you should stress-test the system yourself until you are either satisfied with the stability or conclude that you won't be swapping on RAID.

You can set up RAID in a swap file on a filesystem on your RAID device, or you can set up a RAID device as a swap partition, as you see fit. As usual, the RAID device is just a block device.

3. Hardware issues

This section will mention some of the hardware concerns involved when running software RAID.

3.1. IDE Configuration

It is indeed possible to run RAID over IDE disks, and excellent performance can be achieved too. In fact, today's price on IDE drives and controllers does make IDE something to be considered when setting up new RAID systems.

▼ **Physical stability**   IDE drives have traditionally been of lower mechanical quality than SCSI drives. Even today, the warranty on IDE drives is typically one year, whereas it is often three to five years on SCSI drives. Although it is not fair to say that IDE drives are per definition poorly made, one should be aware that IDE drives of some brand may fail more often that similar SCSI drives. However, other brands use the exact same mechanical setup for both SCSI and IDE drives. It all boils down to: All disks fail, sooner or later, and one should be prepared for that.

■ **Data integrity**   Earlier, IDE had no way of assuring that the data sent onto the IDE bus would be the same as the data actually written to the disk. This was due to total lack of parity, checksums, etc. With the Ultra-DMA standard, IDE drives now do a checksum on the data they receive, and thus it becomes highly unlikely that data gets corrupted.

■ **Performance**   I'm not going to write thoroughly about IDE performance here. The really short story is:

■ IDE drives are fast (12MB/s and beyond).

■ IDE has more CPU overhead than SCSI (but who cares?).

■ Only use one IDE drive per IDE bus, slave disks spoil performance.

▲ **Fault survival**   The IDE driver usually survives a failing IDE device. The RAID layer will mark the disk as failed, and if you are running RAID levels 1 or above, the machine should work just fine until you can take it down for maintenance.

It is very important, that you only use one IDE disk per IDE bus. Not only would two disks ruin the performance, but the failure of a disk often guarantees the failure of the bus, and therefore the failure of all disks on that bus. In a fault-tolerant RAID setup (RAID levels 1, 4, 5), the failure of one disk can be handled, but the failure of two disks (the two disks on the bus that fails due to the failure of the one disk) will render the array unusable. Also, when the master drive on a bus fails, the slave or the IDE controller may get awfully confused. One bus, one drive, that's the rule.

There are cheap PCI IDE controllers out there. You often get two or four busses for around $80. Considering the much lower price of IDE disks versus SCSI disks, I'd say an IDE disk array could be a really nice solution if one can live with the relatively low (around 8, probably) number of disks one can attach to a typical system (unless of course, you have a lot of PCI slots for those IDE controllers).

IDE has major cabling problems though when it comes to large arrays. Even if you had enough PCI slots, it's unlikely that you could fit much more than 8 disks in a system and still get it running without data corruption (caused by too long IDE cables).

3.2. Hot Swap

This has been a hot topic on the linux-kernel list for some time. Although hot swapping of drives is supported to some extent, it is still not something one can do easily.

3.2.1. Hot-swapping IDE drives Don't! IDE doesn't handle hot swapping at all. Sure, it may work for you, if your IDE driver is compiled as a module (only possible in the 2.2 series of the kernel), and you re-load it after you've replaced the drive. But you may just as well end up with a fried IDE controller, and you'll be looking at a lot more down-time than just the time it would have taken to replace the drive on a downed system.

The main problem, except for the electrical issues that can destroy your hardware, is that the IDE bus must be re-scanned after disks are swapped. The current IDE driver can't do that. If the new disk is 100% identical to the old one (wrt. geometry etc.), it may work even without re-scanning the bus, but really, you're walking the bleeding knife's edge here.

3.2.2. Hot-swapping SCSI drives Normal SCSI hardware is not hot-swappable either. It may, however, work. If your SCSI driver supports re-scanning the bus, and removing and appending devices, you may be able to hot-swap devices. However, on a normal SCSI bus you probably shouldn't unplug devices while your system is still powered up. But then again, it may just work (and you may end up with fried hardware).

The SCSI layer should survive if a disk dies, but not all SCSI drivers handle this yet. If your SCSI driver dies when a disk goes down, your system will go with it, and hot-plug isn't really interesting then.

3.2.3. Hot-swapping with SCA With SCA, it should be possible to hot-plug devices. However, I don't have the hardware to try this out, and I haven't heard from anyone who's tried, so I can't really give any recipe on how to do this.

If you want to play with this, you should know about SCSI and RAID internals anyway. So I'm not going to write something here that I can't verify works, instead I can give a few clues:

▼ Grep for remove-single-device in linux/drivers/scsi/scsi.c

▲ Take a look at raidhotremove and raidhotadd

Not all SCSI drivers support appending and removing devices. In the 2.2 series of the kernel, at least the Adaptec 2940 and Symbios NCR53c8xx drivers seem to support this, others may and may not. I'd appreciate if anyone has additional facts here.

4. RAID setup

4.1. General setup

This is what you need for any of the RAID levels:

▼   A kernel. Preferably a stable 2.2.X kernel, or the latest 2.0.X. (If 2.4 is out when you read this, go for that one instead.)

■   The RAID patches. There usually is a patch available for the recent kernels. (If you found a 2.4 kernel, the patches are already in and you can forget about them)

■   The RAID tools.

▲   Patience, pizza, and your favorite caffeinated beverage.

All this software can be found at ftp://ftp.fi.kernel.org/pub/linux. The RAID tools and patches are in the daemons/raid/alpha subdirectory. The kernels are found in the kernel subdirectory.

Patch the kernel, configure it to include RAID support for the level you want to use. Compile it and install it.

Then unpack, configure, compile and install the RAID tools.

Ok, so far so good. If you reboot now, you should have a file called /proc/mdstat. Remember it, that file is your friend. See what it contains, by doing a cat /proc/mdstat. It should tell you that you have the right RAID personality (e.g., RAID mode) registered, and that no RAID devices are currently active.

Create the partitions you want to include in your RAID set.

Now, let's go mode-specific.

4.2. Linear mode

Ok, so you have two or more partitions which are not necessarily the same size (but of course can be), which you want to append to each other.

Set up the /etc/raidtab file to describe your setup. I set up a raidtab for two disks in linear mode, and the file looked like this:

```
raiddev /dev/md0
        raid-level          linear
        nr-raid-disks       2
        chunk-size          32
        persistent-superblock 1
        device              /dev/sdb6
        raid-disk           0
        device              /dev/sdc5
        raid-disk           1
```

Spare-disks are not supported here. If a disk dies, the array dies with it. There's no information to put on a spare disk.

You're probably wondering why we specify a chunk-size here when linear mode just appends the disks into one large array with no parallelism. Well, you're completely right, it's odd. Just put in some chunk size and don't worry about this any more.

Ok, let's create the array. Run the command:

```
mkraid /dev/md0
```

This will initialize your array, write the persistent superblocks, and start the array.

Have a look in /proc/mdstat. You should see that the array is running.

Now, you can create a filesystem, just like you would on any other device, mount it, include it in your fstab and so on.

4.3. RAID-0

You have two or more devices, of approximately the same size, and you want to combine their storage capacity and also combine their performance by accessing them in parallel.

Set up the /etc/raidtab file to describe your configuration. An example raidtab looks like:

```
raiddev /dev/md0
        raid-level        0
        nr-raid-disks     2
        persistent-superblock 1
        chunk-size        4
        device            /dev/sdb6
        raid-disk         0
        device            /dev/sdc5
        raid-disk         1
```

Like in Linear mode, spare disks are not supported here either. RAID-0 has no redundancy, so when a disk dies, the array goes with it.

Again, you just run:

```
mkraid /dev/md0
```

to initialize the array. This should initialize the superblocks and start the raid device. Have a look in /proc/mdstat to see what's going on. You should see that your device is now running.

/dev/md0 is now ready to be formatted, mounted, used and abused.

4.4. RAID-1

You have two devices of approximately the same size, and you want the two to be mirrors of each other. Eventually you have more devices, which you want to keep as stand-by spare-disks, that will automatically become a part of the mirror if one of the active devices breaks.

Set up the /etc/raidtab file like this:

```
raiddev /dev/md0
        raid-level        1
        nr-raid-disks     2
        nr-spare-disks    0
        chunk-size        4
        persistent-superblock 1
        device            /dev/sdb6
        raid-disk         0
```

```
device              /dev/sdc5
raid-disk           1
```

If you have spare disks, you can add them to the end of the device specification:

```
device              /dev/sdd5
spare-disk          0
```

Remember to set the nr-spare-disks entry correspondingly.

Ok, now we're all set to start initializing the RAID.

1. The mirror must be constructed, e.g., the contents (however unimportant now, since the device is still not formatted) of the two devices must be synchronized.

2. Issue the

    ```
    mkraid /dev/md0
    ```

    command to begin the mirror initialization.

3. Check out the /proc/mdstat file. It should tell you that the /dev/md0 device has been started, that the mirror is being reconstructed, and an ETA of the completion of the reconstruction.

4. Reconstruction is done using idle I/O bandwidth. So, your system should still be fairly responsive, although your disk LEDs should be glowing nicely.

5. The reconstruction process is transparent, so you can actually use the device even though the mirror is currently under reconstruction.

6. Try formatting the device, while the reconstruction is running. It will work. Also you can mount it and use it while reconstruction is running. Of course, if the wrong disk breaks while the reconstruction is running, you're out of luck.

4.5. RAID-4

NOTE   I haven't tested this setup myself. The setup below is my best guess, not something I have actually had up running.

You have three or more devices of roughly the same size, one device is significantly faster than the other devices, and you want to combine them all into one larger device, still maintaining some redundancy information. Eventually you have a number of devices you wish to use as spare-disks.

Set up the /etc/raidtab file like this:

```
raiddev /dev/md0
        raid-level      4
        nr-raid-disks   4
        nr-spare-disks  0
        persistent-superblock 1
        chunk-size      32
```

```
        device          /dev/sdb1
        raid-disk       0
        device          /dev/sdc1
        raid-disk       1
        device          /dev/sdd1
        raid-disk       2
        device          /dev/sde1
        raid-disk       3
```

If we had any spare disks, they would be inserted in a similar way, following the raid-disk specifications;

```
        device          /dev/sdf1
        spare-disk      0
```

as usual.

Your array can be initialized with the

```
    mkraid /dev/md0
```

command as usual.

You should see the section on special options for mke2fs before formatting the device.

4.6. RAID-5

You have three or more devices of roughly the same size; you want to combine them into a larger device, but still to maintain a degree of redundancy for data safety. Eventually you have a number of devices to use as spare-disks that will not take part in the array before another device fails.

If you use N devices where the smallest has size S, the size of the entire array will be (N-1)*S. This "missing" space is used for parity (redundancy) information. Thus, if any disk fails, all data stay intact. But if two disks fail, all data is lost.

Set up the /etc/raidtab file like this:

```
raiddev /dev/md0
        raid-level      5
        nr-raid-disks   7
        nr-spare-disks  0
        persistent-superblock 1
        parity-algorithm        left-symmetric
        chunk-size      32
        device          /dev/sda3
        raid-disk       0
        device          /dev/sdb1
        raid-disk       1
        device          /dev/sdc1
```

```
raid-disk       2
device          /dev/sdd1
raid-disk       3
device          /dev/sde1
raid-disk       4
device          /dev/sdf1
raid-disk       5
device          /dev/sdg1
raid-disk       6
```

If we had any spare disks, they would be inserted in a similar way, following the raid-disk specifications:

```
device          /dev/sdh1
spare-disk      0
```

And so on.

A chunk size of 32KB is a good default for many general purpose filesystems of this size. The array on which the above raidtab is used, is a 7 times 6GB = 36GB (remember the $(n-1)*s = (7-1)*6 = 36$) device. It holds an ext2 filesystem with a 4KB block size. You could go higher with both array chunk-size and filesystem block-size if your filesystem is either much larger, or just holds very large files.

Ok, enough talking. You set up the raidtab, so let's see if it works.

Run the

```
mkraid /dev/md0
```

command, and see what happens. Hopefully your disks start working like mad, as they begin the reconstruction of your array. Have a look in /proc/mdstat to see what's going on.

If the device was successfully created, the reconstruction process has now begun. Your array is not consistent until this reconstruction phase has completed. However, the array is fully functional (except for the handling of device failures of course), and you can format it and use it even while it is reconstructing.

See the section on special options for mke2fs before formatting the array.

Ok, now when you have your RAID device running, you can always stop it or re-start it using the

```
raidstop /dev/md0
```

or

```
raidstart /dev/md0
```

commands.

Instead of putting these into init-files and rebooting a zillion times to make that work, read on, and get autodetection running.

4.7. The Persistent Superblock

Back in "The Good Old Days" (TM), the raidtools would read your /etc/raidtab file, and then initialize the array. However, this would require that the filesystem on which /etc/raidtab resided was mounted. This is unfortunate if you want to boot on a RAID.

Also, the old approach led to complications when mounting filesystems on RAID devices. They could not be put in the /etc/fstab file as usual, but would have to be mounted from the init-scripts.

The persistent superblocks solve these problems. When an array is initialized with the persistent-superblock option in the /etc/raidtab file, a special superblock is written in the beginning of all disks participating in the array. This allows the kernel to read the configuration of RAID devices directly from the disks involved, instead of reading from some configuration file that may not be available at all times.

You should, however, still maintain a consistent /etc/raidtab file, since you may need this file for later reconstruction of the array.

The persistent superblock is mandatory if you want auto-detection of your RAID devices upon system boot. This is described in the Autodetection section.

4.8. Chunk sizes

The chunk-size deserves an explanation. You can never write completely parallel to a set of disks. If you had two disks and wanted to write a byte, you would have to write four bits on each disk; actually, every second bit would go to disk 0 and the others to disk 1. Hardware just doesn't support that. Instead, we choose some chunk-size, which we define as the smallest "atomic" mass of data that can be written to the devices. A write of 16KB with a chunk size of 4KB, will cause the first and the third 4KB chunks to be written to the first disk, and the second and fourth chunks to be written to the second disk, in the RAID-0 case with two disks. Thus, for large writes, you may see lower overhead by having fairly large chunks, whereas arrays that are primarily holding small files may benefit more from a smaller chunk size.

▼ Chunk sizes must be specified for all RAID levels, including linear mode. However, the chunk-size does not make any difference for linear mode.

■ For optimal performance, you should experiment with the value, as well as with the block-size of the filesystem you put on the array.

▲ The argument to the chunk-size option in /etc/raidtab specifies the chunk-size in kilobytes. So "4" means "4KB."

4.8.1. RAID-0   Data is written "almost" in parallel to the disks in the array. Actually, chunk-size bytes are written to each disk, serially.

If you specify a 4KB chunk size, and write 16KB to an array of three disks, the RAID system will write 4KB to disks 0, 1 and 2, in parallel, then the remaining 4KB to disk 0.

A 32KB chunk-size is a reasonable starting point for most arrays. But the optimal value depends very much on the number of drives involved, the content of the file system you put on it, and many other factors. Experiment with it, to get the best performance.

4.8.2. RAID-1   For writes, the chunk-size doesn't affect the array, since all data must be written to all disks no matter what. For reads, however, the chunk-size specifies how much data to read serially from the participating disks. Since all active disks in the array contain the same information, reads can be done in a parallel RAID-0 like manner.

4.8.3. RAID-4   When a write is done on a RAID-4 array, the parity information must be updated on the parity disk as well. The chunk-size is the size of the parity blocks. If one byte is written to a RAID-4 array, then chunk- size bytes will be read from the N-1 disks, the parity information will be calculated, and chunk-size bytes written to the parity disk.

The chunk-size affects read performance in the same way as in RAID-0, since reads from RAID-4 are done in the same way.

4.8.4. RAID-5   On RAID-5 the chunk-size has exactly the same meaning as in RAID-4.

A reasonable chunk-size for RAID-5 is 128KB, but as always, you may want to experiment with this.

Also see the section on special options for mke2fs. This affects RAID-5 performance.

4.9. Options for mke2fs

There is a special option available when formatting RAID-4 or -5 devices with mke2fs. The -R stride=nn option will allow mke2fs to better place different ext2 specific data-structures in an intelligent way on the RAID device.

If the chunk-size is 32KB, it means, that 32KB of consecutive data will reside on one disk. If we want to build an ext2 filesystem with 4KB block-size, we realize that there will be eight filesystem blocks in one array chunk. We can pass this information on to the mke2fs utility, when creating the filesystem:

```
mke2fs -b 4096 -R stride=8 /dev/md0
```

RAID-{4,5} performance is severely influenced by this option. I am unsure how the stride option will affect other RAID levels. If anyone has information on this, please send it in my direction.

The ext2fs blocksize severely influences the performance of the filesystem. You should always use 4KB block size on any filesystem larger than a few hundred megabytes, unless you store a very large number of very small files on it.

4.10. Autodetection

Autodetection allows the RAID devices to be automatically recognized by the kernel at boot-time, right after the ordinary partition detection is done.

This requires several things:

1. You need autodetection support in the kernel. Check this.
2. You must have created the RAID devices using persistent-superblock.
3. The partition-types of the devices used in the RAID must be set to 0xFD (use fdisk and set the type to "fd").

NOTE: Be sure that your RAID is NOT RUNNING before changing the partition types. Use raidstop / dev/md0 to stop the device.

If you set up 1, 2 and 3 from above, autodetection should be set up. Try rebooting. When the system comes up, cat'ing /proc/mdstat should tell you that your RAID is running. During boot, you could see messages similar to these:

```
Oct 22 00:51:59 malthe kernel: SCSI device sdg: hdwr sector= 512
 bytes. Sectors= 12657717 [6180MB] [6.2 GB]
Oct 22 00:51:59 malthe kernel: Partition check:
Oct 22 00:51:59 malthe kernel:  sda: sda1 sda2 sda3 sda4
Oct 22 00:51:59 malthe kernel:  sdb: sdb1 sdb2
Oct 22 00:51:59 malthe kernel:  sdc: sdc1 sdc2
Oct 22 00:51:59 malthe kernel:  sdd: sdd1 sdd2
Oct 22 00:51:59 malthe kernel:  sde: sde1 sde2
Oct 22 00:51:59 malthe kernel:  sdf: sdf1 sdf2
Oct 22 00:51:59 malthe kernel:  sdg: sdg1 sdg2
Oct 22 00:51:59 malthe kernel: autodetecting RAID arrays
Oct 22 00:51:59 malthe kernel: (read) sdb1's sb offset: 6199872
Oct 22 00:51:59 malthe kernel: bind
Oct 22 00:51:59 malthe kernel: (read) sdc1's sb offset: 6199872
Oct 22 00:51:59 malthe kernel: bind
Oct 22 00:51:59 malthe kernel: (read) sdd1's sb offset: 6199872
Oct 22 00:51:59 malthe kernel: bind
Oct 22 00:51:59 malthe kernel: (read) sde1's sb offset: 6199872
Oct 22 00:51:59 malthe kernel: bind
Oct 22 00:51:59 malthe kernel: (read) sdf1's sb offset: 6205376
Oct 22 00:51:59 malthe kernel: bind
Oct 22 00:51:59 malthe kernel: (read) sdg1's sb offset: 6205376
Oct 22 00:51:59 malthe kernel: bind
Oct 22 00:51:59 malthe kernel: autorunning md0
Oct 22 00:51:59 malthe kernel: running:
Oct 22 00:51:59 malthe kernel: now!
Oct 22 00:51:59 malthe kernel: md: md0: raid array is not clean —
 starting background reconstruction
```

This is output from the autodetection of a RAID-5 array that was not cleanly shut down (e.g., the machine crashed). Reconstruction is auto-matically initiated. Mounting this device is perfectly safe, since reconstruction is transparent and all data is consistent (it's only the parity information that is inconsistent — but that isn't needed until a device fails).

Autostarted devices are also automatically stopped at shutdown. Don't worry about init scripts. Just use the /dev/md devices as any other

```
/dev/sd or /dev/hd devices.
```

Yes, it really is that easy.

You may want to look in your init-scripts for any raidstart/raidstop commands. These are often found in the standard RedHat init scripts. They are used for old-style RAID, and have no use in new-style RAID with autodetection. Just remove the lines, and everything will be just fine.

4.11. Booting on RAID

There are several ways to set up a system that mounts its root filesystem on a RAID device. At the moment, only the graphical install of RedHat Linux 6.1 allows direct installation to a RAID device. So most likely you're in for a little tweaking if you want this, but it is indeed possible.

The latest official lilo distribution (Version 21) doesn't handle RAID devices, and thus the kernel cannot be loaded at boot-time from a RAID device. If you use this version, your /boot filesystem will have to reside on a non-RAID device. A way to ensure that your system boots no matter what is to create similar /boot partitions on all drives in your RAID; that way the BIOS can always load data from e.g., the first drive available. This requires that you do not boot with a failed disk in your system.

With redhat 6.1 a patch to lilo 21 has become available that can handle /boot on RAID-1. Note that it doesn't work for any other level; RAID-1 (mirroring) is the only supported RAID level. This patch (lilo.raid1) can be found in dist/redhat-6.1/SRPMS/ SRPMS/lilo-0.21-10.src.rpm on any redhat mirror. The patched version of LILO will accept boot=/dev/md0 in lilo.conf and will make each disk in the mirror bootable.

Another way of ensuring that your system can always boot is to create a boot floppy when all the setup is done. If the disk on which the /boot filesystem resides dies, you can always boot from the floppy.

4.12. Root filesystem on RAID

In order to have a system booting on RAID, the root filesystem (/) must be mounted on a RAID device. Two methods for achieving this are supplied below. Because none of the current distributions (that I know of at least) support installing on a RAID device, the methods assume that you install on a normal partition, and then — when the installation is complete — move the contents of your non-RAID root file system onto a new RAID device.

4.12.1. Method 1 This method assumes you have a spare disk you can install the system on, which is not part of the RAID you will be configuring.

▼ First, install a normal system on your extra disk.

■ Get the kernel you plan on running, get the raid-patches and the tools, and make your system boot with this new RAID-aware kernel.
Make sure that RAID-support is in the kernel, and is not loaded as modules.

■ Ok, now you should configure and create the RAID you plan to use for the root filesystem. This is standard procedure, as described elsewhere in this document.

■ Just to make sure everything's fine, try rebooting the system to see if the new RAID comes up on boot. It should.

■ Put a filesystem on the new array (using mke2fs), and mount it under /mnt/newroot.

■ Now, copy the contents of your current root-filesystem (the spare disk) to the new root-filesystem (the array). There are lots of ways to do this, one of them is:

```
cd /
find . -xdev | cpio -pm /mnt/newroot
```

■ You should modify the /mnt/newroot/etc/fstab file to use the correct device (the /dev/md? root device) for the root filesystem.

■ Now, unmount the current /boot filesystem, and mount the boot device on /mnt/newroot/boot instead. This is required for LILO to run successfully in the next step.

■ Update /mnt/newroot/etc/lilo.conf to point to the right devices.
The boot device must still be a regular disk (non-RAID device), but the root device should point to your new RAID. When done, run lilo -r /mnt/newroot complete with no errors.

▲ Reboot the system, and watch everything come up as expected.

If you're doing this with IDE disks, be sure to tell your BIOS that all disks are "auto-detect" types, so that the BIOS will allow your machine to boot even when a disk is missing.

4.12.2. Method 2 This method requires that you use a raidtools/patch that includes the failed-disk directive. This will be the tools/patch for all kernels from 2.2.10 and later.

You can only use this method on RAID levels 1 and above. The idea is to install a system on a disk which is purposely marked as failed in the RAID, then copy the system to the RAID which will be running in degraded mode, and finally making the RAID use the no-longer needed "install-disk," zapping the old installation but making the RAID run in non-degraded mode.

▼ First, install a normal system on one disk (that will later become part of your RAID). It is important that this disk (or partition) is not the smallest one. If it is, it will not be possible to add it to the RAID later on!

■ Then, get the kernel, the patches, the tools etc. etc. You know the drill. Make your system boot with a new kernel that has the RAID support you need, compiled into the kernel.

■ Now, set up the RAID with your current root-device as the failed-disk in the raidtab file. Don't put the failed-disk as the first disk in the raidtab; that will give you problems with starting the RAID. Create the RAID, and put a filesystem on it.

■ Try rebooting and see if the RAID comes up as it should.

■ Copy the system files, and reconfigure the system to use the RAID as root-device, as described in the previous section.

■ When your system successfully boots from the RAID, you can modify the raidtab file to include the previously failed-disk as a normal raid-disk. Now, raidhotadd the disk to your RAID.

▲ You should now have a system that can boot from a non-degraded RAID.

4.13. Making the system boot on RAID

For the kernel to be able to mount the root filesystem, all support for the device on which the root filesystem resides must be present in the kernel. Therefore, in order to mount the root filesystem on a RAID device, the kernel must have RAID support.

The normal way of ensuring that the kernel can see the RAID device is to simply compile a kernel with all necessary RAID support compiled in. Make sure that you compile the RAID support into the kernel, and not as loadable modules. The kernel cannot load a module (from the root filesystem) before the root filesystem is mounted.

However, since RedHat-6.0 ships with a kernel that has new-style RAID support as modules, I here describe how one can use the standard RedHat-6.0 kernel and still have the system boot on RAID.

4.13.1. Booting with RAID as module   You will have to instruct LILO to use a RAM-disk in order to achieve this. Use the mkinitrd command to create a ramdisk containing all kernel modules needed to mount the root partition. This can be done as:

```
mkinitrd --with=
```

For example:

```
mkinitrd --with=raid5 raid-ramdisk 2.2.5-22
```

This will ensure that the specified RAID module is present at boot-time, for the kernel to use when mounting the root device.

4.14. Pitfalls

Never NEVER never re-partition disks that are part of a running RAID. If you must alter the partition table on a disk which is a part of a RAID, stop the array first, then repartition.

It is easy to put too many disks on a bus. A normal Fast-Wide SCSI bus can sustain 10MB/s which is less than many disks can do alone today. Putting six such disks on the bus will of course not give you the expected performance boost.

More SCSI controllers will only give you extra performance, if the SCSI busses are nearly maxed out by the disks on them. You will not see a performance improvement from using two 2940s with two old SCSI disks, instead of just running the two disks on one controller.

If you forget the persistent-superblock option, your array may not start up willingly after it has been stopped. Just re-create the array with the option set correctly in the raidtab.

If a RAID-5 fails to reconstruct after a disk was removed and re- inserted, this may be because of the ordering of the devices in the raidtab. Try moving the first "device ..." and "raid-disk ..." pair to the bottom of the array description in the raidtab file.

Most of the "error reports" we see on linux-kernel, are from people who somehow failed to use the right RAID-patch with the right version of the raidtools. Make sure that if you're running 0.90 RAID, you're using the raidtools for it.

5. Testing

If you plan to use RAID to get fault-tolerance, you may also want to test your setup, to see if it really works. Now, how does one simulate a disk failure ?

The short story is, that you can't, except perhaps for putting a fire axe through the drive you want to "simulate" the fault on. You can never know what will happen if a drive dies. It may electrically take the bus it's attached to with it, rendering all drives on that bus inaccessible. I've never heard of that happening though. The drive may also just report a read/write fault to the SCSI/IDE layer, which in turn makes the RAID layer handle this situation gracefully. This is fortunately the way things often go.

5.1. Simulating a drive failure

If you want to simulate a drive failure, then unplug the drive. You should do this with the power off. If you are interested in testing whether your data can survive with a disk less than the usual number, there is no point in being a hot-plug cowboy here. Take the system down, unplug the disk, and boot it up again.

Look in the syslog, and look at /proc/mdstat to see how the RAID is doing. Did it work?

Remember, that you must be running RAID-{1,4,5} for your array to be able to survive a disk failure. Linear- or RAID-0 will fail completely when a device is missing.

When you've re-connected the disk again (with the power off, of course, remember), you can add the "new" device to the RAID again, with the raidhotadd command.

5.2. Simulating data corruption

RAID (be it hardware or software), assumes that if a write to a disk doesn't return an error, then the write was successful. Therefore, if your disk corrupts data without returning an error, your data will become corrupted. This is of course very unlikely to happen, but it is possible, and it would result in a corrupt filesystem.

RAID cannot and is not supposed to guard against data corruption on the media. Therefore, it doesn't make any sense either to purposely corrupt data (using dd for example) on a disk to see how the RAID system will handle that. It is most likely (unless you corrupt the RAID superblock) that the RAID layer will never find out about the corruption, but your filesystem on the RAID device will be corrupted.

This is the way things are supposed to work. RAID is not a guarantee for data integrity, it just allows you to keep your data if a disk dies (that is, with RAID levels above or equal one, of course).

6. Reconstruction

If you've read the rest of this HOWTO, you should already have a pretty good idea about what reconstruction of a degraded RAID involves. I'll summarize:

- ▼ Power down the system.
- ■ Replace the failed disk.
- ■ Power up the system once again.
- ■ Use raidhotadd /dev/mdX /dev/sdX to re-insert the disk in the array.
- ▲ Have coffee while you watch the automatic reconstruction running.

And that's it.

Well, it usually is, unless you're unlucky and your RAID has been rendered unusable because more disks than the redundant ones failed. This can actually happen if a number of disks reside on the same bus, and one disk takes the bus with it as it crashes. The other disks, however fine, will be unreachable to the RAID layer, because the bus is down, and they will be marked as faulty. On a RAID-5 where you can spare one disk, loosing two or more disks can be fatal.

The following section is the explanation that Martin Bene gave to me, and describes a possible recovery from the scary scenario outlined above. It involves using the failed-disk directive in your /etc/raidtab, so this will only work on kernels 2.2.10 and later.

6.1. Recovery from a multiple disk failure

The scenario is:

- ▼ A controller dies and takes two disks offline at the same time,
- ■ All disks on one scsi bus can no longer be reached if a disk dies,
- ▲ A cable comes loose...

In short: quite often you get a temporary failure of several disks at once; afterwards the RAID superblocks are out of sync and you can no longer init your RAID array.

One thing left: rewrite the RAID superblocks by mkraid—force.

To get this to work, you'll need to have an up to date /etc/raidtab—if it doesn't EXACTLY match devices and ordering of the original disks this won't work.

Look at the sylog produced by trying to start the array, you'll see the event count for each superblock; usually it's best to leave out the disk with the lowest event count, i.e., the oldest one.

If you mkraid without failed-disk, the recovery thread will kick in immediately and start rebuilding the parity blocks—not necessarily what you want at that moment.

With failed-disk you can specify exactly which disks you want to be active and perhaps try different combinations for best results. By the way, only mount the file system read-only while trying this out. This has been successfully used by at least two guys I've been in contact with.

7. Performance

This section contains a number of benchmarks from a real-world system using software RAID. Benchmarks are done with the bonnie program, and at all times on files twice—or more the size of the physical RAM in the machine.

The benchmarks here only measure input and output bandwidth on one large single file. This is a nice thing to know, if it's maximum I/O throughput for large reads/writes one is interested in. However, such numbers tell us little about what the performance would be if the array was used for a news spool, a web server, etc. Always keep in mind, that benchmarks numbers are the result of running a "synthetic" program. Few real-world programs do what bonnie does, and although these I/O numbers are nice to look at, they are not ultimate real-world-appliance performance indicators. Not even close.

For now, I only have results from my own machine. The setup is:

▼   Dual Pentium Pro 150 MHz

■   256MB RAM (60 MHz EDO)

■   Three IBM UltraStar 9ES 4.5 GB, SCSI U2W

■   Adaptec 2940U2W

■   One IBM UltraStar 9ES 4.5 GB, SCSI UW

■   Adaptec 2940 UW

▲   Kernel 2.2.7 with RAID patches

The three U2W disks hang off the U2W controller, and the UW disk off the UW controller.

It seems to be impossible to push much more than 30MB/s thru the SCSI busses on this system, using RAID or not. My guess is, that because the system is fairly old, the memory bandwidth sucks, and thus limits what can be sent thru the SCSI controllers.

7.1. RAID-0

Read is Sequential block input, and Write is Sequential block output. File size was 1GB in all tests. The tests were done in single-user mode. The SCSI driver was configured not to use tagged command queuing.

Chunk size	Block size	Read KB/s	Write KB/s
4k	1k	19712	18035
4k	4k	34048	27061
8k	1k	19301	18091
8k	4k	33920	27118
16k	1k	19330	18179
16k	2k	28161	23682
16k	4k	33990	27229
32k	1k	19251	18194
32k	4k	34071	26976

From this it seems that the RAID chunk-size doesn't make that much of a difference. However, the ext2fs block-size should be as large as possible, which is 4KB (e.g., the page size) on IA-32.

7.2. RAID-0 with TCQ

This time, the SCSI driver was configured to use tagged command queuing, with a queue depth of 8. Otherwise, everything's the same as before.

Chunk size	Block size	Read KB/s	Write KB/s
32k	4k	33617	27215

No more tests were done. TCQ seemed to slightly increase write performance, but there really wasn't much of a difference at all.

7.3. RAID-5

The array was configured to run in RAID-5 mode, and similar tests where done.

Chunk size	Block size	Read KB/s	Write KB/s

8k	1k	11090	6874	
8k	4k	13474	12229	
32k	1k	11442	8291	
32k	2k	16089	10926	
32k	4k	18724	12627	

Now, both the chunk-size and the block-size seems to actually make a difference.

7.4. RAID-10

RAID-10 is "mirrored stripes," or, a RAID-1 array of two RAID-0 arrays. The chunk-size is the chunk sizes of both the RAID-1 array and the two RAID-0 arrays. I did not do a test where those chunk-sizes differ, although that should be a perfectly valid setup.

Chunk size	Block size	Read KB/s	Write KB/s	
32k	1k	13753	11580	
32k	4k	23432	22249	

No more tests were done. The file size was 900MB, because the four partitions involved were 500 MB each, which doesn't give room for a 1G file in this setup (RAID-1 on two 1000MB arrays).

8. Credits

The following people contributed to the creation of this documentation:

- ▼ Ingo Molnar
- ■ Jim Warren
- ■ Louis Mandelstam
- ■ Allan Noah
- ■ Yasunori Taniike
- ■ Martin Bene
- ■ Bennett Todd
- ■ The Linux-RAID mailing list people
- ▲ The ones I forgot, sorry

Please submit corrections, suggestions, etc., to the author. It's the only way this HOWTO can improve.

APPENDIX B

References

Blair, David C. and Marron, M. E. "Evaluation of Retrieval Effectiveness for a Full-Text Document-Retrieval System," *Communications of the ACM*, v28 n3 Mar 1985, p. 289-299.

Codd, E. F. "The Relational Model for Database Management: version 2" c1990 AddisonWesley Pub. Co, Not recommended as a textbook, Date's is better for that, but worthwhile if you want a long paper by Codd. Notice that he places greater emphasis on closure, and design methodology principles in general, than designers of other naming systems such as hypertext.

Date, C.J. *An Introduction to Database Systems*, 4th ed. Reading, Mass.: Addison-Wesley Pub. Co., c1986. Contains a well written substantive textbook sneer at the problems of hierarchical naming systems, and a well annotated bibliography.

Curtis, Ronald and Wittie, Larry. "Global Naming in Distributed Systems," *IEEE Software*, July 1984, p. 76-80.

Feldman, Jerome A., Fanty, Mark A., Goddard, Nigel H. and Lynne, Kenton J. "Computing with Structured Connectionist Network,." *Communications of the ACM*, v31, Feb 1988, p. 170(18).

Fox, E. A., and Wu, H. "Extended Boolean Information Retrieval," *Communications of the ACM*, 26, 1983, pp. 1022-1036.

Gallant, Stephen I., "Connectionist Expert Systems," *Communications of the ACM*, v31 Feb 1988, pl52(18).

Gates, Bill. Comdex '91 speech on "Information at Your Fingertips," available for $8 on videotape from Microsoft's sales department.

Gifford, David K., Jouvelot, Pierre, Sheldon, Mark A., O'Toole, James W. Jr., "Semantic File Systems," *Operating Systems Review*, v25, n5, October 13-16, 1991. They demonstrated that extending Unix file semantics to include nonhierarchical features is useful and feasible. Unfortunately, their naming system lacks closure.

Gilula, Mikhail. *The Set Model for Database and Information Systems*, 1st Edition, c 1994, Addison-Wesley. Provides a Set Theoretic Database Model in which relational algebra is a shown to be a special case of a more general and powerful set theoretic approach.

Joint Object Services Submission (JOSS), OMG TC Document 93.5.1.

Marchionini, Gary, and Shneiderman, Ben. "Finding Facts vs. Browsing Knowledge in Hypertext Systems," *Computer*, January 1988, p. 70.

McAleese, Ray. "Hypertext: Theory into Practice," edited by Ray McAleese, ABLEX Publishing Corporation, Norwood, NJ 07648.

Messinger, Eli, Shoens, Kurt, Thomas, John, Luniewski, Allen. "Rufus: The Information Sponge," Research Report RJ 8294 (75655), August 13, 1991, IBM Almaden Research Center.

Metzler and Haas. "The Constituent Object Parser: Syntactic Structure Matching for Information Retrieval," *Proceedings of the ACM SIGIR Conference*, 1989, ACM Press.

Nelson, T.H. *Literary Machines*, self published by Nelson, Nashville, Tenn., 1981. Did much to popularize hypertext; at the time of writing he has still not released a working product, though competitors such as hypercard have done so with notable success.

Mozer, Nfichael C. "Inductive Information Retrieval Using Parallel Distributed Computation," UCLA.

Pike, Rob and Weinberger, P.J. "The Hideous Name," AT&T Research Report.

Pike, Rob, Presotto, Dave, Thompson, Ken, Trickey, Howard, Winterbottom, Phil. "The Use of Name Spaces in Plan 9," available via ftp from att.com. Plan 9 is an operating system intended to be the successor to Unix, and greater integration of its name spaces is its primary focus.

Potter, Walter D. and Trueblood, Robert P. "Traditional, semantic, and hyper-semantic approaches to data modeling," *Computer*, v21, 1988, p. 53(11).

Rijsbergen, C. J. Van, *Information Retrieval*, 2nd. ed., Butterworth and Co. Ltd., 1979, printed in Great Britain by The Whitefriars Ltd., London and Tonbridge.

Salton, G. "Another Look At Automatic Text-Retrieval Systems," *Communications of the ACM*, v29, 1986, pp. 648-656.

Smith, J.M. and Smith, D.C. "Database Abstractions: Aggregation and Generalization," *ACM Transactions Database Systems*, June 1977, pp. 105-133, ICS Report No. 8406, June 1984.

Corbató, F. J. and Vyssotsky, V. A. "Introduction and Overview of the Multics System," this volume.

Couleur, J.F., Glaser, E.L., and Oliver, G. A. "System Design of a Computer for Time-Sharing Applications," this volume.

Corbató, F.J., Graham, R.M., and Vyssotsky, V. A."Structure of the Multics Supervisor," this volume.

Dunten, S. D., Mikus, L.E. and Ossana, J. F. "Communications and Input-Output Switching in a Multiplex Computing System," this volume.

David Jr., E. E., and Fano, R. M. "Some Thoughts About the Social Implications of Accessible Computing," this volume.

Acceta, M., Baron, R., Bolosky, W., Golub, D., Rashid, R., Tevanian, A. and Young, M. "Mach: A New Kernel Foundation For UNIX Development." In *Proceedings of the USENIX 1986 Summer Conference*, June 1986.

Bach, M. *The Design of the UNIX Operating System*. Prentice Hall, 1986.

Bina, E. and Emrath, P. A Faster fsck for BSD Unix. In *Proceedings of the USENIX Winter Conference*, January 1989.

Card, R., Commelin, E., Dayras, S. and Mével, F. The MASIX Multi-Server Operating System. In *OSF Workshop on Microkernel Technology for Distributed Systems*, June 1993.

SECURITY INTERFACE for the Portable Operating System Interface for Computer Environments - Draft 13. Institute of Electrical and Electronics Engineers, Inc, 1992.

Kleiman, S. "Vnodes: An Architecture for Multiple File System Types in Sun UNIX. In *Proceedings of the Summer USENIX Conference*, pp. 260-269, June 1986.

Fabry, R., Joy, W., McKusick, M. and Leffler, S. "A Fast File System for UNIX." *ACM Transactions on Computer Systems*, 2(3):181-197, August 1984.

Bostic, K., McKusick, M., Seltzer, M. and Staelin, C. "An Implementation of a Log-Structured File System for UNIX." In *Proceedings of the USENIX Winter Conference*, January 1993.

Tanenbaum, A. *Operating Systems: Design and Implementation*. Prentice Hall, 1987.

Additional References

Bachman, C. W. and Williams, S. B. "A General Purpose Programming System for Random Access Memories," *Proceedings of the Fall Joint Computer Conference*, 26, Spartan Books, Baltimore, 1964.

Dennis, J. B. and Van horn, E. C. "Programming Semantics for Multiprogrammed Computations," *ACM Conference on Programming Languages,* San Dimas, Calif., Aug. 1965. To be published in *Comm. ACM.*

Holt, W. "Program Organization and Record Keeping for Dynamic Storage Allocation," *Comm. ACM* 4, pp. 422-431, Oct. 1961.

Nelson, T. H. "A File Structure for the Complex, the Changing and the Indeterminate," *ACM National Conference,* Aug. 1965.

Wilkes, M. V. "A Programmer's Utility Filing System," *Computer Journal 7,* pp. 180-184, Oct.1964.

APPENDIX C

The Loopback Root Filesystem HOWTO

The Loopback Root Filesystem HOWTO by Andrew M. Bishop,
amb@gedanken.demon.co.uk, v1.1, September 24, 1999

This HOWTO explains how to use the Linux loopback device to create a Linux native filesystem format installation that can be run from a DOS partition without re-partitioning. Other uses of this same technique are also discussed.

TABLE OF CONTENTS

1. Introduction
1.1 Copyright
1.2 Revision History

2. Principles of Loopback Devices and Ramdisks
2.1 Loopback Devices
2.2 Ramdisk Devices
2.3 The Initial Ramdisk Device
2.4 The Root Filesystem
2.5 The Linux Boot Sequence

3. How To Create a Loopback Root Device
3.1 Requirements
3.2 Creating the Linux Kernel
3.3 Creating the Initial Ramdisk Device
3.4 Creating The Root Device
3.5 Creating the Swap Device
3.6 Creating the MSDOS Directory
3.7 Creating the Boot Floppy

4. Booting the System
4.1 Possible Problems With Solutions
4.2 Reference Documents

5. Other Loopback Root Device Possibilities
5.1 DOS Hard-disk Only Installation
5.2 LILO Booted Installation
5.3 VFAT / NTFS Installation
5.4 Installing Linux without Re-partitioning
5.5 Booting From a Non-bootable device

1. Introduction

1.1.Copyright

The Loopback Root Filesystem HOWTO Copyright © 1998–99 Andrew M. Bishop (amb@gedanken.demon.co.uk).

This documentation is free documentation; you can redistribute it and/or modify it under the terms of the GNU General Public License as published by the Free Software Foundation; either version 2 of the License, or (at your option) any later version.

This program is distributed in the hope that it will be useful, but WITHOUT ANY WARRANTY; without even the implied warranty of MERCHANTABILITY or FITNESS FOR A PARTICULAR PURPOSE. See the GNU General Public License for more details.

The GNU General Public License is available from http://www.fsf.org/ or, write to the Free Software Foundation, Inc., 59 Temple Place, Suite 330, Boston, MA 02111 USA.

1.2. Revision History

Version 1.0.0	Initial Version (June 1998)
Version 1.0.1-1.0.3	Slight Modifications, kernel version changes, typos etc. (1998 - July 1999)
Version 1.1	Added Copyright Information and Re-Submitted (September 1999)

2. Principles of Loopback Devices and Ramdisks

First I will describe some of the general principles that are used in the setting up of a loopback filesystem as the root device.

2.1. Loopback Devices

A loopback device in Linux is a virtual device that can be used like any other media device.

Examples of normal media devices are hard disk partitions like /dev/hda1, /dev/hda2, /dev/sda1, or entire disks like the floppy disk /dev/fd0 etc. They are all devices that can be used to hold a files and directory structures. They can be formatted with the filesystem that is required (ext2fs, msdos, ntfs etc.) and then mounted.

The loopback filesystem associates a file on another filesystem as a complete device. This can then be formatted and mounted just like any of the other devices listed above. To do this the device called /dev/loop0 or /dev/loop1 etc is associated with the file and then this new virtual device is mounted.

2.2. Ramdisk Devices

In Linux it is also possible to have another type of virtual device mounted as a filesystem, this is the ramdisk device.

In this case, the device does not refer to any physical hardware, but to a portion of memory that is set aside for the purpose. The memory that is allocated is never swapped out to disk, but remains in the disk cache.

A ramdisk can be created at any time by writing to the ramdisk device /dev/ram0 or /dev/ram1 etc. This can then be formatted and mounted in the same way that the loopback device is.

When a ramdisk is used to boot from (as is often done on Linux installation disks or rescue disks), then the disk image (the entire contents of the disk as a single file) can be stored on the boot floppy in a compressed form. This is automatically recognized by the kernel when it boots and is uncompressed into the ramdisk before it is mounted.

2.3. The Initial Ramdisk Device

The initial ramdisk device in Linux is another important mechanism for which we need to be able to use a loopback device as the root filesystem.

When the initial ramdisk is used the filesystem image is copied into memory and mounted so that the files on it can be accessed. A program on this ramdisk (called /linuxrc) is run and when it is finished a different device is mounted as the root filesystem. The old ramdisk is still present though and is mounted on the directory /initrd if present or available through the device /dev/initrd.

This is unusual behaviour since the normal boot sequence boots from the designated root partition and keeps on running. With the initial ramdisk option the root partition is allowed to change before the main boot sequence is started.

2.4. The Root Filesystem

The root filesystem is the device that is mounted first so that it appears as the directory called / after booting.

There are a number of complications about the root filesystem that are due to the fact that it contains all files. When booting the rc scripts are run; these are either the files in /etc/rc.d or /etc/rc?.d depending on the version of the /etc/init program.

When the system has booted it is not possible to unmount the root partition or change it since all programs will be using it to some extent. This is why the initial ramdisk is so useful because it can be used so that the final root partition is not the same as the one that is loaded at boot time.

2.5. The Linux Boot Sequence

To show how the initial ramdisk operates in the boot sequence, the order of events is listed below.

1. The kernel is loaded into memory, this is performed by LILO or LOADLIN. You can see the Loading... message as this happens.

2. The ramdisk image is loaded into memory, again this is performed by LILO or LOADLIN. You can see the Loading... message again as this happens.

3. The kernel is initialized, including parsing the command line options and setting of the ramdisk as the root device.

4. The program /linuxrc is run on the initial ramdisk.

5. The root device is changed to that specified in the kernel parameter.

6. The init program /etc/init is run which will perform the user configurable boot sequence.

This is just a simplified version of what happens, but is sufficient to explain how the kernel starts up and where the initial ramdisk is used.

3. How To Create a Loopback Root Device

Now that the general principles are explained, the method of creating the loopback device can be explained.

3.1. Requirements

To create the loopback root device will require a number of things.

▼   A working Linux system.

▲   A way to copy large files onto the target DOS partition.

Most important is access to an installed Linux system. This is because the loop device can only be created under Linux. This will mean that it is not possible to bootstrap a working system from nothing. The requirement of the Linux system that you use is that you can compile a kernel on it.

Once the loopback device is created it will be a large file. I have used an 80MB file, but while this was sufficient for an X terminal it may not be enough if you want to use it for much else. This file must be copied onto the DOS partition, so either a network or a lot of floppy disks must be used.

The software that you will require includes:

▼   LOADLIN version 1.6 or above.

■   A version of mount that supports loopback devices.

■   A version of the kernel that supports the required options.

▲   All of these should be standard for recent Linux installations.

3.2. Creating the Linux Kernel

I created the loopback device using Linux kernel version 2.0.31. Other versions should also work, but they must have at least the options listed below.

The kernel options that you will need to enable are the following:

▼   RAM disk support (CONFIG_BLK_DEV_RAM).

■ Initial RAM disk (initrd) support (CONFIG_BLK_DEV_INITRD).

■ Loop device support (CONFIG_BLK_DEV_LOOP).

■ fat fs support (CONFIG_FAT_FS).

▲ msdos fs support (CONFIG_MSDOS_FS).

The first two are for the RAM disk device itself and the initial ram disk device. The next one is the loop back filesystem option. The last two are the msdos filesystem support, which is required to mount the DOS partition.

Compiling a kernel without modules is the easiest option, although if you do want modules then it should be possible, although I have not tried it. If modules are used then you should make sure that you have the options above compiled in and not as modules themselves.

Depending on the kernel version that you have you may need to apply a kernel patch. It is a very simple one that allows the loopback device to be used as the root filesystem.

▼ Kernel versions before 2.0.0; I have no information about these.

■ Kernel version 2.0.0 to 2.0.34; you need to apply the kernel patch for 2.0.x kernels as shown below.

■ Kernel version 2.0.35 to 2.0.x; no kernel patch is required.

■ Kernel version 2.1.x; you need to apply the kernel patch for 2.0.x or 2.2.x kernels as shown below, depending on the exact 2.1.x version.

■ Kernel version 2.2.0 to 2.2.10; you need to apply the kernel patch for 2.2.x kernels as shown below.

▲ Kernel version 2.3.x; you need to apply the kernel patch for 2.2.x kernels as shown below.

For 2.0.x kernels the file /init/main.c needs to have a single line added to it as shown by the modified version below. The line that says "loop," 0x0700 is the one that was added.

```
static void parse_root_dev(char * line)
{
        int base = 0;
        static struct dev_name_struct {
                const char *name;
                const int num;
        } devices[] = {
                { "nfs",    0x00ff },
                { "loop",   0x0700 },
                { "hda",    0x0300 },

        . . .
```

```
                    { "sonycd",   0x1800 },
                    { NULL, 0 }
            };


    ...


    }
```

For 2.2.x kernels the file /init/main.c needs to have three lines added to it as shown by the modified version below. The line that says "loop," 0x0700 and the ones either side of it are the ones that were added.

```
        static struct dev_name_struct {
                const char *name;
                const int num;
        } root_dev_names[] __initdata = {
        #ifdef CONFIG_ROOT_NFS
                { "nfs",     0x00ff },
        #endif
        #ifdef CONFIG_BLK_DEV_LOOP
                { "loop",    0x0700 },
        #endif
        #ifdef CONFIG_BLK_DEV_IDE
                { "hda",     0x0300 },

        ...

                { "ddv", DDV_MAJOR << 8},
        #endif
                { NULL, 0 }
        };
```

Once the kernel is configured it should be compiled to produce a zImage file (make zImage). This file will be arch/i386/boot/zImage when compiled.

3.3. Creating the Initial Ramdisk Device

The initial ramdisk is most easily created as a loopback device from the start. You will need to do this as root; the commands that you need to execute are listed below, they are assumed to be run from root's home directory (/root).

```
        mkdir /root/initrd
        dd if=/dev/zero of=initrd.img bs=1k count=1024
        mke2fs -i 1024 -b 1024 -m 5 -F -v initrd.img
        mount initrd.img /root/initrd -t ext2 -o loop
```

```
cd initrd
[create the files]
cd ..
umount /root/initrd
gzip -c -9 initrd.img > initrdgz.img
```

There are a number of steps to this, but they can be described as follows:

1. Create a mount point for the initial ramdisk (an empty directory).
2. Create an empty file of the size required. Here I have used 1024kB, you may need less or more depending on the contents, (the size is the last parameter).
3. Make an ext2 filesystem on the empty file.
4. Mount the file onto the mount point; this uses the loopback device.
5. Change to the mounted loopback device.
6. Create the files that are required (see below for details).
7. Move out of the mounted loopback device.
8. Unmount the device.
9. Create a compressed version for use later.

Contents of the initial ramdisk   The files that you will need on the ramdisk are the minimum requirements to be able to execute any commands.

/linuxrc	The script that is run to mount the msdos file system (see below).
/lib/*	The dynamic linker and the libraries that the programs need.
/etc/*	The cache used by the dynamic linker (not strictly needed, but does stop it complaining).
/bin/*	A shell interpreter (ash because it is smaller than bash). The mount and losetup programs for handling the DOS disk and setting up the loopback devices.
/dev/*	The devices that will be used. You need /dev/zero for ld-linux.so,
/dev/hda*	To mount the msdos disk and /dev/loop* for the loopback device.
/mnt	An empty directory to mount the msdos disk on.

The initial ramdisk that I used is listed below, the contents come to about 800kB when the overhead of the filesystem are taken into account.

```
total 18
drwxr-xr-x   2 root     root         1024 Jun  2 13:57 bin
drwxr-xr-x   2 root     root         1024 Jun  2 13:47 dev
drwxr-xr-x   2 root     root         1024 May 20 07:43 etc
drwxr-xr-x   2 root     root         1024 May 27 07:57 lib
-rwxr-xr-x   1 root     root          964 Jun  3 08:47 linuxrc
drwxr-xr-x   2 root     root        12288 May 27 08:08 lost+found
drwxr-xr-x   2 root     root         1024 Jun  2 14:16 mnt

./bin:
total 168
-rwxr-xr-x   1 root     root        60880 May 27 07:56 ash
-rwxr-xr-x   1 root     root         5484 May 27 07:56 losetup
-rwsr-xr-x   1 root     root        28216 May 27 07:56 mount
lrwxrwxrwx   1 root     root            3 May 27 08:08 sh -> ash

./dev:
total 0
brw-r--r--   1 root     root        3,   0 May 20 07:43 hda
brw-r--r--   1 root     root        3,   1 May 20 07:43 hda1
brw-r--r--   1 root     root        3,   2 Jun  2 13:46 hda2
brw-r--r--   1 root     root        3,   3 Jun  2 13:46 hda3
brw-r--r--   1 root     root        7,   0 May 20 07:43 loop0
brw-r--r--   1 root     root        7,   1 Jun  2 13:47 loop1
crw-r--r--   1 root     root        1,   3 May 20 07:42 null
crw-r--r--   1 root     root        5,   0 May 20 07:43 tty
crw-r--r--   1 root     root        4,   1 May 20 07:43 tty1
crw-r--r--   1 root     root        1,   5 May 20 07:42 zero

./etc:
total 3
-rw-r--r--   1 root     root         2539 May 20 07:43 ld.so.cache

./lib:
total 649
lrwxrwxrwx   1 root     root           18 May 27 08:08 ld-linux.so.1 ->
                                          ld-linux.so.1.7.14
-rwxr-xr-x   1 root     root        21367 May 20 07:44 ld-linux.so.1.7.14
lrwxrwxrwx   1 root     root           14 May 27 08:08 libc.so.5 -> libc.so.5.3.12
-rwxr-xr-x   1 root     root       583795 May 20 07:44 libc.so.5.3.12

./lost+found:
total 0

./mnt:
total 0
```

The only complex steps about this are the devices in dev. Use the mknod program to create them, use the existing devices in /dev as a template to get the required parameters.

The /linuxrc file

The /linuxrc file on the initial ramdisk is required to do all of the preparations so that the loopback device can be used for the root partition when it exits. The example below tries to mount /dev/hda1 as an msdos partition and if it succeeds then sets up the files /linux/linuxdsk.img as /dev/loop0 and /linux/linuxswp.img as /dev/loop1.

```
#!/bin/sh
echo INITRD: Trying to mount /dev/hda1 as msdos
if /bin/mount -n -t msdos /dev/hda1 /mnt; then
    echo INITRD: Mounted OK
    /bin/losetup /dev/loop0 /mnt/linux/linuxdsk.img
    /bin/losetup /dev/loop1 /mnt/linux/linuxswp.img
    exit 0
else
    echo INITRD: Mount failed
    exit 1
fi
```

The first device /dev/loop0 will become the root device and the second one /dev/loop1 will become the swap space.

If you want to be able to write to the DOS partition as a non-root user when you have finished then you should use mount -n -t msdos /dev/hda1 /mnt -o uid=0,gid=0,umask=000,quiet instead. This will map all accesses to the DOS partition to root and set the permissions appropriately.

3.4. Creating The Root Device

The root device that you will be using is the file linuxdsk.img. You will need to create this in the same way that the initial ramdisk was created, but bigger. You can install any Linux installation that you like onto this disk.

The easiest way might be to copy an existing Linux installation into it. An alternative is to install a new Linux installation onto it. Assuming that you have done this, there are some minor changes that you must make.

The /etc/fstab file must reference the root partition and the swap using the two loopback devices that are setup on the initial ramdisk.

```
/dev/loop0      /       ext2    defaults 1 1
/dev/loop1      swap    swap    defaults 1 1
```

This will ensure that when the real root device is used the kernel will not be confused about where the root device is. It will also allow the swap space to be added in the same way a swap partition is normally used. You should remove any other reference to a root disk device or swap partition.

If you want to be able to read the DOS partition after Linux has started then you will need to make a number of extra small changes.

▼ Create a directory called /initrd, this is where the initial ramdisk will be mounted once the loopback root filesystem is mounted.

■ Create a symbolic link called /DOS that points to /initrd/mnt where the real DOS partition will be mounted.

▲ Add a line into the rc file that mounts the disks. This should run the command mount -f -t msdos /dev/hda1 /initrd/mnt, this will create a "fake" mount of the DOS partition so that all programs (like df) will know that the DOS partition is mounted and where to find it. If you used different options in the /linuxrc file then obviously you should use them here also.

There is no need to have a Linux kernel on this root device since that was already loaded earlier. If you are using modules however then you should include them on this device as normal.

3.5. Creating the Swap Device

The root device that you will be using is the file linuxswap.img. The swap device is very simple to create. Create an empty file as was done for the initial ramdisk and then run mkswap linuxswap.img to intialize it.

The size of the swap space will depend on what you plan to do with the installed system, but I would recommend between 8MB and the amount of RAM that you have.

3.6. Creating the MSDOS Directory

The files that are going to be used need to be moved onto the DOS partition. The files that are required in the DOS directory called C:\LINUX are the following:

▼ LINUXDSK.IMG The disk image that will become the root device.

▲ LINUXSWP.IMG The swap space.

3.7. Creating the Boot Floppy

The boot floppy that is used is just a normal DOS format bootable floppy. This is created using format a: /s from DOS. Onto this disk you will need to create an AUTOEXEC.BAT file (as below) and copy the kernel, compressed initial ramdisk and LOADLIN executable.

▼ AUTOEXEC.BAT The DOS automatically executed batch file.

■ LOADLIN.EXE The LOADLIN program executable.

■ ZIMAGE The Linux kernel.

▲ INITRDGZ.IMG The compressed initial ramdisk image.

The AUTOEXEC.BAT file should contain just one line as below.

```
\loadlin \zImage initrd=\initrdgz.img root=/dev/loop0 ro
```

This specifies the kernel image to use, the initial ramdisk image, the root device after the initial ramdisk has finished and that the root partition is to be mounted read-only.

4. Booting the System

To boot from this new root device all that is required is that the floppy disk prepared as described above be inserted for the PC to boot from.

You will see the following sequence of events.

1. DOS boots.

2. AUTOEXEC.BAT starts.

3. LOADLIN is run.

4. The Linux kernel is copied into memory.

5. The initial ramdisk is copied into memory.

6. The Linux kernel is started running.

7. The /linuxrc file on the initial ramdisk is run.

8. The DOS partition is mounted and the root and swap devices set up.

9. The boot sequence continues from the loopback device.

When this is complete you can remove the boot floppy and use the Linux system.

4.1. Possible Problems With Solutions

There are a number of stages where this process could fail, I will try to explain what they are and what to check. DOS booting is easy to recognize by the message that it prints MS-DOS Starting ... on the screen. If this is not seen then the floppy disk is either not bootable or the PC is not bootable from the floppy disk drive.

When the AUTOEXEC.BAT file is run the commands in it should be echoed to the screen by default. In this case there is just the single line in the file that starts LOADLIN.

When LOADLIN executes it will do two very visible things: first it will load the kernel into memory, second it will copy the ramdisk into memory. Both of these are indicated by a Loading... message.

The kernel starts by uncompressing itself; this can give crc errors if the kernel image is corrupted. Then it will start running the initialization sequence, which is very verbose with diagnostic messages. Loading of the initial ramdisk device is also visible during this phase.

When the /linuxrc file is run there are no diagnostic messages, but you can add these yourself as an aid to debugging. If this stage fails to set up the loopback device as the root device then you may see a message that there is no root device and the kernel aborts.

The normal boot sequence of the new root device will now continue and this is quite verbose. There may be problems about the root device being mounted read-write, but the LOADLIN command line option 'ro' should stop that. Other problems that can occur are that the boot sequence is confused about where the root device is; this is probably due to a problem with /etc/fstab.

When the boot sequence has completed, the remaining problem is that programs are confused about whether the DOS partition is mounted or not. This is why it is a good idea to use the fake mount command described earlier. This makes life a lot easier if you want to access the files on the DOS device.

4.2. Reference Documents

The documents that I used to create my first loopback root filesystem were:

▼   The Linux kernel source, in particular init/main.c.

■   The Linux kernel documentation, in particular Documentation/initrd.txt and Documentation/ramdisk.txt.

■   The LILO documentation.

▲   The LOADLIN documentation.

5. Other Loopback Root Device Possibilities

Once the principle of booting a filesystem in a file on a DOS partition has been established there are many other things that you can now do.

5.1.DOS Hard-disk Only Installation

If it is possible to boot Linux from a file on a DOS hard disk by using a boot floppy then it is obviously also possible to do it using the hard disk itself. A configuration boot menu can be used to give the option of running LOADLIN from within the AUTOEXEC.BAT. This will give a much faster boot sequence, but is otherwise identical.

5.2. LILO Booted Installation

Using LOADLIN is only one option for booting a Linux kernel. There is also LILO that does much the same but without needing DOS. In this case the DOS format floppy disk can be replaced by an ext2fs format one. Otherwise the details are very similar, with the kernel and the initial ramdisk being files on that disk.

The reason that I chose the LOADLIN method is that the arguments that need to be given to LILO are slightly more complex. Also it is more obvious to a casual observer what the floppy disk is since it can be read under DOS.

5.3. VFAT / NTFS Installation

I have tried the NTFS method, and have had no problems with it. The NTFS filesystem driver is not a standard kernel option in version 2.0.x, but is available as a patch from http://www.informatik.hu- berlin.de/~loewis/ntfs/. In version 2.2.x the NTFS driver is included as standard in the kernel.

The only changes for the VFAT or NTFS options are in the initial ramdisk; the file /linuxrc needs to mount a file system of type vfat or ntfs rather than msdos.

I know of no reason why this should not also work on a VFAT partition.

5.4. Installing Linux without Re-partitioning

The process of installing Linux on a PC from a standard distribution requires booting from a floppy disk and re-partitioning the disk. This stage could instead be accomplished by a boot floppy that creates an empty loopback device and swap file. This would allow the installation to proceed as normal, but it would install into the loopback device rather than a partition.

This could be used as an alternative to a UMSDOS installation; it would be more efficient in disk usage since the minimum allocation unit in the ext2 filesystem is 1kB instead of up to 32kB on a DOS partition. It can also be used on VFAT and NTFS formatted disks, which are otherwise a problem.

5.5. Booting From a Non-bootable device

This method can also be used to boot a Linux system from a device that is not normally bootable.

- ▼ CD-ROM
- ■ Zip Disks
- ▲ Parallel port disk drives

Obviously there are many other devices that could be used, NFS root filesystems are already included in the kernel as an option, but the method described here might also be used instead.

APPENDIX D

Linux Partition HOWTO

Linux Partition HOWTO by Kristan Koehntopp, kris@koehntopp.dev2.4,
November 3, 1997

This Linux Mini-HOWTO teaches you how to plan and layout disk space for your Linux system. It talks about disk hardware, partitions, swap space sizing; positioning considerations, file systems, file system types and related topics. The intent is to teach some background knowledge, not procedures.

TABLE OF CONTENTS

1. Introduction
1.1 What is this?
1.2 What is in it? and related HOWTO documents

2. What is a partition anyway?
2.1 Backups are important
2.2 Device numbers and device names

3. What Partitions do I need?
3.1 How many partitions do I need?
3.2 How large should my swap space be?
3.3 Where should I put my swap space?
3.4 Some facts about file systems and fragmentation
3.5 File lifetimes and backup cycles as partitioning criteria

4. An example
4.1 A recommended model for ambitious beginners

5. How I did it on my machine

1. Introduction

1.1. What is this?

This is a Linux Mini-HOWTO text. A Mini-HOWTO is a small text explaining some business related to Linux installation and maintenance tutorial style. It's mini, because either the text or the topic it discusses are too small for a real HOWTO or even a book. A HOWTO is not a reference: that's what manual pages are for.

1.2. What is in it? and related HOWTO documents

This particular Mini-HOWTO teaches you how to plan and layout disk space for your Linux system. It talks about disk hardware, partitions, swap space sizing and positioning considerations, file systems, file system types, and related topics. The intent is to teach some background knowledge, so we are talking mainly principles and not tools in this text.

Ideally, this document should be read before your first installation, but this is somehow difficult for most people. First timers have other problems than disk layout optimization, too. So you are probably someone who just finished a Linux installation and is now thinking about ways to optimize this installation or how to avoid some nasty miscalculations in the next one. Well, expect some desire to tear down and rebuild your installation when you are finished with this text.

This Mini-HOWTO limits itself to planning and laying out disk space most of the time. It does not discuss the usage of fdisk, LILO, mke2fs or backup programs. There are other HOWTOs that address these problems. Please see the Linux HOWTO Index for current information on Linux HOWTOs. There are instructions for obtaining HOWTO documents in the index, too.

▼ To learn how to estimate the various size and speed requirements for different parts of the filesystem, see "Linux Multiple Disks Layout mini-HOWTO," by Gjoen Stein.

■ For instructions and considerations regarding disks with more than 1024 cylinders, see "Linux Large Disk mini-HOWTO," Andries Brouwer.

▲ For instructions on limiting disk space usage per user (quotas), see "Linux Quota mini-HOWTO," by Albert M.C. Tam

Currently, there is no general document on disk backup, but there are several documents with pointers to specific backup solutions. See "Linux ADSM Backup mini-HOWTO," by Thomas Koenig for instructions on integrating Linux into an IBM ADSM backup environment. See "Linux Backup with MSDOS mini-HOWTO," by Christopher Neufeld for information about MS-DOS driven Linux backups.

For instructions on writing and submitting a HOWTO document, see the Linux HOWTO Index, by Tim Bynum. Browsing through /usr/src/linux/Documentation can be very instructive, too. See ide.txt and scsi.txt for some background information on the properties of your disk drivers and have a look at the filesystems/ subdirectory.

2. What is a partition anyway?

When PC hard disks were invented people soon wanted to install multiple operating systems, even if their system had only one disk.

So a mechanism was needed to divide a single physical disk into multiple logical disks. So that's what a partition is: A contiguous section of blocks on your hard disk that is treated like a completely separate disk by most operating systems.

It is fairly clear that partitions must not overlap: An operating system will certainly not be pleased if another operating system installed on the same machine were overwriting important information because of overlapping partitions. There should be no gap between adjacent partitions, too. While this constellation is not harmful, you are wasting precious disk space by leaving space between partitions.

A disk need not be partitioned completely. You may decide to leave some space at the end of your disk that is not assigned to any of your installed operating system yet. Later, when it is clear which installation is used by you most of the time, you can partition this left over space and put a file system on it. Partitions cannot be moved nor can they be resized without destroying the file system contained in it. So repartitioning usually involves backing up and restoring all file systems touched during the repartitioning. In fact it is fairly common to mess up things completely during repartitioning, so you should back up anything on any disk on that particular machine before even touching things like fdisk.

Well, some partitions with certain file system types on them actually can be split into two without losing any data (if you are lucky). For example there is a program called "fips" for splitting MS-DOS partitions into two to make room for a Linux installation without having to reinstall MS-DOS. You are still not going to touch these things without carefully backing up everything on that machine, aren't you?

2.1. Backups are important

Tapes are your friends for backups. They are fast, reliable and easy to use, so you can make backups often, preferably automatically and without hassle.

Step on soapbox: And I am talking about real tapes, not that disk controller driven ftape crap. Consider buying SCSI: Linux does support SCSI natively. You don't need to load ASPI drivers, you are not losing precious HMA under Linux and once the SCSI host adapter is installed, you just attach additional disks, tapes and CD-ROMs to it. No more I/O addresses, IRQ juggling or Master/Slave and PIO-level matching.

Plus proper SCSI host adapters give you high I/O performance without much CPU load. Even under heavy disk activity you will experience good response times. If you are planning to use a Linux system as a major USENET news feed or if you are about to enter the ISP business, don't even think about deploying a system without SCSI. Climb off soapbox.

2.2. Device numbers and device names

The number of partitions on an Intel based system was limited from the very beginning: The original partition table was installed as part of the boot sector and held space for only four partition entries. These partitions are now called primary partitions. When it became clear that people needed more partitions on their systems, logical partitions were invented. The number of logical partitions is not limited: Each logical partition contains a pointer to the next logical partition, so you can have a potentially unlimited chain of partition entries.

For compatibility reasons, the space occupied by all logical partitions had to be accounted for. If you are using logical partitions, one primary partition entry is marked as "extended partition" and its starting and ending block mark the area occupied by your logical partitions. This implies that the space assigned to all logical partitions has to be contiguous. There can be only one extended partition: no fdisk program will create more than one extended partition.

Linux cannot handle more than a limited number of partitions per drive. So in Linux you have 4 primary partitions (3 of them useable, if you are using logical partitions) and at most 15 partitions altogether on an SCSI disk (63 altogether on an IDE disk).

In Linux, partitions are represented by device files. A device file is a file with type c (for "character" devices, devices that do not use the buffer cache) or b (for "block" devices, which go through the buffer cache). In Linux, all disks are represented as block devices only. Unlike other Unices, Linux does not offer "raw" character versions of disks and their partitions.

The only important thing with a device file is its major and minor device number, shown instead of the file's size:

```
$ ls -l /dev/hda
brw-rw----   1 root       disk        3,    0 Jul 18  1994 /dev/hda
                                       ^    ^
                                       |    minor device number
                                   major device number
```

When accessing a device file, the major number selects which device driver is being called to perform the input/output operation. This call is being done with the minor number as a parameter and it is entirely up to the driver how the minor number is being interpreted. The driver documentation usually describes how the driver uses minor numbers. For IDE disks, this documentation is in /usr/src/linux/Documentation/ ide.txt. For SCSI disks, one would expect such documentation in /usr/src/linux/Documentation/scsi.txt, but it isn't there. One has to look at the driver source to be sure (/usr/ src/linux/driver/scsi/sd.c:184-196). Fortunately, there is Peter Anvin's list of device numbers and names in /usr/src/linux/Documentation/devices.txt; see the entries for block devices, major 3, 22, 33, 34 for IDE and major 8 for SCSI disks. The major and minor numbers are a byte each and that is why the number of partitions per disk is limited.

By convention, device files have certain names and many system programs have knowledge about these names compiled in. They expect your IDE disks to be named / dev/hd* and your SCSI disks to be named /dev/sd*. Disks are numbered a, b, c and so on, so /dev/hda is your first IDE disk and /dev/sda is your first SCSI disk. Both devices represent entire disks, starting at block one. Writing to these devices with the wrong tools will destroy the master boot loader and partition table on these disks, rendering all data on this disk unusable or making your system unbootable. Know what you are doing and, again, back up before you do it.

Primary partitions on a disk are 1, 2, 3 and 4. So /dev/hda1 is the first primary partition on the first IDE disk and so on. Logical partitions have numbers 5 and up, so /dev/ sdb5 is the first logical partition on the second SCSI disk.

Each partition entry has a starting and an ending block address assigned to it and a type. The type is a numerical code (a byte) which designates a particular partition to a certain type of operating system. For the benefit of computing consultants partition type codes are not really unique, so there is always the probability of two operating systems using the same type code.

Linux reserves the type code 0x82 for swap partitions and 0x83 for "native" file systems (that's ext2 for almost all of you). The once popular, now outdated Linux/Minix file system used the type code 0x81 for partitions. OS/2 marks its partitions with a 0x07 type and so does Windows NT's NTFS. MS-DOS allocates several type codes for its various flavors of FAT file systems: 0x01, 0x04 and 0x06 are known. DR-DOS used 0x81 to indicate protected FAT partitions, creating a type clash with Linux/Minix at that time, but neither Linux/Minix nor DR-DOS is widely used any more. The extended partition, which is used as a container for logical partitions, has a type of 0x05, by the way.

Partitions are created and deleted with the fdisk program. Every self respecting operating system program comes with an fdisk and traditionally it is even called fdisk (or FDISK.EXE) in almost all OS'es. Some fdisks, notably the DOS one, are somehow limited when they have to deal with other operating systems' partitions. Such limitations include the complete inability to deal with anything with a foreign type code, the inability to deal with cylinder numbers above 1024 and the inability to create or even understand partitions that do not end on a cylinder boundary. For example, the MS-DOS fdisk can't delete NTFS partitions, the OS/2 fdisk has been known to silently "correct" partitions created by the Linux fdisk that do not end on a cylinder boundary and both the DOS and the OS/2 fdisk have had problems with disks with more than 1024 cylinders (see the "large-disk" Mini-Howto for details on such disks).

3. What Partitions do I need?

3.1. How many partitions do I need?

Okay, so what partitions do you need? Well, some operating systems do not believe in booting from logical partitions for reasons that are beyond the scope of any sane mind. So you probably want to reserve your primary partitions as boot partitions for your MS-DOS, OS/2 and Linux or whatever you are using. Remember that one primary partition is needed as an extended partition, which acts as a container for the rest of your disk with logical partitions.

Booting operating systems is a real-mode thing involving BIOS's and 1024 cylinder limitations. So you probably want to put all your boot partitions into the first 1024 cylinders of your hard disk, just to avoid problems. Again, read the "large-disk" Mini-Howto for the gory details.

To install Linux, you will need at least one partition. If the kernel is loaded from this partition (for example by LILO), this partition must be readable by your BIOS. If you are using other means to load your kernel (for example a boot disk or the LOADLIN.EXE MS-DOS based Linux loader) the partition can be anywhere. In any case this partition will be of type 0x83 "Linux native."

Your system will need some swap space. Unless you swap to files you will need a dedicated swap partition. Since this partition is only accessed by the Linux kernel and the Linux kernel does not suffer from PC BIOS deficiencies, the swap partition may be positioned anywhere. I recommend using a logical partition for it (/dev/?d?5 and higher). Dedicated Linux swap partitions are of type 0x82 "Linux swap."

These are minimal partition requirements. It may be useful to create more partitions for Linux. Read on.

3.2. How large should my swap space be?

If you have decided to use a dedicated swap partition, which is generally a Good Idea [tm], follow these guidelines for estimating its size.

In Linux RAM and swap space add up (this is not true for all Unices). For example, if you have 8MB of RAM and 12MB swap space, you have a total of about 20MB virtual memory.

When sizing your swap space, you should have at least 16MB of total virtual memory. So for 4MB of RAM consider at least 12MB of swap, for 8MB of RAM consider at least 8MB of swap.

In Linux, a single swap partition cannot be larger than 128MB. That is, the partition may be larger than 128MB, but excess space is never used. If you want more than 128MB of swap, you have to create multiple swap partitions.

When sizing swap space, keep in mind that too much swap space may not be useful at all. Every process has a "working set." This is a set of in-memory pages which will be referenced by the processor in the very near future. Linux tries to predict these memory accesses (assuming that recently used pages will be used again in the near future) and keeps these pages in RAM if possible. If the program has a good "locality of reference" this assumption will be true and prediction algorithm will work.

Holding a working set in main memory only works if there is enough main memory. If you have too many processes running on a machine, the kernel is forced to put pages on disk that it will reference again in the very near future (forcing a page-out of a page from another working set and then a page-in of the page referenced). Usually this results in a very heavy increase in paging activity and in a substantial drop of performance. A machine in this state is said to be "thrashing" (for you German readers: That's "thrashing" ("dreschen," "schlagen," "haemmern") and not trashing ("muellen")).

On a thrashing machine the processes are essentially running from disk and not from RAM. Expect performance to drop by approximately the ratio between memory access speed and disk access speed.

A very old rule of thumb in the days of the PDP and the Vax was that the size of the working set of a program is about 25 percent of its virtual size. Thus it is probably useless to provide more swap than three times your RAM.

But keep in mind that this is just a rule of thumb. It is easily possible to create scenarios where programs have extremely large or extremely small working sets. For example, a simulation program with a large data set that is accessed in a very random fashion would have almost no noticeable locality of reference in its data segment, so its working set would be quite large.

On the other hand, an xv with many simultaneously opened JPEGs, all but one iconified, would have a very large data segment. But image transformations are all done on one single image; most of the memory occupied by xv is never touched. The same is true for an editor with many editor windows where only one window is being modified at a time. These programs have — if they are designed properly — a very high locality of reference and large parts of them can be kept swapped out without too severe performance impact.

One could suspect that the 25 percent number from the age of the command line is no longer true for modern GUI programs editing multiple documents, but I know of no newer papers that try to verify these numbers.

So for a configuration with 16MB RAM, no swap is needed for a minimal configuration and more than 48MB of swap is probably useless. The exact amount of memory needed depends on the application mix on the machine (what did you expect?).

3.3. Where should I put my swap space?

Mechanics are slow, electronics are fast. Modern hard disks have many heads. Switching between heads of the same track is fast, since it is purely electronic. Switching between tracks is slow, since it involves moving real world matter.

So if you have a disk with many heads and one with less heads and both are identical in other parameters, the disk with many heads will be faster. Splitting swap and putting it on both disks will be even faster, though.

Older disks have the same number of sectors on all tracks. With these disks it will be fastest to put your swap in the middle of the disks, assuming that your disk head will move from a random track towards the swap area.

Newer disks use ZBR (zone bit recording). They have more sectors on the outer tracks. With a constant number of rpms, this yields a far greater performance on the outer tracks than on the inner ones. Put your swap on the fast tracks.

Of course your disk head will not move randomly. If you have swap space in the middle of a disk between a constantly busy home, partition and an almost unused archive partition, you would be better off if your swap were in the middle of the home partition for even shorter head movements. You would be even better off if you had your swap on another otherwise unused disk, though.

Summary   Put your swap on a fast disk with many heads that is not busy doing other things. If you have multiple disks: Split swap and scatter it over all your disks or even different controllers.

Even better, buy more RAM.

3.4. Some facts about file systems and fragmentation

Disk space is administered by the operating system in units of blocks and fragments of blocks. In ext2, fragments and blocks have to be of the same size, so we can limit our discussion to blocks.

Files come in any size. They don't end on block boundaries. So with every file a part of the last block of every file is wasted. Assuming that file sizes are random, there is approximately a half block of waste for each file on your disk. Tanenbaum calls this "internal fragmentation" in his book *Operating Systems*.

You can guess the number of files on your disk by the number of allocated inodes on a disk. On my disk

```
# df -i
Filesystem        Inodes   IUsed   IFree  %IUsed Mounted on
/dev/hda3          64256   12234   52022    19%  /
/dev/hda5          96000   43058   52942    45%  /var
```

there are about 12000 files on / and about 44000 files on /var. At a block size of 1KB, about 6+22 = 28MB of disk space are lost in the tail blocks of files. Had I chosen a block size of 4KB, I would have lost 4 times this space.

Data transfer is faster for large contiguous chunks of data, though. That's why ext2 tries to preallocate space in units of eight contiguous blocks for growing files. Unused preallocation is released when the file is closed, so no space is wasted.

Noncontiguous placement of blocks in a file is bad for performance, since files are often accessed in a sequential manner. It forces the operating system to split a disk access and the disk to move the head. This is called "external fragmentation" or simply "fragmentation" and is a common problem with DOS file systems.

ext2 has several strategies to avoid external fragmentation. Normally fragmentation is not a large problem in ext2, not even on heavily used partitions such as a USENET news spool. While there is a tool for defragmentation of ext2 file systems, nobody ever uses it and it is not up to date with the current release of ext2. Use it, but do so on your own risk.

The MS-DOS file system is well known for its pathological management of disk space. In conjunction with the abysmal buffer cache used by MS-OS the effects of file fragmentation on performance are very noticeable. DOS users are accustomed to defragging their disks every few weeks and some have even developed some ritualistic beliefs regarding defragmentation. None of these habits should be carried over to Linux and ext2. Linux native file systems do not need defragmentation under normal use and this includes any condition with at least 5 percent of free space on a disk.

The MS-DOS file system is also known to lose large amounts of disk space due to internal fragmentation. For partitions larger than 256MB, DOS block sizes grow so large that they are no longer useful (this has been corrected to some extent with FAT32). ext2 does not force you to choose large blocks for large file systems, except for very large file systems in the 0.5 TB range (that's terabytes with 1 TB equaling 1024 GB) and above, where small block sizes become inefficient. So unlike DOS there is no need to split up large disks into multiple partitions to keep block size down. Use the 1KB default block size if possible. You may want to experiment with a block size of 2KB for some partitions, but expect to meet some seldom exercised bugs. Most people use the default.

3.5. File lifetimes and backup cycles as partitioning criteria

With ext2, Partitioning decisions should be governed by backup considerations to avoid external fragmentation from different file lifetimes. Files have lifetimes. After a file has been created, it will remain some time on the system and then be removed. File lifetime varies greatly throughout the system and is partly dependent on the pathname of the file. For example, files in /bin, /sbin, /usr/sbin, /usr/bin and similar directories are likely to have a very long lifetime: many months and above. Files in /home are likely to have a medium lifetime: several weeks or so. File in /var are usually short lived: Almost no file in /var/spool/news will remain longer than a few days, files in /var/spool/lpd measure their lifetime in minutes or less.

For backup it is useful if the amount of daily backup is smaller than the capacity of a single backup medium. A daily backup can be a complete backup or an incremental backup.

You can decide to keep your partition sizes small enough that they fit completely onto one backup medium (choose daily full backups). In any case a partition should be small enough that its daily delta (all modified files) fits onto one backup medium (choose incremental backup and expect to change backup media for the weekly/monthly full dump - no unattended operation possible).

Your backup strategy depends on that decision. When planning and buying disk space, remember to set aside a sufficient amount of money for backup! Unbacked up data is worthless! Data reproduction costs are much higher than backup costs for virtually everyone!

For performance it is useful to keep files of different lifetimes on different partitions. This way the short-lived files on the news partition may be fragmented very heavily. This has no impact on the performance of the / or /home partition.

4. An example

4.1. A recommended model for ambitious beginners

A common model creates /, /home and /var partitions as discussed above. This is simple to install and maintain and differentiates well enough to avoid adverse effects from different lifetimes. It fits well into a backup model, too: Almost no one bothers to backup USENET news spools and only some files in /var are worth backing up (/var/spool/mail comes to mind). On the other hand, / changes infrequently and can be backed up upon demand (after configuration changes) and is small enough to fit on most modern backup media as a full backup (plan 250 to 500MB depending on the amount of installed software). /home contains valuable user data and should be backed up daily. Some installations have very large /homes and must use incremental backups.

Some systems put /tmp onto a separate partition as well, others symlink it to /var/tmp to achieve the same effect (note that this can affect single user mode, where /var will be unavailable and the system will have no /tmp until you create one or mount /var manually) or put it onto a RAM disk (Solaris does this for example). This keeps /tmp out of /, a good idea.

This model is convenient for upgrades or reinstallations as well: Save your configuration files (or the entire /etc) to some /home directory, scrap your /, reinstall and fetch the old configurations from the save directory on /home.

5. How I did it on my machine

There was this old ISA bus 386/40 sitting on my shelf that I abandoned two years ago because it no longer cut it. I was planning to turn it into a small X-less server for my household LAN.

Here is how I did it: I took that 386 and put 16MB RAM into it. Added a cheap EIDE disk, the smallest I could get (800MB) and an ethernet card. I added an old Hercules because I still had a monitor for it, installed Linux on it and there I have my local NFS, SMB, HTTP, LPD/LPR and NNTP server as well as my mail router and POP3 server. With an additional ISDN card the machine became my TCP/IP router and firewall, too.

Most of the disk space on this machine went into the /var directories, /var/spool/mail, /var/spool/news and /var/httpd/html. I put /var on a separate partition and made this one large. There will be almost no users on this machine, so I created no home partition and mounted /home from some other workstation via NFS.

Linux without X plus several locally installed utilities will be fine with a 250MB partition as /. The machine has 16MB of RAM, but it will be running many servers. 16MB swap should be in order, 32MB should be plenty. We are not short on disk space, so the machine will get 32MB. Out of sentimentality a MS-DOS partition of some 20MB is kept on it. I decided to import /home from another machine, so the remaining 500+ MB will end up as /var. This is more than sufficient for a household USENET news feed.

We get:

```
Device         Mounted on                        Size
/dev/hda1      /dos_c                            25MB
/dev/hda2      - (Swapspace)                     32MB
/dev/hda3      /                                 250MB
/dev/hda4      - (Extended Container)            500MB
/dev/hda5      /var                              500MB

homeserver:/home /home                           1.6 GB
```

I am backing up this machine via the network using the tape in homeserver. Since everything on this machine has been installed from CD-ROM all I have to save are some configuration files from /etc, my customized locally installed *.tgz files from /root/Source/Installed and /var/spool/mail as well as /var/httpd/html. I copy these files into a dedicated directory /home/backmeup on homeserver every night, where the regular homeserver backup picks them up.

Index

 A

Absolute file name, 84
Access control in JFS, 230-231
Active item list (AIL), 268-269
Administration of XFS, 262
AG, 223
AG free inode list, 224
Air drops (ReiserFS), 248
AIX VFS, 76
AIX, use of LVM, 138
Algorithms, allocation, 203
Allocation algorithms for file system manager, 203
Allocation group. *See* AG
Allocation groups, headers used in XFS, 274
Allocation of disk space using space manager, 259-260
Allocation strategies, 66-68
Allocation vs. buffering issues in XFS, 278-279
Alpha (platform), 7, 21
API, 8
Application programming interface. *See* API
Arcangeli, Andrea, 138
Arch/ directory, 17

Architecture-dependent code (in source code), 16, 17
ARM (platform), 21
Arrays, RAID layering, 171
Asynchronous commits in ReiserFS, 247
Asynchronous writing, meta-data, 68
Attribute manager in XFS, 260-261
Autodetection in RAID, 297-298

 B

B+-tree, defined, 66
B+-trees, use of in JFS, 226-227
Backup of super-block, 186
Bakun, Andy, 138
Bash shell, 6
Basket of inodes, 59
Bdflush kernel daemon, 32-33, 268
Benchmarks for RAID performance, 304-306
Bibliography, 307-312
Bishop, Andrew, 315
Block address numbers, in allocations, 66-67
Block alignment, use of in ReiserFS, 235-236

Block allocation,
      ext2fs, 187-188
      map for JFS, 222-223
      methods, 66-67
Block buffer sizes, 29
Block device support (software RAID), 166
Block devices, defined, 29
Block group defined, in ext2fs, 185
Block group number, in super-block, 193
Block number assignment (ReiserFS), 249
Block size,
      ext2fs, 183-185
      JFS, 228
      super-block, 193
Block-based allocation, 66-67
Blocks bitmap,
      defined, 200
      group descriptor, 194
Blocks per group, in super-block, 193
Bogomips reading (at boot), 18
/boot directory, RAID limitations, 170
Boot floppy, creating, 323
Boot sequence for Linux, 316-317
Booting the system, 324
Brueggeman, Steve, 138
BSD, 76
B-tree
      defined, 66
      mapping use in XFS, 277
BUF files, in fs/ subdirectory, 77
Buffer cache, 29-32, 79
Buffer cache maintenance, 32
Buffer cache manager for XFS, 259
Buffer types, 31
Buffering vs. allocation issues in XFS, 278-279
Buffers, 29

C

Caches, 29
Caldera, 6
Card, Rémy, ext rewrite,182
Check/recover a file system, 221
Check_media_change (files), 40
Chunk size
      described, 296
      for different RAID levels, 296-297
Ckraid command (RAID), 173
Ckraid -fix command (RAID), 172
Clean buffers, 31
Clear_inode (super-block), 63
Coding conventions, 20-21
Coding issues in ReiserFS, 250-251

Compilation commands (kernel), 19-20
Configuration commands (kernel), 19
Configuration commands for RAID 0 and 1, 168-170
Configuration of ReiserFS, 253-254
Contributing to kernel, 20-21
Create (inodes), 46
Create a file system, JFS utility, 221
Crusoe (platform), 21

D

D_alias (dentry), 54
D_child (dentry), 54
D_compare (dentry), 56
D_count (dentry), 53
D_covers (dentry), 53
D_delete (dentry), 56
D_dsubdirs (dentry), 54
D_flags (dentry), 53
D_hash (dentry), 53, 56
D_iname (dentry), 55
D_inode (dentry), 53
D_invalidate (dentry), 56
D_iput (dentry), 56
D_lru (dentry), 54
D_mounts (dentry), 53
D_name (dentry), 54
D_op (dentry), 55
D_parent (dentry), 53
D_reftime (dentry), 55
D_release (dentry), 56
D_revalidate (dentry), 56
D_sb (dentry), 55
D_time (dentry), 54
Data block allocation in XFS, 275
Data block logging in ReiserFS, 247
Data block size in ext2fs, 190-191
Data blocks (in inodes), 40
Data corruption simulation, 303
Data, moving with a volume group, 146
Datablocks field, in inode, 192
Dcache path (inodes), 41
Debugfs utility, 188
Default_file_ops (inodes), 46
Delete_inode (super-block), 61-62
Dense files, JFS support for, 228-229
Dentry
      functions, 55-56
      object, in VFS, 79
      structure, 52-53
Dentry cache
      data structures, 80

file system performance, 79
functions, 81
Dentry_unused list, 56
Dentrys (file system), 52
/dev/md0 driver configuration (RAID), 168
DEV files, in fs/ subdirectory, 77
Device files, defintion and uses, 331-332
Directory
defined, 3, 25, 183-184
in JFS, 229
Directory file entries, 194
Directory file structure in ext2fs, 202
Directory organization in JFS, 228
Dirty buffers, 31
Dirty inodes list, 60
Disk block structure (ReiserFS), 241-242
Disk failure, RAID protection against, 171
Disk quota operations (dq_op), 59
Disks
removing from a volume group, 146
spare, 287
Distributions, 6
Doucette, Doug, 257
DPT controller (RAID), 164-165
Drive failure simulation, 302
Drivers/ directory, 17
Drops, use of in ReiserFS, 248-250
Dumpe2fs utility, 188

 E

E2fsck, 185, 188-190
EFS file system, 256
Elevator algorithms, 237
Entry name, defined, 25
Error handling in ext2fs, 204-205
/etc/lilo/conf, 19
/etc/lilo/config, 19
/etc/raidtab command (RAID), 168
/etc/rc.d/rc.local command (RAID), 168
EXE files, in fs/ subdirectory, 77
Ext2fs,
allocation method, 68
bitmaps, 200
blocks, 184-185
deficiencies, 68-69
directories, 183-184
directory file structure, 202-203
error handling, 204-205
features, 182-183
file size, how to change, 194
file system check, 185
file system debugger, 190

flags, 185-186
group descriptor defined, 193-194
group descriptor structure, 199-200
inode defined, 192
inodes, 185-186
library, 188-189
meta-data, 188
physical layout, 191
physical structure, 186-187
reserved space, 185
revisioning mechanism, 186
source code, 205-217
super-block, 186, 192-193, 196-199
tools, 189-191
utilities, 188
Extended file system (ext), 2
Extent
addressing structure, 66
defined, 66
Extent allocation descriptor (in JFS). *See* Xad.
Extent descriptors, mapping use in XFS, 277-278

F

F_async (files), 39
F_awin (files), 36
F_count (files), 36
F_dentry (files), 36
F_error (files), 37
F_flags (files), 36
F_gid (files), 36
F_list (files), 35
F_mode (files), 36
F_op (files), 36
F_owner (files), 36
F_pos (files), 36
F_raend (files), 36
F_ralen (files), 36
F_reada (files), 36
F_remax (files), 36
F_uid (files), 36
F_version (files), 37
Fdisk command, 145
Fdisk program, 332
File
fields, 35-37
functions, 37-40
lifetimes, 336
name size in ext2fs, 182
object in VFS, 79
recovery in JFS, 69
File attributes in ext2fs, 182
File control data structures, 66

File creation semantics, ext2fs, 182
File size, how to change, 194
File storage in XFS, 260
File structure, defined, 35
File system
    ambiguities, 49
    block size, 58
    connecting to a disk, 82-84
    defined, 3, 34
    lock, 60
    performance issues, 63-64
    registration, 50
    remounting, 62-63
    space reservation in ext2fs, 185
    static, 68-69
    unregistration, 50
File system (ext2) physical structure, 186-187
File system check program. *See* Fsck
File system checker program, 189
File system configuration, optimizing, 63-64
File system consistency check, in ext2fs, 185
File system debugger, in ext2fs, 190
File system directories, in ext2fs, 183-184
File system functions, 24
File system hierarchy, 25-28
File system manager, allocation algorithms, 203
File system mounting, 81-82, 84
File system naming operations in XFS, 261-262
File system objects, 28-29
File system size, ext2fs, 182
File system structure in XFS, 278
File_operations structure, 86
Fileboundaries in ReiserFS, 235-236
Files
    access to, 84-85
    defined, 25, 33
    JFS, 229
    limit of open, 65
Fileset allocation map inodes, 224-225
First inode, in super-block, 193
Flags
    in ext2fs, 185-186
    inode transactions (XFS), 267-268
    super-block, 59
    using RAID, 172
Flush (files), 39
Flushing of dirty inodes in XFS, 268-269
Flushpage (inodes), 49
Follow_link f (inodes), 48
Fork() function, 18
Format command, RAID disk, 169
Free blocks, in super-block, 193
Free inodes, in super-block, 193
Free Software Foundation, 5

Freelist, data block (XFS), 275
Fs.h source files, 86-118
Fs/ directory, 17
Fs/ subdirectory, files and purposes, 76-77
Fs/ext2/file.c source file, 130-132
Fs/ext2/super.c source file, 113-130
Fs_flags (file system), 51
Fsck command, RAID, 172
Fsck time, 71-72
Fsck, 69
Fstab file, described, 288
Fsync (files), 39

G

General Public License. *See* GPL
Get_block (inodes), 48
GNU gcc compiler, 6, 20
GNU Parted, 138
GNU tools, 5
GPL, 4, 5
Granularity issues in ReiserFS, 236
Group descriptor structure in ext2fs, 199-200

H

Hash table, 30-31
Hot-swapping, 290
HP-UX VFS, 76
HURD, 185

I

I/O device, raw, 64
I/O efficiency in ReiserFS, 236-237
I_attr_flags (inodes), 45
I_broot_bytes counter in XFS, 266-267
I_bytes counter in XFS, 266-267
I_dentry (inodes), 43
I_flags (inodes), 44-45
I_flock (inodes), 44
I_generation (inodes), 45
I_hash (inodes), 43
I_list (inodes), 43
I_mmap (inodes), 44
I_nrpages (inodes), 43
I_pages (inodes), 44
I_sem (inodes), 44
I_shared_lock (inodes), 44

I_state (inodes), 44
I_version (inodes), 43
I_writecount (inodes), 45
IA64 (platform), 21
IAG free list, 224
IAG, 223
ICP-Vortex controller (RAID), 164-165
IDE configuration with RAID, 288-289
Iget function, 41, 61
Include/ directory, 17
In-core structure in XFS, 278
In-core super-block, description, 270
Independent code (in source code), 16-17
Index inode. *See* inode
Init/ directory, 17-18
Inline functions, 20
Inode allocation group. *See* IAG
Inode allocation map for JFS, 223-224
Inode allocation on demand (XFS), 275
Inode allocation, in-core (XFS), 264-265
Inode bitmap
        defined, 200
        group descriptor, 194
Inode data structure, in-core (XFS), 262-263
Inode fields, in ext2fs, 192
Inode hash table path, 41
Inode life cycle, in-core (XFS), 263-264
Inode locking mode (XFS), 267
Inode numbers, accessing file, 84-85
Inode object, in VFS, 79
Inode operations, 85-86
Inode pointer, to access files, 85
Inode table, group descriptor, 194
Inode transaction flags (XFS), 267-268
Inode_operations structure, 85-86
Inodes
        as building blocks, 40
        bitmap vs. freelist in XFS, 276
        defined, 34, 41
        ext2fs, 185-186
        fields, 43-45
        flushing of (XFS), 268-269
        functions on, 45-46
        in cache, 41
        in directory entry, 194
        JFS, 220-221
        numbering of (XFS), 277
        recycling of (XFS), 269
        ReiserFS, 242
        structure, 42-43
        structure (ext2fs), 200-202
Input/output. *See* I/O
Installation of ReiserFS, 251-252
Installation tips for XFS, 279-280

Integer file handle, 85
Intel (platform), 7
Intelx86 (platform), 21
Internal nodes, in JFS, 227-228
Internet
        ReiserFS patch, 251
        use as resource, 5
Ioctl (files), 39
Ipc/ directory, 17
Iput, 56
Irix operating system, 256
Iu_broot field (XFS), management of, 266
Iu_data field (XFS), management of, 265-266
Iu_extents field (XFS), management of, 266

 J

Java, 9
JFS, 12, 25
JFS
        access control, 230-231
        advantages, 69-70
        allocation method, 68
        block allocation map, 222-223
        defined, 220
        directories defined, 229
        download from the Internet, 220
        extent-based allocation, 66
        features and other file systems, 225-226
        files defined, 229
        how it works, 70-71
        inodes, 220-221
        internal nodes, 227-228
        leaf nodes, 227
        logs defined, 230
        mount command, 82
        set up at boot time, 222
        super-blocks, 220
        support for sparse and dense files, 228-229
        use of B+-trees, 226-227
        utilities, 221-222
        variable block size, 228
Jiffies, 55
Journaling features in ReiserFS, 246-247
Journaling file system. *See* JFS

 K

Kernel, definition, 3
Kernel/ directory, 18
Kernel/ subdirectory, 17

Key structure in ReiserFS, 239-240
kHTTPd, 9
Kiobuf (I/O device), 64-65
Kswapd daemon, 33

 L

Leaf nodes, in JFS, 227
Least recently used. *See* LRU
Lib/ directory, 18
Lib/ subdirectory, 17
Libext2fs library, 188-189
LILO, 19-20
Limit value default (for open files), 65
Limit(1) command, 65
Limitations of RAID, 170-171
Linear mode, RAID, 291-292
Link, defined, 25
Link, inodes, 47
LINKNAME command, 27
Links, in tree hierarchy, 26-28
Linux documentation project, 283
Linux loader. *See* LILO
Liquid drops (ReiserFS), 248
Llseek (files), 38
Locality_id key in ReiserFS, 239-240
Lock (files), 40
Lock manager for XFS, 259
Locked buffers, 31
Locking, super-block, 58
Log manager for XFS, 258-259
Logging file systems. *See also* JFS
Logging, transactions, 64
Logical volume commands, 144
Logical volume manager. *See* LVM
Logical volume
    creating striped, 145-146
    removing from a volume group, 146
Logical volumes, 138
    changing size, 141
Logs, in JFS, 230
Lookup (inodes), 47
Loopback root device
    creating, 317-324
    defined, 315
    other uses, 325-326
    software requirements, 317
LRU list, 30, 54, 80
LV. *See* Logical volumes
Lvchange command, 146
Lvcreate command, 145-146
Lvdisplay command, 146
Lvextend command, 141

LVM
    adding a disk to volume groups, 145
    benefits of using, 141
    block devices, 138-139
    creating a logical volume, 145
    creating a volume group, 145
    creating physical volumes for, 145
    development, 138
    for online disk storage, 138
    how it works, 141-142
    internal structure, 142
    registerering physical volumes, 145
    source code, 146-162
    storage organization, 140
    use by XFS, 257
    volume groups, 138
LVM commands
    examples of, 143
    for mapping, 141
LVM driver, 142
Lvm.h source code, 146-162

 M

M68000 (platform), 21
Magic number, in super-block, 193
Mail Transportation Agent. *See* MTA
Make bzImage, 19
Make bzlilo, 19
Make config, 19
Make menuconfig, 19
Make xconfig, 19
Marxmeier, Michael, 138
Mauelshagen, Heinz, 146
Md driver, internal structure, 173-180
Memory management, 33
Memory manager directory, 18
Meta-data
    asynchronous writing, 68
    ext2fs, 188
    logging file systems, 71-73
Minix file system, 59
Minix operating system, 2, 6
MIPS (platform), 7, 21
Mirroring of disks, RAID, 167
Mirroring, RAID limitations, 171
Mkbootdisk utility, 20
Mkdir (inodes), 47
Mke2fs command, 297
Mke2fs utility, 188
Mknod (inodes), 47
Mm/ directory, 18
Mm/ subdirectory, 17

Mmap (files), 39
Mode field, in inode, 192
Molnar, Ingo, 282
Motorola 68000 (platform), 7
Mount command, 59, 82
Mount count, in super-block, 193
Mounting a file system, 81-82
Mounting a file system, sequence, 84
Mp3.com, use of ReiserFS, 234
Ms_rdonly flag, 59
MSDOS directory, creating, 323
MTA, 2

N

Name, in directory entry, 194
Name field (file system), 51
Name length, in directory entry, 194
Name space
    definition, 3
    use of in ReiserFS, 234-235
Name space manager in XFS, 261-262
Namei() function, 84
Names, defined, 34-35
Native file system (ext2fs), 68
Net/ directory, 19
Networking support (in subdirectory), 19
Neuffer, Michael, 165
Next (file system), 51
Node layout in ReiserFS tree, 245-246
Nodes
    in ReiserFS tree, 238-239
    structure of internal (ReiserFS), 242
    structure of leaf (ReiserFS), 243-245
Notify_change (super-block), 62
NULL pointer, in VFS, 83

O

Object_id key in ReiserFS, 239-240
Object-oriented programming, 234
Oestergaard, Jakob, 283
Offset key in ReiserFS, 239-240
OLTP and RAID, 168
Open (files), 39
Open files (on file system), 60
Open source, 5, 6
Open_namei() function (from fs/namei.c) source
    code, 132-136
Optimization of files in ReiserFS, 245
Optimization strategies, 63-64

OSF/i operating system, 138
Owner information field, in inode, 192

P

Page cache, 79
Parent directory, 47
PA-RISC (platform), 21
Partitions
    defined, 329-330
    how many to use, 332-333
    how to use, 330-332
    resizing of, 138
PATHNAME command, 28
PCI controllers for RAID, 164-165
Performance issues
    dentry cache, 79
    file system, 63-64
Performance optimizations in ext2fs, 187-188
Performance under RAID, 166-168
Persistent super-block, described, 296
Physical volume commands, 144
Physical volumes, 138
    creating for LVM, 145
    registering with LVM, 145
Platforms, 7
Pointers (inodes), 40
Poll (files), 38
Portable operating system interface. *See* POSIX
POSIX, 7
Power failure, RAID, 172-173
PowerPC (platform), 7
PPc (platform), 21
Prealloc_block field, 195
Prealloc_count field, 195
Preserve lists, use in ReiserFS, 237, 241
Private_data (files), 37
Process resource limits, defined, 65
Provenzano, Chris, 2
Prune_dcache, 54
Ps command, 32
Put_inode (super-block), 61
Put_super (super-block), 62
PV. *See* Physical volumes
Pvcreate command, 145
Pvmove command, 146

Q

Qstr argument, 56

R

RAID
boot messages, 298-299
booting on, 299
hardware, 164
how to set up, 290-291
implementation steps, 168
limitations, 170-171
performance benchmarks, 304-306
protection against disk failure, 171
reconstruction of degraded, 303
recovery from failure, 303-304
software, 164
testing procedures, 302-303
RAID as a module, boot procedure, 301
RAID controllers
PCI, 164-165
SCSI to SCSI, 165
RAID devices, configuration of, 166
RAID levels, 166-168
RAID levels, what current patches support, 285-287
Ramdisk device, defined, 315-316
RDBMS, I/O devices, 64
Read (files), 38
Read_inode (super-block), 61
Read_super (file system), 52
Read-aheads, in ext2fs, 187
Readdir (files), 38
Readlink (inodes), 48
Readpage (inodes), 48
RedHat, 6
RedHat installation media (for XFS), 279
Redundancy, RAID configurations, 167-168
Reiser, Hans, 234
ReiserFS, 12
allocation method, 68
configuration on Linux kernels, 253-254
Relative file name, 84
Release (files), 39
Remount_fs (super-block), 62-63
Rename (inodes), 47
Revalidate (files), 40
Revision level, in super-block, 193
Rmdir (inodes), 47
Root (/), 20
Root device, creating, 322-323
Root file system
defined, 316
mounting on a RAID device, 299-301

 S

S_blocksize field (super-block), 58
S_dev field (super-block), 58
S_dirt field (super-block), 59
S_dirty field (super-block), 60
S_files field (super-block), 60
S_flags field (super-block), 59
S_ibasket fields, 59
S_list field (super-block), 58
S_lock field (super-block), 58
S_magic field (super-block), 59
S_mounted inode in accessing files, 85
S_op field (super-block), 59
S_root field (super-block), 59
S_type field (super-block), 59
S_vfs_rename_sem field (super-block), 60
S_wait field (super-block), 58
SAN, 24
Scheduler function, 18
SCSI controllers for RAID, 165
Second extended file system (ext2fs), developed, 3
Selective flushing in ReiserFS, 247
Server, number of disks, 138
Set up commands for RAID, 290-291
Set up suggestions, 336-337
SGI, development of XFS, 256
Shared buffers, 31
Silicon Graphics Inc. *See* SGI
Size field, in inode, 192
SMP configure, 17
Software RAID, 166-170
hardware concerns, 288-290
how to, 281-306
Solaris VFS, 76
Solid drops (ReiserFS), 248
Source code
directories, 17-19
ext2fs, 205-217
lvm.h, 146-162
md_k.h, 173-180
open_namei() function (from fs/namei.c), 132-136
tree structure, 12-16
Source file
fs.h, 86-118
fs/ext2/file.c, 130-132
fs/ext2/super.c, 113-130
Space manager for XFS, 259-260
Sparc (platform), 7, 21
Sparse files
JFS support for, 228-229
XFS, 256
Stallman, Richard, 5

Start command, RAID, 169
Statfs (super-block), 62
Static file systems, 68-69
Storage area network. *See* SAN
Striped logical volume, creating, 145-146
Striping
    logical volumes, 145-146
    RAID,168
Structures in ReiserFS, 241-245
Super_operations structure
    ext2, 83
    VFS, 83
Super-block
    buffer (XFS), 270
    calls used, (XFS), 271-272
    defined in XFS, 269
    ext2fs, 186
    fields, 58-60
    fields (XFS), 273
    functions, 60-63
    JFS, 220
    location of (XFS), 272
Super-block structure,
    description, 57-58
    ext2fs, 196-199
    VFS, 78
SuSe, 6
Swap device creating, 323
Swap space, size, 333-334
Symbolic links. *See* Symlinks
Symlink (inodes), 47
Symlinks, 84
Symlinks, in ext2fs, 183
Synchronous updates, in ext2fs, 183
System calls
    inode operations, 85-86
    VFS-handled, 79-80
System failure, I/O, 64

T

Tasklets, 9
Timer.c function, 18
Timestamps field, in inode, 192
Tools, ext2fs, 189-191
Torvalds, Linus, 2, 6
Transactions
    definition, 64
    ReiserFS, 246-247
Transmeta Crusoe (processor), 8
Tree hierarchy, 25-28
Tree name, defined, 26
Tree structure, source code, 12-16

Trees
    ordering within, 239
    structure of in ReiserFS, 238-239
Ts'o, Theodore, ext rewrite,182
Tune2fs program, ext2fs, 184
Tune2fs utility, 188
Tuning issues in ReiserFS, 248
Tweedie, Stephen, ext rewrite, 182

U

U.generic_sbp field (super-block), 60
Ulimit(1) command, 65
Umount system call, 62
Umount_begin (super-block), 63
Unified name space. *See* Name space
Uniqueness key in ReiserFS, 239-240
Unlink (inodes), 47
Unshared buffers, 31
Update command, 32
/usr directory, RAID limitations, 170
Utilities, ext2fs, 188
Utilities, used in JFS, 221-222

V

Venema, Wietse, 2
VFS, 28-29
    common file model, 78
    how it works, 78-86
    organization, 30
    source code location, 76
    switch, 76
VFS files, in fs/ subdirectory, 77-78
VFS layer, 2
Vfsmount structures, 57
VG. *See* Volume groups
Vgcreate command, 145
VGDA, 141
Vgextend command, 145
Vgreduce command, 146
Viro, Alexander, 76
Virtual file system. *See* VFS
Virtual memory, 29
Virtual memory, file system check, 221-222
Volg. *See* Volume groups
Volume group
    adding a disk to, 145
    creating, 145
    moving data within, 146
    removing a disk, 146

removing a logical volume, 146
Volume group commands, 144
Volume group descriptor area. *See* VGDA
Volume groups, 138

 W

Write (files), 38
Write_inode (super-block), 61
Write_super (super-block), 62
Write-ahead logging in ReiserFS, 246

Writepage (inodes), 49

 X

Xad, 226-227
XFS, 12
XFS components, 258
XFS design and development goals, 256-257
Xfs_mount structure, 278
Xia file system (Xiafs), 3

INTERNATIONAL CONTACT INFORMATION

AUSTRALIA
McGraw-Hill Book Company Australia Pty. Ltd.
TEL +61-2-9417-9899
FAX +61-2-9417-5687
http://www.mcgraw-hill.com.au
books-it_sydney@mcgraw-hill.com

CANADA
McGraw-Hill Ryerson Ltd.
TEL +905-430-5000
FAX +905-430-5020
http://www.mcgrawhill.ca

**GREECE, MIDDLE EAST,
NORTHERN AFRICA**
McGraw-Hill Hellas
TEL +30-1-656-0990-3-4
FAX +30-1-654-5525

MEXICO (Also serving Latin America)
McGraw-Hill Interamericana Editores S.A. de C.V.
TEL +525-117-1583
FAX +525-117-1589
http://www.mcgraw-hill.com.mx
fernando_castellanos@mcgraw-hill.com

SINGAPORE (Serving Asia)
McGraw-Hill Book Company
TEL +65-863-1580
FAX +65-862-3354
http://www.mcgraw-hill.com.sg
mghasia@mcgraw-hill.com

SOUTH AFRICA
McGraw-Hill South Africa
TEL +27-11-622-7512
FAX +27-11-622-9045
robyn_swanepoel@mcgraw-hill.com

**UNITED KINGDOM & EUROPE
(Excluding Southern Europe)**
McGraw-Hill Education Europe
TEL +44-1-628-502500
FAX +44-1-628-770224
http://www.mcgraw-hill.co.uk
computing_neurope@mcgraw-hill.com

ALL OTHER INQUIRIES Contact:
Osborne/McGraw-Hill
TEL +1-510-549-6600
FAX +1-510-883-7600
http://www.osborne.com
omg_international@mcgraw-hill.com

INTRODUCTION TO THE CD-ROM

IMPORTANT USER INFORMATION

I am writing this at the end of June, 2001. The contents of the CD-ROM were prepared at of beginning of May 2001. All of the file systems discussed in this book, *Linux File Systems*, as well as the LVM patch have been included on the companion CD-ROM along with the pure Linux kernel 2.4.4.

CAUTION: Some of the file systems included on the CD-ROM, like JFS, have been released into non-beta versions since these files were prepared. It is therefore *imperative* that you first check for up-dated versions before you patch your kernel.

The versions included in this CD-ROM, however, are known to patch the kernel correctly and to work without major problems. In other words, the versions inlcuded in this CD-ROM form a congruent and harmonic set of versions which will work beautifully with each other.

To apply the file system patches to the supplied kernel, follow the instructions on kernel compiling in Chapter 2 of this book.

Moshe Bar

The GNU License

Linux is written and distributed under the GNU General Public License which means that its source code is freely-distributed and available to the general public.

GNU GENERAL PUBLIC LICENSE

Version 2, June 1991

Preamble

The licenses for most software are designed to take away your freedom to share and change it. By contrast, the GNU General Public License is intended to guarantee your freedom to share and change free software--to make sure the software is free for all its users. This General Public License applies to most of the Free Software Foundation's software and to any other program whose authors commit to using it. (Some other Free Software Foundation software is covered by the GNU Library General Public License instead.) You can apply it to your programs, too.

When we speak of free software, we are referring to freedom, not price. Our General Public Licenses are designed to make sure that you have the freedom to distribute copies of free software (and charge for this service if you wish), that you receive source code or can get it if you want it, that you can change the software or use pieces of it in new free programs; and that you know you can do these things.

To protect your rights, we need to make restrictions that forbid anyone to deny you these rights or to ask you to surrender the rights. These restrictions translate to certain responsibilities for you if you distribute copies of the software, or if you modify it.

For example, if you distribute copies of such a program, whether gratis or for a fee, you must give the recipients all the rights that you have. You must make sure that they, too, receive or can get the source code. And you must show them these terms so they know their rights.

We protect your rights with two steps: (1) copyright the software, and (2) offer you this license which gives you legal permission to copy, distribute and/or modify the software.

Also, for each author's protection and ours, we want to make certain that everyone understands that there is no warranty for this free software. If the software is modified by someone else and passed on, we want its recipients to know that what they have is not the original, so that any problems introduced by others will not reflect on the original authors' reputations.

Finally, any free program is threatened constantly by software patents. We wish to avoid the danger that redistributors of a free program will individually obtain patent licenses, in effect making the program proprietary. To prevent this, we have made it clear that any patent must be licensed for everyone's free use or not licensed at all.

The precise terms and conditions for copying, distribution and modification follow.

GNU GENERAL PUBLIC LICENSE TERMS AND CONDITIONS FOR COPYING, DISTRIBUTION AND MODIFICATION

0. This License applies to any program or other work which contains a notice placed by the copyright holder saying it may be distributed under the terms of this General Public License. The "Program", below, refers to any such program or work, and a "work based on the Program" means either the Program or any derivative work under copyright law: that is to say, a work containing the Program or a portion of it, either verbatim or with modifications and/or translated into another language. (Hereinafter, translation is included without limitation in the term "modification".) Each licensee is addressed as "you".

Activities other than copying, distribution and modification are not covered by this License; they are outside its scope. The act of running the Program is not restricted, and the output from the Program is covered only if its contents constitute a work based on the Program (independent of having been made by running the Program). Whether that is true depends on what the Program does.

1. You may copy and distribute verbatim copies of the Program's source code as you receive it, in any medium, provided that you conspicuously and appropriately publish on each copy an appropriate copyright notice and disclaimer of warranty; keep intact all the notices that refer to this License and to the absence of any warranty; and give any other recipients of the Program a copy of this License along with the Program.

You may charge a fee for the physical act of transferring a copy, and you may at your option offer warranty protection in exchange for a fee.

2. You may modify your copy or copies of the Program or any portion of it, thus forming a work based on the Program, and copy and distribute such modifications or work under the terms of Section 1 above, provided that you also meet all of these conditions:

    a) You must cause the modified files to carry prominent notices stating that you changed the files and the date of any change.

    b) You must cause any work that you distribute or publish, that in whole or in part contains or is derived from the Program or any part thereof, to be licensed as a whole at no charge to all third parties under the terms of this License.

    c) If the modified program normally reads commands interactively when run, you must cause it, when started running for such interactive use in the most ordinary way, to print or display an announcement including an appropriate copyright notice and a notice that there is no warranty (or else, saying that you provide a warranty) and that users may redistribute the program under these conditions, and telling the user how to view a copy of this License. (Exception: if the

Program itself is interactive but does not normally print such an announcement, your work based on the Program is not required to print an announcement.)

These requirements apply to the modified work as a whole. If identifiable sections of that work are not derived from the Program, and can be reasonably considered independent and separate works in themselves, then this License, and its terms, do not apply to those sections when you distribute them as separate works. But when you distribute the same sections as part of a whole which is a work based on the Program, the distribution of the whole must be on the terms of this License, whose permissions for other licensees extend to the entire whole, and thus to each and every part regardless of who wrote it. Thus, it is not the intent of this section to claim rights or contest your rights to work written entirely by you; rather, the intent is to exercise the right to control the distribution of derivative or collective works based on the Program.

In addition, mere aggregation of another work not based on the Program with the Program (or with a work based on the Program) on a volume of a storage or distribution medium does not bring the other work under the scope of this License.

3. You may copy and distribute the Program (or a work based on it, under Section 2) in object code or executable form under the terms of Sections 1 and 2 above provided that you also do one of the following:

a) Accompany it with the complete corresponding machine-readable source code, which must be distributed under the terms of Sections 1 and 2 above on a medium customarily used for software interchange; or,

b) Accompany it with a written offer, valid for at least three years, to give any third party, for a charge no more than your cost of physically performing source distribution, a complete machine-readable copy of the corresponding source code, to be distributed under the terms of Sections 1 and 2 above on a medium customarily used for software interchange; or,

c) Accompany it with the information you received as to the offer to distribute corresponding source code. (This alternative is allowed only for noncommercial distribution and only if you received the program in object code or executable form with such an offer, in accord with Subsection b above.)

The source code for a work means the preferred form of the work for making modifications to it. For an executable work, complete source code means all the source code for all modules it contains, plus any associated interface definition files, plus the scripts used to control compilation and installation of the executable. However, as a special exception, the source code distributed need not include anything that is normally distributed (in either source or binary form) with the major components (compiler, kernel, and so on) of the operating system on which the executable runs, unless that component itself accompanies the executable.

If distribution of executable or object code is made by offering access to copy from a designated place, then offering equivalent access to copy the source code from the same place counts as distribution of the source code, even though third parties are not compelled to copy the source along with the object code.

4. You may not copy, modify, sublicense, or distribute the Program except as expressly provided under this License. Any attempt otherwise to copy, modify, sublicense or distribute the Program is void, and will automatically terminate your rights under this License. However, parties who have received copies, or rights, from you under this License will not have their licenses terminated so long as such parties remain in full compliance.

5. You are not required to accept this License, since you have not signed it. However, nothing else grants you permission to modify or distribute the Program or its derivative works. These actions are prohibited by law if you do not accept this License. Therefore, by modifying or distributing the Program (or any work based on the Program), you indicate your acceptance of this License to do so, and all its terms and conditions for copying, distributing or modifying the Program or works based on it.

6. Each time you redistribute the Program (or any work based on the Program), the recipient automatically receives a license from the original licensor to copy, distribute or modify the Program subject to these terms and conditions. You may not impose any further restrictions on the recipients' exercise of the rights granted herein. You are not responsible for enforcing compliance by third parties to this License.

7. If, as a consequence of a court judgment or allegation of patent infringement or for any other reason (not limited to patent issues), conditions are imposed on you (whether by court order, agreement or otherwise) that contradict the conditions of this License, they do not excuse you from the conditions of this License. If you cannot distribute so as to satisfy simultaneously your obligations under this License and any other pertinent obligations, then as a consequence you may not distribute the Program at all. For example, if a patent license would not permit royalty-free redistribution of the Program by all those who receive copies directly or indirectly through you, then the only way you could satisfy both it and this License would be to refrain entirely from distribution of the Program.

If any portion of this section is held invalid or unenforceable under any particular circumstance, the balance of the section is intended to apply and the section as a whole is intended to apply in other circumstances.

It is not the purpose of this section to induce you to infringe any patents or other property right claims or to contest validity of any such claims; this section has the sole purpose of protecting the integrity of the free software distribution system, which is implemented by public license practices. Many people have made generous contributions to the wide range of software distributed through that system in reliance on consistent application of that system; it is up to the author/donor to decide if he or she is willing to distribute software through any other system and a licensee cannot impose that choice.

This section is intended to make thoroughly clear what is believed to be a consequence of the rest of this License.

he distribution and/or use of the Program is restricted in certain countries either by patents or by copyrighted interfaces, nal copyright holder who places the Program under this License may add an explicit geographical distribution limita-
ling those countries, so that distribution is permitted only in or among countries not thus excluded. In such case,
ncorporates the limitation as if written in the body of this License.

9. The Free Software Foundation may publish revised and/or new versions of the General Public License from time to time. Such new versions will be similar in spirit to the present version, but may differ in detail to address new problems or concerns.

Each version is given a distinguishing version number. If the Program specifies a version number of this License which applies to it and "any later version", you have the option of following the terms and conditions either of that version or of any later version published by the Free Software Foundation. If the Program does not specify a version number of this License, you may choose any version ever published by the Free Software Foundation.

10. If you wish to incorporate parts of the Program into other free programs whose distribution conditions are different, write to the author to ask for permission. For software which is copyrighted by the Free Software Foundation, write to the Free Software Foundation; we sometimes make exceptions for this. Our decision will be guided by the two goals of preserving the free status of all derivatives of our free software and of promoting the sharing and reuse of software generally.

NO WARRANTY

11. BECAUSE THE PROGRAM IS LICENSED FREE OF CHARGE, THERE IS NO WARRANTY FOR THE PROGRAM, TO THE EXTENT PERMITTED BY APPLICABLE LAW. EXCEPT WHEN OTHERWISE STATED IN WRITING THE COPYRIGHT HOLDERS AND/OR OTHER PARTIES PROVIDE THE PROGRAM "AS IS" WITHOUT WARRANTY OF ANY KIND, EITHER EXPRESSED OR IMPLIED, INCLUDING, BUT NOT LIMITED TO, THE IMPLIED WARRANTIES OF MERCHANTABILITY AND FITNESS FOR A PARTICULAR PURPOSE. THE ENTIRE RISK AS TO THE QUALITY AND PERFORMANCE OF THE PROGRAM IS WITH YOU. SHOULD THE PROGRAM PROVE DEFECTIVE, YOU ASSUME THE COST OF ALL NECESSARY SERVICING, REPAIR OR CORRECTION.

12. IN NO EVENT UNLESS REQUIRED BY APPLICABLE LAW OR AGREED TO IN WRITING WILL ANY COPYRIGHT HOLDER, OR ANY OTHER PARTY WHO MAY MODIFY AND/OR REDISTRIBUTE THE PROGRAM AS PERMITTED ABOVE, BE LIABLE TO YOU FOR DAMAGES, INCLUDING ANY GENERAL, SPECIAL, INCIDENTAL OR CONSEQUENTIAL DAMAGES ARISING OUT OF THE USE OR INABILITY TO USE THE PROGRAM (INCLUDING BUT NOT LIMITED TO LOSS OF DATA OR DATA BEING RENDERED INACCURATE OR LOSSES SUSTAINED BY YOU OR THIRD PARTIES OR A FAILURE OF THE PROGRAM TO OPERATE WITH ANY OTHER PROGRAMS), EVEN IF SUCH HOLDER OR OTHER PARTY HAS BEEN ADVISED OF THE POSSIBILITY OF SUCH DAMAGES.

END OF TERMS AND CONDITIONS

Appendix: How to Apply These Terms to Your New Programs

If you develop a new program, and you want it to be of the greatest possible use to the public, the best way to achieve this is to make it free software which everyone can redistribute and change under these terms.

To do so, attach the following notices to the program. It is safest to attach them to the start of each source file to most effectively convey the exclusion of warranty; and each file should have at least the "copyright" line and a pointer to where the full notice is found.

<one line to give the program's name and a brief idea of what it does.> Copyright © 19yy <name of author>

This program is free software; you can redistribute it and/or modify it under the terms of the GNU General Public License as published by the Free Software Foundation; either version 2 of the License, or (at your option) any later version.

This program is distributed in the hope that it will be useful, but WITHOUT ANY WARRANTY; without even the implied warranty of MERCHANTABILITY or FITNESS FOR A PARTICULAR PURPOSE. See the GNU General Public License for more details.

You should have received a copy of the GNU General Public License along with this program; if not, write to the Free Software Foundation, Inc., 675 Mass Ave, Cambridge, MA 02139, USA.

Also add information on how to contact you by electronic and paper mail.

If the program is interactive, make it output a short notice like this when it starts in an interactive mode:

Gnomovision version 69, Copyright © 19yy name of author Gnomovision comes with ABSOLUTELY NO WARRANTY; for details type `show w'. This is free software, and you are welcome to redistribute it under certain conditions; type `show c' for details.

The hypothetical commands `show w' and `show c' should show the appropriate parts of the General Public License. Of course, the commands you use may be called something other than `show w' and `show c'; they could even be mouse-clicks or menu items--whatever suits your program.

You should also get your employer (if you work as a programmer) or your school, if any, to sign a "copyright disclaimer" for the program, if necessary. Here is a sample; alter the names:

Yoyodyne, Inc., hereby disclaims all copyright interest in the program `Gnomovision' (which makes passes at compilers) written by James Hacker.

<signature of Ty Coon>, 1 April 1989
Ty Coon, President of Vice

This General Public License does not permit incorporating your program into proprietary programs. If your program is a subroutine library, you may consider it more useful to permit linking proprietary applications with the library. If this is what you want to do, use the GNU Library General Public License instead of this License.